ALSO BY BILL MAHER

Does Anybody Have A Problem with That?
Politically Incorrect*'s Greatest Hits*

The New New Rules: A Funny Look at How
Everybody but Me Has Their Head Up Their Ass

New Rules: Polite Musings from a Timid Observer

When You Ride Alone, You Ride with bin Laden:
What the Government Should Be Telling Us
to Help Fight the War on Terrorism

True Story: A Novel

WHAT THIS COMEDIAN SAID WILL SHOCK YOU

BILL MAHER

SIMON & SCHUSTER

NEW YORK   LONDON   TORONTO   SYDNEY   NEW DELHI

For the writers

I know Twitter is X now,

I don't care,

I call it Twitter and always will.

CONTENTS

INTRODUCTION xi

1 PARTIES 1

2 KNOWLEDGE 18

3 MEDIA 41

4 FREE SPEECH 52

5 GENERATIONS 61

6 REPUBLICANS 79

7 DEMOCRATS 97

8 FRAGILITY 115

9 CANCEL CULTURE 132

10 COPS 149

11 SCAMERICA 156

12 DRUGS 168

13 RELIGION 176

14 MONEY 194

15 GUNS 220

16 TIME 226

CONTENTS

17 **EARTH** 236

18 **RACE** 255

19 **IMMIGRATION** 273

20 **SHOWBIZ** 282

21 **HEALTH** 295

22 **LOVE** 308

23 **TRUMP** 329

24 **CIVIL WAR** 342

Acknowledgments 357

Index 359

INTRODUCTION

Real Time with Bill Maher started in February 2003, on a network I was grateful had patience. Because it wasn't very good that first season, and one reason was: the ending of the show wasn't right. For some reason, I had the dumb idea to end *my* show with other people performing. New comics, who I wanted to present to America. Like I was Ed Sullivan.

I blame the pot.

Because, really, the big ending for your own show should not be a pass-off. If people are watching a show with your name in the title, finish it up with what you do best, which in my case is a straight-to-camera commentary on something people want to hear your take on. (Even if they don't know they want to hear it yet, but I'll get to that in a minute.)

And so I started doing that in the second half of 2003, our "second season." I'd basically done the same thing every Friday night when *Politically Incorrect* was on five days a week, and I always called such a monologue at the end of the show "the editorial." Some people still call it a new rule, because on *Real Time* it comes at the end of the "New Rules" segment and segues into it with a "New rule . . . " opening. But it's a completely different animal. New rules are short thoughts about anything—they can be silly, serious, of-the-week or timeless. The ones I reject sound like bad open-mic night.

But the editorial is a ten-minute thought piece, with laughs. Always with laughs. I've told my brilliant writers who work on it with me every week: you can be bad, I can always edit that out—just don't be earnest. Because anyone can be earnest, and usually when they are it kind of makes me puke. I define "earnest" as a) saying something obvious (or at least obvious to your tribe); b) not being funny about it; and c) acting like it's an issue that affects you personally way more than it does.

Real Time has always attempted to be a show about ideas. The people who know *of* it, but don't know *it*, talk to me about the show like we're investigative journalists; we are not. We don't break stories, we break new ways of looking at stories. And that is especially true of the editorials—I always want them to introduce novel ways of thinking about something. These editorials do not aim to tell people what they want to hear, what they think they already know. They often start off getting people to say, "Yeah, you go, boy," and halfway through have them saying, "Hey, wait a minute . . . " At least they do when I've done my job right. We are only Team Real on *Real Time*, not Team "This Party" or Team "This Philosophy."

The twenty-first century in America has been a political nightmare because the partisan hate has reached a fever pitch. Yes, the two sides always opposed each other, but I remember the late twentieth century, and it wasn't this bad. We had a lot of people yelling at each other on TV in the nineties (quite a bit of it on my old show), but at least we could stand to sit in the same room.

Now what we have are factions that only want to hear the bits that allow them to feel superior to the deplorable people on the other side. People not only don't want to hear a countering view, they often want to make those offering it disappear—either actively, by canceling them, or passively, by ignoring them. I'm sure I've lost fans over the years for not toeing the line they wished I would toe; I do not miss them. This show is not for them. My show, and this book, is for those with an open mind and those who recognize that, especially now, there's ample crazy on both sides.

I wish it were not so. Things were easier for me, and it was easier for people to understand me, during the Bush-Obama years. Before wokeness, at first a noble directive to remain alert to injustice, morphed into an ugly authoritarianism, and often in support of bad ideas.

One reason I did this book is because it's almost impossible to understand where I'm coming from *without* it; it's not like one of those books where you can get the gist in a few excerpts. I'm sure watching *Real Time* can sometimes make it appear to viewers that I'm all over the map politically, and there's a reason for that—I'm serving many masters as the host of the show: on any one given night, depending on who I'm talking to—and sometimes debating with—one aspect of an issue can dominate the discussion and all the audience will hear is a sliver of what I'd like to say on that issue. I have to allow multiple guests to have their say, and also, in a freewheeling debate format, people just cut you off a lot before you can express the full scope of your take. Or we just run out of time and have to move on to the next topic—it is, after all, a show in which I'm trying to catch the audience up on what I think they should know about what happened in that week; that is Job One. So philosophical coherence can get lost in all that, and this book hopes to remedy that.

But the danger is not equal—I've tried to be clear that I don't think it is. The things I never liked about Republicans, I still don't like: they're too religious; they're fiscal hypocrites who hate when America spends money it doesn't have, except when they're in office, and then it's always perfectly OK; they're largely in denial about racism; and they're insufficiently alarmed about the environment. We are losing an estimated 150 species a day, and I don't think they care.

And then they got worse. They added to that shitty mixtape the embracing of a sociopath, Donald Trump, and being largely accepting of the idea that a right-wing coup is a legitimate response to losing a presidential election. They seem to have adopted that unholy paradox from the

Vietnam War: they had to "destroy the village to save it." They think what the Left is doing is so fundamentally wrong for the country that they are willing to jettison the essence of the country—democracy—to save it. And you just can't have one party dominated by a policy of "Elections only count when we win them, because the other side is nuts."

Even when the other side *is* nuts, it still must be handled within the democratic process. I understand the argument the Right is making: "Oh, we may be upending the norms of politics and government . . . perhaps we no longer understand what democracy is . . . but you on the left no longer understand what *humans* are . . . and you are upending even more fundamental norms, of life itself. For example, you don't seem to know what a woman is, and we just can't trust the country to people that divorced from reality."

Yes, I get that argument. It's why I say in one of the editorials: "Let's get this straight: it's not me who's changed, it's the Left, which is now made up of a small contingent who've gone mental and a large contingent who refuse to call them out for it. But I will."

This is a crucial point: wokeism in its current form is not an extension of liberalism, it is more often its opposite; it is not mostly an expanding of traditional liberalism but an undoing of it.

Tim Scott, running in 2023 as a Black Republican, sounded more like Obama talking about race when he was president than Obama or any Democrat does today. Democrats changed that, not me. There are hundreds of colleges with Black-only dorms and graduation ceremonies, which doesn't exactly seem to jibe with the spirit of diversity that I thought *we* thought was so important at college.

A common rebuttal to this from Democrats is, "Oh sure, there's crazy stuff on the left, but it's just a fringe, just a few crazies that don't amount to anything significant." I don't know how to put this gently, so I'll just say it: you're wrong.

And this is the problem with being in tightly sealed information bubbles: they don't show you anything that makes you aware of the stuff your side is doing that you actually might not like. Matt Taibbi put it well when he wrote, "Media firms work backward. They first ask 'How does our target demographic want to understand what's just unfolded?'" adding, "Media companies need to get out of the audience-stroking business."

This is what I'm always trying to do: break through the bubbles. When people say to me, "You make fun of the Left more these days" . . . well, yes, they're a lot funnier than they used to be, and I'm a comedian. But also: If I don't, where else are liberals going to hear it?

Yale University has over 5,000 "administrators" (not professors), and Stanford in 2020 had 10,896 "managerial and professional staff" and 1,789 "administrative and technical staff." Does that sound crazy to you? It sure does to me. That's what's going on at colleges these days, and it has fundamentally changed the nature of higher education. But are you going to hear about it on MSNBC? I doubt it.

There's a children's book called *Every Body*, which includes lines like "Before you were born, a group of white men started making up lots of ideas about bodies that weren't true. They said that one kind of body was the best, and that being fat was bad and skinny was good. They were wrong, but lots of people listened to them."

I'm sure there are people who applaud that, but to me, it showcases all that is wrong with the Left today: making everything racial, using children as frontline troops in culture wars and blithely denying patent realities: obesity *is* bad for your health.

The *Los Angeles Times* editorial page condemned a proposal to simply allow city authorities to prohibit homeless tents within five hundred feet of *schools*. (Not to be outdone, Oregon now fines *you* for the crime of asking the homeless to move off the street, possibly in front of where you're trying to run a business.)

MrBeast is one of the biggest stars on YouTube, staging massive stunts that are often charitable giveaways that then pay for themselves when those stunts generate millions of views. In 2023 he did one entitled "Funded Cataract Surgery for 1000 People"—and for this *he* was the bad guy. A reporter for the *Washington Post* tweeted, "What needs curing is society's view of disabled people," that this was "systemic ableism" and that MrBeast "seems to regard disability as something that needs to be solved."

The *Atlantic* ran a piece entitled "Separating Sports by Sex Doesn't Make Sense," which included lines such as "Maintaining the binary in youth sports reinforces the idea that boys are inherently bigger, faster and stronger than girls in a competitive setting."

The *Atlantic* is not fringe. Neither is the *Washington Post* or the *Los Angeles Times*, so please stop pretending the reality-challenged are a meaningless few. That boys are inherently bigger, faster and stronger than girls is not an "*idea*"—it's an obvious verity. The *Atlantic* author talks of "researchers"—I assume writing in the *New England Journal of WTF?*—who hypothesize that "the gap they did find between boys and girls was likely due to socialization, not biology."

This is madness. Separate dorms for separate races? Keeping home-less people *on* the street? Keeping blind people blind, operating on children's genitalia more wantonly than any other nation now does, cheating women athletes out of winning in their sport? This is your idea of compassion? This is what you think liberalism is?

Please. Seeing is better than not seeing. Separating sports by sex makes perfect, obvious sense. Obesity is not good. Don't present me with a menu of delirium and then call me a "conservative" because I don't want to jump on the Crazy Train with you.

I know that some people think it's me, that I've "taken the red pill." This was another reason I wanted to do this book: it forced me to read over all the editorials we've done from 2003 till the strike shut us down in 2023, and it was very instructive. I knew *things* had changed a lot in twenty years—but had I? That was my special focus in researching myself.

And plainly, in the first decade of the show, the amount of space given to bashing Republicans and what they were doing wrong greatly exceeded the critiques of the Left—but that's because the Left wasn't doing anything particularly nutty or obnoxious. Obama was a one-man scorched-earth policy for comedy—which was great for the country, he wasn't a buffoon—but tough on comedians, especially any right-wing comedian trying to find the funny in Nancy Pelosi. Even if you disagreed with her policies, she's smart and tough—that's not funny. We had Sarah Palin, a comedy gold mine. It wasn't a fair fight.

But things change. They've changed a lot in the era *Real Time* has been on. I remember doing jokes about how fragile millennials were in the Bush-Obama years and hearing guests on the show opine that the new generation coming up—Gen Z—was going to backlash all that. But it turned out, they didn't backlash at all. They supercharged it and brought new levels of oversensitivity, victim culture and sheer nonsense that I refuse to pretend is an extension of liberalism.

The fact that someone could believe that the obvious physical differences between the sexes derive from socialization speaks of a fundamental problem we have today: parents raise their kids as peers, telling them they're little geniuses, and then we all wind up pretending the predictable brain farts that would emerge from a child are actual debatable ideas. It reminds me of monarchical states where a five-year-old inherits the throne and then all the courtiers have to rationalize and carry out the whims of a toddler. Kind of like the Trump White House.

So if it seems like I don't like either side . . . kinda. I like individuals, but I believe when historians look back on this period in American history, they will not divide us into the camps into which we currently divide ourselves.

They will see the same pathologies and unappealing traits on both sides—traits that simply manifest themselves differently. We don't look back on the Romans or the Egyptians and talk about the subsects that brought down their reigns, even though surely they had their internal debates. Historians tend to talk about them *as a people* at a certain time in history and where their minds were collectively. I think they will write about us in the same way.

For example, I think future historians will characterize twenty-first-century Americans as anti-science. The denial about ecological collapse from the Right will strike them that way. But so will pregnant men and censoring the idea that Covid could have originated in a lab because that's "racist."

Both sides are smug. America is a very successful nation, and history shows that when a nation reaches an apex, there seems to be no way of preventing one deleterious side effect: it makes people act like spoiled, entitled assholes who forget what real hardship is and obsess about bullshit. Again, that manifests on both sides, just differently.

Large numbers on both sides will believe anything you send them in an email that denigrates the "other" side or supports their own. Both sides like to cancel people they don't agree with. Both sides are completely fact-free on a host of issues that they nevertheless speak about with great confidence. Although, importantly, with more dire consequences from those on the Right.

Yes, important point: the consequences of the Right's intellectual degeneration are worse both in the short term (we could lose America being run "the old way"—you know, with elections and the rule of law and stuff) and in the long term (we reach a tipping point from the environmental destruction, like if we kill *all* the bees). So there's that.

In 1994 I wrote a piece for *Playboy* magazine called "The Reluctant Conservative," which included this: "I'm more conservative than I ever thought I would be, but when I am I try to own up to the fact that it comes from cynicism about how effective government can really be. It comes from lost idealism, from my brain winning and my heart losing. I go with it when it would be stupid not to, but it's nothing to crow about. It should not be forgotten that being liberal is what a nation should aspire to, just as it is what a person should aspire to. Liberal means open-minded, willing to try new things, eager to get to the next place."

That's from thirty years ago, and I feel fundamentally the same. So I don't take very seriously this idea that I took some red pill. For five years, every Democrat I had on *Real Time* laughed at my "alarmism" when I said Trump would never concede losing an election but we saw how that turned out.

I've always tried to look at every issue, every candidate, every election, anew and dispassionately—it was simply my honest judgment that every Democrat for president was more sane, compassionate and practical than the Republican. I still think Al Gore and John Kerry would have been better than George W. Bush, that Obama was better than McCain or Romney would have been, and that Hillary would have been better, and Biden is better, than Trump.

But the Democrats are without a doubt a nuttier mess than they have ever been before. Here's Obama in 2018 talking about the excesses of his own side: "The average American doesn't think that we have to completely tear down the system and remake it. There are a lot of persuadable voters and . . . a lot of Democrats . . . who just want to see things make sense. They just don't want to see crazy stuff."

Ah, yes, the "crazy stuff" doctrine. And how to implement it in an age where the other side is even more dangerous. That's the challenge we find before ourselves as a nation, and the challenge I personally find in going out there every week without the protection of a "team." But the audience has been incredibly loyal, and for that I am eternally grateful. We have a great mutual trust built on love of honesty, not on "You can count on me to sing your tune."

Here's a snippet from the editorial I did on the occasion of turning sixty:

My relationship with the audience is the relationship of my life. Kids? I don't have time for kids, I've got to rewrite this editorial. It's always been where I put my energy. It's what I love most. That's my truth; that's the way I was born; that's what my body is telling me to do, and always has. It's why I've always treated the audience like they're my friend—and I mean a real friend. I trust them enough to say things they may not want to hear. We don't agree on everything, and we don't have to, because friends don't leave each other over that. We even fight sometimes, because honesty is love, and friends don't bullshit each other.

I know, you get that already. Or else you wouldn't be reading this.

1

PARTIES

UNQUALIFIED SUCCESS

Name almost any job: dental hygienist, rodeo clown, dog walker, mall Santa, chicken-sexer—they all demand some kind of definable skill set. The one exception is member of Congress.

You can be in jail and get this job. You can be deranged and get this job. If you have a heart attack, they just let your wife start doing it. All you need is a smile and a flag pin. I'd say all you need is a pulse, but dead people have been elected to Congress; much more is required of an immigrant taking the citizenship test. In forty-eight states you can't vote if you're *in* prison, but in every state, you can run for Congress *from* prison.

Unremarkable people can get a remarkable life in Congress, and that's what keeps the average backbencher sticking with party-dictated bullshit. It guarantees them something that's bigger than faith, family, country or objective reality: they get to keep the best job they could ever get with absolutely nothing to recommend their lazy, ignorant ass for it.

College degree? You don't even need a high school degree. Lauren

Boebert didn't get one, and she sits on the Budget Committee. If she wasn't in Congress, she could probably get a shift at a truck stop, dusting the jerky.

But then she wouldn't have two paid-for offices, one in DC, one in her district. She wouldn't have a staff that answers the phone for her and kisses her ass all day. No one would put her on TV and ask her opinions. She couldn't go on exotic paid-for trips—I mean, fact-finding missions.

If you want to know what is so great that it can make someone say anything they're told to say, it's this: the title, the office, the staff, the attention, the good table at the restaurant. "Congressperson" is literally the only job in the world you can get with so much prestige and so many perks while being a complete doofus with absolutely no skills, knowledge or qualifications.

Mike Johnson, I guess, could mop up puke at the Sonic, but it would take him all day. But in Congress, puke-mopper Mike Johnson is a big deal. A man of respect. When he walks in and asks for the best table, they know what to say: "Sir, this is PetSmart, the Cheesecake Factory is next door."

A job in Congress is just so much better than racking the weights at CrossFit, which is what Marjorie Taylor Greene did before she set her crazy eyes on the prize. And once you've got the gig, it's yours for life. The reelection rate in the House for incumbents in 2022 was 95 percent—that's better job security than a pedophile priest has.

In 2022, a video went viral of a Walmart employee quitting her job very publicly. She got on the PA and let it all out: "Fuck this company, fuck this position, and fuck that big lazy bitch Chris Price, I fucking quit!" Texas representative Chip Roy also once told Congress to take *his* job and shove it. He said: "This institution is a sham. And we should adjourn and shut this place down."

But Chip Roy will never quit. Because there are no other jobs where a moron gets paid to ride around in a limo. Chip gets paid a hundred and seventy-five grand a year, free medical, a great pension, with half the year off, plus a million-and-a-half-dollars-a-year "allowance" for decorating the office, or, um, "sundries." Oh, also: Lobbyists blow him. And he gets to be on TV for doing nothing, which as we all know, is the American dream.

And by "doing nothing," I mean literally. Once you get elected, you don't have to actually do anything. There's no year-end performance review. Nobody calls you into an office and says, "I don't think this is working out." You have, essentially, no boss.

Well, except for the voters. That's the one thing you must do to keep all these perks coming: if your district is full of people who think the election was rigged, or vaccines have microchips in them, or men can have babies, you have to agree, and then repeat it in Congress. And they do.

Nancy Mace is a House member from South Carolina, the first woman to graduate from the Citadel. After January 6, she was outraged and stood up to her party, giving a dozen interviews in a single day condemning Trump. Soon after, she wouldn't even talk about it. Then she voted to oust Liz Cheney for making the exact same case she herself had made.

A lot of people in America think she's a patriot, but she looks to me like a supplicant for the corner office. She supported an insurrection for the "likes."

OWNING THE FIBS

George Santos is the somehow-elected Republican House member from Long Island who represents a growing segment of American society: liars.

Now, if you're sort of hazy on the details of Santos's life, don't worry, so's he. When they film his biography, it'll start with "Based on a false story." He lied about his schooling, his career, his sexuality, his charity work—what kind of family raises a person like this? We don't know because he lied about them too. He lies like a goose shits—if he's not doing it that very moment, he's about to.

Santos said he attended the prestigious Horace Mann prep school;

they have no record of him. Nor does NYU, where he said he got an MBA, or Baruch College, where he falsely claimed to have graduated in the top 1 percent of his class and starred on the volleyball team. I'd say you can't make this shit up, but he just made this shit up.

And it raises a lot of questions, starting with: If you're going to lie, why volleyball? He also claimed he ran an animal charity that neutered three thousand stray cats. He didn't, but again, what a strange thing to brag about.

OK, so it's easy to make fun of George Santos, but we shouldn't be missing the bigger picture with him—because this man has pioneered something completely new in American politics. Of course, we've seen liars before, but it was always about tacking from the fringes to the center of your own party—what Mitt Romney called "shaking the Etch A Sketch." Santos, however, is the first to realize that since we are all in our hermetically sealed media bubbles now, you can pretend to be everything to voters in *both* parties, and no one on either side will notice.

Some of Santos's lies appeal to far-right Republicans, like being all in on Trump's election denying. Or making the white power sign in the halls of Congress. Or claiming he was a Wall Street wunderkind who made millions working at Goldman Sachs, which, of course, he didn't, or that he was a luxury yacht broker, which, of course, he wasn't.

But Santos's district is not a Republican district: Biden won it by eight points. So how did a Trump-loving, election-denying white nationalist get elected in a Democrat-leaning district? Simple—he told them what they wanted to hear too.

Liberals love identity politics and victimhood, so George said he had a brain tumor. He also said he was one of the first New Yorkers hospitalized for Covid. He said he lost four coworkers in the famous Pulse nightclub shooting in 2016.

George has said he's from Brazil, which is overwhelmingly Catholic, but when he ran in New York he said he was Jewish and that his grandparents fled Ukraine to escape the Nazis. That's right, his Jewish Ukrainian forefathers escaped the Holocaust by being born Catholic in

Brazil. His immigration policy is "We must stop people like me from getting into this country."

Also, he claims to be half Black, although I doubt it's the half that wears a blazer with a fleece vest. Oh—and he's gay. Or at least he is since he divorced the woman he was married to up until two weeks before the campaign started.

Yes, George knows where the sweet spots are with Democrats too. He once said, "I'm very much gay." What does that mean, "very much gay"? You have a blue checkmark on Grindr?

For Republicans, George bragged that he "personally attended the insurrection" on January 6 and tweeted hashtags like #DemsAreDestroyingAmerica. But that obviously didn't matter to plenty of Democrats in his district. What mattered is that he's a brave, sad, proudly gay, half-Black, Latino Holocaust victim. With a brain tumor. Vote for him? I'm surprised they didn't have him host the Oscars.

Everybody keeps asking, "How could a guy like this happen?" I'll tell you how: because no one cares anymore about substance. It's all tribalism. The only thing that matters is "Is he on our team?" "Is he doing our schtick?" Santos is just the first one to realize you could do both sides' schtick and get away with it because people have completely tuned out anything that doesn't already fit their narrative. Republicans love a winner, and Democrats love someone whose life story makes you want to kill yourself.

WORLD WAR ME

America in our current age suffers acutely from a particular disease of the mind, which is: everything proves what we already believed, and everything goes back to the thing we already hate. All issues today, from pandemic to war, become a stress test for our reflexive partisanship: Can you take a vastly complex situation that is 100 percent *not* about your thing and somehow still make it about your thing? And our answer is: watch me.

Americans will put anything new in our mouths and nothing new in our heads. So naturally Republicans blamed Putin's invasion of Ukraine on Biden being the worst president ever, and Democrats blamed it on Trump's being the worst president ever. Which he was; there is that.

But I'm not sure I can follow Biden's logic all the way when he dragged January 6 into this by saying, "Look, how would you feel if you saw crowds storm and break down the doors of the British Parliament, kill five cops, injure a hundred and forty-five? Or the German Bundestag? Or the Italian parliament? I think you'd wonder."

OK, but if Putin thought Trump was really that supportive of him, why didn't he invade when Trump was in office? It's at least worth asking that question if you're not locked into one intransigent thought.

Nikole Hannah-Jones is the curator of the 1619 Project, which posits racism as the deciding factor in pretty much every single issue in America—or, apparently, anywhere. She said, "We should care about Ukraine. But not because the people appear white . . . all people deserve to be free and to be welcomed when their countries are at war."

Of course. Agreed. And the people there don't *appear* white—they are. Maybe it should be a reminder that when two of the whitest people in the world fight each other, racism is bad, but other things are bad too. It's not like an avocado, you don't have to put it in everything.

Republican presidential hopeful Nikki Haley knows why the mess in Ukraine happened: "The reason Ukraine is in this situation . . . is the United States has been completely and totally distracted . . . We have to stop this national self-loathing that's happening in our country." Of course! Self-loathing! I hate myself for not thinking of that!

Can you guess what Pat Robertson thought was behind the war in Ukraine? I'll give you a hint: in 1980, 1990, 2006 and 2020, Pat predicted the end of the world due to some troubling story in the news. So it wasn't out of character for Pat to say, practically with his dying breath, that Putin "went into the Ukraine, but that wasn't his goal. His goal was to move against Israel."

Because that's where the Bible says the world will end—in Israel. It's where Pat's flight to Jesusville departed from. By way of Ukraine. Who's booking this trip, Delta?

And then it gets really strange: QAnon John says, "I don't see this 'invasion' of Ukraine as a 'bad' thing. I see it as a clearing out of a very corrupt center of operations for the Cabal." Ah yes, the Cabal, that's the pedophile ring of elitist baby-eaters that QAnon believes is the real problem in the world, and naturally when war breaks out, it's really about that.

No wonder the government puts chips in the vaccine to track you people.

Vanity Fair wants you to know that "the fight for Ukraine is also a fight for LGBTQ rights," and conversely Colonel Mitchell Swan, a Republican who ran for Congress in Georgia, said, "Allowing transgender individuals to serve sends a message to our adversaries that we are more focused on social experimentation than on the defense of our nation."

I see. Transgender, that's the key to the Ukrainian situation. Yeah, Putin was on the fence about invading, and then one night he was watching a *M*A*S*H* rerun and saw Corporal Klinger in a dress and said, "Send in the tanks!"

Fox News's Monica Crowley's obsession has always been cancel culture, and so naturally she said, "Between the fierce Ukrainian resistance and the sanctions . . . Russia is being canceled." Wait, the Ukrainians shouldn't resist an invasion because that makes them part of cancel culture? But isn't *their* country what's getting canceled?

Justin Bieber once visited Anne Frank's attic in Amsterdam and wrote in the guest book: "Anne was a great girl. Hopefully she would have been a Belieber." That's what all these people sound like. Don't take this personally, but don't take everything personally. Ukraine is not mostly about your pet grievances—it's about Vladimir Putin's.

And Putin is bad—very, very bad. He pushes people out of windows and cheats at hockey. But he's still better than the guy who brings every conversation back to Bitcoin. My pet cause is PETA, People for the Ethical Treatment of Animals, but I don't think Ukraine got invaded because we haven't neutered enough cats.

And I guarantee you that right now, somewhere, some guy who can't get it up is telling a girl, "This never happened before Ukraine."

PRUDE AWAKENING

In 2021, CNN described a night out with Republican congressman Matt Gaetz this way: "The partygoers, at times dressed in formal wear from a political event they'd just left, mingled and shared drugs like cocaine and ecstasy. Some had sex."

Wait a minute: Wild hotel-suite parties—shouldn't that be a Democratic thing? Shouldn't Democrats be the party of free love and fun and forgetting where you parked your car? Republicans can't be the "conservative," stick-up-your-ass party and then take our drugs and fuck our women. JFK used to have nude pool parties in the White House. Now the politician who comes closest to carrying on that legacy is Matt Gaetz?

Republicans can't spend decades chastising liberals for being too permissive about sex and drugs and then be completely silent about their recent embrace of both.

And Gaetz isn't the only one: former Republican House speaker John Boehner now sells pot for a living—my old job. Marjorie Taylor Greene was reportedly into "polyamorous tantric-sex," and Ashli Babbitt, the MAGA warrior who died storming the Capitol, turns out to have been in a throuple with her husband and another woman. And don't get me started on Trump.

Even their spiritual advisers are freaks. Jerry Falwell Jr. apparently likes to relax after a hard day at Bible college by watching the pool boy do the missus. I know Republicans are lazy and they love outsourcing, but come on. This is a long way from when his father made it a national issue that one of the Teletubbies was purple = gay, duh.

What happened? Republicans always sounded like Grover Norquist when he said of a Kansas congressman caught in a strip club: "Because

Politico did an exposé on his lap dance with a naked lady in a strip club, he's not the kind of person you can ask your sister to vote for anymore."

That's the Republican Party I know! So uptight they could grind diamonds in their ass. While liberals used their asses the way God intended: to smuggle drugs.

You could always count on Republicans to be the fuddy-duddies, the wet blankets, the bores. The "Moral Majority." Nixon started the war on drugs, and Nancy Reagan never stopped spitting her stupid catchphrase "Just Say No" about it. Her husband had a commission to root out pornography. If it was fun, Republicans were against it.

They got apoplectic over Clinton getting a blow job. They invented abstinence-only education. Mitt Romney has never seen himself naked. John Ashcroft once covered the tits on a statue. Rick Santorum wears a sweater vest.

Newt Gingrich once said Democrats were "the party of total hedonism, total exhibitionism, total bizarreness, total weirdness." Well, on a good night, yes. And frankly, Newt, knowing that you believe what I did on an average Friday night was morally reprehensible just made it all the more fun.

I don't want to live in a world where liberals are the uptight ones and conservatives do drugs and get laid. Once upon a time, the Right were the ones offended by everything. They were the party of speech codes and blacklists and moral panics and demanding some TV show had to go.

And now that's liberals? Yes, it is. *We're* the fun suckers now, sucking the fun out of everything: Halloween, the Oscars, childhood, Twitter, comedy. It's like woke kids on campus decided to be all the worst parts of a Southern Baptist, and that's wrong. Because it's cultural appropriation.

If Democrats had always policed morality as hard as they do now, they'd be down a lot of heroes: no FDR, no JFK or RFK, no LBJ, no Clinton, no Martin Luther King Jr. Democrats are now the party that can't tell the difference between Anthony Weiner and Al Franken.

Or Katie Hill, an up-and-coming Democratic congresswoman from California who had to resign because, like Ashli Babbitt, she was found to be in a throuple. And pictured holding a bong, which was too much for our new puritanical Democratic Party. Quite the opposite, a woman in a throuple holding a bong should be the Democrats' logo: You're the throuple people, the bong people, the tantric sex gurus—not Matt Gaetz! You did fucking in the mud and bra burning and "turn on, tune in and drop out" before it was cool, and they're the party that won't bake wedding cakes for gay people. It's time to switch back.

Because frankly, you're not good at being us, and being you sucks.

PUNCH-DRUNK GOV

When someday soon an actual brawl breaks out on the floor of Congress, don't say I didn't tell you it was coming. And oh yes, it's coming—the kind of thing we've seen many times from all over the world. It could be its own show called *Parliament Fights*, where a perfectly normal debate in some country's legislative house devolves into an actual brawl.

When Americans see bad things happen overseas we always think, "It will never happen here." We thought that about terrorism, and mask-wearing, and being one of those countries where people shit in the street.

And when we saw brawling in the very places where people are supposed to come together to work out their differences politely, we said, "Ha ha, foreigners are funny! Countries where democracy is barely a thing and men have too much hair on their knuckles—that will never be us!"

Oh, it be us. It be us real soon.

A recent study examined 365 incidents of physical fights in parliaments across the globe between 1990 and 2018 and discovered the key to where the fighting takes place. Here's who doesn't have parliament fights: countries with authoritarian rulers. Because they just wouldn't allow it. And also, because they're too busy clapping for the dictator.

And the other kind of country that doesn't throw punches? Real democracies—like we used to be. The places where fights break out are the countries that aren't sure which one they are. That's where we're heading.

And while I believe that, as citizens, we need to find a way to love and respect each other again, for Congress it's possible that bus has sailed. Which is why I'd like to suggest that our political leaders learn a lesson from the people who work in one of America's most successful industries—show business—and understand something very fundamental: you can get great things done and still hate each other's fucking guts.

I say this because it would be easier to name great movies where the principals *didn't* hate each other. The editor of *Mad Max: Fury Road* said Charlize Theron and Tom Hardy "didn't want to touch each other, they didn't want to look at each other, they wouldn't face each other if the camera wasn't actively rolling." But the movie works!

Director Roman Polanski hated his leading lady Faye Dunaway so much he refused to give her a bathroom break, so she pissed in a cup and threw it in his face. The movie they made together? *Chinatown*. Which ironically is about hoarding water.

At the end of *An Officer and a Gentleman*, Richard Gere whisks Debra Winger away, but when the cameras stopped, he couldn't wait to drop her. And on *Terms of Endearment*, Winger hated Shirley MacLaine so much she farted in her face.

Eddie Murphy and John Landis stuck it out on *Coming to America*, but when it was over Eddie said that Vic Morrow, who had been decapitated in a stunt gone wrong on a previous Landis movie, had "a better chance of working with Landis [again] than" he did.

Actors have many times hated each other so much they refused to be on the set together at the same time, even in a scene they were both in.

America loves Bill Murray. But you know who doesn't? Everyone who's ever worked with him. Well, everyone who's ever worked with Ted Cruz hates him—why can't this work for government? The list of people who sucked it up and said "I know we hate each other, but we've got a movie to make" is long and impressive.

And it's not just movies: your favorite TV stars hate each other too! On *Star Trek*, Captain Kirk feuded constantly with Mr. Spock, and he's *still* feuding with Mr. Sulu. And it's no secret there was no love lost between Kim Cattrall and the other ladies on *Sex and the City*, and yet they just found a way to work together again on a show about how men are always the problem.

Government needs to learn how to do the same thing. Yes, here in terrible, horrible, immoral show business, we hate each other, and yet we still do our jobs: turning your children communist and gay.

DON'T TREAD ON FREE

Many years ago, on a television network far, far away, I expressed support for libertarianism, because back then it meant that I didn't want big government in my bedroom or my medicine chest, and especially not in the second drawer of the nightstand on the left side of my bed. And I still believe that.

But somewhere along the way libertarianism morphed into this creepy obsession with free-market capitalism based on Ayn Rand's *Atlas Shrugged*, a novel that's never been read all the way through by anyone with a girlfriend.

Paul Ryan once said Ayn Rand taught him "what [his] value systems are." And I believe him, because her book has a strange appeal to people who are kind of smart but not really. She wrote things like "Money is the barometer of a society's virtue" and "The question isn't who is going to let me; it's who is going to stop me"—which sounds like something a Batman villain says. It's all stuff that seems very deep when you're nineteen years old, about how government is a dirty trick played by the weak on the strong. And I can see how if you're a privileged college kid, you read it and think, "Yeah, that's right—I *don't* need anything! So shut up, Dad, and pay my tuition."

And then one day you graduate and pack up your things and realize that your copy of *Atlas Shrugged* belongs in the same milk crate as your beer helmet and the T-shirt that looks like a tuxedo.

Which is not to say that there aren't a lot of people freeloading off the government, or that there aren't libertarian notions that I applaud, like reinstating Fourth Amendment protections against search and seizure, and shutting down the American empire—but libertarians have to stop ruining libertarianism, or at least do a better job of explaining the difference between today's libertarian and just being a selfish prick.

Like, when you see a stoplight your reaction should be "Great. An easy way to ensure we don't all crash into each other," not "How dare the government tell me when I can and cannot go!"

"Seat belts? I refuse to live in a nanny state—I'm an individual, and I want to soar, free as an eagle, right through the windshield."

Same thing with meat inspectors—who needs 'em? "People can sniff their own meat! And if a few die, the word will get around town: 'Don't order the T-bone at the Ponderosa,' and then the Ponderosa closes—problem solved, thanks to the free market!"

Too many of today's libertarians don't believe the government should be regulating banks, or guns, or civil rights, or even helping out after natural disasters. And they're aggressively hostile to environmental protection. But I like air. And water. I'm practically addicted. Libertarians also hate Medicare and Social Security—and there are problems with those programs. But it beats stepping over lepers and watching human skeletons shit in the river, and I also like not seeing things like that. I guess I'm just selfish that way.

What I'd really like to see is libertarianism restored to its proper place in the political firmament—because Americans retain a strong libertarian streak, and I think that's a good thing. Hollywood made a movie a few years ago about the evils of violence in football called *Concussion*, and it tanked, probably because when it comes to football, our view is: let's enjoy this national pastime instead of indulging in that other national pastime, which is telling strangers how to live their lives.

Football is a body-crushing, brain-wrecking game—but we all know that now, so either ban it or shut up about it. And I say that as someone who is not callous to the suffering: when I see a receiver go over the middle and get hammered, I always think two things: one, "I hope that didn't cause permanent damage," and two, "Did he get enough for the first down? Because we needed that play . . . Oh, he didn't even hold on? Jesus Christ, what are we paying you for??"

I would feel bad about the violence in football if the reason I watched the game was specifically to see injuries—you know, like NASCAR. But that's not the reason. I watch football because it's a great game, and an unfortunate side effect is young men smashing into each other like demolition derby cars full of meat. And loving it. Yes, they do seem to be loving it. This is a sport where the players love celebrating so much they have rules about penalizing *that*.

Paul Walker died joyriding. I don't get car love; I don't think driving is like sex—I think it's like commuting. But that's me. He was doing what he loved.

Some people smoke cigarettes, some ski too fast, some date Chris Brown. Americans spend a lot of their time working on relationships—unfortunately, they're other people's. If Rihanna wanted to get back with Chris Brown or Hillary wants to stay with Bill, that's their call, not yours. You don't get to stop strangers from doing what, or who, they love, even if it's not what, or who, you would do.

Just days after David Bowie's death, someone dug up an old interview with a retired groupie named Lori Mattix where she revealed that she'd lost her virginity to Bowie when she was fifteen, in a hotel suite, on hash and champagne, which in 1972 was considered part of a complete breakfast.

To hear Lori tell it, she was a more-than-willing partner, and he was a gentle and knowing lover. And he was wearing a kimono. And he was David fucking Bowie. Which is not a bad way to lose your virginity considering most deflowerings involve Michelob, a van and crying. If there's a victim here, it's the poor guy who had to fuck Lori Mattix *next*: How do you follow David Bowie in a kimono? Talk about "pressure, pushing down on me . . . "

But according to the Internet's social justice warriors, this was horrible and Lori would be better off today if she'd lost her virginity to a loser named Dan from Algebra II class. Sure, *Lori* says she loved it, and still loves it, and has never regretted it for a second. But she's wrong, because she only asked herself; she should be asking a blogger or a women's collective in Winnipeg, because they know better than Lori how Lori should feel.

I thought we'd all come to accept this mantra, "Live in the moment." I guess not. Sometimes, when you're young and in the moment, the moment includes recklessness. Who can say that when they were young and felt invincible they didn't do stuff that compromised their health later on? I certainly did. And I pity the fool in 1983 who would have tried to take the Jack Daniel's out of my hand.

INTENTIONAL POUNDING

One more thing about football . . .

In January of 2023, an event happened on the football field in Cincinnati that seemed to capture everything that's wrong with our national psyche, and a few things that are right. It was a highly consequential meeting between two playoff-bound teams, the Bengals and the Bills, and the outcome would determine each team's standing going into the playoffs. For the players who worked so hard and sacrificed so much to get there, this game had to be played.

But it wasn't. Because early in the game on a kickoff play, defensive back Damar Hamlin collapsed after a routine tackle. Paramedics rushed the field, and then an ambulance came, and everyone held their breath: this was no ordinary injury, and he could have died. What's good about what happened here is: he got the best, quickest medical care possible, and it saved his life; everyone agreed his life was the priority, not the game; and players didn't feel the need to be so macho they completely brushed it off.

Here's what's bad:

1. **GROUPTHINK.** Players get hurt all the time in football, even carted off the field. So when it happened, the announcers, the fans, the

NFL brass, all seemed to be leaning toward continuing play—the players went back to the locker rooms to get their heads straight, but it seemed too important a game to just toss aside. And what about the fans? The ones who bleed for their teams all season long, and who suffered through years of losing, and who count on the football season for passion and relief in lives that are often lacking in both—the ones watching on TV, and the ones who made all those plans you have to make to get out to the stadium. It seemed cruel and unnecessary to just send them home with just the ticket stub.

But about a half hour in, after a couple of camera shots of players on the sideline crying, the game was canceled, and in minutes it went from debatable to unthinkable that this game could be played. The next day, sports analyst Skip Bayless said he thought maybe it should have been played and he was practically canceled for just entertaining the idea. Because this is a nation of sheep.

2. **STUPID LOGIC.** Everyone on TV kept saying the same thing: "The game is not important—Damar Hamlin's life is important." Absolutely. Of course. And it's great it had a happy ending. But what the fuck does that have to do with playing the rest of the game after he was already in the hospital?

If you just heard the commentary, you would have thought we were asking him to suit up again and go back in the game. The inability to do two things at once—to recognize his life is more important than the game and that playing the game doesn't "dishonor" him, is depressing. Playing the rest of the game would have had zero effect on the thing we were all saying was most important—his life. The doctors in the emergency room weren't distracted because they were watching the game out of the corners of their eyes while they worked. Everyone talked about it like it was a zero-sum situation where playing the game would somehow take away from his care or in some way make us think his life wasn't more important than football.

You know who got this? Damar Hamlin. The first thing he wrote when he woke up was not "How am I?" or "Am I going to be OK?" It was "Did we win?" No, Damar, your team didn't win, because they didn't play, because you live in Stupidland.

3. **OVERREACTION.** The only appropriate reaction in America is over-reaction. I thought football was played no matter what, come rain or snow or whatever. It's a violent sport, we've established that, but it's also still voluntary—players are injured in every single game, and the announcers say, "We'll step away," which means we go to a commercial for Nationwide insurance while they scrape the body parts off the field, and we all hope—or, if it's your thing, pray—they'll be OK. And the fact that on this night the player in question turned out to be OK made it all the more ridiculous that everyone acted like the World Trade Center got hit again.

4. **HYPOCRISY.** This was a freak accident that did not have much to do with football—obviously if you collapse from a heart issue after a routine play, something else is going on with your health. But what *is* routine is players retiring with chronic traumatic encephalopathy (CTE) and then often not being able to function in life; some have even killed themselves because of it. Happily, Damar now seems fine. Unless he plays again and gets hit in the head so many times during his career that later in life he has CTE and finds life unbearable because of it. If they really cared about people getting grievously injured, they wouldn't have can-celed the game—they would cancel the sport. But again, they shouldn't, because we all should be able to make those choices in life. Life is about trade-offs, and they should always be ours to make.

5. **WEAKNESS.** There's no crying in football.

2

KNOWLEDGE

COMFORTABLY DUMB

Some years ago I was on CNN and said I didn't think Sarah Palin would ever be president, but I "wouldn't put anything past this stupid country." We went to a break, and when we came back Wolf Blitzer said, "People are already complaining that you're calling the United States a stupid country, giving you a chance to clarify." To which I said, "I don't need to clarify. It is."

I used to say our elections went on far too long, but you know what? No. Americans are dumb; they need the extra time. I used to think we should do it like the British, where an election takes five weeks, or France, where the official length of the campaign is two weeks. I've been to France; it takes that long to get a waiter to notice you. And these are people who will spend three days shopping for a cheese that goes with pears. Their idea of fast food is a snail. When they cooked Joan of Arc, she was still pink in the middle.

But we're not them. Americans are far too dim and distracted to responsibly make a choice in just weeks or even months. Americans actually think it's a brag to say that they're cynical about politics and therefore they don't follow it. Don't flatter yourself. Cynical comes when you know too much; you, on the other hand, haven't bothered to learn anything.

And it's odd, because Americans *are* capable of learning. Noam Chomsky once observed of listening to a sports call-in show, "It's plain that quite a high degree of thought and analysis is going into that. People . . . know all sorts of complicated details . . . on the other hand, when I hear people talk about, say, international affairs or domestic problems, it's at a level of superficiality that's beyond belief."

Which I found quite amazing. Noam Chomsky listens to sports call-in shows?

But his point is valid. We're not clueless, we just apply our brainpower to bullshit. Before people go out for a taco, they'll spend an hour on Yelp researching to find the most authentic one. All for something that'll be out of your body in fifteen minutes. They'll use six different websites to get a plane ticket for a weekend trip, but they don't care who runs the world for four years.

And for a people who are so amazingly unaware of so much of what's important, there's nothing this country loves to do more than "raise awareness." I think it's time to raise awareness that, when it comes to raising awareness, we raise too much of it, and it's making us crazy, anxious and depressed.

We're so aware 24/7 of every bad thing that could possibly happen that we've completely run out of colors. Purple is now the color for Alzheimer's, lupus, epilepsy, fibromyalgia and the opioid crisis. I used to like that color—now it scares the shit out of me.

Everything you can buy now comes in a pink version to raise awareness of breast cancer, including a pink drill bit for fracking, which is probably giving us cancer. Staples sells pink breast-cancer-awareness pens, paper clips, scissors—even a pink stapler *shaped* like a ribbon.

Walking the aisles there is like a visit to the Cancer Museum. Am I a terrible person because I'd like to buy office supplies without needing a drink afterward?

And football players with pink shoes? Let me go on record and say I am against breast cancer. But I'm trying to escape for a few hours—can I just watch the game without thinking about cancer? We've all heard about it. It's like raising awareness for death.

"Hey, what's that black ribbon for?"

"Death."

"What's that?"

"It's when you're not alive anymore—would you like to know more?"

Did you know that the month of March contains World Glaucoma Week, National Poison Prevention Week, International HPV Awareness Day and World Down Syndrome Day? And that March is also National Colorectal Cancer Awareness Month, Brain Injury Awareness Month, Bleeding Disorders Awareness Month, and National Deep-Vein Thrombosis Awareness Month? That's March for you, it comes in like a brain injury and goes out like deep-vein thrombosis.

The month of May brings us Salt Awareness Week—a whole week to be aware of salt. I thought we were. Is there someone out there thinking, "Why do restaurants always put the cocaine right next to the pepper?"

Budweiser pulled their ads from 2021's Super Bowl and donated the money to raise awareness about Covid, which by then I was pretty aware of. Hey, Budweiser, you weren't put on Earth to raise my awareness—you were put on Earth to lower it.

Humans need to zone out sometimes. That's why marijuana is so popular. And meditating. It's not a "privilege" to take a break from everyone else's problems—it's an imperative. Not every ad on TV needs to chastise me for not doing enough because I'm sitting around watching TV. I can't even watch *The Price Is Right* without thinking about cutting my dog's balls off.

Crew members on the major airlines now wear Black Lives Matter pins during the flight. But you can support a movement without being constantly reminded of it. Can I just get a rum and Coke and hold the white guilt trip until we land? Must we use every available platform as an issue billboard—clothing, commercials, social media, sporting events, award shows . . . milk?

I feel like this whole goddamn thing started with milk. Someone in the eighties looked at a milk carton and said, "What a waste—not using milk as a vehicle for missing children to plead with you to put down the shredded wheat and get out there and crack my cold case!"

But I'm not a PI. And I don't have a lab where I can cure cancer. Must we be sad about everything all the time, most of which we can't do anything about? The ribbons, the flags, the ads, the hashtags—it's like that person on the plane in the next seat who won't take a hint that you don't want to talk.

BY THE TIME I GET TO PHONICS

As I've traveled this country on weekends doing stand-up, during election years I see the political ads that are running in the local TV markets, and I think, "How can this possibly work on people?"

Political campaigns used to turn out two kinds of ads: the positive, or what I like to call "the Village People ad," where you're seen with a cop, a construction worker, a military guy and a minority; and the negative, the ones that look like they were shot by Navy SEALs wearing night-vision goggles, where you make your opponent look like someone who killed their spouse on an episode of *Dateline*.

When candidates in political ads say, "I approve this message," they should have to add at the end, "You dumb fucks."

"I'm Brad Turnbull and I approve this message . . . you dumb fucks." "Vote for me, because I'm meeting with firemen!" "I'm meeting with teachers!" "I'm meeting with cops," "I'm talking to kids," "I'm talking to *Black* kids," "I'm wearing a hard hat and looking concerned," "I'm pointing to the border wall with my thumb!"

Come on, that's my thumb, you must know I got this!

After all, didn't you hear me say I'm "strong on values" and "good for jobs"? That I'm "fighting for you" and "on your side" and am going to "get things done" and "shake things up"? And that I have a plan—details to follow—to "clean things up"? My God, my sleeves are rolled up, what more evidence do you need that I'm a good guy?

Unlike my opponent, who's always cackling maniacally. And who "lives in Washington." Good guys live in America, which is great and pure; bad guys live in Washington—gross—and are "career politicians."

There's a phenomenon psychologists call the Dunning-Kruger effect: the tendency of ignorant people to think they're much smarter than they are. Usually it's harmless and just leads to rock bands making concept albums about robots. But it gets scary when it leads to a president who says, "I like [reading] as little as possible. I don't need, you know, two-hundred-page reports on something that can be handled on a page."

That was Donald Trump who said that, but it could have been Reagan. Or George W. Bush. The anti-intellectual trend has only grown over the years in the Republican Party. Trump seemed to be actually proud that he made decisions as president without learning anything. Which made him the perfect president for a nation perpetually looking at its phone.

Illiteracy wasn't Trump's shame, it was his bond with us; a subliterate president for a subliterate country. A country where a majority of adults get their news from Facebook, and 46 percent of teenagers are "almost constantly" online. Mostly with Andrew Tate.

Before we tackle any of our daunting specific problems here in America, we have to figure out how a country can solve *any* problem if so many of its people are so intractably, astoundingly, mind-numbingly stupid. And I'm not saying that as hyperbole or just out of frustration. I mean this country just might be empirically, verifiably too fucking dumb to continue as an ongoing enterprise.

Jay Leno used to do a classic bit called "Jaywalking" where he asked ordinary citizens the kind of questions we used to consider common knowledge, and in the Internet age that bit has been updated and is still a useful indicator of where exactly we are on the birdbrain chart.

Here are some of the answers given on a TikTok site called Project Better:

QUESTIONER: Who's the first person to land on the sun?
ANSWER: Lance something . . . Lance— Armstrong?

QUESTIONER: What is the biggest city in the world?
ANSWER: I think it's, like . . . Asia?

QUESTIONER: If you were born in 2021, how old would you be?
ANSWER: Twenty-one.

QUESTIONER: What country is Venice, Italy, located in?
ANSWER: Gosh, I'm going to be a teacher, so I should know this . . . Paris?

QUESTIONER: Where is Queen Elizabeth from?
MAN: Egypt.
WOMAN: Brazil.

So you tell me: If a country is only as strong as its people, what can the future possibly hold for a population this moronic? Being a full-grown adult and thinking a human could walk on the sun? Or that the biggest city in the world is . . . Asia? When, plainly, it's Europe.

This country simply has no education standards anymore—they will let you out of a public high school and give you a diploma and you don't have to actually know anything. Which used to be the mission of schools: knowing things. I know it's super important to stop the grooming of our kids—or, I don't know, to start it—and certainly critical race theory must be stricken from the curriculum—or, who knows, maybe included in all of it—but while we're having those fights, could someone please notice that the kids don't actually know anything?

When asked "Does the Earth go around the sun, or the sun around the Earth?" 28 percent of Americans said the sun, where Lance Armstrong landed, revolves around the Earth. And the Earth revolves around

NASCAR. Americans know they live in the greatest country on Earth, but a quarter of them can't name one branch of its government, and less than half can name all three. A full 80 percent think Ramadan is those noodles college kids eat. A quarter of Americans say they haven't read a book in the past year, and the other three-quarters are lying.

Lately, the hottest thing in publishing has been adult coloring books, which you can find in the bookstore in the section marked "Seriously?" People will always say, "I love to read," but don't dig too deep into that. What they mean is they went to Barnes & Noble to buy a cat calendar and on the way out picked up another book on cooking in the Instant Pot. Or a self-help book. Or one of the many stories of a boy who dies and meets Jesus in heaven and comes back to life. Or something that's really for juvenile readers, like Harry Potter or *Twilight*. There's reading, and then there's reading: *The Da Vinci Code* is to literature what candy corn is to vegetables.

Facebook, Instagram, TikTok—these are not places to read in the sense of garnering real and valuable information; they're what *replaced* reading so you'd have more time to take pictures of your dick. Sorry, but staring at your phone doesn't make you a reader any more than watching fireworks makes you an astronomer, or getting a tramp stamp makes your ass a museum.

ENDLESS SUMMER

One of the big losers in our War on Knowing Things is summer. How can summer, the time of year when we traditionally give our brains a rest, retain its specialness if stupid season now runs all year round? How can you feel good about earning a vacation for your mind if we've retired from the job of thinking altogether?

If America insists on being at peak stupid at all times, how is my guilty-pleasure time of year supposed to outdo that? How can you enjoy casual Fridays when everyone already dresses like shit all the time? Flip-flops used to be a summer thing—now they're a year-round disgusting thing. It's not special to wear a swimsuit all day when your everyday pants have an elastic waistband. I saw a guy at a funeral in February wearing cargo shorts and a "Who Farted?" T-shirt. May he rest in peace.

It used to be that you worked hard and behaved responsibly for most of the year, and then when June came: school's out, brain's out. No reading except for trashy novels on the beach, no studying, no thinking—and the movies were all stupid.

We used to keep the sequels and superhero bullshit between Memorial Day and Labor Day—that was the deal. Then when September came, the serious movies came out. Films. And we accepted that: we'd had our fun with robots and car crashes, and then in the fall we knew it was time to go see the one where Meryl Streep teaches gay Holocaust survivors how to box. But now all year long is robots and talking raccoons.

Summer songs were different too: you could do the moody stuff in the winter, but summer you had to keep it light: doo doo doo, dah dah dah—stuff like that. The deepest a summer lyric got was "I like big butts and I cannot lie." But now all year round, half the songs have no lyrics, it's just noises people make during sex and odes to "the booty."

Time was, even casual conversations in the summer adhered to an unwritten code: keep it stupid. It's summer—we earned this; don't be an asshole and start talking about serious stuff! Keep it to "Is it hot enough for you?" "When do you think the ice cream truck's coming back?" and "What's the best way to get sand out of your ass?"

And this was all great—because you'd earned it! Even if you got a summer job, it was a weird gig you did for a few months. Or as it's now called, "a job."

EARNING CURVE

A few years ago, a second-grade teacher in Arizona posted her pay stub and it went viral, probably because she's one of the people we trust to care for and educate our children and she was making 320 bucks a week. We pay such lip service to kids: they're "the future," "our greatest natural resource," "we'd do anything for them"—but then we nickel-and-dime their teachers. If we really think children are our future, shouldn't the people who mold their minds make more than the night manager at GameStop?

Elisabeth Milich, the teacher who posted her pay stub, wrote, "I buy every roll of tape I use, every paper clip I use, every Sharpie I grade with, every snack I feed kids who don't have them." How do people, even the burdened taxpayer, justify this? Teachers are tired of being told what Sarah Palin once said of a teacher, that "her reward's in heaven." Maybe, but the rent's due here on Earth.

Five years ago in West Virginia a revolt started: teachers were just asking for a 5 percent pay raise—not a lot, but it helps when you have to pay for your own paper, your own pencils, and now your own bullets. Here's an idea: don't give teachers guns, give them a living wage. They're not asking for the world, just enough of a raise so they don't have to drive an Uber three nights a week. And yes, it turns out, teachers actually do drive Ubers. And work as cashiers at Hardee's on weekends, and sell their blood plasma to make ends meet.

But teaching isn't supposed to be a "side hustle."

If we really cared about kids, it wouldn't be so hard for states to pass laws against marrying them. That's right, fun fact: child marriage is legal in almost every state. What? Yes! True! In America you don't even have to start your own crazy religion to have sex with children, you can just marry them. And that's *every* state, not just the Waffle House states. More than two hundred thousand children were married in America over the past fifteen years—some as young as ten. In five states, there is *no* minimum age to marry. It's "Me Too" for Hollywood, but we're OK with *this*?

During the pandemic, when parents had to take over the job of educating their children at home, 69 percent of parents admitted that being a teacher is a harder job than their own. And 80 percent said they had a "newfound respect" for teachers.

Great—but how about we go beyond giving teachers "newfound re-spect"? How about we also give them a) that whole "enough money to live on" thing, and b) the benefit of the doubt?

Ask any teacher what their number one complaint is, and they'll tell you: it's overbearing parents sticking their noses in and doing their kids' work for them and trying to adjust grades and undermining disci-pline. Parents, you have *two* kids and you want to strangle them—can you imagine having to deal with an entire classroom full of tiny, sticky strangers?

It used to be the teacher would send home a report about the behav-ior of the child. Now it's the behavior of the teacher that gets judged. I've heard it from teachers many times: parents saying things like, "But my daughter studied really hard for this test." *Yes, but she got all the answers wrong.* That's what matters in life: results. Not just trying. Not just par-ticipating.

When everybody gets a trophy, the only people who win are the people who make trophies. If children don't learn that life can be full of disappointments, they won't be ready for Democratic primaries or their friends' improv shows.

If your kid gets a D, don't blame the teacher. Tell your child, "You should have worked harder and buckled down more—now go to your room and do whatever it is you do in there on your webcam." And the next time there's a classroom disagreement where a teacher says one thing and your kid says another . . . side with the teacher! I mark the onset of American decline to the moment parents started siding with their children instead of with the teachers.

Kids may be cute, but they're also relentlessly manipulative little weasels who can only be contained with a unified front. Mom, Dad, and the teacher used to form an iron triangle. Kids couldn't get away with shit, and they were so much healthier for it.

In the future, if a teacher takes your kid's phone, just tell that teacher, "Thank you. Thank you for doing something I lacked the balls to do years ago."

TUITION ACCOMPLISHED

Let's get real about what "higher education" in America really is: a racket that sells you a very expensive ticket to the upper middle class. President Biden's American Families Plan was one of his administration's centerpiece legislative proposals, asking the taxpayers to pony up hundreds of billions so that everyone can go to college, and billions more for subsidized childcare so our kids can go to school while *we* go to school. The theory being that all this education trickles down and eventually gets to Florida.

The Right calls Biden's plan social engineering, which is over-the-top, but Biden's plan *is* an endorsement of a particular idea: that the more time humans spend in classrooms staring at blackboards, the better. Liberals see more school the way Republicans see tax cuts: as the answer to everything. They imagine going to college is the way to fight income inequality, but actually it does the reverse.

If you have a bachelor's degree, you make about 65 percent more than someone who doesn't, and with a master's degree, it's more like 100 percent more. And the unemployment rate of college grads is about half what it is for high school grads. I know "free college" is now a left-wing thing, but is it really liberal for someone who doesn't go to college, and makes less money, to pay for people who do go and make more?

Especially since colleges have turned into giant, luxury day care centers with overpaid babysitters anxious to indulge every student whim. The University of Missouri has a river grotto inspired by the *Playboy* mansion, and Texas Tech has one of the largest water parks in the country, which includes a twenty-five-person hot tub, tanning deck, water-slide and "lazy river."

A third of students now spend less than five hours a week studying, and when they do it's for their onerous magna cum bullshit course load of Sports Marketing, History Through Twitter, Advanced Racist Spotting, Intro to Microaggressions and You Owe Me an Apology 101. In 2019 we issued almost as many undergrad degrees in "visual and performing arts" as computer and information sciences, and more than in math. Say what you want about Lori Loughlin, at least she understood that one good scam deserves another.

In the immortal words of her daughter Olivia Jade, "I don't know how much school I'm going to attend . . . but I do want the experience of, like, game days and partying."

Yeah, I'm not paying for that.

In 1960, colleges awarded A's to 15 percent of the students. Now it's 45 percent, and it's not because they got smarter. It's because of Adderall. But also because colleges now are businesses selling a consumer product for hundreds of thousands of dollars, and they want to give the customers what they want: a magical piece of paper called a diploma.

In the Middle Ages, the Catholic Church famously sold indulgences, which were just tickets to heaven that you could buy. Now another priesthood—of academia—sells a different ticket to heaven, and because it's so necessary, colleges can charge whatever they want. Since 1985 the average cost of college has risen 500 percent. It doubles every nine years. Every year it increases at four times the rate of inflation.

And yet, no one knows how to change a tire.

But that's only the beginning of the scam. A wannabe librarian needs a master's degree just to get an entry-level job filing books. I've heard this so many times from nurses and teachers and administrators, rolling their eyes when relating how they needed to take some bullshit course in order to advance in their field, when really they already learned what they needed to know by working the job.

But in the grift that is our higher education, when you want to move up . . . hold on there, not so fast. Tollbooth ahead. You need to pay for more "education" before we decide if you can do what you already do. This is what Scientology does: makes you keep taking "courses" to move up to the Bridge to Total Freedom.

The answer isn't to make college free. The answer is to make it more unnecessary. Which it is for most jobs. So that the many millions of Americans who either can't afford to or just don't want to go don't feel shut out. Because the system we have sets up this winner-loser dynamic and breeds resentment that working hard has less value than sitting around in the "lazy river," and that in turn feeds into our widening political division. Or as Trump once put it, "I love the poorly educated."

FRAT BOY SLIM

It's always struck me as strange that college campuses are where political correctness is the most stringently enforced, and yet smack in the middle of it all are frat houses: little Vatican Cities of depravity that seem to enjoy diplomatic immunity from civilization. There was a time when fraternities fit in with society as a whole, but that day is long gone—if you don't believe me, go back and watch *Animal House*. In 1978, watching a guy deciding whether he should have sex with an out-cold high school girl was something we all considered hilarious. And Bill Cosby still thinks so.

Revenge of the Nerds from 1984 has a scene where the guys break into a sorority and install cameras so they can watch the girls shower—and again, we all laughed. But when Penn State's Kappa Delta Rho frat got caught basically pulling the same stunt in 2015, no one was laughing. For one thing, institutions that go out of their way to have no women around always lead to abuse and madness and lighting farts. Scientology is bad, but at least it admits women; every ten years, someone has to pretend-marry Tom Cruise.

The fact is, any enterprise that has a history of excluding women almost always descends into sexual deviancy, at least at my bathhouse. Whether it's the Boy Scouts, the Taliban, Wall Street, the Penn State locker room or the US military with its enormous rape problem, sooner or later, a bunch of innocent folks get fucked. Show me any culture that's traditionally hostile to women and I'll show you a culture that's screwed up.

Oh, and there's one other little thing about fraternities that's bad: they kill people. Every year, some kid dies when the hilarious dangle-the-pledge-over-the-wood-chipper prank goes awry. Since 1970, there's been at least one hazing-related death every year as pledges routinely endure alcohol poisoning, sleep deprivation, waterboarding, being dressed in diapers, being buried in trash or being force-fed cat food. Jesus, why not just pledge ISIS?

A cult is a cult, and that's what a fraternity is: a place where they strip you of your personality and rebuild it in their image. That's why when a girl says, "I'm dating a frat guy," no one ever asks, "Oh yeah, what's he like?"

"I just told you—he's a frat guy."

Of all the bad things fraternities do, the absolute worst is that they take young people at the exact moment when they should be learning to be individuals and turn them into shit-eating, orders-following group-thinkers.

My college had a lot of fraternities, but it never occurred to me to join one, because finally in my life I was able to live on my own, away from family and among women; it had no appeal when some frat guy said, "Hey, how about coming with me to live with a bunch of dudes? Come on, we'll stick a carrot up your butt."

And this is where someone says, "But, Bill, fraternities are a tradition." So was throwing virgins in a volcano for a while. If you think "tradition" is a good enough reason to paint your face, or degrade women, or drink yourself sick, then maybe college isn't for you to begin with.

GOWN AND OUT

Every year at graduation time we witness the ritual of commencement addresses, when America's overrated gasbags and wisdom-free celebrities are invited by star-fucking universities to come to their school and tell a bunch of spoiled, stoned, debt-laden brats things like "Your only limit is your own imagination" and "The world will be a better place for having you in it."

But I say, why not level with the kids? Why not tell them the truth for once: Kids, you are not the future, you can't be anything you want to be and the only way you can follow your dreams "wherever they take you" is if your dreams involve the blender at Jamba Juice or wearing a Spider-Man costume in Times Square. Your parents just spent a quarter million dollars to send you to drinking camp, and the average student who takes loans now owes thirty-seven grand in debt—jeez, if you'd spent that on a minivan, at least you'd have somewhere to sleep.

But cheer up, because if you think it's bad now, take solace in the thought that in twenty-five years it's going to be so much worse! And so, I offer you here a glimpse into the future by way of what a commencement address in the year 2049 might sound like:

Graduates, parents, faculty, distinguished guests, masculine identifiers, feminine identifiers and cyborgs: Let me first say what an honor it is to be here today at the University of California, Goldman Sachs, and to join you in celebrating such an exciting time to be alive! 2049! This could be the year that we finally decide how we're going to handle pronouns!

Now, of course it's easy to get nostalgic for how things used to be under the first President Seacrest, back before Canada built a wall to keep us out, and back when a person starting out in life could still get a studio apartment in San Francisco for under two million dollars. A month. Well, now that same apartment is unaffordable for all but the top executives at Exxon-Google and Huffington Porn.

I'd love to tell you that the world is your oyster—but the oysters are all dead. Along with most species—but when that happened, did we give up and just start eating jellyfish? Well, yes. Of course we did. What else could we do? We can't all afford plankton! My point is, we're resilient: I believe it was former Miami Dolphins coach Don Shula who said, "Success is not forever, and failure is not fatal." Miami was a city that once existed in Florida.

And when it sank, we didn't panic—because we don't panic! Did we panic during the Zika epidemic of 2028?! No, and many of the pinheaded babies born that year have gone on to become fine Republican congressmen! Did we panic when Jesus returned to Earth, took one look

*at us and said, "Fuck you," and left? No! We rallied around President
Gaga and took solace in the words of Chief Justice Khaled, "We da best!"
Hats in the air!*

GRADDY ISSUES

As an Ivy League graduate who knows the value of a liberal education,
I have one piece of advice for the youth of America: Don't go to college.
And if you have to go, don't go to an "elite" college, because as recent
events have shown, it just makes you stupid.

There are few, if any, positives to come out of the massacre in Israel
on October 7, but one of them is opening America's eyes to how higher
education has become indoctrination into a stew of bad ideas, among
them the simplistic notion that the world is a binary place where everyone is either an "oppressor" or "oppressed." In the case of Israel, "oppressors" being babies and bubbes.

The same students who'll tell you that words are violence, and silence is violence, were very supportive when Hamas went on a rape and
murder rampage worthy of the Vikings. They knew where to point fingers: at the murdered. And then it was off to ethics class!

I recognize that a certain amount of foolishness is expected of college kids, but mixing Jägermeister and tomato juice isn't the same as
siding with terrorists. Thirty-four student groups at Harvard signed a
letter that said "the apartheid regime is the only one to blame," proving
they don't know what constitutes apartheid. They don't know much of
anything, but it doesn't deter them from having an opinion. They've convinced themselves Israel is the most repressive regime in history, because
students at upper echelon colleges today have no knowledge of history,
or even a desire to know it, and actual history doesn't come up in their
Intersectionality of Politics and Gender Queer Identities class.

Now, to be fair, at least five of the student groups have rescinded
what they signed, saying they didn't read the letter closely—and they
promised not to make that mistake again after they graduate and start

running the world. I actually believe them—that they didn't read the letter closely. I think they scanned it, saw it was blaming Israel, and went
back to surfing TikTok.

Because college life today is a day spa combined with a North Korean
reeducation camp, with the added perk that the people on campus who
fear being graded badly are the professors, not the students. The fact
that college presidents, who usually love to speak out about anything,
couldn't find their voice to condemn the worst attack on Jews since the
Holocaust says a lot about who really controls colleges and, why, if ignorance is a disease, Harvard Yard is the Wuhan wet market.

Not that colleges didn't always have professors with radical beliefs—
I know, because I used to sell them weed. But the reason why despis-
ing Israel became pretty much a requirement of the American left is
colleges—"elite" colleges, the mouth of the river from which this and all
manner of radical left, illiberal—yes, illiberal—nonsense flows.

Supporting all-Black (that is, segregated) dorms and graduation
ceremonies and orientation programs—which occur on hundreds of
campuses—is illiberal. So is the racism against Asian applicants, and
so is chasing speakers off of campus for not espousing the One True
Opinion.

When the First Amendment watchdog group Foundation for Individual Rights and Expression began ranking colleges based on their
commitment to free speech, Harvard came in dead last. There is only
one set of acceptable beliefs on campus, and it's policed hard. The old
dorm room bull sessions? It's less risky shooting the shit in Scientology.

John Stuart Mill wrote that "he who knows only his own side of the
case knows little." To which today's college students respond: "'He' and
'his' are cis pronouns that commit violence against queer and BIPOC
communities, so who cares what John Stuart Mill says, whoever he is.
Oh, and Thomas Jefferson was a slaveholder. He might've done some
other stuff too, but that wasn't on the test."

Elite schools should no longer be called elite—just say "expensive"
now. Which may be why they breed a particular brand of detestable

graduate, a personality type that doesn't tend to emerge from Chico State. Sure, they occasionally turn out someone decent, but for every Barack Obama there are two Josh Hawleys, the former debate-team jerkoff who had no friends, that no one likes today, and yet somehow manages to win a statewide popularity contest. Box-checking brown-nosers who don't actually believe anything, except that tricking stupid people is fun. That's why it's so repulsive when they pander for votes from Mama June and flat earthers because they just hate elitists!

Yes, consider these truck-driving He-Men from the tool aisle at Sam's Club who went to Ivy League schools: Vivek Ramaswamy? Yale and Harvard. Ron DeSantis? Yale and Harvard. Ted Cruz? Princeton and Harvard. There's a special magic that links Harvard types and being utterly face-punchable: Pat Robertson, George Bush, Tom Cotton, Mike Pompeo, Bill O'Reilly, Steve Bannon, Jared Kushner. Not to mention a large percentage of the current and recently past Supreme Court. It may seem that men like these and the kids who signed the Harvard letter have nothing in common, but actually I think they do: they all came out of an Asshole Factory.

And some, I assume, are good people.

To the older folks I say: college today is not the college you remember. And to the younger I say: don't do it. You don't need four years and a lifetime of crippling debt to learn to hate America when you can just watch five minutes of "Selling Sunset." If your parents have 300 grand they absolutely need to flush down the toilet, put it in crypto, or buy a van, go to a national park and feed yourself to a bear. Any legacy dipshit can go to Penn. But a bear? That's hard to get into.

CIV VICIOUS

For all the progressives and academics who refer to Israel as an "outpost of Western civilization" like it's a bad thing, please note: Western civilization is what gave the world pretty much every goddamn liberal precept that liberals are supposed to adore: individual liberty, scientific inquiry, rule of law, religious freedom, women's rights, human rights, democracy, trial by jury, freedom of speech . . . please, somebody stop us before we enlighten again.

And since one can find all these concepts in today's Israel and virtually no where else in the Middle East, if anything, the world would be a better place if it had more Israels.

Of course, this message falls on deaf ears to the current crop who reduce everything to being only about victims or victimizers—so Israel is lumped in as the toxic fruit of the victimizing West. The irony being that all marginalized people live better today because of Western ideals, not in spite of them.

Martin Luther King used Henry David Thoreau's essay "Civil Disobedience" to help shape the Civil Rights Movement. The UN's Universal Declaration of Human Rights owes its core to Rousseau and Voltaire. Cleisthenes never showed up for a sexual harassment seminar, but without him, there's no democracy. The cop who murdered George Floyd got twenty-one years for violating his Fourth Amendment rights, an idea we got directly from John Locke—a brilliant thinker who no one in college would ever study anymore because he's so old and so white and so dead. So Western.

That's how simple the woke are—it's never about ideas; if it was, would they be cheering on Hamas for their "liberation"—liberation? Liberated to do what? More freely preside over a country where there are no laws against sexual harassment, spousal rape, domestic violence, homophobia, honor killings or child marriage? This is who "progressives" think they should stand with? Women in Gaza would be lucky to get "colonized" by anybody else.

And for the record, the Jews didn't "colonize" Israel, or anywhere, ever, except maybe Boca Raton. Gaza wasn't seized by Israel like India or Kenya was by the British Empire, and the partitioning of the region wasn't decided by Jews, it was decided by a vote of the United Nations in 1947, with everyone from Russia to Haiti voting for it. But apparently they don't teach this at Drag Queen Story Hour anymore.

Now, it's true that for too long we didn't study enough Asian or African or Latin American history—but part of the reason for that is, frankly, there's not as much to study. Colleges replaced courses in Western Civ— Boo! Eye roll! Dead white men, amiright?—with "World Civilization" classes, which is fine in theory, but what it meant in practice is you read "Queer Poetry of the African Diaspora" instead of Shakespeare.

And I'm sure there's value in both, but as usual, America only ever over-corrects, and so we're at this place where the words "Western Civ" became a kind of shorthand for "white people ruined everything." But they didn't ruin everything—yes, they didn't live up to their own ideals for far too long, and they committed barbarous acts, but people back then were all beastly, not just the white ones, depending on who had the power.

But it was the Western Enlightenment that gave rise to the notion that the law of the jungle was something that should be curbed. Henry David Thoreau, Ralph Waldo Emerson, Jean-Jacque Rousseau, John Stuart Mill—three-named old dudes like that were the OG social justice warriors. The ideas that came through Athens, Rome, London, Paris and Philadelphia are what make life good for most people in free societies today: That individuals have value; that even the powers that be must submit to the rule of law; that punishment should not be "cruel and unusual"; that accused people get a trial. That there's such a thing as a war crime.

Why is it that every other culture gets a pass, but the West is exclusively the sum of the worst things it's ever done? You think only white people "colonize"? Historians estimate that the very non-Western Mr. Genghis Khan killed forty million people. And that was in the thirteenth century. He single-handedly may have reduced the world's population by 11 percent. On the other hand, he kind of made up for that because he was such a prolific colonizer of vaginas that today an estimated sixteen million people are his direct descendants.

FACTS OF STRIFE

The Christmas of 2023 was different than all others for me, in that every time I would see a Nativity scene on someone's lawn or at the mall, I couldn't help but think about where that manger really is. It's in the West Bank, on Palestinian land, controlled by the Palestinian Authority. In 1950, the little town of Bethlehem was 86% Christian. Now it's overwhelmingly Muslim.

Point being, things change. To 2.3 billion Christians, there can be no more sacred site than where their savior was born—but they don't have it anymore, and yet no Crusader army has geared up to take it back.

Things change. Countries. Boundaries. Empires. Palestine was under the Ottoman empire for four hundred years, but today an Ottoman is something you put under your feet. The city of Byzantium became the city of Constantinople became Istanbul. Not everybody liked it, but you can't keep arguing the call forever.

The Irish had their entire island to themselves, but then the British decided to start an empire and, well, the Irish lost their tip. They blew each other up over it for thirty years, but eventually everybody comes to an accommodation. Except the Palestinians.

Was it unjust that even a single Arab family was forced to move upon the founding of the Jewish state? Yes. But it's also not rare, happening all through history, all over the world, and mostly what people do is, at some point, make the best of it. After World War II, twelve million ethnic Germans got shoved out of Russia and Poland and Czechoslovakia because being German had become kind of unpopular. A million Greeks were shoved out of Turkey in 1923, a million Ghanaians out of Nigeria in 1983, almost a million French out of Algeria in 1962.

Nearly a million Syrian and Afghan refugees moved to Germany eight years ago—was that a perfect fit?

No one knows more about being pushed off land than the Jews themselves, including being almost wholly kicked out of every Arab country they once lived in. In the seventy years from 1948 to 2018, the Jewish population of Morocco went from 265,000 to 2,150; Tunisia, from 105,000 to 1,050; Egypt from 75,000 to 100 and Syria from 30,000 to 100; Algeria, from 140,000 to less than 50, Iraq from 135,000 to less than 10. Libya from 38,000 to . . . zero.

Yes, TikTok fans, ethnic cleansing happened both ways.

In *Fiddler on the Roof*, the family is always moving, to stay one step ahead of the Cossacks, but they deal with it. When they're leaving Anatevka, they say "Ah, it wasn't so great anyway—like other countries don't have roofs you could fiddle on?" That's not how they really felt, but they were coping; they coped. Because sometimes that's all you can do.

History is brutal, and humans are not good people. History is sad, and full of wrongs, but you can't make them unhappen, because a paraglider isn't a time machine. People get moved, and yes, colonized.

Nobody was a bigger colonizer than the Muslim army that swept out of the Arabian desert in the century after Mohammed's death and took over much of the world, and they didn't do it by asking. There's a reason Saudi Arabia's flag is a sword. Kosovo was the cradle of Christian Serbia, then it became Muslim. They fought a war about it in the 1990s, but stopped. They didn't keep it going for seventy-five years.

There were deals on the table to share the land called Palestine in 1947, 1993, 1995, 1998, 2000 and 2008, and East Jerusalem could have been the capitol of a Palestinian state that today might look more like Dubai than Gaza. Arafat was offered 95% of the West Bank and said no. Of course the deals weren't perfect—no deals are—but eventually most people decide to make a start somewhere in order to forge a better future for their children.

The Palestinian people should know: your leaders, and the useful idiots on college campuses who are "allies," are not doing you any favors by keeping alive the "river to the sea" myth. Where do you think Israel is going? Spoiler alert: nowhere. It's one of the most powerful countries in the world, with a $500 billion economy, the world's second largest tech sector after Silicon Valley and nuclear weapons. They're here, they like their bagel with a schmear, get used to it.

What happened to Palestinians after the Hamas attack on October 7 is horrible; attacks by Israeli settlers against Palestinian neighbors in the West Bank are horrible. But wars end with negotiation, and what the media glosses over is: it's hard to negotiate when the other side's bargaining position is "you all die and disappear."

The chant "from the river to the sea"? OK, I looked at a map: the river . . . the sea . . . Oh, I get it. It means you get all of it. Not just the West Bank which was basically the original UN partition deal you rejected. Because you wanted all of it, and always have, even though it's indisputably also the Jews' ancestral homeland, and so Arab armies attacked, in 1948, and lost. And attacked again, in 1967, and lost. And attacked again in 1973, and lost. As my friend Dr. Phil says, "How's that working for ya?"

Look at what Mexico used to own—all the way up to the top of California—but no Mexican is out there chanting "From the Rio Grande to Portland, Oregon." Because they chose a different path. They got real and built a country that's the world's fourteenth biggest economy. Because they knew the United States wasn't going to give back Phoenix any more than Hamas will ever be in Tel Aviv.

One of the leaders of Hamas said two months after the attack: "Save yourselves time and imaginary dreams. In a few years, Allah willing, you will have to discuss the situation in the region after Israel."

I'm sorry, who's the one with imaginary dreams? If I give you the benefit of the doubt and say your plan for a completely Jew-less Palestine isn't that all the Jews should die . . . a big if . . . what is the only other option?

They move. You move all the Jews. OK, I must warn you: there's going to be some kvetching. And we do this moving with what, a fleet of trucks called Jew-Haul? And to where are we moving this entire country? Texas? Sure, they have room, and I guess we could put the Wailing Wall on the border and kill two birds with one stone . . .

Or we could just get serious.

3

MEDIA

LOVE FACTUALLY

A few years ago, after it was found out that Facebook had wrongly given out the personal information of fifty million people, there was a movement started called #DeleteFacebook. Well, it #Didn'tFuckingWork.

Facebook has only gotten bigger, and since social media is where the world increasingly gets its news, maybe we should take a moment to remember how the whole thing got started. And it wasn't because Mark Zuckerberg had a calling to birth a world with a more informed populace.

It's because he started a website that gave college dudes the chance to rate women whose pictures he hacked from Harvard's databank. Yes, the most powerful man in the news business got there by inventing a "Hot or Not" site.

Of course, on the bright side, Facebook has solved many crimes. Like the ones where the genius thieves post pictures of the heist—because that's what Facebook does: it makes you stupider. Because there are only so many hours in a day, and you can only get so much accomplished if you're constantly checking to see what everybody you ever met had for lunch.

Facebook should be called Timesuck.

Of course, the world has always had a lot of gullible people who'll buy anything. Have you been to Salt Lake City? But at least Americans used to get their news from actual news organizations—now they get it from chain emails and chat rooms and Facebook posts written by lunatics and sadists.

Instead of "all the news that's fit to print," you click on a link from your cousin Jody who runs the Tilt-A-Whirl. Why waste money on a subscription to a newspaper when they'd just blow it on war correspondents?

People used to get their news from newspapers, because professional newsrooms took separating fact from fiction seriously, and they hired people who knew how to do that. But now people get their news on Facebook by "sharing," or as it used to be called, "hearsay." And that's what's so great about social media news sources! You're not *telling* lies—you're just *sharing* them. And anyway, lies are the new truth. Facebook—all social media—is the place where thinking went to die. All the time people used to just waste by reading books and newspapers? Now they're "sharing." Isn't it great that we share?

Putin thinks it's great—that's why he only had to spend 150 grand on the 2016 election, because we spread his propaganda for him.

Of course, a lot of "sharing" isn't really sharing either: it's humble-bragging. "So embarrassed! Didn't realize there was a hole in the knee of my jeans and my penis was showing . . ."

For something called "sharing," there's an awful lot of "here's something I want you to know I have." "Look at me." "Look how talented my kids are." "Look what great concert seats I have." "Look, I'm in Italy and you're in Pacoima."

And the Russians saw this. And they took our "everyone needs to smell my every brain fart" culture and used it as the engine for spreading their bullshit. For the purpose of starting cockfights. Except we're the cocks: brainless birds pecking at each other.

There is an entire building in St. Petersburg filled with a Russian "troll army": hundreds of employees of their defense department sitting in front of computers, pretending to be Americans and creating thousands of tweets, memes, news site "comments" and flat-out fake stories designed not to take sides on any issue but just to get us fighting about it. To create chaos, the better to elect a chaos candidate.

A Russian-created meme from 2016 said, "Up to 5.7 million illegals may have voted in 2008 election." That, of course, is ridiculous, but it nevertheless reached ten million American voters by way of Facebook, millions more through Twitter and one guy on Bing. Hillary Clinton spent over a billion dollars on her campaign, and the Russians beat her with 150 grand because they were able to turn Facebook into Fakebook. Or maybe a more apt name would be Shit-Starter. Because that's what their meddling was meant to do—start shit.

We can all stop asking the question "Why isn't our government functioning?" Because truth is dead, and the Internet killed it.

Remember back in the early nineties when we read about this new thing called the Internet that could put the totality of world knowledge right at our fingertips? Then someone discovered it could deliver free porn, and we quickly had something else at our fingertips. But bare breasts on the net are not the problem: at least some of those are real. The problem is that the Information Superhighway quickly became Bullshit Boulevard.

Before the Internet, you only had to put up with your wingnut uncle on Thanksgiving. Now he's forwarding you proof that Trump won Arizona and Epstein was murdered by the QAnon Shaman. The street-corner nut with the sandwich board used to be laughed at; now he's linked to.

A student in a social media focus group once said, "If the news is important, it will find me." Except it doesn't, and that's how we wound up with President Donald Trump. It's not surprising that it can't find you, since on social media news competes with videos of Russian car crashes, creepy clowns and a rabbi doing the Mannequin Challenge.

And you know how they say "you can't make this shit up"? It turns out you can. We know that in 2016, the top fake news on Facebook generated more shares, clicks and comments than the real news. Millions of people believed some straight-up bullshit that the Pope had endorsed Trump—when in fact, after Trump won, what the Pope said was "I'm praying for his enlightenment." To which God said, "I've done a lot of miracles, but gimme a break."

More than ever, politicians are living an entirely fact-free lifestyle, because when they're confronted on *their* lies now, they just say, "Oh, I see what you're doing by fact-checking me—I just don't care. Because my fans don't care."

When Trump—to take one of a thousand examples—said he saw American Muslims cheering after the 9/11 attacks and it was later proved it never happened, he just owned it more. George Santos took notice. These guys are like Pinocchio, except when they tell a lie their balls grow bigger.

This is new. That liars have stopped caring if they get caught. Bill Clinton had to get all weaselly when he got caught, but in today's world he'd just say, "Nope, I've never even *heard* of a blow job. That woman sucking my penis right now? I was bitten by a snake and she's getting the venom out."

And all of this for what? I never got the whole point of staying in touch with so many people I don't really care about. Maybe it's because I grew up on classic rock, where the songs were always about moving on: "Papa Was a Rollin' Stone" . . . "Free Bird" . . . "Ramblin' Man" . . . "Go Your Own Way."

Now *no one* moves on, and I don't get why that is. You don't need to follow Gary from high school who was your lab partner in chem class—you forgot chem, you can forget him. You don't need his "status update." His status is he never left town.

And guess what? Because of Facebook, you haven't either. Just remember, not everyone you've ever crossed paths with is meant to be in your consciousness forever. Some people come into your life, touch you and then leave. But enough about scoutmasters.

CHARLATAN'S WEB

Since so much of what passes for today's journalism is anything but, how about some new rules for identifying actual news:

When an Internet headline reads, "You won't believe . . . ," yes, you will, and no, it's not news. When anyone is demanding an apology, unless they have hostages, that's not news. And when the offended group is identified as "the Internet," "Twitter" or "people," it's nobody. Guarantee, when you click on the story you find out "the Internet" is three losers with a combined Twitter following of *their mom.*

I used to think something was "news" if a journalist reported it, but really we live in a world where it's "news" if Kesha's tit flops out, because Twitter will respond and then a "journalist" "reports" on "the controversy."

If a boob flops in the forest and no one is around to hear it, it doesn't make a sound . . . but if three jackasses tweet about it, it's news.

When Jennifer Lawrence appeared along with her male costars coatless to promote her movie *Red Sparrow*, the headline from *Elle* online was "Jennifer Lawrence's Latest 'Red Sparrow' Photocall Has Twitter Calling Out Gender Inequality."

Because the men were wearing coats but she wasn't. And even though that was her choice, someone with eleven followers didn't like it, and so the "story" was reported in the *New York Times*, the *Washington Post*, the *New York Post*, Fox News, the BBC, *Vanity Fair*, the *Chicago Tribune*, the *Guardian* and the *National Review*.

Now, these esteemed news organizations aren't saying *they* think it's a big deal, because they're serious journalists: they'd rather be writing about Syria and the oceans dying. But oh, the humanity, Jennifer Lawrence didn't have a coat! Wrap her up! Wrap her up!

And this isn't an outlier—this is a constant and prominent part of today's "journalism": creating some bullshit nonissue that a few trolls will predictably go apeshit over, and then reporting on those unrepresentative tweets like all of America is talking about nothing else. Here are some real headlines in the "serious" press:

"Twitter Is Outraged that 'Scream 6' Doesn't Feature Neve Campbell."

"Twitter Is Outraged Over Kamala Harris' Vogue Cover."

"Twitter Is Outraged Over 'Idol' Judges Eliminating Half-Blind Contestant on His Birthday."

No it isn't, it's the same three people, and it's not hard to find three people who are mad at *anything*. I could say "Good morning" on Twitter and three people would fire back, "Good in *your* privileged world, Bill Maher!"

No wonder "fake news" resonates so much with Trump fans—because so much of it *is* fake. Just nonsense made to keep you perpetually offended with an endless stream of "controversies" that aren't controversial and "outrages" that aren't outrageous.

Because places like the *Huffington Post* and the *Daily Beast* and *BuzzFeed* and *Salon* make their money by how many clicks they get—yes, the people who see themselves as morally superior are actually ignoring their sacred job of informing citizens of what's important and instead sowing division for their own selfish ends.

WRONG DIVISION

You know why nobody talks around the water cooler anymore? It's because as a culture, we no longer have enough in common to talk *about*.

And that's because the thing that was supposed to unite the world—the Internet—became too adept at doing the opposite: serving us "personalized content."

Do you know what I saw on my news feed this morning? No, you don't, because mine isn't the same as yours. People get news feeds now that just spit back customized stories based on what we've clicked on in the past. So I, for example, might see a lot of stories about pot, American history and, of course, Christian Mingle, whereas Hunter Biden gets ads for antiviral software. And antiviral medication.

Welcome to the brave new world of microtargeting—which, admittedly, is often harmless. No one gets hurt if my computer tells me "You bought James Taylor's *Greatest Hits*—you might also enjoy this pillow and these sleeping pills." Or "You've shown an interest in nipple slips—here's every picture ever of Tara Reid."

News feeds now track the news you're interested in and show you less of everything else, never burdening you with contradictory information or telling you anything new. That's what makes it "news"!

But only seeing the stuff that confirms the opinions you already have isn't news. It's Fox News. One reason so many Americans are apathetic about climate change is that their news sources simply ignore it as an issue. I mean, come on, it's depressing—and I agree, it is. I don't enjoy reading about climate change either. But I do want to know about it so I can plan when exactly to kiss my ass goodbye.

I recently saw a headline that said, "Jellyfish Taking Over Ocean." Which I found alarming. So I read the article, and apparently jellyfish are the cockroaches of the sea and will happily eat all the toxic shit we're putting in the ocean, which is killing everything else down there. But the jellyfish say, "Oil? We fucking love it! Plastic? I had some for lunch."

Yes, jellyfish: five hundred million years of yuchh—and now their time has come. And no one will hear about it unless a jellyfish washes up on a beach and exposes its nipple.

The news media lost trust because they became eyeball-chasing clickbait whores who bump the story about climate change for the one about grizzly bears in a Jacuzzi.

You can be mad at me for "giving a platform" to people like Kellyanne Conway, but Donald Trump is the apotheosis of the alt-right, and the media gave him the biggest platform ever. MSNBC, his supposed nemesis, covered every Trump rally in 2016 like we put a game show host on the moon. They made him look like he was president before he was.

Even during the primaries, Trump got three times the coverage of the entire rest of the field—although Marco Rubio was able to break through one week because he gave a very important speech about how Trump had a small cock.

There is an answer to this. When TV started, there was an understanding between the folks who owned the airwaves (the American people) and the folks who made TV (the Jews). And that understanding was that the news wasn't supposed to make money, it was something that corporations gave us as a public service. It was a "loss leader"—not a profit center in itself, but the prestige and goodwill it generated made up for the other shit they aired.

What's really sad is, they're selling out now for so little: from 2020 to 2022, CBS News was 2.5 percent of Paramount Global's revenue; CNN was 3 percent of Warner Bros. Discovery; and ABC and NBC News were less than 1 percent of Disney and Comcast, respectively.

Guys, take one for the team, it's not that much. It'll pay off in the long run.

THE APPY HOOKER

The tycoons of social media have to stop pretending they're friendly nerd-gods building a better world and admit they're just tobacco farmers in T-shirts, selling an addictive product to children. Because let's face it: checking your "likes" is the new smoking.

The term "brain hacking" refers to how everything Silicon Valley develops is purposely designed to make us feel compelled to check in constantly. Former Facebook executive Tristan Harris says, "They want you to use it in particular ways and for long periods of time. Because that's how they make their money. Every time I check my phone, I'm playing the slot machine to see, 'What did I get?' This is one way to hijack people's minds and create a habit, to form a habit . . ."

When I heard this—that Apple, Google and Facebook are essentially drug dealers—I thought: "Where have I heard that before?" Oh yeah, it was on the famous *60 Minutes* episode where tobacco executive Jeffrey Wigand admitted, "We're a nicotine delivery business," and Mike Wallace said, "And that's what cigarettes are for?" Wigand: "Most certainly. It's a delivery device for nicotine."

Yup, it was never about "smooth tobacco flavor"; it was about the nicotine and other drugs that cigarette makers deliberately put in to make it addictive. The moral rot in this country began when corporate America decided it wasn't enough just to successfully sell your product. People needed to be addicted to it. Keebler's cookies are not really made by elves in a tree—they're engineered in labs, like all processed food, with precise combinations of salt, sugar and fat that are specifically designed to *not* satisfy. The reason you can't eat just one pretzel is the salt is like the nicotine in the cigarette: it's the drug, and the pretzel is the delivery system. That's how twisted pretzels are.

Food companies aren't in the "satisfying hunger" business; they're in the "Finish the whole bag!" business. They're in the "We own you" business—"You are our junkie slave, you can't resist this shit, just put it in the cart and shut up before we make you suck our dick for it."

And so with your phone: every time you check it you're pulling that slot machine handle because you might get a reward. Facebook purposefully holds back the likes sometimes so you'll keep checking. Because you don't exist until you get a smiley face. And then that's not enough—you need a thumbs-up. Or better, a *giant* thumbs up. This is why the average person interacts with their phone over 2,600 times a day. It wants all your attention, all the time. It's not so much a service as it is Glenn Close in *Fatal Attraction*: "I'm not going to be *ignored*, Dan."

Pedestrian deaths are up because people in the crosswalk looking down are getting run over by drivers looking down. The whole damn country is constantly looking down. There's something being crushed out there, but it ain't candy. Philip Morris just wanted your lungs; the App Store wants your soul.

Today's phones make people assholes. Whenever someone starts in on how evil smartphones are, there's a pat answer coming back about how people have always freaked out about the latest technology corrupting young minds: "C'mon, they said it about radio and the telephone and TV."

Yeah, it sounds like that argument might be right—but it's not. Not if you think about it for more than two seconds.

I don't remember lugging a TV under my covers so I could watch *Huckleberry Hound* until the screen asked me "Are you still watching?" I looked forward to seeing *I Dream of Jeannie* once a week, but it didn't throw off my circadian rhythm. I liked *McHale's Navy*, but I wasn't addicted to it; I didn't watch it when I drove.

Radio to TV was a difference in degree; smartphones are a difference in kind—less like TV or radio and more like a pacemaker. Something you can't live without.

No other device has ever commanded our constant attention the way the smartphone does. There was no hard-core pornography on my family's twenty-four-inch Zenith television set—sadly—and we didn't have to worry that maybe my sister was on the landline with a strange man who was posing as another teenager but was really fifty.

A former VP at Facebook said he felt "tremendous guilt" because "the short-term, dopamine-driven feedback loops that we have created are destroying how society works." TV didn't do that. *Psychology Today* says the average high school kid now has the same level of anxiety as the average psychiatric patient in the early 1950s, and that's directly related to social media.

Increasingly, studies are linking phones to not just anxiety but depression, bullying, hate speech, fake news, sleep disturbance, relationship problems and photographs of knees on the beach. TV didn't do all that either. And TV didn't turn people into assholes: shady, needy, passive-aggressive, mean and fake: fake outraged, fake brave, fake pretty, fake supportive—phones make people fake their lives instead of living their lives. It's more important to get a picture of you looking like you're having a good time than actually having a good time. And the pathetic addiction to "likes."

"Did they like my picture? Maybe it wasn't good enough . . . maybe that means *I'm* not good enough!"

Phones have ruined self-esteem, comedy clubs, concerts, childhood, attention spans, sleep cycles, using toilet time to reflect and falling off cliffs. Oh, and dating, which has been reduced from a quest for true love to looking at a menu: "I think I'll have the Kelly tonight."

Phones make people bullies. Angrier, more vitriolic, more racist online than they would ever dream of being if they had to say those things to someone's face.

The phone made us passive-aggressive to our friends and hyper-aggressive to total strangers. It has two settings: "I'll kill you" or "You're dead to me."

Not that if "You're dead to me" was the message you wanted to send to someone you'd bother sending it, because even texting is too confrontational for most people now. We don't engage with our friends when we disagree, we just walk away. Don't like something? Delete it. Don't want to talk to someone? Don't reply. Just ghost them. Ghosting—it's the electronic equivalent of going out for a pack of smokes and never coming back.

Cell phones have obliterated courtesy—the fundamental building block of developing any real relationship. We all see it—groups of friends out together at a bar or eating in a restaurant and they're all staring down at their phones. Imagine how rude that would be if, instead of a phone, you brought a magazine to the table and read it during dinner with a "friend."

Many is the night I've wanted to say to someone, "Can you just put the phone down for a minute? After all, we haven't seen each other in weeks and . . . we *are* having sex."

4

FREE SPEECH

GULP, FICTION

Twitter and Facebook have been in the news a lot lately for, depending on your point of view, either nobly protecting us from "misinformation" or unfairly limiting our right to read diverse positions. But even if the information we were protected from was always wrong—and it most definitely was not—the idea we can clean up Twitter and Facebook and protect you from fake news is ridiculous. It would be like trying to fact-check the graffiti on the bathroom wall of a dive bar: "We called this number and we *didn't* have a good time!"

Keeping you safe and sorting out the lies from the truth is not the job of Twitter or Facebook—it's yours.

Do lies spread faster than they used to? Yes, but this must have always been a somewhat similar problem since Jonathan Swift said, "Falsehood flies, and the truth comes limping after it," in 1710. People lie; that's what they do. And every age is the Misinformation Age. And whenever a new means of communication comes along, some people reach immediately for the censor button.

In 1858, the *New York Times* thought we couldn't handle the transatlantic telegraph, saying it was "superficial" and "too fast for the truth." In 1487, the Pope issued an order to stop "the misuse of the printing press for the distribution of pernicious writing." You know, fake news, like how the Earth is round.

In 1938, radio was the hot medium of the day, and lots of people got plenty worked up about *it*—especially after Orson Welles presented what was obviously a fictitious drama about a Martian invasion of New Jersey and thousands of people thought it was real and panicked. You can't censor away that level of naïveté: the Martians had the whole universe to invade and they chose New Jersey?

Lies are ubiquitous, and in that way, are quite analogous to germs and viruses. Deluded people think you can germ-proof the world and never have to be in contact with the pathogens that can do you harm, but you can't; you have to have a strong immune system. It's the reason babies who live in sterile environments are more likely to develop allergies than babies who are allowed to exist in the world as it is, messy and impure.

Lies are all around you: develop a better bullshit detector. That's a better solution than *me* giving up what *I'm* allowed to read. Who decides that?

In 2021, sixteen thousand doctors, scientists and researchers signed a petition called the Great Barrington Declaration that listed legitimate dissenting opinions about how our government was handling the Covid crisis—and many of those esteemed doctors were banned or downgraded from Google, Twitter, YouTube . . . Why are your doctors more worth hearing from than my doctors? Who decides what gets the "no evidence for that" sticker slapped on it?

Most people in this country still have a religion. They believe they have an imaginary best friend in the sky who listens and responds to them when they "pray." Nobody throws up a warning label on that that says, "There's no evidence for this." And sometimes, misinformation is just history's first draft.

Conservatives do seem to have a special talent for embracing the real eye-roll stuff, like wildfires are started by Jewish space lasers, or Bill Gates put microchips in the vaccine, or that the 2020 election was "rigged." But 41 percent of Democrats in 2021 believed the hospitalization rate if you got Covid unvaccinated was over 50 percent, when it was actually less than 1 percent. Somebody's "misinformation" got to those people.

We have to get past this endless, unforgiving, zero-tolerance mindset bent on punishing and disappearing anyone caught saying the "wrong" thing. The right response to speech you don't like is more speech, not the lazy, cowardly response of canceling people and shutting them up.

We've all become very adept at saying things that are technically true but lack context, or that leave out half the story, because so few people are really interested in the truth; they're interested in the piece of the truth that backs up *their side*. If we're going to ban "untruth," does that include the half-truth? The quarter-truth? And don't the wokest people in the world believe that what really matters in today's world is "your truth"?

So, of course, ban kiddie porn, and libel, and personal threats, and calls for insurrection—that's a no-brainer because they're *already illegal*. Just as it would be illegal in an actual town square to whip out your dick, so should it be in the digital square. And so should bots and deepfakes be banned, and anything else that isn't really the people who they say they are.

But that's an entirely different thing than actual people expressing an opinion, as repugnant or offensive or misguided as some opinions may be.

This is still America, where people have the right to express what they think, including to be wrong, to lie and, yes, to be an asshole.

And if you think you know everything and no one else could possibly have some other truth, you should be glad for that protection. Because you're an asshole.

CAL JAZEERA

In 2014 I gave the commencement address at Berkeley's winter gradua-tion, despite strong protests against my appearance. Here was my report on that:

Now that it's been a month since I gave the commencement address at Berkeley, someone has to check in with the people who tried to have my speech canceled and make sure they made it through OK. Also, since they were protesting me for once saying that Islam is "the only religion that acts like the Mafia and will kill you if you say the wrong thing or draw the wrong picture," and then two jihadists gunned down twelve people in Paris for saying the wrong thing and drawing the wrong pic-ture, you have to tell me: Where do I go to protest *you*?

Bill Donohue is the head of the Catholic League, and as such, he's called me an anti-Catholic bigot so many times, it's now my ringtone. Bill also once took umbrage at my stance on pedophilia—I'm against it—and threatened to punch me in the nose. Because whether you're represent-ing the Prince of Peace or the Religion of Peace, threatening violence is a great way to drive home the point that you're secure in your medieval beliefs.

Last week, Mr. Donohue wrote that it was too bad *Charlie Hebdo*'s publisher "didn't understand the role he played in his tragic death," which is like saying the rape victim didn't understand that her clothes were too sexy. And that's the great irony of Bill Donohue: he's a staunch advocate for a religion that considers masturbation a sin, and yet he's a huge jerk-off.

Glenn Greenwald says "anti-Muslim speech," like the cartoons in *Charlie Hebdo*, are "a vital driver" in "bombing . . . and occupying Muslim countries and killing . . . the innocent." Wow, newspaper cartoons did all that? Wait till they get to the horoscopes and the crossword. It reminds me of one of the protest signs I saw up at Berkeley. It said "Islamophobia Kills." The phobia kills? Or maybe more the AK-47s and the beheadings?

In much of Europe, denying the Holocaust is a crime. It shouldn't be.

The French arrested an anti-Semitic comedian for his comments about the *Hebdo* attack, which were vile, but opinions shouldn't be illegal. Everyone can always come up with a reason why the thing that bugs *you* should get a waiver—but free speech only works if there are no waivers.

SAVING PRIVATE LYIN'

Apple, the company that made it possible for men to send a woman a picture of their penis from thousands of miles away, released an update in 2021 that allows them to hack into your phone without your consent in order to snoop through all your pictures just in case you're a pedophile. Or as Matt Gaetz put it, "I'm switching to Samsung."

Now, let me be clear, I'm *against* pedophilia—that's why I joined QAnon. But nosing through everybody's private photo stash is casting an awfully wide, intrusive net. It's like if the company that sold you a safe said, "Oh, and we're going to stop by sometimes when you're not home to make sure you're not keeping naked pictures of kids in it."

This is the very definition of unreasonable search and seizure, which can and will be abused to find evidence of other illegal stuff on our phones. In my case, drugs. Our phones should be like our wallets or purses—private. What about probable cause? What about the Fourth Amendment?

In 2014 a sad asshole named Donald Sterling lost the team he owned, the LA Clippers, because he was taped in his home asking his mistress not to flaunt her relationships with Black players. When President Obama was asked about the Sterling episode, he said, "When ignorant folks want to advertise their ignorance . . . just let them talk."

But Sterling didn't advertise—he was bugged. And while he may not be worth defending, the Fourth Amendment is. That's the one that says we have the right to be secure in our person, in our homes, in our property. Well, not if bitching to your girlfriend in your home loses you your property.

In an op-ed in the *Washington Post*, Kathleen Parker offered one way of dealing with the modern world's ubiquitous invasions of privacy: give up.

She wrote, "If you don't want your words broadcast in the public square, don't say them." Really? Even at home we have to talk like a White House press spokesman? She then looked on the bright side by saying, "Such potential exposure forces us to more carefully select our words and edit our thoughts."

Always editing? I'd rather be a Mormon. I would listen to a hundred stupid boyfriends if that was the price of living in a world where I could also hear interesting and funny people talk without a filter. Perhaps most chilling of all, Parker said, "Speaking one's mind isn't really all it's cracked up to be," which is quite a statement, since her job is speaking her mind. It's like your AA sponsor telling you sobriety is overrated.

So let me get this straight: we should concede that there's no such thing as a private conversation anymore, so therefore remember to lawyer everything you say before you say it, and hey, speaking your mind was overrated anyway, so you won't miss it.

I would miss it. Does anyone really want there to be no place where we can let our hair down and not worry if the bad angel in our head occasionally grabs the mic?

What about the bathroom? Not a public bathroom, of course I expect to be taped and photographed in there. But my bathroom at home: Would it be OK if that was kind of a cone of silence where I could invite friends in to speak freely?

Who wants to live in a world where the only privacy you have is inside your head? That's what life in East Germany was. That's why we fought the Cold War. So we'd never have to live in some awful limbo where you never knew who, even among your friends, was an informer—and now we're doing it to ourselves!

Well, don't. Don't be part of the problem. Because we're humans—we're not that good; we're not ready to live in a world where everything has to come out perfectly on the first take. There's a reason houses have doors on them and windows have shades.

CRASS WARFARE

Ever since Donald Trump came on the political scene and injected words like "pussy" and "motherfucker" and "shit" into common use, something changed in American political discourse. Oh sure, Dick Cheney once told a senator to go fuck himself, and Joe Biden called Obamacare "a big fucking deal," but those comments were off mic, not intended for public consumption, and considered gaffes.

But Andrew Dice Trump didn't even try to clean it up publicly, and the voters have decided that not only don't they mind their leaders swearing, they kind of like it when a politician drops the façade and talks the way we all talk.

Well, be careful what you wish for, because a future State of the Union address could sound like this:

Mr. Speaker, Madam Vice President, fellow citizens: I stand before you tonight to report that the state of our union is fucking awesome. Thanks to the programs we put in place, inflation has been kicked in the taint, we are job-creating like a motherfucker, and our deficit is shrinking like a cock on a cold morning.

But I know that even though the economy is strengthening and the stock market is up, too many working families still feel like they're taking it in the ass. And that shit needs to stop.

For too long, we've been borrowing money like a bitch in heat, and when that happens small business owners get skull-fucked. I recently completed a listening tour, and hauling ass around this great nation, I talked to everyone, from the shit-kickers in Texas to the clit-lickers in San Francisco, and the one thing they all have in common is debt.

I met a hardworking single mom named Cindy Walker in Ann Arbor, and when I explained to her that just servicing the interest on the debt is why we don't have money for education and health care, she looked at me and said, "Mr. President . . . fuck! That is dumber than dogshit! Don't you ass-clowns in Washington do anything all day, or are you so busy rimming each other you don't have time to think about the little guy?!"

And she's right! I know! Being in debt is like fucking a fat guy: it's hard to get out from under it.

Here with us tonight is Bob Guggins from Park Ridge, New Jersey; Bob's story is America's story. He busted his nut sack for twenty-seven years assembling brake pads, until the company decided to move the factory to Mexico, and Bob was shit-canned and left holding his dick in his hand. Which is why, if this Congress asks me to raise taxes, I'll say no. And they'll push and I'll say no, and they'll push again and I will say to them, "Lick my balls, no new taxes!"

Also with us tonight is Shirley Fowler, a widowed mother of four who, along with her husband, Bud, worked hard and played by the rules. But Bud was killed in a fertilizer plant explosion due to a rollback in workplace regulations, and now Shirley's life is a shit show. By day she labors for minimum wage wiping down the sneeze guard at Shakey's, and by night she works the pole at a country music strip club called Puss 'n' Boots, giving tug jobs in the parking lot for extra cash. Let us make this pledge tonight: that in the richest country in the world, no one should have to do a lap dance or suck a dick to make ends meet!

Last year when Diane and I were campaigning in Ohio, I met a sixth-grade teacher in Chagrin Falls, and, well, she looked like she'd had a hard day, so I gave her a hug. And I asked her what was wrong. She pointed at her classroom and said to me, "Mr. President, these kids don't know shit. They deserve an education that doesn't suck balls." We can do better!

We also must do better caring for our wounded warriors, like air force veteran Sergeant Jeff Monroe, who lost a leg fighting in Syria, but instead of bitching about it like a little cunt, Jeff worked with blade-runner technicians and this year ran in the Boston Marathon.

It is for soldiers like Sergeant Monroe that tonight I am asking this Congress for one hundred billion dollars in increased military spending: let every nation know that if you fuck with the United States, you are fucking with the most balls-out, badass swinging dicks the world has ever seen, and we will not hesitate to tear off your head and shit down your neck.

My friends, there are those in these uncertain times who say America's best days are behind us, but I say: Fuck that! Fuck that! Fuck that!

There's a term our eleven-year-old, Tyler, likes to use: "BDE." It stands for "big dick energy," and I know if we pledge with all our strength to harness the big dick energy in each of us, then America's greatest days are still ahead.

Thank you, God bless you, and God bless the United motherfucking States of America.

5

GENERATIONS

GOING POSTAL

If someone knows of a story that better captures what's wrong with today's "journalism" than the saga of what happened at the *Washington Post* in 2022, please keep it to yourself, because it would be too depressing.

The shitstorm at the *Post* started when one of their best reporters, David Weigel, retweeted—not tweeted, retweeted—this joke: "Every girl is bi. You just have to figure out if it's polar or sexual."

The comedian who actually wrote the tweet called it "a banal throwaway joke"—which is exactly what it is. Throwaway, as in, if you don't like it, throw it away. For eons, each sex has made jokes about how the other is crazy, and no one but the perpetually offended thinks it means anything more than that the sexes get frustrated over how differently we each see the world, and yes, we relieve some of that frustration with humor. And, scene . . .

Nevertheless, Weigel pulled down his retweet and wrote, "I apologize and did not mean to cause any harm." And that was the end of that. I'm joking, of course. The unlicensed day care center that is today's "newsroom" went apeshit. You see, the *Post* has another writer named Felicia Sonmez, and she's . . . a lot. For example, she tweeted about Kobe Bryant's 2003 rape trial hours after his helicopter crashed.

And despite the fact that Felicia says Dave Weigel is a "good friend," she resurrected the tweet he took down with a screenshot and demanded to know what the *Post* was going to do about this unacceptable evil that must not be allowed to stand, sarcastically writing, "Fantastic to work at a news outlet where tweets like this are allowed!"

Yes, can you imagine a world that allows jokes you don't like?

Of course, the leadership at the *Post* folded like a Miami condo and suspended Weigel without pay for a month and denounced the offending retweet as a gross violation of their values—free speech apparently not being one of them.

Then a third *Post* reporter offered up the idea—of course, on Twitter, because why do anything privately?—that hey, maybe everyone was overreacting and we should all just calm down. And then it was really on. Felicia demanded that the *Post* also discipline *that guy*, and tweeted about that. I assume she's tweeting about this right now.

For days, she raged with the fire of a thousand burning bras, sending a gazillion tweets calling for more to be done against Weigel, mocking her bosses, attacking colleagues and letting the world know how much the *Washington Post* sucked. And this endless bickering and infighting continued online in public view until the bell rang and they all went to seventh period.

Now, note that I haven't yet told you what age Felicia Sonmez and her quarreling coworkers are. Why? Because I didn't have to. Because you can't imagine someone my age acting like this in an office. Around the same time, the *New York Times* ran an op-ed entitled "Why Are We Still Governed by Baby Boomers?"

This is why. Because too many millennials/Gen Z–ers are overly sensitive, overly fragile and have no sense of priorities. I'm sure many boomers would love to retire, but they can't; they're like the grand-mother who'd much rather be watching *Judge Judy* but has to raise her grandkids because her own kids are too fucked up to manage it.

You think my generation is an eye-roll? I'm going to let you in on a little secret about the younger generations: no one wants to hire you. Your sense of entitlement is legendary and—with notable exceptions—your attention span and work ethic stink.

Here's a story you never stop hearing around Hollywood: unquali-fied little shit who's been here all of six months doesn't understand why they're not a producer yet.

This *Washington Post* story had such resonance because it's be-havior we all recognize. There's a war going on within the millennial generation—I know, because I'm friends with the good ones. But the crybabies, unfortunately, are still winning. They complain they haven't taken over yet—well, stop, because in many ways you already have. The fact that the *Post*'s initial response was to punish not Felicia but one of their best reporters for a silly joke shows that the kindergarten is already in charge.

Fifty years before this nonsense went down at the *Washington Post*, the paper had given the world a master class in investigative journal-ism covering the Watergate break-in. I have to wonder how the *Post*'s newsroom of today would handle that story—or how they're currently handling any story.

All this time spent blubber-tweeting over a retweet begs the ques-tion: Don't you have anything better to do? Aren't you supposed to be reporters digging up stuff? Are there no more vital issues going on in America right now?

This is why millennials are not in charge—because if someone named Deep Throat called the paper today and wanted to meet in a parking ga-rage, this crew of emotional hemophiliacs would have an anxiety attack and report to HR that they didn't "feel safe."

If there's a silver lining to this story, it's that eventually the *Post* did fire Felicia Sonmez, so maybe there is a line that equates to just too much nonsense—but that generation needs to move that line much closer to sanity and find it much sooner. Because Democracy dies in dumbness.

GOODBYE, MR. STRIPS

In November 2018, Stan Lee died, and a few days later I posted a blog that was in no way an attack on Mr. Lee but took the occasion of his death to express my dismay at people who think comic books are literature and superhero movies are great cinema, and who in general are stuck in an everlasting childhood. I wasn't even aware that I had ruffled so many capes until I saw that forty thousand Twitter followers unfollowed me in one day—a personal best.

Director Kevin Smith accused me of "taking a shot when no shots are fuckin' necessary." Except, again, my shot wasn't at Stan Lee, it was at the idea that comics aren't just for kids—they are. That's why they sell them next to the Pokémon cards and not on the aisle with the condoms and lube. If you're an adult playing with superhero dolls—I'm sorry, I mean "collectible action figures"—why not go all the way and drive to work on a Big Wheel?

Other people tweeted things like, "I learned about social justice and racial tolerance by reading comic books." OK, but now you have pubic hair: *Read James Baldwin.* Read Toni Morrison. Read Michael Eric Dyson. Even a book as dumb as the Bible gets this: "When I was a child, I spoke as a child, I understood as a child, I thought as a child: but when I became a man, I put away childish things." Including my X-Men bedsheets.

Bragging that you're all about the "Marvel Universe" is like boasting that your mother still pins your mittens to your sleeves. You can, if you want, like the exact same things you liked when you were ten, but if you do, you can't claim to have grown up. That was the point of my blog: it wasn't that I'm glad Stan Lee is dead—it's that I'm sad you're alive.

There's nothing wrong with a man writing comic books, but there is something wrong with adults thinking they're profound.

The folks at Stan's company, "Team Stan," wrote an open letter to me and said, "You have a right to your opinion that comics are childish and unsophisticated. Many said the same about Dickens, Steinbeck, Melville and even Shakespeare."

Um, no, they didn't. No one ever said *King Lear* or *Moby-Dick* was childish and unsophisticated—if you ever read a book without pictures, you'd know that. Team Shakespeare should write *you* an open letter. Hamlet, Howard the Duck, same diff. "To thine own self be true," meet "Hulk smash."

And if someone says you're being childish and you react by throwing a tantrum, you're not Iron Man. You're irony, man.

Grown-ups these days cling so desperately to their childhood that when they do attempt to act their age, they have a special word for it: "adulting." Hey, world, look at me: "I just made my own doctor's appointment! #Adulting." "Ate vegetables at dinner! #Adulting." "Today I wiped my own ass . . . I guess I'm turning into my dad!"

GREEN FAKERS

Greta Thunberg has shown the world that she is the conscience of her generation. Unfortunately, while she may be its conscience, she doesn't represent it. I really wish you did, Greta, but you don't.

Greta Thunberg: around fifteen million followers on Instagram. Kylie Jenner: over four hundred million.

Seriously, who is the real "influencer" in that generation? The model citizen? Or the model? The young woman who refuses to fly . . . or the one who refuses to fly commercial? Greta gets where she's going on a sailboat, powered by the wind. Kylie takes a private jet, powered by Exxon. And she's twenty-seven times more popular.

Now, this is not a screed against comfort or capitalism—I'm fond of both.

And I also fly private (see chapter 17). And I give Kylie credit: like her dad, she's a self-made woman.

But Kylie embodies and embraces a lifestyle that is pretty much the opposite of carbon-neutral, and the younger generations love it. Kylie posts things like a tour of her shoe closet, which houses "well over a thousand pairs." She also has entire rooms of things she's only worn once—yay!

In polls, young people always claim to be more concerned about climate change than other generations, but they don't act like it. They throw around buzzwords like "sustainable" and shame people who forget to bring a cloth bag to Trader Joe's, but one of their favorite YouTubers is MrBeast, who's famous for stunts like "I Gave My 40,000,000th Subscriber 40 Cars." Jason Derulo celebrated his twenty-two millionth follower by eating twenty-two hamburgers.

The cognitive dissonance between planet-destroying conspicuous consumption and planet-saving rhetoric is breathtaking. Kids, you say you love Greta and her message, but everything else you love is a climate disaster.

Far from rejecting consumerism, young people are so obsessed with labels that venerable fashion houses like Balenciaga have pivoted from selling couture dresses to rich women, to selling $400 baseball hats to teenagers. And where does a twentysomething get the money to pay $400 for a hat that borrows the Bernie Sanders logo because you're, like, a socialist and stuff? From Mommy and Daddy, of course, those huge assholes who ruined the planet. Oh, and also maybe by trading Bitcoin, the mining of which is worse for the environment than actual mining.

Cryptocurrency uses more energy than Netflix, Apple, Facebook, Microsoft and Google combined, and more than some entire nations, and yet young people couldn't love it more if it apologized for old tweets. Ninety-four percent of crypto buyers are either millennials or Gen Z, which makes it ring a little hollow when you're out there chanting for us to "put the planet ahead of profits." And what do crypto fans say about this? They say, "Well, yes, it uses too much energy now, but in the future . . ." Ah yes, the future. Same thing my generation said: Let them handle it in the future. I'll get mine now.

Like Bitcoin, the smartphone is a huge contributor to carbon emissions, because the Cloud isn't an actual cloud, of course; it's a vast network of servers using energy, and all that liking, following and subscribing requires lots of fossil fuels. And yet you'd need the jaws of life to pry a phone out of the hands of anyone under thirty.

What would it take to convince Gen Z and millennials to give up their phones? A pollster once asked that: 43 percent said it would take $5 million. To give up their phone. One in ten said they'd sacrifice a finger for it. That deserves a "high four"!

I know it would be fire to be able to both live like Kylie and also save the planet, but you can't do both. In 2020, when Australia was devastated by wildfires, Greta reminded us in a tweet that "we still fail to make the connection between the climate crisis and increased extreme weather events."

Kylie too was moved by the disaster and tweeted about how the loss of animal life breaks her heart. Then she quickly followed up with a post of her new $1,500 Louis Vuitton mink slippers. It's always so sad when fire kills potential slippers.

People need to make a choice: Do you want to be progressive or excessive? Team Drastic or Team Plastic? When Kylie's lifestyle becomes uncool and unpopular, and you stop loving Bitcoin and stop thinking that stuffing your face is harmless, I'll take you seriously—until then, shut up about how older generations ruined the planet.

We get it—boomers dropped the ball on the environment. We did. We dropped it like it was hot. But have you picked it up? I wish your generation were better than mine, I really do—but the sad truth is, we're completely the same: lots of talk, but at the end of the day, hopelessly seduced and addicted to pigging out on convenience, luxury and consumption.

So that's it. You can be either the fake-tits-and-private-jet generation or the one that saves the planet. But you can't be both. Because fake tits are not biodegradable.

ERR A PARENT

I know it seems like I'm being harsh on the younger generations, but here's the interesting thing about that: whenever I talk to anyone in those generations about these critiques, they never push back against them. Their response is always "I know, we suck."

"You're on your phone too much." "I know!"

"You have too much anxiety for no good reason." "That's so true!"

"You do too much virtually and not enough in person." "I agree!"

It baffles me that they seem to realize all this about themselves but are helpless to change it. But I really do feel for them, and since 2019 marked the first graduating class of Gen Z, I thought they deserved a special commencement address to memorialize the occasion:

Honored alumni, legacy students, parents, grandparents, stepparents, third wives and drunken uncles: I know it's traditional at commencement ceremonies to break the ice with a joke, so, here goes: A man walks into a bar. Of course, it doesn't have to be a man. It absolutely could be a woman, but then, who am I to write a joke about a female when I don't have firsthand experience of a woman's struggle? So a nonbinary, non-gender-conforming humanoid walks into a bar and orders a drink, and the bartender says, "You took too long, we closed twenty minutes ago."

Well, I see that about 50 percent of you are texting, so I can tell already this will be somewhat pointless, but it is my job as your graduation speaker to tell you that you're a very special group of young people and the future belongs to you.

But let's not kid ourselves. You're not that special, and the future belongs to China and our robot overlords. But OK, let me see if I can fake it: "You're the smartest, you're the best, and thanks to that photography degree you have now, you're gonna change the world!"

Now I want you to look in the gallery today and find your two best friends: Mom and Dad. They're the ones who worked and sacrificed to scrape together the half a million in bribes needed to get you into this seventy-thousand-dollar-a-year keg party they call a college.

And, parents, I'm here today to tell you that the results of your parenting have been incredible—for the pharmaceutical industry. Because these kids are fucked up and need drugs. They need drugs for the crushing levels of anxiety they have, brought on by the knowledge that after the way you pampered and spoiled them, life is going to crush them like the white kid in a spelling bee.

I'm just trying to be your friend, which is someone who tells you the truth, and the truth is: The world is unfair. It's not like college. It's like the Electoral College. And you kids are about to enter freshman year of life, and that can be unsettling, much like the slap in the face that your parents should have given you the first time you swore at them. But they didn't, and so you became the "Hey, buddy" generation: "Hey, buddy, could you put your shoes on?" . . . "Hey, buddy, could you get in the car?" But in real life, not everyone is your buddy.

And that's why you're fucked. No, I mean really fucked. Because no one ever told you "no" or "you're wrong" or "you're in the way" or "that's not good enough" or "wait," so you think the whole world is supposed to be your safe space, where everything is wonderful and nobody ever gets their feelings hurt. Well, I have some bad news for you: Mr. Rogers is dead.

And so, new graduates, as you look back at where you've been and ahead to where you're going, I want you to turn to your parents now and take this moment to tell them, "Thank you."

Thank you for murdering any chance I had of actually making it in the real world. Thank you for covering the walls of my childhood room with fake certificates and made-up bullshit like "Third-Grade Gym Superstar" and "Most Improved Finger Painter" and "World Champion Paste-Eater." Thank you for the trophies I got for just showing up and for the temper tantrums you let me throw in the cereal aisle. And thank you for bitching out every teacher who ever gave me a B instead of an A. Even though I really deserved a C.

MOMMIE NEAREST

The best gift an American kid can give his parents is to sit them down and say, "Mom, Dad . . . we need some space." Now, it's true, I never had kids, but maybe that gives me some objectivity, and what I see in Zillennials is these kids are more anxious than a squirrel on crystal meth. And that's not because human offspring have changed; it's because the parents have.

If millennials were the generation with helicopter parents who hovered over them, Gen Z are the kids with bulldozer parents who don't just hover but clear the way of all obstacles for their kids. In both cases, too protective, too always on the case, too always just *there*—and it's not good for anybody. Not the teachers. Not the parents. Not the kids.

And it doesn't even end when the kids leave the house. Parents go on job interviews with their kids now. A study a few years ago found that 30 percent of employers had gotten résumés written by applicants' parents. Fifteen percent reported fielding complaints when they didn't hire the kid—*from the parent*. And yet somehow our reading and math scores are falling behind China's. Weird.

This topic has been much in the news because there are now families going against the grain who want to raise children guided by the radical concept of occasionally letting them out of their sight—a movement that's been dubbed "free-range parenting." Or as we used to call it, "parenting."

Actually, we didn't even call it that, because "parenting" wasn't a word, because being a parent wasn't a job description. In the seventies "parenting" meant you woke up, went to your kids' room . . . and if they were alive, you were done for the day. Crib monitors? Why? What are they gonna do, turn into werewolves in the middle of the night?

But that's not how most parents see it these days, when kids are routinely picked up by the cops for walking home alone from the park, which is all of two blocks away. I walked farther than that to school every day when I was that age, and nobody cared; in fact, my mother always looked a little disappointed when I came back.

What kind of country do we live in where the sight of a kid walking alone in his own neighborhood requires a call to 911? Parents act like every time their kids leave the house they're being chased down the street by a clown with his dick out, when, truth is, probably the most dangerous thing out there in the fresh air is the fresh air.

When did we get this idea that children should never endure even the slightest risk or experience any disappointment? If the ice cream truck doesn't come, the parents panic and double-strap the kids in the car and rush over to Baskin-Robbins, where they disinfect the table and test the cones for gluten. Fun!

Studies confirm that all this excess time with kids is not having a positive effect. Kids free to engage the world on their own a bit wind up coming out happier and more creative than the ones who have to put on a helmet to take out the garbage.

Let the little bastards breathe a little! Do you know that American kids now spend 90 percent of their leisure time at home? Plopped on the couch watching TV, playing video games. We're not raising citizens; we're fattening veal calves. And all because we think outside is where the baby snatchers are and inside is where it's safe.

Right, inside—where the pornography is at their fingertips 24/7. I have news for you, that's the thing that's really going to fuck them up for the rest of their lives. When I was a kid, it was a thrill to find an old *Playboy* in the neighbor's garage, but now every ten-year-old can whip out his phone and in seconds be looking at a team of Japanese businessmen ejaculating on a squid.

SELFIE SCHTICK

The idea that certain people do certain things better than others, and it's OK to reward them for it, is called meritocracy—and it's the opposite of guaranteed outcomes. Equality of outcomes, as opposed to equality of opportunity: that was Trophy Syndrome. Now they call it "equity."

America is a country whose children score low in math and science but off the charts in self-esteem. A study of eight developed countries found that US students were dead last in math skills but number one in *confidence* in math skills, even though they suck at it. Yes, we're number one in thinking we're number one.

The idea that kids have too little self-esteem is antiquated. It's a Zombie Lie, one of those ideas that perhaps was true in the past but now is not, and yet people keep saying it. Kids now have too *much* self-esteem, and it's turning them into angry, screaming grievance collectors. All of that childhood tolerance is resulting in grown-up tyrants. It's no wonder that by the time they get to college, just having to listen to an opinion they don't agree with is considered an act of "violence."

This is what happens when no one ever loses and everyone gets a prize. You can run the wrong way on the field and score five goals for the other team, and you're still a winner. Even though you're actually a big fucking loser. No wonder today's NBA players give each other high fives when they *miss* a foul shot.

We tell our children they don't have to fix their flaws, because it's the world's job to accept everything about them and love it. Like they say on reality shows, the most important thing is just "you doing you." But what if "you" is a big asshole?

Remember that song about how "learning to love yourself is the greatest love of all"? Yeah, that was a bad idea. To teach children that there is nothing better than falling madly, head-over-heels, leaving-notes-on-your-own-windshield in love with yourself. And also that any-one who doesn't agree that you are fabulous and perfect in every way is just a hater and they can suck it.

Parents put notes in their kids' lunch boxes that say "I love you" when there's already something in the lunch box that lets kids know you love them: food.

Every time a parent takes the kid's side over the teacher's, or asks a child where *they* want to go for dinner, or doesn't say "Be quiet when adults are talking," you're creating the monsters of tomorrow. The grown-up version of every pain-in-the-ass kid who ever sat behind you on a plane kicking the back of your seat while the parents did nothing.

"Little Logan is just exploring." No, little Logan is being a dick, and if you won't shove him in the overhead bin, I will.

The result of this kind of thinking is that American kids now have a totally deluded and unearned belief in their charm, brains and talent. It's not only that the entire generation wants to be famous, it's that they think *not* being famous isn't fair. If you think I'm exaggerating, let me quote from a 2021 article in *Rolling Stone* that lamented how streaming has not given us equality of outcomes in the music industry.

The article tells us that more than 1.6 million artists released songs between January 2019 and July 2020—forty thousand tracks a day on Spotify—and yet, *Rolling Stone* complains, "today's streaming landscape looks a lot like the music industry used to . . . a small class of artists . . . see not just the majority of activity, but damn near all of it."

Yes, these are called the good ones. Of course, an occasional big talent can fall through the cracks, but in general, it's simply the case that most people who try their hand at music write the songs that *don't* make the whole world sing.

Rolling Stone whines that "nearly all the streams went to artists in the top ten percent with the bottom 90 percent pulling in just .6 percent of streams." Whoa, let me get this straight—talented artists people like are listened to more than untalented ones that they don't like? Yes, meritocracy! If people don't like your song, your mommy can't make them listen to it.

You know why 99 percent of artists aren't getting heard? Because music is hard and most people suck at it. For more details, Google "reality." *Rolling Stone* actually writes the sentence, "In a perfect world, the bottom one percent of artists would get one percent of activity." No, they wouldn't, that's a stupid world I don't want to live in.

Who taught you this nonsense? And when you grumble that "streaming hasn't just upheld the gap between music's haves and have-nots, it's widened it," you're making my case for me—because streaming allows the public to sample everybody. There are no more gatekeepers, so you can't gripe that no one heard your song because no label would sign you. We tore that wall down, and the result was the same: some musicians are have-nots because, yes, they may have a voice, but *we have ears*.

It reminds me of the early audition rounds of the old *American Idol* where contestants are all attitude and image, as if to say, "Can we not focus so much on the talent and just skip to the part where I'm an idol?" Fifty-four percent of Gen Z and millennials say they would become an influencer "given the opportunity."

According to the *Los Angeles Times*, "content creators are the fastest-growing type of small business in the US." By one estimate, over fifty million people worldwide now consider themselves to be online creators or influencers. When we used to ask kids, "What do you want to be when you grow up?" they'd say "Firefighter" or "Astronaut." Now most six-year-olds would probably say "I wanna be Instagram-famous, bitch!"

And why not? The supposedly media-savvy millennials and Gen Z–ers really do buy stuff just because some ding-dong holds it up on Instagram or opens a box of it on YouTube. They laugh at boomers buying crap on QVC, but they're doing the same thing. Grandma's buying Tupperware, and they're selling mascara to each other. The only difference is, she's suffering from dementia—what's your excuse?

I keep hearing that there are no good jobs out there. Well, there certainly are many shitty jobs out there, but there are also millions of openings in professional and business services, education, health, construction, retail, manufacturing—America right now has more job openings than at any time in its history, and more than there are people looking.

A lot of the time "there are no good jobs out there" just means "I want to be a Kardashian." It means "I want my job to be 'I'm me, and people pay to watch that!'" What's the fallback career to that, marijuana tester?

We spent decades dismantling the patriarchal notion that women should stay home and not work, and then the Kardashian phenomenon happened and now it seems like millions want to . . . um, stay home and not work. This generation's financial plan is hitting the jackpot.

Paris Hilton recently made a return to the limelight, revealing that the ditzy party girl we knew back in the day was just her playing "a character," and that there was really more to her than sex tapes, driving drunk, carrying around a little dog and saying "That's hot." I mean, what about her work on the Human Genome Project? Some people thought we owed Paris an apology.

I'm not one of them. I just can't be living in this time when we're madly on the hunt for anything with the slightest whiff of white privilege and then feel bad for Paris Hilton.

Quite the reverse; maybe Paris is the one who owes *us* an apology for being patient zero for today's vapid, entitled, famous-for-nothing culture. She kind of birthed the world where every fifteen-year-old with a phone aspires to be an "influencer"—she's the face that launched a thousand little shits. Paris is who led directly to the Kardashians, and then to Housewives and Teen Moms and Snookis and a generation of young girls who look up to the "role models" who managed to turn an unenthusiastic blow job into an empire.

Young people think, "Talent? My talent is being *me*, and *you* wanting to live my life." For the generations who are always on about "This is my voice!" and "I have something to say!" an awful lot of that something is about lip gloss.

Seventy-two percent of Gen Z–ers say they'd like to be an online celebrity. They don't even want to achieve something that makes them famous because that would involve that pesky step of developing some sort of talent or skill—no, getting followers, that *is* the achievement. I'd say "Take a good long look at yourself," but plainly that's all they do all day.

It doesn't feel sustainable. We can't all be *The Truman Show*. Most of the time what vloggers are reporting on in their travels is just themselves. "This just in: we woke up." Getting paid to do nothing is their highest goal, so spoiled by parents who told them, "All you have to do is do you," they think it's fascinating for us to watch them order eggs at a diner. But how long can we go on selling each other our life stories as the basis for an economy?

It's hard to wrap my head around the level of narcissism of so many people trying to make a living by taking pictures of themselves, like they're their own paparazzi. Home movies have never been interesting—that's as true in the YouTube era as it was back when kids had to sit through Uncle Morty's Super 8 footage of his trip to Cypress Gardens. But at least he didn't ask us to hit the "like" button and "subscribe" to it.

AGE AGAINST THE MACHINE

Do you know the reason why advertisers in this country love the eighteen-to-thirty-four demographic? Because it's the most gullible. A third of people under thirty-five say they're in favor of abolishing the police—not defunding, but doing away with a police force altogether, which is less of a policy position and more of a leg tattoo. Thirty-six percent of millennials think it might be a good idea to try communism.

But much of the world did try it. I know, millennials think that doesn't count because they weren't alive when it happened, but it did happen, and there are people around who remember it. Pining for communism is like pining for Betamax or MySpace.

So when kids say, "You're old, you don't get it"—get *what*? Abolish the police? And the border patrol? And get rid of capitalism? Twenty percent of Gen Z agree with the statement "Society would be better off if all property was owned by the public and managed by the government," and another 29 percent say they "don't know" if that's a good idea. Here's who does know: anyone who wasn't born yesterday.

The problem isn't that I don't get what you're saying because I'm old; the problem is that your ideas are stupid. If you say, "Let's eat in the bathroom and shit in the kitchen," yeah, that's a new idea, but I wouldn't call it an improvement.

You think someone who's eighty is hopeless because they can't use an iPhone? Maybe the one who's hopeless is the one who can't *stop* using it.

You think I'm out of it because I'm not on Twitch? Maybe I "get" Twitch, but I just think people watching other people play video games is a giant waste of time.

In America, ageism is the last acceptable prejudice. It's completely forbidden to tell any joke about race, gender, religion, weight—but age? Have at it. Did you ever go down the greeting card aisle at CVS? Every card for anyone over sixty is the same joke: "Happy birthday. I'm surprised you can read this without your glasses!"

Now, the excuse for this prejudice has always been "We're a young country." I've been hearing that my whole life: "America's a young country." Well, I'd just like to say this to America: Sorry, but you're not that young anymore. Powdered wigs were a long time ago. It's time you grew up. It's time to stop doing stupid, teenage, immature things, and number one on that list is not understanding the most fundamental trade-off in life: you're beautiful when you're young, wise when you're old.

This is the only country in the world dumb enough not to get this most basic, intuitive, obvious, file-it-under-"duh" concept: that if, as they say, you learn something new every day, it stands to reason someone who's logged ten thousand more days is going to be, in general, wiser. Life is a series of patterns. You don't see it the first time because it's not a pattern yet, but by the third time, you go, "OK, I get it now."

Is there anything more self-defeating than not using old people as a resource? Not taking advantage of their accumulated knowledge? Everywhere else in the world elders are sought for guidance. In America, elders are sought for TikTok pranks.

In Greece, "old man" is a compliment, not something you scream after "Get out of my way." In India, young people touch old people's feet to show reverence. Japan has a national holiday called Keiro no Hi: "Respect for the Aged Day."

Of course societies need youthful energy and fresh eyes on problems, and it takes young people to start a revolution. But Joe Biden turned out to be the right man for the moment precisely because he *is* old. "Been there, done that" can be a virtue. As president, he's gotten things done on wealth inequality, Afghanistan, racial justice and climate change that keyboard warriors only dream about while muttering, "OK, boomer."

Young, dumb and full of cum—there's a season for that, but right now I'll take old, stooped and full of soup.

Addendum:

Respectable news sources report that there's a phenomenon occurring where people in nursing homes are now fucking like rabbits on an adjustable bed. We know this because the Centers for Disease Control reports that syphilis and chlamydia in seniors have nearly tripled over the past decade. Apparently, seventy is the new sixty-nine, and so are eighty and ninety, and the old folks' home is the new freshman dorm. These days when Grandma yells "Bingo," it's because an old vet just found her G-spot.

And you know what? I say great—no country in the world disrespects the elderly more than this one; the least we can do is let them go out with a bang. As long as they don't mix up the Astroglide and the Poligrip, I'm for it.

6

REPUBLICANS

REPUBLICAN GUARD

One thing you gotta say about Republicans: they're tight. In 2016, three Republican congressmen—past majority leaders Paul Ryan and Kevin McCarthy, and Steve Scalise—were caught on tape in what they believed was a private conversation admitting they thought Trump was on Putin's payroll. They laugh about it, and then Ryan says, "No leaks, all right? This is how we know we're a real family here . . ."

That's how they are. What happens in Harlan Crow's steam room stays in Harlan Crow's steam room—"this is how we know we're family." A crime family, sure, but a family.

What I want to know now is: Was there another conversation Republicans had in private where they agreed that there was something Trump could have done when he was president that would have made them say "That goes too far, we're out"? Because, obviously, *Trump being on Putin's payroll* wasn't that.

But was there something—that is, did they have a safe word? We all know what that means in the bedroom: an agreed-upon, specific word that people engaging in during rough sex to let their partner know, "OK, I'm not playing anymore—I really want you to stop." So it has to be an offbeat word that would never come up during actual sex. For example, Melania uses "I'm coming."

But for most garden-variety freaks it's a word like, oh, I don't know, "pineapple"—you say "pineapple" so that way when the dominatrix is choking you, you don't have to say, "Stop, you whore, you're killing me," and she doesn't have to say, "Wait, *really* stop or pretend stop?"

And when Trump was in the White House, I wanted to think that Republicans had that with him, since any dominatrix will tell you: most of their customers are successful, older white guys with power and authority they know they don't really deserve—in other words, Republicans.

If you asked me in 2015, when the Trump nonsense began, what I thought the safe word for Republicans would be, I would have said "Mexicans are rapists" or "John McCain wasn't a war hero." But it was soon evident that the line was not going to be drawn on matters of behavior: mocking the handicapped, bragging about your dick at debates, grabbing pussies—all good.

Then once he was in office, it became apparent the line would also not be drawn at . . . norms. Practices so universally agreed upon to be the right thing to do that we never thought we needed to codify them into law: releasing your taxes, not putting family members in the cabinet, having press briefings, siding with Americans instead of Russians.

And then we moved on to breaking actual laws—not answering subpoenas, using campaign funds for hush money to mistresses, withholding foreign aid to allies and domestic aid to states.

So we found out what *wouldn't* make Republicans say "pineapple." The good news is, we also found out what *did* make at least some of them say it. For Liz Cheney, Mike Pence, Bill Barr, Mitch McConnell, Mitt Romney and a few others, there was a bridge they would not cross: trying to steal the election. All of those Republicans have forthrightly declared Trump lost in 2020, and essentially pronounced him a huge asshole for continuing to claim that he didn't.

These are what I call "good-as-it-gets Republicans." Chris Christie is also one of them, and Chris and I had a good laugh on *Real Time* in 2023 when I told him that to his face. But it's actually a very important concept.

George W. Bush was not my idea of a good president, but I never worried that he was going to lock up his political opponents. Or reporters. Or me. Bush was wrong on most things, but he wasn't trying to enrich George W. Bush. He condemned Islamophobia—actual Islamophobia—after 9/11, and he did a lot for AIDS in African countries without calling them shitholes. He was willing to lose Dick Cheney as a friend and supporter because he wouldn't pardon Scooter Libby—because it wasn't always just about loyalty. He stood with Obama when Obama took his job and said, "We want you to succeed."

If you can't see the difference between that and Trump, Democrats are doomed. Democrats should really get over themselves and stop insisting every Republican is a monster. Chris Christie is not a monster, although he could play one in a movie without special effects.

No matter who is on the ballot in the next presidential election—in any foreseeable presidential election—if that person has an "R" by their name, I guarantee they will be in the race. One of the most predictable headlines you'll ever see is "Race Tightens as Election Day Draws Near." There are many reasons for this, but the bottom line is: Republicans are about half the country and always can win, no matter who they run. And if you think Trump is as bad as it could get, remember the first rule of modern Republican politics: they always go lower. Because the party has no bottom, unless you count Lindsey Graham.

Republicans are the masters of nominating the "you've got to be fucking kidding me" candidate. Palin? Herschel Walker? Marjorie Taylor Greene? George Santos? Is there anyone who couldn't be nominated by this party? The person who seems completely ridiculous today is Congressman Ridiculous tomorrow.

So given how Republicans try to out-hillbilly each other for the nomination, here are some dark-horse contenders I see in their future as acceptable candidates for the Republican base:

Ted Nugent, known as the Motor City Madman. Which is a huge plus, because he's got "madman" right in his name. In addition, terrorists will have a hard time targeting a president who dresses entirely in camouflage, and when he's president, no more of that "pardoning the Thanksgiving turkey" bullshit.

Charlie Sheen. He's got the Trump swagger, and like most Republican candidates, he's had multiple marriages. And like Dick Cheney, he once shot someone "by accident." Negatives include that he might try to snort the campaign trail.

Andrew Dice Clay. For decades, he's been called misogynist, racist and homophobic—or what Republican primary voters call "a good start." He was inexplicably popular at the same time Ronald Reagan was inexplicably popular and speaks in a vernacular that the Republican base understands: nursery rhymes.

Thor. He's blond and white and solves all his problems with a hammer.

Face-Ripper Monkey. Remember him? The chimp that got mad and ripped off someone's face in San Francisco back in 2013? Well, Face-Ripper Monkey has everything that appeals to Trumpers: His very existence disproves evolution, and he's not a "Washington insider." In fact, he's not an "insider" at all. Face-Ripper Monkey doesn't wait around for government to solve his problems. He acts—he doesn't do nuance. He goes with his gut. And for your face. Face-Ripper Monkey is aggressive, independent, and he's not afraid to prove his toughness with direct, commonsense solutions. Like ripping off people's faces.

VLADDY ISSUES

In today's merger-crazy economy, everybody needs a partner. That's how we got the likes of ExxonMobil, GlaxoSmithKline and JPMorgan Chase.

We live in the age of get bigger or get eaten. In fact, I look forward to the brave new day when there will be only two companies: Apple-zon and GoldmanGoogle-Mart.

At GoldmanGoogle-Mart, I only have to imagine the words "I think I need more dog food," and seconds later, a robot drone shoves it in my pants.

The Republican Party certainly understands the concept of merging to survive. In recent years they were facing a serious demographic problem: America was becoming younger and browner, and they were becoming whiter and deader. They had lost the popular vote in six of the last seven presidential elections and realized they couldn't win by themselves, so they did what any smart corporation would do—they merged with a giant oil company: Russia. Yes, the Republican Party and Russia merged to form . . . the Trumpcussia Group!

Two great corporations, now operating out of the same evil lair.

Oh sure, Republicans used to hate Russia as much as they hated taxes, welfare and sexually active women, but fiddle-faddle, 40 percent of Republicans now say they either approve of Russian interference in our elections or don't object strongly. Some even wear "I'd rather be a Russian than a Democrat" T-shirts. See, it's funny, because they're traitors. I guess the new saying is "Better red than . . . well-read."

When Donald Trump met Putin in Helsinki in 2018 and took *his* side against *our* intelligence agencies, it was like if after 9/11 Bush stood on the rubble at the World Trade Center and shouted into the bullhorn, "Bin Laden is innocent and the FBI will hear from all of us soon!"

How did the party of Ronald "Russia is an evil empire" Reagan become the party of Putin? How did Russia flip an entire political party? And not the one that was supposedly soft on Russia.

For such a fundamental shift to occur in an entire party, there has to be something more going on here. I think the dirty little secret about the Republicans and their newfound love for baseball, apple pie and Mother Russia is that it's about race. Ann Coulter once tweeted, "In 20 years, Russia will be the only country that is recognizably European." As far back as 2013, Matt Drudge called Putin "the leader of the free world." David Duke described Russia as "the key to white survival."

Today's Republicans have, to put it charitably, mixed feelings about the melting pot—and Russia? That pot don't melt. Russia is one of the last places on Earth to say, "Fuck diversity! We're here, we're white, get used to it."

I remember going to London in the eighties, and everyone was white. The closest thing to an Afro was the hat on the guards at Buckingham Palace. Now London looks like New York and the mayor is brown. To an old-school liberal, that's progress. But not everyone sees it that way.

In the recent World Cup, the French national team didn't look like the old France, it looked like the new France. Germany let in a million Syrians—the Fatherland is now the Brotherland. You know how many Syrian refugees Russia has taken in? Two. Martin Sheen has more refugees in his pool house.

But Russia? Their basketball team looks like the team that plays against the Globetrotters. They have a drink called a white Russian that's actually the whitest drink there is: "Let's see, I want to get drunk, but I also want a glass of milk."

Russia is the last honky oasis, and Republicans love it. Russian kids don't learn the words to "Despacito," and a Barack Obama does not become president there.

Funny, wingnuts accused Obama of being a foreign agent who took over America, but when a foreign power actually did meddle in our elections, it was the proudly white one, and their response was: "Come right in." To the members of the Grand Old Party, Russian meddling in our elections isn't a breach of national security; it's just white people helping white people.

But since it's now acceptable to merge your party with a foreign power, I'd like to be the first to suggest that if it's OK to bring in Russia as their ringer, Democrats get to bring in their own country, and I pick China: DNC, meet MSG! Wok the vote, baby! When they go low, we go lo mein. Who better to hack voting machines than the country whose children assemble them?

If you're gonna turn over your party to a foreign power, at least pick the right one. Russia? Are you kidding? It's like the Republicans looked over all the companies they could merge with and picked Sears. China is the future and Russia is a mobbed-up, has-been petro-state run by men in purple satin shirts. Their main exports are videos of bears blocking traffic and wives. The male life expectancy in Russia is lower than in *North Korea*. Their GDP is smaller than Italy's—it's like merging with a Halloween store.

GULLIBLE'S TRAVAILS

It used to be an unwritten rule of both parties that you're entitled to your own opinion but not your own facts. But that was before Republicans discovered you *can* have your own facts. In fact, we just pulled a fresh batch out of the oven. There's a large part of the Republican base that will believe anything—so can we stop sending reporters to diners to figure them out? They're not there for breakfast, they literally think there are clouds in the coffee.

Two years after the 2016 election, 83 percent of Republicans still definitely believed or were "unsure" whether five million people had voted illegally in that election. Something Trump just completely made up. He even appointed a voter fraud commission, based on his own fraud—"Hey, you remember that bullshit I made up? I want you to get to the bottom of it."

And even his own commission couldn't back him up.

But it didn't matter—this isn't about ideology anymore. And this isn't about actual Republicans either: those guys are gone. George Bush the First quit the NRA in 1995 when some gun nuts called the Bureau of Alcohol, Tobacco and Firearms "jackbooted thugs"—he said it "deeply offended" his sense of decency and honor.

But when Alex Jones said children faked their own deaths at Sandy

Hook, it didn't deter Trump from telling him, "Your reputation is amazing. I will not let you down." They're soul mates. "You say twisted crap to crazy people and so do I! We should grab a pussy sometime!"

I never liked Rush Limbaugh, but I would take a return to his nineties-era demagoguery any day. It turned out that Rush was just a gateway drug, to which they eventually built up a tolerance and then needed something stronger, which was Glenn Beck. Which led to Alex Jones. And now there is literally nothing too stupid and conspiratorial a third of the country won't swallow: A cabal of Satan-worshiping pedophiles is secretly controlling the world? Sounds right.

In 2023, John Durham finally completed his investigation into whether the FBI had been "spying" on Trump. There was no spying. It was just the bureau checking out whether someone on the Trump campaign was communicating with Russia, based on the tiny fact that everybody in the Trump campaign was communicating with Russia. Investigation—it's what the FBI does. It's in their *name*.

One way we measure the health of a society is by how conspiratorial it is. Communist countries and Arab dictatorships were always places where you could sell any conspiracy theory because there was no trust in the institutions. Like us now.

FALSE AMBIVALENCE

Americans like to say of politicians, "They're all bad!" because it makes you sound like you're justifiably jaded by the entire process, but really it's a stupid person's idea of a smart thing to say. It's a cheat that says you're above it all when you're really just too lazy to tell shit from Shinola. It's the central fraudulent idea that allowed an "outsider" like Trump to be elected. It's one step up from "I don't vote because it only encourages them."

A pair of highly respected scholars named Norm Ornstein and Thomas Mann have been analyzing Congress for half a century, always criticizing both parties in equal measure. But then, around 2012, they started writing something very different, summed up in their article

"Let's Just Say It: The Republicans Are the Problem." They wrote, "The Republican Party has become an insurgent outlier . . . ideologically extreme . . . scornful of compromise, unmoved by conventional understanding of facts, evidence and science."

All presidents lie to a degree, but Trump was in a world of his own: He's Bob Beamon at the '68 Olympics, breaking the long jump record by *two feet*! He's Babe Ruth, hitting sixty home runs when the previous record holder had twenty-seven. Tom Brady playing in ten Super Bowls.

Bill Clinton left office with a budget surplus. Obamacare was paid for, and Obama's bank bailouts—necessary because of a Republican recession—were paid back. Reagan, W. and Trump all ran up huge debt, and their party continues to practice trickle-down economics long after evidence has shown it not to work. Yes, evidence. Only one side generally trades in political reality anymore.

Al Gore conceded the 2000 election for the good of the country. Would Bush have? And we know about Trump. Trump fired the head of the FBI for doing his job with the Russia investigation—then he had the Russians over to the Oval Office and laughed about it. That's not a bipartisan problem. If Obama had done it, he'd be in supermax now trading cigarettes with Jared from Subway.

And are you really going to tell me both sides are equally to blame for the state of the environment?

For people who say both parties are basically the same, voter suppression is the starkest example of how that's not true. This is 100 percent a Republican thing. They know their policies aren't as popular, so they came up with an effective, time-tested political tactic called "cheating": I can't make you want to vote for me, but maybe I can keep you from voting for the other guy. That's their credo: "May the best man lose anyway."

A few years ago a Republican chair of North Carolina's redistricting committee named David Lewis said, "I think electing Republicans is better than electing Democrats, so I drew the map to help foster what I think is better for the country."

Wow, talk about saying the quiet part out loud. They don't even think they *should* play fair. It must have been such a relief for these cheaters to stop pretending and just say it. Like when Mom finally admits the Hitachi Magic Wand isn't for her back.

Texas has very similar demographics to California, but one reason Democrats' goal of turning Texas blue never happens is a federal court has ruled seven times that Texas Republicans drew their congressional districts with "racially discriminatory intent."

Power, you see, is a lot like owning rabbits: the more you have, the easier it is to get a lot more. The more justices Republicans get to pick, the more those justices protect unlimited campaign spending and voter suppression laws, which helps more Republicans get elected. Power begets power.

Trump loves to say the system is rigged—but he leaves out the part that it's rigged *for* Republicans. The Electoral College helps Republicans. The fact that every state gets two senators helps Republicans. Mike Enzi of Wyoming represents 287,000 people; Alex Padilla of California represents 20 million.

Why is Wyoming even a state? There's not even a river or any other kind of natural border separating it from the other states. It's just a square. It's like they copy-pasted Colorado and then forgot to put people in it. Do we really need two Dakotas? It's like when there's a Starbucks right across the street from another Starbucks. It's greedy. You're greedy, Dakotas. Four senators for you?! It's like a little person going up to the buffet and taking half the food.

We all failed to notice that as more Americans moved to coastal cities in pursuit of high-paying jobs as influencers, rural red states became overrepresented. Which is why every election year we have to hear what's on the mind of everyone in a diner in Iowa. Meanwhile, nobody ever talks to the loser at the Coffee Bean in West Hollywood—does America's vast army of unemployed screenwriters not count?

The Constitution is not on the side of liberals: George W. Bush and Trump both lost the popular vote—they shouldn't have been picking

Supreme Court justices at all. Had the Democrats who actually won the popular vote been in the Oval Office, there would now be a seven-to-two liberal majority on the court.

Republicans in Texas were able to draw those districts with "racially discriminatory intent" because they won the statehouse. Democrats lost a thousand state legislature seats in the Obama years: that's the ball game. To win elections so you can protect voting rights, you need to win elections.

In 2016, when Supreme Court justice Scalia died, Mitch McConnell said that, since the seat had become vacant in an election year, the Senate would not even consider a nomination from Obama, which he found in article 1, section 4 of his ass.

Mitch was essentially saying, "Even though I know the Constitution is clear that when a Supreme Court slot comes open, the sitting president gets to fill it, and it's my job as a senator to make that happen, that's the old America—a nation of laws. This is the new America now, with only one law: *make me.*"

GLORY DAZE

In June of 2013, right before they took their summer break, the Supreme Court dropped a big one: they gutted the 1965 Voting Rights Act, which is the law that forced certain states—let's just say the ones where you might find grits for sale at the gas station—to get permission from the Justice Department before they made any changes in their voting laws. Why? Because in the past these states had been naughty and had prevented minorities from voting, with little tricks like poll taxes and literacy tests.

But the conservatives on the court, all excited from being born yesterday, said racism had been cured and that laws against voter suppression were unnecessary relics of a bygone era. There was no evidence anymore that Black people needed special protections—come on, it's 2013, Ice-T plays a cop on *Law & Order* now!

During arguments for the case, Justice Roberts actually asked, with a straight face: "Is it the government's submission that the citizens of the South are more racist than the citizens of the North?" Well . . . in the 2012 election, 66 percent of whites in Vermont voted for a Black president, and only 10 percent of whites in Mississippi did. So maybe a tad. And the South, after all, was responsible for *enslaving* Black people. And Jim Crow. And the KKK. And lynchings. And Paula Deen lives there. So I'm gonna go with "yes."

And what happened after the court changed the law? Within forty-eight hours Texas, Alabama, Mississippi, Arkansas, South Carolina and Virginia all moved to make it harder for minorities to vote.

Same thing with the *Citizens United* ruling: President Obama said at his 2010 State of the Union speech that the Supreme Court had "open[ed] the floodgates for special interests . . . to spend without limit in our elections," and Justice Alito famously was shown mouthing the words, "Not true."

Turns out . . . true! Left to their own devices, the filthy rich—I'm sorry, I mean "America's job creators"—did indeed sway elections with billions from God knows where. Creepy billionaire Sheldon Adelson alone spent $150 million in 2012, money he mainly got from owning a casino in China. Just as the Founders envisioned.

And yet Justice Kennedy, writing for the majority from his tower in Whoville, said, "Independent expenditures, including those made by corporations, do not give rise to corruption"—or even "the appearance of corruption." Which is true, except for always.

This highlights a real problem with today's conservatives: they're just too sentimental about how wonderful America is. Racism? That's over. Moneyed interests—they couldn't corrupt us if they tried! Conservatives act like they're tough-as-nails realists, but they cry at fireworks, and they get a warm, morning-in-America feeling thinking about lighthouses and farmers and the smell of pie, always falling to pieces over flags and anthems and commercials for pickup trucks, Route 66 and porch swings, barbershops that still offer a shave . . . old barns and pictures of wheat give them a hard-on. That's why they love the paintings of Thomas Kinkade, with his vision of America as one big Hobbit village of fairy-tale cottages.

And they just can't believe that Americans, God's chosen and wonderful people—maybe you've heard, we're exceptional—would ever do anything so corrupt as . . .

Yeah, we would.

Twice in three years the court believed in us, and twice Americans basically said what John Belushi said in *Animal House*: "You fucked up; you shouldn'ta trusted us." For the party that thinks of itself as the tough guys, they're such pussies for Americana bullshit.

And somehow, the people who wrap themselves in the flag are always the ones most clueless about what it represents. Like the way Trump turned taking a knee at football games—a respectful protest about police brutality—into a patriotism pissing match. The nerve of these young Black men kneeling while an *American Idol* runner-up sings the "bombs bursting in air" song! How *dare* you exercise your freedoms while we're honoring them! We will not stand for not standing!

Trump literally said that soldiers have died and we need to stand because "they were fighting for our national anthem." Oh for God's sake, no one ever died for the anthem! Although some have died trying to sing it.

But for conservatives, the anthem is like their senior prom theme song. It makes them all misty-eyed, the way I get when I hear Captain & Tennille's "Do That to Me One More Time." Remember John Boehner? He'd cry like a little bitch if he saw a tiny American flag in his club sandwich or if someone mentioned small-business owners. Jesus.

But nothing triggers that soft, mushy part of a right-winger more than the military. They love the military the way eight-year-old girls love horses—wholly and completely, with a slight tinge of sexual frustration. They get a tingle in their taint when the Blue Angels fly overhead. They cry during the president's Martian-fighting speech in *Independence Day*. They see a guy in uniform at the mall and say, "Thank you for your service," even though the guy's thinking, "I'm a security guard, dipshit."

In his heroic battle against a grieving widow, Donald Trump once sent his chief of staff General Kelly out to talk to the media and offer us a lesson about honor. And when that honor lesson included blatantly lying on behalf of the president, General Kelly was criticized—which President Trump's spokesperson said was "highly inappropriate."

That's right, it is highly inappropriate to ever question a general. In North Korea. But I thought this was America. This impulse to tell people not to protest against the police, not to question the generals—this is not American. And that's the problem with all this fetish patriotism. It starts with goose bumps, but it ends with goose steps.

GALL PASS

Someone has to tell me what's magic about a capital "R," the kind that goes after your name if you're a Republican. Because if you have one of those, you can get away with pretty much anything when it comes to selling out, cursing out or compromising your own country.

Bill O'Reilly once asked Trump why he always defended Putin, who O'Reilly said was a killer—a reasonable question, since the last two guys who were as cozy as Putin and Trump held their bilateral talks on Brokeback Mountain. But Trump took Putin's side over America, saying, "We got killers here too—you think our country is so innocent?" If a Democrat said that before the Super Bowl, Fox News would never shut up about it.

But if you have the magic "R" by your name, no problem.

Trump repeatedly said he was going to donate to military charities, then didn't, then lied about it. He compared our intelligence agencies to Nazis. He said John McCain, who spent five years in a Vietnamese prison, wasn't a war hero, because, "I like people who *weren't* captured." He stood in front of the Wall of Heroes at the CIA and talked about his television ratings.

I gotta say to all you flag-waving right-wingers who always say, "I'm not gonna just stand here and let you run down America": you absolutely just stand there when Trump runs down America. Trump could go to the Tomb of the Unknown Soldier and say, "Well, maybe if he'd done something he wouldn't be so unknown," and Republicans would be OK with that too.

If you have the magic "R" after your name, you can drive a Hummer through a day care center and Newsmax will say the babies were asking for it.

Meanwhile, in the alternative universe where a Democrat is president, Obama once said, "We have not been perfect," and for eight years, Republicans screamed that he was on a nonstop apology tour. They lost their shit whenever there was a picture of him committing high crimes like saluting with coffee in his hand, even though George Bush once did it holding a dog. Bush, the president who sat frozen for seven minutes after being told the words, "The country is under attack." And Republicans defended *that*.

And we all just accept this. America is the Republican Party's bitch, and they can criticize and betray her, but you can't. Even though Obama spent two terms talking up the troops, talking up the country, telling us how much he loved it, saying, "In no other country is my story even possible"—didn't matter. Conservatives all nodded when Rudy Giuliani said, "I do not believe that President Obama loves America." As opposed to Giuliani, who happened to be mayor on 9/11, so that made him "America's Mayor," a savior whose great act of heroism was nothing fell on his head.

In 1968, when President Lyndon Johnson was trying to end the war in Vietnam, candidate Richard Nixon actively, purposefully undermined the peace talks, because he wanted the war to go on so he could have it as an election issue. You'd think the "America First" crowd would find that a bridge too far. Dick Cheney once outed a CIA agent, just to say "fuck you" to her husband. Reagan sold weapons to Iran, the country right-wingers all want to bomb now, in brazen defiance of American law, and instead of being impeached, he was elevated to sainthood and now rides horses in heaven with Jesus.

Why do Republicans get away with this? Why do they have Patriotic Immunity? America is like a dysfunctional family where the Democrats are the older, mature son who works hard but somehow is never good enough, and the Republicans are the young asshole son who's a huge fuckup but no matter how many times he crashes the Camaro, Daddy buys him a new one.

Again, I say to the "not much difference between the parties" people: actually, there's more of a difference between the parties now than ever. And here's why: Democrats, for all their flaws, still see democracy as the essence of America—they see America and democracy as inextricably linked. They believe that one without the other is unthinkable.

Republicans? Thinkable!

Republicans now seem to be OK with America continuing to exist as a country but without being a democracy. Democracy doesn't die in darkness—it dies in plain sight because enough people think democracy is a luxury America can no longer afford. That's pretty much the position of the Republican Party now—that you can vote for anyone you like, but it doesn't count if it's not us. Heads we win, tails we coup.

Utah senator Mike Lee said: "We're not a democracy. Democracy isn't the objective; liberty, peace, and prosperity are. We want the human condition to flourish. Rank democracy can thwart that." Which is a weird idea for a campaign ad: "Vote for Mike Lee, because voting is bad." But beyond that, this is a true sea change in American politics, and Mike Lee isn't the only one saying it out loud.

A big talking point from conservatives these days is that "the Founding Fathers feared mob rule!" This from the party that on January 6 encouraged a literal mob to attempt to rule.

If you violently attack the US Capitol, kicking in doors, breaking windows, killing cops, chasing duly elected representatives out of the building, all with the intent of overturning a lawful election and hanging the vice president for certifying it—you know, in the name of patriotism—maybe you've lost the thread of exactly what it is you're supposed to be loyal to. I'm no constitutional scholar, but I'm pretty sure it doesn't say, "In case of an election loss, break shit and install your guy anyway."

And please stop imagining you're blowing our minds when you

point out that "America is not a direct democracy, it's a republic!" Duh. Of course, even at the time of America's founding, direct democracy, where everyone who could vote gathered in the square like in ancient Athens and put a white or black pebble in a big pot . . . was impractical.

So democracy added the idea of representatives, and with the addition of a constitution that guided us and protected minorities, we became a republic—that is, an improved type of democracy, not something apart from democracy. But still a system where we vote, the votes count and the winners, with reasonable restraints, are put in charge. That's the best, albeit imperfect, way to do this thing called government, and we all used to get that. But now many Republicans have decided that democracy *is* what's wrong with America.

A lot of people drive themselves crazy asking Republicans for evidence that Biden somehow stole the election, but that's a fool's errand: in the circular logic of today's Right, the evidence that the election was stolen *is* that they lost.

The "logic" goes like this: We all know America should be made great again, and one side wanted it made great again—it said so right on their hats. So, logically, the other side wanted America to stay bad. And there's no way Jesus, who loves America, would let that happen.

Same thing with "voter fraud," which has been studied a million times, all with the same result: it's negligible and doesn't affect elections. Again, missing the point: the evidence of voter fraud is that sometimes Democrats win.

This is madness. Democrats and Republicans have certainly always had their differences: taxes, guns, abortion, wearing cowboy boots with a suit. But neither ever really doubted that our system of accepting electoral loss was what made America different from so many countries who could never get that right—it was, as much as anything, what made America great.

Despite the fact that in a democracy, the people who win, yes, sometimes get things wrong. Maybe that's why Churchill called democracy the worst system of government, except for all the others. The Left today is getting lots of things wrong: police departments gutted, kids taught crazy shit, unpopular thought being scrubbed, trying to reframe America as irredeemably racist—so I get the panic. But solutions short of junking democracy can and must handle this. What do tough guys and true patriots do in times of panic? They don't panic!

But conservatives now sound creepily like the generals in some country where they finally experimented with democracy for the first time and . . . well, they didn't like it so much: "I'm afraid we let the voters decide, and, well, they fucked up. So we'll be taking over again."

When a country slides into authoritarian rule, you don't get a text alert. Things will look the same on the surface. The buses will still be running, the cops will still be patrolling. You can still get your hair done. Your favorite show is still on TV—unless maybe it's *Real Time*. Americans are always worried that when we lose our freedom it'll look like the movie *Red Dawn*, with tanks in the street. But that's not how a republic always ends.

When Rome stopped being a republic, it didn't stop having a senate, and if we stop being a republic, neither will we. It'll just be more like "student government." Because that's what dictators do. Russia has a pretend parliament, and so do China and North Korea.

We keep the names on the institutions, but we just change what's inside. We still have trials, we just don't have witnesses. You can still subpoena people, they just don't show up. There's still an EPA, it just works for the coal companies now. It's like the way TV channels sometimes completely change format but keep the name. The Learning Channel has Honey Boo Boo and *America's Worst Tattoos*, and I don't think you can really call that learning.

7

DEMOCRATS

I'M WITH GRRR!

Part of the appeal of a Donald Trump, or any number of egregious dopes Republicans have backed, is that such a candidate sends a message to Democrats, and that message is: "This is how much we don't want what you're selling."

The fact that Republicans have no shame in their game and will vote for any monster with an "R" by their name is their way of signaling how serious they are about blocking what Obama called "the crazy stuff." They're like the bad guy in action movies who shoots one of his own men and then says, "I liked him, but I had to make a point." That's why you can be a really bad dude today in Republican politics, and it's not a deal-breaker.

Judge Roy Moore was in his thirties and was still going to the mall and picking up teenage girls.

Eric Greitens was Missouri governor, then in 2022 a Senate candidate, despite the fact that his ex-wife says he beat her and the kids, and he was charged with tying up a woman he was having an affair with, taking nude pictures and threatening to blackmail her with them. As governors do. I mean, John Edwards was creepy, but there was no begging to be untied. Al Franken took a "gag" picture, but he didn't go Phil Spector on anyone.

And then there was Herschel Walker. A lot was written in 2022 about how shocking it was that Republicans could stand behind Senate candidate Walker—did it mean they'd lost all sense of integrity?

Really? Just now? Integrity died a long time ago after a long battle with tribalism. Integrity is survived by hypocrisy and fear of the other party.

Where to begin with Walker? First off, he's just a fucking idiot on a scale almost impossible to parody—although on *Real Time* we did once present his book called *Herschel Walker, Science Talker*, because he says things like, "If man descended from apes, why are there still apes?"

Then there's the lying and the crazy and the violence. Not only did he write a book about having twelve different personalities, he wrote it with two other people. He admits that he used to play Russian roulette. He used to threaten to blow his wife's brains out, a lot, and seems to have never met a family member he hasn't threatened to kill. He threatened to kill his girlfriend, and he stalked a Dallas Cowboys cheerleader. He threatened to *shoot cops*.

He claimed to *be* a cop; he wasn't. Claimed to be an FBI agent; he wasn't. Claimed to be valedictorian of his high school; he wasn't. Claimed to graduate in the top 1 percent of his college class; never graduated. Claimed to have once supervised six hospitals; it's amazing that he had the time, given his job at the FBI. When the pandemic hit, he tried to sell a dry mist Covid cure that "would kill any Covid on your body." Because one of his personalities is Dr. Oz.

And then during his 2022 campaign, three secret children were unearthed, one of whom said of Herschel: "He has 4 kids 4 different women, wasn't in the house raising one of them." He's very pro-family, just not his. He's 100 percent against abortion, no exceptions, but his ex-girlfriend has proof he paid for hers. Then he got her pregnant again and tried to get her to abort that one. His campaign slogan was "Stop me before I kill again."

Voting for Herschel Walker was a way to say to Democrats: "All that socialism and identity politics and victimhood and oversensitivity and cancel culture and white self-loathing and forcing complicated ideas about race and sex on kids too young to understand it . . . literally, anything would be better than that."

There is an entire species of political ads on the right where the candidate just shoots something they don't like. Many of these ads make no mention of policy at all, it's just "Truck . . . gun . . . gun . . . truck . . . me like these things you like—vote me!" But among the ones that use actual words, I noticed that in the Republican ads, the candidates can't say the word "conservative" enough, and in the Democrats' ads, they never use the word "liberal."

Democrats might want to think about what that means. Because the implication is you're embarrassed by what liberalism has become, that the term is now so irredeemably coupled with woke nonsense that you dare not invoke it. Which is a shame, because despite the truly alarming drift of their fringe, voting Democrat is still usually voting for a superior product. Better than the one that doesn't believe in democracy or climate change.

But what does it say about your brand if you don't want to say what you are? So much of liberal politics nowadays is identity politics, and yet it seems we found the one thing liberals won't identify as: liberals.

DONKEY WRONG

There is a fundamental problem with the Democratic Party: they look weak. Running from a fight when you should be in there throwing punches.

Democrats should learn the lesson that's staring them in the face every day in the person of Donald Trump: voters don't care about how smart you are, just don't be a pussy. Trump did better with Hispanics after calling them rapists and killers, and he once said to a crowd in Iowa, "How stupid are the people of Iowa?"—and then won Iowa in a landslide, as the people cried, "It's about time somebody leveled with us about how stupid we are." Their attitude is, "Insult me, lie to me—just lead me."

Hillary had the right plan for coal country: get them off coal. She said, "Now we've got to move away from coal and all the other fossil fuels, but I don't want to move away from the people who did the best they could to produce the energy that we relied on." Everything about that plan and that statement was right, but she did what Democrats always do—the second there was the slightest backlash, she backpedaled, saying, "It was a misstatement because what I was saying is . . ."

Stop. You already lost.

She got 26 percent of the vote in West Virginia. But it wasn't a misstatement, it was the truth, and she should have said: "You heard me, coal is dead, and it's about goddamn time. It's dirty, it's killing the environment and it's killing *you*." Instead of pretending it's a great thing that a West Virginia man can die in a hole looking for rocks just like his daddy did and his daddy before that, how about "We're the party that's gonna get you *out* of the hole!" What happened to selling the American dream of a *better* life for your kids?

But Democrats are to political courage what Velveeta is to cheese. Republicans are all claws and sharp teeth and fangs when they fight. The Democrats' weapon of choice is adaptive coloration: "I'm a leaf, don't eat me . . . Vote for me, I'm the same pattern as the couch."

How about this for an ad: "Democrats support abortion. So do Republicans—when they need one for their girlfriend."

I used to think the reason I never saw prominent Democrats on Fox News was they weren't invited. I thought they were banned from appearing on the network, like I am. But no, they're invited. Most of them just don't go.

Republicans never shy away from coming on *Real Time*, and they come with a smile on their face, despite knowing that much of the audience is against them. They don't care, because it's an opportunity to expose people to their side of the story. So what if there are groans! Groans don't kill you.

Democrats are like Mormons if Mormons only proselytized in Utah. But for a hundred years, Mormons have gone all over the world with one goal: to spread their faith to people who don't want it. Savages with their own weird gods, like the French. But that's how you build a brand. Look at Samoa—16.9 percent of it is Mormon. Do they look Mormon? Was it an easy sell when the guys with white shirts and clip-on ties showed up?

Nineteen percent of all voters—Democrat and Republican—said Fox News was their main source of campaign news. That's ahead of every other source; it's more than ABC, CBS and NBC combined. We all know Fox News sucks: it's ruined bow ties and pillow commercials and Tulsi Gabbard, and turned your grandpa into a dick. He's crabby now, and he only leaves the house once every four years. But unfortunately, it's to vote. You have to get *inside* the bubble.

Democrats call themselves the resistance? Then fight behind enemy lines. That's what a "resistance" does. That's the difference between blowing up a tank and tweeting about it. Get out of your echo chamber and infiltrate theirs.

Also, stop pouting about voter suppression and using it as an excuse to lose elections. Yes, the Republicans' game is making voting such a hassle for the people they want to keep out of the booth that those people just give up and don't vote. And, of course, no one should have to jump through hoops to vote.

But it's also not impossible. Especially if you're young, the group who vote the least and have the most time: if you can stand in line for a damn phone, you can stand in line to vote. If you can find the after-party, you can find the polling place. If you have time to get a tattoo, you have time to get registered. Picture ID? Yeah, it's a pain in the ass, but you take pictures of every other fucking thing in your life; think of it as a selfie for democracy. It's what you'll have to do if you ever want to see that "blue wave." "Blue Wave"—sounds like an off-brand aftershave at the Dollar Store. Blue Wave: from the makers of Hillary Clinton's Inevitable.

YOU, ME AND DECREE

Regulation should be a good issue for Democrats—and as a party, it needs to be, because it's certainly one with which they're associated.

The average voter probably agrees that banks and chemical plants and drug companies need watching. Telling a company "You can't dump the waste from your hog farm straight into the water supply"—we're mostly all for that. But Democrats have become a parody of themselves—just making rules to make rules, because it makes you feel like you're a better person. Making sure that everything bad "never happens again," which you can never fully do and which just makes everyone else's life a drag.

Democrats keep trying to pass federal legislation requiring car manufacturers to install a motion sensor that would remind drivers they left their kid in the backseat. Really. It's called the Hot Cars Act, because Turn Around, Dipshit was too on-the-nose. But if someone's too high to remember their kid, you think they're gonna see a little yellow light?

Sadly, this is something done mostly by crackheads and people who, yes, do it on purpose. And after every one of us winds up bearing the cost for cars to install this alarm, do you know who's going to ignore it? Crackheads and people who do it on purpose.

A sensor light is not going to fix this problem, and Democrats no longer possess the common sense to understand that not every problem in the world can be fixed with a regulation.

My dashboard doesn't need any more indicators. "Is your seat belt on?" "Are your tires inflated?" "Is your oil changed?" Jeez, if I wanted to be nagged this much I'd get married.

There were over thirteen million new cars sold in America last year—are we really going to require them all to install sensors, the cost of which will be passed on to the consumer, to prevent something less likely than being struck by lightning? And should reminding you not to forget your baby really be Toyota's problem?

Where does this stop? Chunks of toilet ice fall out of the sky from airplanes all the time, and one of them is going to kill some unlucky fucker someday. Why not the Piss Ice Act, requiring all vehicle roofs to be reinforced to withstand a urine iceberg dropped from thirty thousand feet?

Honolulu banned looking at your phone while crossing the street. But wait—what if I'm getting an important message, like that I've left my baby in a hot car?!

And here's where someone says, "But if it saves one life . . ."

Yes, you could put kids in bubble wrap all day and it would save some, but would it be worth it? We're never going to get this down to zero until we get rid of kids altogether. And I keep signing the petition, but it never happens.

Until then, all this will accomplish is to feed into the Republican message that Democrats don't want to help people, they just want to micromanage their lives. And I hate to tell you, but we're *all* in an over-heating vehicle. It's called Earth. That's why I say to Democrats, "Either go big or go home."

Yes, I understand you have a thousand good ideas for how I should live my life, check my privilege and sort my recycling, and we'll get to that. But in the meantime, the movement to childproof the world has made Republicans the "party of freedom" and Democrats the "party of poopers."

Do you have to inject yourselves into everything—from where you can throw a Frisbee to who can braid hair? This is why so many people were triggered by Covid policies: they were already sick of rules. Democrats have to stop thinking that what the voters dream about is to be hassled.

But don't tell that to the advocacy groups who also want every future car in America to only start when the driver blows into a Breathalyzer. Great, my other car is a Karen. It's also not safe to drive when you're crying—should we make a car that follows your texts and stops the engine when you get dumped? Racism is bad; how about a car that won't start until you play a message about tolerance from George Takei?

In California, we make just about every business under the sun put up signs that say, "Warning: Detectable amounts of chemicals known to cause cancer may be found around this facility." No shit. We live in LA. It's called "air." If you buy a shed at Costco, it comes with this warning: "**WARNING:** THIS PRODUCT CAN EXPOSE YOU TO WOOD DUST, WHICH IS KNOWN TO THE STATE OF CALIFORNIA TO CAUSE CANCER." That's right, California think's you're going to snort your shed.

I don't want to blow Pinocchio. I just want to put the lawn mower away. And this is all so unnecessary, because it is possible to regulate without making people want to regurgitate.

A BEAUTIFUL GRIND

Progress—real progress that actually changes the lives of real people—comes mainly from dull, patient plodders who put in their ten thousand hours mastering the details of public service. It comes from people trapped in tiny rooms at three a.m. with stale pizza and cold coffee, crafting laws line by line that few will ever read or thank them for. I know it's not the sexy answer, but change comes from people like Henry Waxman.

What if I told you there was a single member of Congress who brought the tobacco industry to its knees, paved the way for less expensive generic drugs, expanded Medicaid to include pregnant women and children, put the teeth into the Clean Air and Safe Drinking Water acts and wrote most of Obamacare? You probably wouldn't know who it was—even though I just told you: Henry Waxman.

You always hear things like "The insurance companies wrote Obamacare!" Sure, they had their input, but no, most of it was written by Henry Waxman. And not just the Affordable Care Act. Nursing home reform. Food safety reform. AIDS research.

Basically, if you ate it, drank it, breathed it or fucked it and it didn't kill you, you have Henry Waxman to thank. When it came to actually making people healthier between 1975 and 2015, he did everything but get the cigarettes out of firing squads.

As one top Republican said, "Fifty percent of the social safety net was created by Henry Waxman when no one was looking."

And that's the thing about being a workhorse instead of a show horse: no one is looking. Waxman never went on the Sunday talk shows; he didn't do TV at all. The camera didn't love him and the feeling was mutual. We asked him once to do *Real Time* and he said, "No—I'm too busy."

I fucking love that.

Henry Waxman didn't even put himself on the cover of his own book. He could have published *Relentless: Taking Back America from the Takers Who Took It*, but that wasn't his style. His style was getting stuff done.

Liberals, to paraphrase Ted Kennedy, see wrong and try to right it, see suffering and try to heal it, see war and try to stop it. But how does that actually happen? It's easy to spray-paint "fuck you" on a federal building. It's a little harder to work inside and actually make shit happen.

There's definitely something about getting in the street that makes a powerful statement: that we care, that we're not afraid and that we feel so strongly we're willing to use a porta-potty. We're liberals, damn it: tanned, rested and gluten-free, and the type of people who will throw a trash can through a Starbucks window and then climb through and say, "While we're here, can I get a double mocha grande, very little foam?"

Done peacefully, street protests can move the needle on how the public sees an issue. It's an important piece of the equation, but while I'm sure it's fun to wear your *V for Vendetta* mask, let's be clear: as a means of actually effecting change, it's right up there with holding your breath until you get a pony.

Someone breathing bad air just wants someone in the government to take responsibility and clean up the toxic waste dump that's so close to where they live. Who actually gets that done?

People don't live in the world of political philosophies and endless intersectional theorizing, they live in the world of: Is there going to be hot lunch at school? No lead in the toys? A higher minimum wage? An end to human trafficking?

John Kerry always looks tired because things like the Iran nuclear deal or the Paris Accords don't just plan themselves. The irony of Hillary Clinton being done in by her emails was that if you actually read them they'd bore you to tears, because that's what a policy wonk meticulously doing her job looks like.

Kerry, Hillary, Barney Frank, John Lewis, Nancy Pelosi, Obama—these are the wonks who never satisfy the radicals but know how to make actual progress, as opposed to doing progressive theater. It's not the screamers and the tweeters, it's the worker bees with the name tags and the binders.

The unheralded grinders who push the boulders up history's hill.

I hate to have to put it this way, but mostly you have to *make* Republicans do the right thing. The guy breaking the windows of a Starbucks in Portland doesn't do that. A guy like Waxman has.

Pundits have always referred to Republicans as the Daddy Party, which makes the Democrats the Mommy Party: the nurturers, the caretakers, the compassionate ones. Democrats worried about your health care and education, and Republicans were all about security and fiscal responsibility. And Republicans used to take their role very seriously: the no-nonsense, keep-you-safe, pay-the-bills party.

But Republicans really aren't the Daddy Party anymore. They're more like the Absentee Father Party: going through a midlife crisis, making bad decisions with an abundance of pretend confidence. It's like the entire party is wearing a toupee.

But for so many who are just trying to survive in this American family, they have to come to terms with the reality that the Daddy Party is the Deadbeat Dad Party, and the man who's been the leader of the party since 2015 is a hot mess. And you know what happens when Daddy's a useless piece of crap? Mom has to take over.

That's why Democrats are no longer the Mommy Party—they're the *Single* Mom Party. They're the party that has to work two jobs because Daddy went out for cigarettes and never came back. The Single Mom Party is the only one that cares about the kids' future. The Republicans are the party of "pollute all you want now, because tomorrow's not our problem, we'll be gone."

WHAT TO EXPECT WHEN YOU'RE NEGLECTING

I know liberals think this country is full of dumb white people, but in our democracy, dumb white people make up a substantial portion of the vote. The median voter is a white person in their fifties who didn't go to college, whose favorite TV show is *NCIS*, and whose pronouns are: "What?" "I don't know what the fuck you're talking about" and "Get away from me."

In 2008, Republicans only won four Virginia counties by more than 70 percent; in the 2021 governor's election there they did it in *forty-five* counties.

And these were some of the headlines in liberal media telling Democrats what the reason was for that:

"Glenn Youngkin's win proves white ignorance is a powerful weapon."

"Racism still works in Virginia."

"It's not the messaging, folks. This country simply loves white supremacy."

I haven't worked up an *official* Democratic campaign slogan for 2024 yet, but I'll tell you what I have ruled out: "Vote Democrat, Because White People Suck." It's like trying to get laid by saying, "You're ugly—do you wanna dance?" You're alienating a whole lot of people. Particularly whites without a college degree, which is most of them. In a country that's still about 70 percent white. I'd say "do the math," but math is a form of white supremacy.

It doesn't have to be that way. You can find ways to stand up for everybody without being David Duke.

And I say this to Democrats as a friend: your paranoia about being seen as racist has crippled your ability to think clearly, and in a host of ways actually has set the cause of Black advancement back.

In 2022, an 85 percent Latino congressional district on the border with Mexico, which had always voted heavily Democratic, flipped to the Red Team; the campaign manager for the losing Democrat said, "We gave up a reliably Democratic congressional seat for no reason at all. We deserve to know why."

Well, aside from your terrible attitude, I'm going to tell you why. Because these voters stopped seeing your candidate as their lawyer—that's why. Their message to you was "I'm an American now—I'm here. Be my lawyer, not the lawyer for the migrants showing up in my backyard."

With apologies to *Law & Order*: In the American political system, the people are represented by two separate yet equally stupid groups: the Republicans, who normalize constitutional crimes, and the Democrats, who pit identity groups against each other. These are their stories.

If you're in court, you need a good representative. And the other place the term "representative" comes up is Congress.

Asian-Americans' support for Democrats is down sixteen points since the 2020 election. A lot of that is because, in the name of achieving equity in schools, Democrats in deep-blue cities have made it a mission to eliminate the advanced programs at which Asian kids excel. Asian parents said, "OK, I wish all kids well—but I need someone who acts like *my* lawyer."

If you're a parent and wanted schools to reopen a lot sooner than they did after Covid shutdowns, or think maybe your kid is getting a bad education partly because it's nearly impossible to fire a lousy teacher, you very well might be saying: "Congratulations, teachers, you got yourself a good lawyer—the Democratic Party's got your back one hundred percent. But I've noticed my kid is kind of an idiot, so I may be looking for new 'representation.'"

President Biden wants to cancel hundreds of billions in student debt. Good news for those students, or ex-students—but the poorer two-thirds of American kids who don't get a college degree will say, "Why should the people who didn't go to college and so make less money subsidize the people who did go and make more? You want me to chip in so some liberal arts college can build a bigger rock wall? Fine, but you're not *my* lawyer."

Yes, I know, Democrats: every fiber of your being tells you the people you really want to reach are Guatemalan teenagers and bloggers in Gaza. But they can't vote. To a lot of folks you come across as the "Cares About Everybody but Me" party.

When the Democrats passed their big trillion-dollar bill to rebuild our roads and bridges in 2021, six ultra-woke Democrats voted no because it didn't go far enough to address climate change, which I'm sure is true—but what does? This was free money from the federal government that would actually improve their constituents' lives. I can see a voter saying, "You know, Squad, I agree with you on climate change, but as long as it *is* happening, we also need money for getting the water pumped out of the subway. Can we do that before we build the workers' paradise?"

A Universal Basic Income sounds pretty good to a lot of people struggling without a college degree, and a number of cities have been running pilot programs in guaranteed income. However, the West Hollywood program had to be suspended because it was unconstitutional. They set up a program where twenty-five residents were to get a thousand bucks a month for eighteen months—but only if you identified as LGBT. Why? Because they need money more than any other people? Because no one in West Hollywood will hire a gay person?

When he ran in 2020 Bernie Sanders said he'd legalize marijuana on his first day as president—but that the business of selling pot would be awarded first to those who suffered most from the Drug War, and I can't argue with that instinct: the Drug War *has* been a horrendous instrument of prejudice and punishment for racial minorities. It only seems fair they jump the line for weed franchises, the way Indians did for casinos.

But it's also what's holding up Republican support for legalizing weed nationally, which would be good for everybody. And those are the hard, practical choices the Democrats have to weigh: redress the past, or reach out to the gettable white voter who says, "I'd like a shot at getting in the pot business . . . but to do that I'm gonna need a lawyer who fights for *me*."

For decades, liberals have said about abortion, "If only men could get pregnant, this wouldn't even be an issue," and "Abortion rights are women's rights." Well, that's wrong now. When the wokey end of the progressive spectrum talks about "women," they prefer terms like "birthing people" or "people who menstruate." Because somewhere a trans man is pregnant, and I say good for him, and I'll be looking for his story somewhere in a future issue of *Ripley's Believe It or Not!*. Yes, let's take the first fucking word a human animal understands—"mama"—and replace it with something best understood by four Trotskyites at Berkeley.

As with all these issues, the wavering voter is saying to her lawyer, the Democratic Party, "So happy for you that you have so many other clients and that you care so much about their problems, and all the pro bono work you do—but you're supposed to be *my* lawyer!"

If the Democrats want to win, they need to be like the lawyers you see on billboards: "You Hurt? We Fight!" . . . "Injured? Get the Gorilla!" . . . and my favorite, "Just Because You Did It Doesn't Mean You're Guilty." It doesn't? I think it does.

But that's the thing about a lawyer—their clients don't care if they're full of shit, they care about winning.

STOP MAKING DENSE

In 2020, a year that was so much about making people aware of racism, the Democratic Party's share of minority votes went down. The message to Democrats from so much of the country seemed to be "We don't like Trump, but we still can't bring ourselves to vote for you." If Cracker Jack was made of popcorn and dog shit and half the people threw out the popcorn, popcorn should want to know why.

Liberals can either write off half the country as irredeemable, or they can ask: What is it about a "D" next to a candidate's name that makes it so toxic? Ruben Gallego, Democratic congressman from Arizona, was once asked how his Democrats could do a better job connecting to Latinos, and he said, "First, start by not using the term 'Latinx.'" Which the vast majority of Latinos have never heard of, and when they do, they don't like it.

Who likes it? Pandering white politicians who mistake Twitter for real people and don't get it that "Latinx" is like "fetch": you can try to make it happen, but it's never going to. Even the country's oldest Latino civil rights group came out against it. Yet Congresswoman Alexandria Ocasio-Cortez keeps defending it, saying, "Gender is fluid. Language is fluid."

Yes, and Latino voters are fluid, and more of them now than ever are "identifying" as Republican.

James Clyburn said: "'Defund the police' is killing our party." Pennsylvania Democrat Conor Lamb says Democratic rhetoric "needs to be dialed back. It needs to be rooted in common sense." That's the crux of the problem: Democrats too often don't come across as having common sense to a huge swath of Americans—and these are people who follow QAnon. Democratic members of Congress tweeting things like "Cancel rent, cancel mortgage" and "No more policing, incarceration" and "Capitalism is slavery."

Politics in this country is binary. You have to wear everything anyone on your side does. Republicans are "the party of" election denying and separating kids from their parents at the border, and Democrats are "the party of" every hypersensitive, social-justice-warrior, woke, bullshit story in the news. The party that disappears people . . . or tries to. The party that makes people apologize for ridiculous things.

In 2019 I read about how NBC held an "emergency meeting" to determine if Mario Lopez should be fired from his job at *Access Hollywood*. I thought, "Holy shit, did he sexually assault someone?" No, he went on a podcast, and when the host brought up the trend of liberal parents letting toddlers pick their gender identity, he said, "My God, if you're three years old and you're saying . . . you think you're a boy or a girl . . . I just think it's dangerous as a parent to make that determination."

Cue the groveling apology, followed by America saying, "Uh, I think Mario is right—maybe kids shouldn't make big life decisions while you still need to make choo-choo noises to get food in their mouth."

I can do this all day—cite stories big and small that are endlessly on people's news feeds that add up to a constant drip drip drip of "these people are nuts."

Everybody heard about that story out of San Francisco about a guy who got on a crowded elevator with a female professor, and when she asked what floor, he said, "Women's Lingerie." You know, a little joke. For which he earned a formal complaint because it left her "shaken."

Shaken? Who are these jellyfish? Like the woman who almost derailed Biden's campaign because he kissed the back of her head before she went out to make a speech. She said her "brain couldn't process what was happening." Really? Your brain couldn't process that—like string theory or wormholes? An old man was trying to show support in his old-man way. She said she was "embarrassed, shocked, confused"—well, then the outside world isn't for you, and certainly running the country isn't.

Trump got more votes the *second* time he ran. Democrats kept saying in both campaigns, "You can't possibly think Trump is preferable to what we're selling," and almost half the country said: "Yes. We. Can." They said, "In fact, our primary reason for voting for him is to create a bulwark against *you*. Because I just want to have our schools be like they were only five years ago, not battlegrounds using children as cannon fodder in your culture war bullshit . . . because your side thinks silence is violence, and looting is not . . . because you're 'the party of' chasing speakers off college campuses and making everyone walk on eggshells and replacing 'Let's not see color' with 'Let's see it always and everywhere.'"

Formerly the position of the Ku Klux Klan.

I talked to a guy in the Midwest once who told me this story about the day he went out to his car in the supermarket parking lot but couldn't back out because a mother and her very young daughter were standing behind his car, which was next to their car, which had a Hillary bumper sticker on it. And the little girl was screaming at her mother, who was profusely apologizing to the child. And he said to me, "I just can't let people like that take over this country."

That's what a lot of people vote on. Not policy. Not your "plan" to fix some problem they doubt any plan can fix.

The majority of Americans are actually with the Democrats on the issues: raising the minimum wage, sensible gun laws, path to citizenship, abortion rights, pro-environment, pro-democracy. But when Democrats lose, it's usually because they reminded voters of a man who's taken his balls and put them in his wife's purse.

One of the first things Biden did in office was getting through a Covid "relief" package that sent $1,400 to, well, everybody. Without a single Republican vote. Did his approval rating soar to great heights as a result of that? It did not. You can give the people all the goodies Joe Manchin will allow, and it doesn't seem to buy their love. Why? Why is the party that supports so many issues that benefit the middle class still considered "out of touch" by 61 percent of Americans? In plain English, because nobody likes a snob.

Hillary Clinton didn't have anyone on rural research or outreach when she ran in 2016. Until the race tightened just before the election, and then they hired one. And where was his office? Brooklyn. True story.

Politics is local, not locally sourced. It's not artisan—it's Art and Stan. Your microaggression culture doesn't play in the Rust Belt. If a staffer hands you a speech that says "menstruating people" instead of "women," don't say that. Say "women."

And don't put anyone fresh out of college in charge of the campaign. They've been given participation trophies their whole life, so they don't know how to win. James Carville knew how to win, and when he blamed Democratic losses in the '21 off-year election on "stupid wokeness," AOC fired back that wokeness "is a term almost exclusively used by older people these days, so that should tell you all you need to know."

What? This is a term folks like AOC brought out only very recently and had been proudly displaying at every march since! In 2020 the *Guardian* declared "woke" "the word of our era." I guess they didn't get the memo from the Mean Girls Club: "Uggh, please, we don't use that emoji anymore."

And what a great strategy, to never miss an opportunity to remind older voters—you know, the ones who actually vote—how lame and clueless and hopelessly uncool they are.

But OK, fine, what word would you like us to use for the plainly insane excesses of the Left that are *not* liberalism but something completely different? Because you can't take the word "liberal" from us and think it should cover things like teaching third-graders they're oppressors. That's all your new thing.

A more pertinent question to ask about the word "woke" might be "Why, in such a short time, has it gone from a rallying cry to a pejorative?" If the word only made you think of rational, deserving causes like teaching a less whitewashed version of American history, AOC would still want to own it.

But it became an eye-roll because it makes you think of people who wake up offended and take orders from Twitter. And their oversensitivity and arrogance have grown tiresome.

8

FRAGILITY

THE SORROW AND PETTY

In 2016, conservatives won the White House, both houses of Congress and almost two-thirds of governorships and state legislatures. Social justice warriors, on the other hand, caught Steve Martin calling Carrie Fisher "beautiful" in a tweet and made him take it down. I'm not making that up. Here's Steve's offensive tweet: "When I was a young man, Carrie Fisher was the most beautiful creature I had ever seen. She turned out to be witty and bright as well."

How could he! Steve, we thought we knew you, but this? You noted her appearance first, and *then* that she was witty and bright? What a monster.

This has become a hallmark of stupid wokeness: getting offended for people who themselves would not be offended.

Democrats have gone from the party that protects people to the party that protects feelings. From "Ask not what your country can do for you" to "You owe me an apology." Republicans apologize for nothing,

Democrats for everything—can't we find a balance? Because I can't keep up anymore with who's on the shit list.

At the Golden Globes a few years ago, Michael Keaton mixed up the titles of two movies that have a Black cast, *Hidden Figures* and *Fences*, and said "Hidden Fences." Because he's a Klansman. Cue the outrage. And then the apology: "I screwed up . . . It makes me feel so badly that people feel badly. If somebody feels badly, that's all that matters." No, that's not all that matters—in fact, things like this don't matter at all.

The iconic, proudly gay designers Dolce and Gabbana offered an opinion some years ago that, when it comes to how-a you make-a da bambino . . . they're old-school Italians and don't approve of what they called "synthetic children." Because, you know, synthetics, they just don't breathe like cotton. Well, naturally, they had to be disowned, disavowed and, if allowed, probably dismembered.

For folks who take such pride in their love of diversity, liberals increasingly seem to tolerate none in their own ranks. I don't agree with Dolce and Gabbana, but what's the point of attacking people who are 95 percent on your side?

But no, it's easier to get all fake outraged over the hateful antigay speech of two men who bedazzle codpieces for a living. Ellen DeGeneres and Martina Navratilova were furious, and Courtney Love said she planned to burn her Dolce and Gabbana—and then breathe in the melting polyester, because hey, you never know what might get you high.

But Dame Elton John was the angriest of all, tweeting, "How dare you refer to my children as synthetic?" My hair, yes, but not my children. ISIS throws gay people off buildings; maybe there are bigger battles to fight. You can't sell handbags now if you only agree with Elton John *almost* all the time?

How deeply stupid has the Far Left become when gay designers can't get along with gay musicians, and when vegans attack vegetarians for not being pure enough: "Cheese-eater. Burn him!" I see agnostics and atheists bitching at each other—why is this even a thing? Do you believe in a talking snake? Me neither, we're on the same team!

NEW WORLD ORDER

Instead of putting a Bible in hotel rooms, we should start putting a dictionary in there. Because apparently nobody knows what words mean anymore. George Carlin famously had the seven words you can't say on TV; here are my eight words people need to stop redefining: "hate," "victim," "hero," "shame," "violence," "survivor," "phobic" and "white supremacy."

Comedian Hannah Gadsby characterized Dave Chappelle's controversial Netflix special as "hate speech dog-whistling." Well, "dog whistle" refers to when someone puts things in code because they're afraid to come out and say what they really think—that's what you get from Dave Chappelle? That he's afraid to say what he really thinks?

And it's not "hate speech" just because you disagree with it. "Hate speech" doesn't mean "speech I hate." Nor is it "phobic," which means to fear something irrationally, like "arachnophobia" for fear of spiders, or "germophobia" for fear of germs. But now it's used as a suffix for anything you just don't like.

I've been called "commitment-phobic." No, I don't fear commitment—I just don't want it. Other people do—great! I don't call them "single-phobic." I don't like bowling. I'm not "bowling-phobic." And if I talk about how wrong I think it is to force women to live their lives under a burka all day, that's not being Islamophobic—I just don't like it. And I bet some women don't either.

Also in the category of "we just don't like it, so we're pretending it's something else" is the word "violence." In 2020 there was a staff "mutiny" at the CBS drama *All Rise* when some of the writers—I'm sorry, I meant "victims"—took issue with a scene where two women are in an elevator and a naked man gets on, and they just continue talking calmly. And if you think that's offensive, you should see how the guy pushed the button.

But the writers found the scene objectionable and sent off an email saying, "Two women would not calmly continue a conversation with a naked white guy running into the elevator. That is violence . . ." No, it's not. Violence usually involves leaving a mark of some kind. This is comedy. The depiction of the women not being fazed by a naked man is a joke to make a point about how blasé we've all become about the craziness of the big city. Obviously.

Of course, innumerable things can *lead* to violence, but sorry, you can't take that word and use it for stuff that's just scary to you. Or just verbal, which is something I literally learned in kindergarten. "Sticks and stones may break my bones, but . . ."—if you don't know how that one ends, you need to repeat kindergarten.

Social justice warriors who are fond of governing by hashtag like to say, "Silence is violence." And we know that . . . because it rhymes?

The words "victim" and "survivor" have likewise traveled a long way from their original usage. The guy who, as a baby, was photographed for an iconic Nirvana album cover sued Nirvana for "lifelong damages." I never thought I'd have to say this to a baby, but stop being such a fucking baby. You're not a victim. There's no reason you can't have a normal, happy life just because people look at you and think "Baby penis."

In 2010, the *New York Times* used the term "white supremacist" on seventy-five occasions. In 2020? Over seven hundred times. Now, some of that to be sure is because Trump came along and emboldened the faction of this country that is truly white supremacist—it is of course still a real thing.

But it shouldn't apply to something like the SAT test, which more and more colleges are getting rid of because it's "racist." Now, if anyone found that the SAT test is slanted in such a way as to stack the deck in favor of Caucasians, this would be appropriate. If there were questions on the test like, "If Biff and Chip are sailing a yacht traveling at 12 knots to an Ed Sheeran concert on Catalina, and Catalina is 26 miles away, how many White Claws should they bring?" then maybe.

But of course, the SAT doesn't have questions like that, so it becomes the kind of ludicrous exaggeration that makes lovers of common sense roll their eyes. Now, when it comes to snowflakes there's no whinier little bitch than Trump himself—but this kind of stuff does tend to stick to the Left a lot more.

Have you ever heard a parent call their child their "hero"? What party are they probably in? "My kid is my hero." Why? He's six, did he pull someone out of a burning building? "My hero—look at the way he shares his Ritalin!" Do you realize how stupid it sounds to imply you want to grow up to be your kid?

And then there's "shaming." That definition has been rewritten to mean "anything that suggests I'm not 100 percent perfect." It's not fat "shaming" to call bullshit on the idea that a person can be healthy at any size. Adele was shamed for *losing* weight, like she was a traitor to—what, unhealthiness?

This is the essence of why word inflation is a problem: you can try to change reality by changing the words, but ultimately it just stops you from dealing with it.

STAND BY YOUR BRAND

In modern America, not only do we change the meaning of words— entire institutions become the reverse of what they always were, and what they're supposed to be, and morph into their opposite. But they keep the old title.

The ACLU has long been synonymous with freedom of speech: they defended it for even the most hated groups, like the Nazis and the Klan— even the Jehovah's Witnesses. It was never about *what* you were saying, it was about the liberal principle of your right to say it. Well, they have new guidelines now, namely that before taking a case, ACLU lawyers should consider if the case might cause "offense to marginalized groups" or if a potential client's "values are contrary to our values."

"Contrary to our values"? Your values are free speech and defending the First Amendment! Those are your values! Your whole purpose in life is not to be worried about "offense to marginalized groups"—because we understand that free speech is an even more important value than never being offended. Because you're the ACLU, not UCLA!

The Boy Scouts of America used to be an organization . . . for boys.

Because girls have cooties. But now the Boy Scouts accepts girls, which I guess is "inclusive," but it ignores the very important need for boys to sometimes get together *as boys* to fart in a sleeping bag and laugh at that, which girls don't find funny. It also ignores the fact that there has also always been a scout troop for girls too—you may have heard of it: the *Girl* Scouts? Can't anything just be what it is anymore?

For decades *Playboy* was the go-to whack-off magazine for heterosexual men, with reviews of movies that came out six months ago and a lot of information about stereos. And fiction by Kurt Vonnegut! But mostly the masturbation thing. Which was facilitated by pictures of naked women. Who were naked.

But in 2016, *Playboy* did away with the nudity; yes, they took the tits out of *Playboy*. And in 2021 put a gay man on the cover. Which I guess we're supposed to celebrate, even though by then we already had a dozen magazines for gay guys—thirteen if you count *Martha Stewart Living*. Do we really need LGBTQ representation in *Playboy*? There's a transgender teenager on every show on television except reruns of *Voyage to the Bottom of the Sea*.

The same thing is going on with the *Sports Illustrated* swimsuit issue, which now celebrates all kinds of bodies except, you know, the good kind. Was it really such a crime against humanity to have one magazine, once a year, that was about finding creative ways for supermodels to hide their nipples? Now it looks like it's edited by the Huffington Post. Jeez, you have every other magazine—do you hate Dad that much? If he can't rub one out in the garage, what's he supposed to do in there, actually sand something? This is not progress—you haven't reformed the soft-core, gentleman masturbator, you've driven him to CreepyPorn.com.

TLC stands for "The Learning Channel." They used to have shows about, you know, learning. In recent years their offerings have included: *Cake Boss, Gypsy Sisters, Toddlers & Tiaras, Extreme Couponing, What Not to Wear, My Teen Is Pregnant and So Am I, 1000-lb Sisters* and *Alaskan Women Looking for Love*. And that's just the shows about the Palins.

The "A" in A&E stands for "Arts." They used to show the symphony. Now they have *Deep Fried Dynasty*, *Hoarders*, *Storage Wars*, *Ghost Hunters* and *Psychic Kids*. You know, for people who find The Learning Channel too intellectual. The History Channel has no history, and MTV has no music. I'm just saying, you can buy a petting zoo and turn it into a bondage dungeon, but then you gotta change the sign!

And I would add to this list the Republican Party, which used to stand for something quite specific—being heartless squares, but something. Oh, and patriotism. They always wanted you to know they loved America more than you. America-first, love-it-or-leave-it, flag-pin-in-the-lapel, thank-you-for-your-service America. But Fox News's Tucker Carlson became so valuable to the Kremlin during the first year of the Ukraine war that they put out a memo asking their propaganda outlets to replay as much of Tucker Carlson as possible. *In Russia.*

After the Capitol riot on January 6, 147 Republican lawmakers in a congressional vote objected to the certification of an election they knew was legitimate. OK, you can't be super-patriots who love America and also run on a platform of "Let's ignore the vote" and "Russia first." You can't represent a form of government you yourself don't believe in. If you do, then you have to get another name, like maybe the Trump Party. He's pretty modest about putting his name on things, but maybe he'll license it just this once.

CRIER BEWARE

To recap: we now have words—like "violence" and "victim"—that no longer mean what they mean; we have institutions that betray their very raison d'être; and we also now have entire lists of words and phrases we're not supposed to say at all, lest someone be "triggered" by hearing them.

Several universities in recent years have even compiled lists of terms we should be warned about or get rid of altogether, including: "balls to the wall," "no can do," "you guys," "master," "white paper," "man in the middle," "gyp," "off the reservation," "peanut gallery," "insane" and "virgin." "Virgin"? We can't say "virgin"? As opposed to what—"person experiencing not getting laid?"

You'd think that one would take the cake for oversensitivity, but the students at Brandeis said, "Hold my baby bottle." They made a list of expressions they don't want to hear because they remind them of violence. Terms like "killing it," "beating a dead horse" and, yes, even "trigger warning." I guess they don't teach irony in college anymore.

I think we need to put a trigger warning on trigger warnings, because they're not working. And that's not my opinion; a study in 2023 from Flinders University analyzed a dozen other studies on trigger warnings and they all came to the same conclusion: not only don't they protect your feelings, but if you actually have been traumatized by something they're warning you about, a trigger warning makes it worse. It's like if seat belts were made out of broken glass.

Now, for those of you who have been living on an offshore oil rig for the last ten years and don't know what I'm talking about, a trigger warning is kind of a "close your eyes, here comes an ouchie" that, like so many bad ideas in recent years, got started on college campuses. Students started demanding them so they could get ready in case something in a book or a piece of art or a history lesson reminded them that life includes bad things and not just good, and that sometimes people are mean. You can't have that just sprung on ya!

Unfortunately, at some point the trigger warning escaped from campus and got out into the real world, and now it's everywhere. Warnings at the top of Reddit threads, and Facebook and Twitter and Instagram posts. Warnings before your favorite serial killer series and before news articles.

Disney put an advisory on the movie *Dumbo*, warning viewers about stereotypes, because otherwise you might think it was a documentary about flying elephants. Turner Classic Movies still wants to show you classic movies, but . . . "Before we do, first there are a few parts we'd like you to feel really bad about—now enjoy the show!"

Theaters do it now too. The storied Guthrie Theater in Minneapolis tipped off their crowd that a play included simulated gunshots, strobe lights and haze—in case you'd ever been groped by a thick fog.

A theater in Brooklyn alerted the audience to expect moments of darkness and violence. And this was for *Oklahoma!* My senior class in high school put on *Oklahoma!*, and I thought it was corny and provincial *then*—I can't imagine the fragility of someone who needs to be warned about it. How do these people get to the airport, let alone through childhood?

London's Globe Theatre felt the need to tell the audience that its production of *Romeo and Juliet* includes suicide. OK, but *Romeo and Juliet* has been in your Netflix queue since 1597. You've had four hundred years to prepare. And also, it does kind of give away the ending. I don't understand how a society that's so in love with spoiler alerts can also be into trigger warnings: tell me what's gonna happen—but don't tell me!

And again, all the research shows that these trigger warnings don't even work. What they do is reinforce the idea that trauma is central to your identity and that you should let it define you instead of dealing with it, dispatching it and moving beyond it. People wonder why the younger generations have so much anxiety—it's this stuff!

Lots of things make us uncomfortable; you know what makes me uncomfortable? People who start every conversation with "As a person who" or "As a survivor of." I'm triggered every time I see a trigger warning because I'm reminded of how weak my country has become. It's like wearing a mask on your mind.

There is an alternate way of dealing with anxiety, and let me put it in comic book terms, so the kids can relate: Bruce Wayne was afraid of bats, so what did he do? He became Batman! That's the way to go!

WINDSOR NOT

One more thing about the words and phrases we're not supposed to say: how about "Your Royal Highness"?

How do Meghan and Harry do it? How do they still command the loyalty of the most liberal quarters and endlessly bitch about their illiberal royal family but still keep the duke and duchess titles? Still perfectly OK with being called "Your Highness"? I thought being born into privilege was déclassé now?

The social justice warriors have been surprisingly forgiving about the idea that some people are born exalted above the rest of us, to be bowed to and carted around in golden carriages. The same people who never tire of pointing out behaviors and bygone attitudes that just don't cut it anymore . . . where have they been on the subject of royalty in the modern world? Seduced by the pageantry, are ya? What is this bullshit that some people are "royal" and others are to be lorded over by a bunch of inbred twits who happened to win the 23 and Me lottery? What could be more antithetical to liberalism than calling another human "Your Highness"?

Meghan, Harry: if you really wanted to be as modern and new and independent as you claim, you'd burn your boats completely and say, "It's the twenty-first century, I hereby declare this birthright nonsense from the Middle Ages stupid. Please stop referring to us as 'Duke' and 'Duchess' and using the term 'Your Highness.' I'm an actress, he's a nice guy, we're not 'highnesses'—no humans are higher by birth, and to suggest so with these titles is just gross."

ALT FRIGHT

If I had to put one thing in a time capsule to let future humans know how it all went so wrong for us in the twenty-first century, I think I would choose the now infamous video from Yale in 2015 where a spoiled-brat college student is screaming at a professor because the professor's wife wrote an email suggesting that maybe Yale should chill out a little bit on being the Halloween costume police.

That's it. Just an email about Halloween costumes. And not even by him, by his wife. And the reaction from this child was:

"Who the fuck hired you? You should step down! If that is what you think of being headmaster, you should step down! It is *not* about creating an intellectual space! It *is not*! Do you *understand* that? It's about creating a *home* here! You are *not doing that*!"

You can't deny the passion—she is adamant that untouchables must be allowed to vote. Oh wait, that's Gandhi; this girl can't sleep at night because there's no school policy against a white girl dressing up as Pocahontas.

How about this for Halloween: if it's too much for your fragile sensibilities, and you're worried about seeing someone wearing something that's on the Forbidden Costume List, just stay the fuck home. Halloween is supposed to be outrageous! It's a festival of the sacrilegious and a celebration of the grotesque, from zombies to ghouls to bobbing for apples in other people's saliva. Halloween was always fun because it *wasn't* PC; not being PC is almost the whole point of the holiday. But now everything has to turn into a federal case of snowflakes vs. humor.

And in that there is no small degree of irony, because Halloween should be a day that conservatives hate, not liberals, as it embodies everything conservatives fear, like paganism, gay pride, women dressing provocatively and kids demanding free handouts, which is a little too close to socialism. And it's gay Christmas. Men dressed as women, women dressed as men, adults dressed as Harry Potter and everything is slutty: slutty nurse, slutty pirate, slutty pizza rat, slutty Bishop Desmond Tutu, slutty Saudi assassin . . .

Think about the things that angry up the Fox News base—what's the single, overarching message of that network? Weirdos are coming for your shit. Well, that's what happens on October 31. People dressed as pimps and hookers walking up your driveway and witch-cackle doorbells that sound like Hillary.

And yet every year the caterwauling we have to endure about Halloween comes from *the Left*—lists of costumes you'd better not wear lest a night of irreverent dress-up spiral into something that resembles fun.

Even the sexy *Handmaid's Tale* costume was pulled lest someone be offended by the ironic take on a character that doesn't exist from a fictional world that never happened. You'd think that a *Handmaid's Tale* costume would be acceptable since it derives from a completely woke-approved show that condemns the patriarchy, but no, Buzzkill—I mean BuzzFeed—says no *Handmaid's Tale* either because "it hits a little too close to home right now."

This is the life philosophy of Zillennials: things that are interesting might also contain something that could cause a moment of discomfort, so ban all of it. It's not your fault, kids—your parents ruined you by over-protecting you, and now you're these assholes.

That's the craziest part of all of this: being irreverent, unclenched and playful should be the province of the young—but it's not. Boomers are supposed to be the "get off my lawn" crowd, but when someone in a "problematic" costume shows up at your door, it's literally Gen Z telling them, "Get off my lawn." Except, it's not even your lawn. Because you live at your parents' house. When did liberals become the Fun Police? We went from "Yes we can" to "Oh no you didn't."

Halloween is not just a fun holiday, it's a necessary psychic venting: societies going back thousands of years knew you had to have some re-lease valve on the calendar to flirt with the macabre and let the demons out to role-play so they wouldn't come out later for real. Mexico has Day of the Dead, Japan has Obon, Haitians have Fèt Gede. It's not a coinci-dence that Carnival comes right before Lent and Halloween before All Saints' Day, much the way getting blown at a bachelor party comes be-fore the wedding day.

So here's an idea, clickbait websites: I won't tell you how to harvest and sell my personal data, and you don't tell me what I can wear on Hal-loween.

You know what day I want to cancel? November 1, All Scolds' Day, when the Good People announce which costumes the Bad People wore. Among the costumes in recent years declared verboten by the usual-suspect websites were: hula girls, Indian chiefs, Southern belles, Daniel Boone, geishas, ninjas, Gypsies, mobsters and terrorists. Also Cleopatra.

And pirates offend one-eyed people and you can't dress as a hobo because it makes light of the homeless. You can't dress as Quasimodo because that offends hunchbacks, and you can't dress as an escaped mental patient because that offends Kanye. And of course nothing that resembles a mariachi band, because that would be "cultural appropriation."

TRIBUTE BANNED

Of all the violations of the woke penal code, "cultural appropriation" just might be the dumbest of all. Not everything that merely alludes to another culture is racist, or "cultural appropriation." Really. Imagine there's no countries—it isn't hard to do.

Justin Timberlake once apologized for the sin of giving someone a compliment. He tweeted that an African-American, Jesse Williams, inspired him and then said: "I apologize to anyone that felt I was out of turn. I have nothing but LOVE FOR YOU AND ALL OF US."

Oh good. Because life knows no sin greater than the one he was being accused of, "the idea that white people shouldn't adopt things from other ethnic groups. How dare you mix and match cultures to produce something new? Where do you think you are, in some kind of melting pot?

At the pandemic-delayed summer Olympics in 2021, surfing was added as a sport. Good, surfers deserve to be recognized as athletes. I'm sorry, what I meant to say is "No, that's cultural appropriation!"

The Associated Press wrote the headline: "Olympic Surfing Exposes Whitewashed Native Hawaiian Roots." The AP said that for Hawaiians, probably two of them, including surfing in the Olympics would be "... an extension of the racial indignities seared into the history of the game and their homeland" when "white outsiders" took over their "spiritual art form."

Or people just having fun in the ocean.

First of all, there are twenty-five thousand islands in the Pacific: How do we know a Hawaiian was the first to stand on a board in the water? It seems like something anyone in any ocean would eventually get around to. And if you're a surfer, it doesn't matter if you're Black, white or in between, you all taste the same to sharks.

But let's say a Hawaiian did invent surfing: Should they have kept it to themselves? Most of human history is a horror story, but the good parts are about different groups coming together and sharing—it's sort of the whole point of the Olympics. Which itself comes from Greece, where wrestling was invented, as a way for completely heterosexual men to get to know each other.

Badminton has roots in India, tennis comes from France, skiing comes from Scandinavia and tae kwon do comes from Korea. Judo was "appropriated" from the Far East, and skateboarding from the Far Out.

What is this new rule that the first to do something are the only ones who get to have it? Jewish people spent most of their history wandering, but when they see other people milling around today they don't say, "Can you not, that's sort of our thing."

Change is not synonymous with progress. Newer doesn't automatically mean better. This new idea that each culture must remain in its own separate silo is not better, and it's not progress. In fact, it's messing with one of the few ideas that still really do make this melting pot called America great.

Not everything is about oppression. Stealing natural resources from Indigenous peoples: yes, that's exploitation. But I swear, not one Beach Boys song resulted in any Hawaiian having fewer waves to surf. Not one African record buyer stopped purchasing local music after Paul Simon made *Graceland*. But lots of white buyers in America were turned on to it and then bought African music.

And today, Korean boy bands make Western-style music. And that's the great thing about cultural mixing—it makes things better for everyone. BTS can be a hit in America, and I can get kimchi on a taco. Isn't that better than everyone walling themselves off from outsiders? I thought walls were supposed to be bad.

And then there's the nonsense that's been going on in Hollywood lately with the casting police either apologizing for, or calling on others to apologize for, playing roles they label as "appropriation."

James Franco was cast in 2022 to play Fidel Castro, and John Leguizamo posted, "No more appropriation . . . Boycott! This F'd up! I don't got a prob with Franco but he ain't Latino!"

OK, but John Leguizamo is Colombian-American. He ain't a Venetian, but he played one in *Romeo and Juliet*. He ain't a French little person, but he played one in *Moulin Rouge*. He ain't an Italian plumber, but he played one in *Super Mario Bros.*

Because he's an actor—why the hell do you think people become actors? Because they want to spend their life *not* being who they are.

"Appropriating" sounds like an unforgivable sin until you remember *that's what acting is.* That's why acting jobs are called "roles." Sean Penn won an Oscar for playing gay civil rights martyr Harvey Milk. At the time, it was considered a courageous act of solidarity for a straight male movie star to play a homosexual. Now it's the opposite.

Eddie Redmayne played a transgender woman in *The Danish Girl* but now calls that "a mistake" because "many people don't have a chair at the table." Zombie lie! Yes, that was true in the past, many people didn't have a chair; now they do. Things change, try to keep up. And what does it have to do with playing trans? Does it then work the other way? Can trans actors only play trans characters? Because that's not going to be a good deal for them.

And isn't the best acting always about making us feel our common humanity beyond separate identities? Isn't that why we applauded a Black George Washington in *Hamilton*? But I'm guessing Ryan Gosling as Frederick Douglass would be "problematic"; ditto Shia LaBeouf as Shaft.

Why don't we just go by merit and let the best actor win—which seems like what happened when Ana de Armas was cast to play Marilyn Monroe, even though she's Cuban. Hey, maybe *she* should play Fidel Castro, and James Franco can play Marilyn Monroe—then we can all stay in our lanes.

Is this what diversity and inclusion look like now—everybody staying in their lane?

Lawrence of Arabia was gay; Peter O'Toole wasn't. I can live with that, because he was so cool, he almost made *me* gay. Emma Stone caught hell for playing a Hawaiian, Jake Gyllenhaal for playing a Persian, Gal Gadot for just *wanting* to play Cleopatra and Johnny Depp for playing an American Indian, even though he's not an actual Comanche.

And spoiler alert: he's also not actually a drunken pirate. OK, bad example.

Tom Hanks now says that if *Philadelphia* were made today, he wouldn't do it, because the character was gay, and he's not. Well, besides the fact that this would force all gay actors to reveal their sexuality even if they didn't want to, great actors—among whom Tom is one—try hard to keep their private lives private so we don't think of their real lives when we see them in a movie that attempts to transport us into a different world. Could you really look at Amber Heard now and not think of her divorce trial? Should she only play bed-shitters now?

What's Daniel Day-Lewis really like? I haven't a clue. I'm not sure he even exists offscreen. Which is why he's so great, because when he plays Lincoln I only see Lincoln. I don't think, "Well there's a British heterosexual!" But Hanks says, "I don't think people would accept the inauthenticity of a straight guy playing a gay guy," because "we're beyond that now." And don't get him started on *Bosom Buddies*.

Does Forrest Gump get thrown under the bus too because Tom isn't really mentally challenged?

Steven Spielberg recently remade *West Side Story* and bent over backward to respect ethnicities, and ended up pleasing nobody. And it's too bad, because the original musical was created by Stephen Sondheim, Arthur Laurents and Leonard Bernstein: three gay Jews. And if you can't trust gay Jews to write about hot-blooded Puerto Rican teenagers, who can you trust? Next you're going to tell me street gangs don't even dance.

And now we have a movie *about* Bernstein, with Bradley Cooper playing him. I mean, if he can get through the picket lines.

You see, like Rachel Brosnahan playing Mrs. Maisel and Helen Mirren playing Israeli prime minister Golda Meir, Bradley is sadly a gentile, and that's the new sin in Hollywood, being a non-Jewish actor portraying a Jew. Because that's always been a big problem in Hollywood—not enough Jews.

The woke even have a word for this troubling new phenomenon: "Jewface." Do you see what I mean about their having their heads up their asses? The word you're using to fight antisemitism is "Jewface"? It sounds like something Mel Gibson says at a traffic stop.

And as far as "we're beyond that"? No, that implies progress, but this is the opposite. This is regression. And it's typical of so much wokeness that doesn't build on liberalism, it undoes it. Empathy—putting yourself in someone else's place so you can understand them better—used to be the very heart of liberalism.

Now it's considered offensive. "Don't even try to put yourself in my shoes, because you could never know!" What a bunch of bullshit. Of course no one can ever know exactly what another person's struggle is, but we try.

Black Like Me was a 1960s book about a white man who darkened his skin and went out into society because he wanted to understand what his Black brothers and sisters were up against. Today all the woke mob would see about it is a guy who did blackface.

But we're now living in a world where white novelists like the author of *American Dirt* aren't allowed to imagine what it would be like to be a Mexican immigrant—even though trying to inhabit the life of someone else is almost the very definition of empathy, the bedrock of liberalism.

9

CANCEL CULTURE

THE GREAT SUPPRESSION

Some people think I've changed—I assure you I have not. I'm still the same unmarried, childless, pot-smoking libertine I always was—I have many flaws, but you can't accuse me of maturing.

Let's get this straight: it's not me who's changed, it's the Left, which is now made up of a small contingent who've gone mental and a large contingent who refuse to call them out for it. But I will.

And when I do, in this ridiculous new era of mind-numbing partisanship, it makes me an instant hero to Republicans, who ignore all my critiques of what they're doing and only trumpet the part where I identify nutty woke shit. The same thing happened in reverse to Darth Vader's daughter Liz Cheney, who is now a hero to liberals because she recognizes Biden didn't steal the 2020 election. What a sad commentary on our politics, when simply acknowledging reality is now seen as a profile in courage.

People sometimes say to me, "You didn't used to make fun of the

Left as much." Yeah, because they didn't used to give me so much to work with. The oath of office I took was to comedy—and if you do goofy shit, wherever you are on the spectrum, I'm going to make fun of you because that's where the gold is. And the fact that the audience is laughing at it should tell you something important: it rings true.

When normal people read that San Francisco has basically legalized shoplifting, they think, "Democrats have gone nuts." They think, "You know, that Ted Cruz guy seems like a real stiff, but at least he believes in the concept of 'shopping with money.'"

It's not my fault the party of FDR and JFK is turning into the party of LOL and WTF.

Liberals always talk about how the Right needs to rein in its crazies, but the Left has some crazy-reining-in to do too. And lest you think I'm creating a false equivalency, I'm not: because on the right, unlike the left, they've actually managed to carve out a place for their crazies.

Unfortunately, that place is elected government. All the more reason not to drive people into their arms with crazy political correctness.

If you're part of today's woke revolution, you need to study the part of revolutions where they spin out of control because the revolutionaries get so drunk on their own purifying elixir they imagine they can reinvent the very nature of human beings.

Communists thought selfishness could be cast out of human nature. Russian revolutionaries spoke of "the new Soviet man," who wasn't motivated by self-interest but instead wanted to be part of a collective. No, it turns out he wanted to be on a yacht in a Gucci tracksuit holding a vodka and a prostitute, not standing in line all day for a potato.

The problem with communism—and with some very recent ideologies here at home—is that its proponents think you can change reality by screaming at it, that you can bend human nature by holding your breath. But that's the difference between "reality" and "your mommy."

Lincoln once said that you can "repeal all past history, [but] you still cannot repeal human nature." But he's canceled now, so fuck him.

Yesterday I asked ChatGPT, "Are there any similarities between to-day's Woke Revolution and Chairman Mao's Cultural Revolution of the 1960s?" and it wrote back, "How long do you have?"

Because, again, in China we saw how a revolutionary thought he could do a page-one rewrite of humans. Mao ordered his citizens to throw off the "Four Olds": old thinking, old culture, old customs and old habits. So your whole life went in the garbage overnight, no biggie, and those who resisted this were attacked by an army of purifiers called the Red Guard who went around the country putting dunce caps on people who didn't take to being a new kind of mortal being. A lot of pointing and shaming went on—and about a million dead—and the only way to survive was to plead insanity for the crime of being insufficiently radical, then apologize and thank the state for the chance to see what a piece of shit you are, and of course, submit to "reeducation." Or as we call it here in America, "freshman orientation."

There's a law professor at the University of Illinois Chicago named Jason Kilborn whose "crime" was that on one of his exams, he used a hy-pothetical case where a Black female worker sued her employer for race and gender discrimination, alleging that managers had called her two slur words—the type of real-world case these law students may one day confront. And knowing the extreme sensitivity of today's students, he didn't write the two taboo words on the test—just the first letter of each.

He was teaching his students how to fight racism in the place where it matters most, the criminal justice system. But because he merely alluded to those words—again, in the service of a good cause—he was banned from campus, placed on indefinite leave and made to wear a dunce cap.

OK, not really a dunce cap, but our version: eight weeks of sensitiv-ity training, weekly ninety-minute sessions with a diversity trainer, and having to write five self-reflection papers. A grown-ass man. A liberal law professor—if you can't see the similarities between that and Mao's Cultural Revolution, the person who needs reeducation is you.

Yes, we have our own Red Guard here, but they do their rampaging on Twitter.

Here's a cute example from a couple years ago: the guitarist from Mumford & Sons tweeted that he liked a book—a book that apparently had not been approved by the revolution. So, of course, he had to delete the tweet, then "take time away from the band"—oh my God, you mean it could have affected Mumford & Sons? And then the cringing apology: "I have come to better understand the pain caused by the book I endorsed."

Pain? From a book? Unless he hit the drummer over the head with it, I wouldn't worry about that. What happened to "I can read whatever the fuck I want—don't worry, I'm a musician, it won't happen again."

There was once a very different musician named John Lennon who wrote a song called "Revolution." People who didn't really listen to the lyrics thought it was a rah-rah call *for* revolution, but in fact, it was the opposite. The song acknowledged that we all *want* to change the world, but cast a jaundiced eye on methods like throwing in with Chairman Mao of China.

Now, there was a guy who understood how good intentions can turn into the insane arrogance of thinking your revolution is *so* fucking awesome, and your generation so mind-bendingly improved, that you have bestowed upon the world a new kind of human, you're welcome. With communists, that new human was no longer selfish; in America today, that human is no longer male or female. And obesity is not something that affects health, you can be healthy at any size—really, we voted on it. I've spent three decades on TV mocking Republicans who say climate change is "just a theory," and now I've got to deal with people who say "You know what else is just a theory? Biology."

Addendum: the guitarist from Mumford & Sons, Winston Marshall, later recanted his recant, and good for him. I'm hopeful a backlash to this insanity has begun.

THE MENDACITY OF DOPE

Here's one way to explain Donald Trump: in an age dominated by the professionally offended, we secretly envy the man who's able to speak his mind with complete abandon, never concerned about the repercussions and never apologizing for it. Whereas the rest of us really live two lives: there's the real us, the person in the kitchen or a bar who speaks frankly and openly with trusted friends, and then there's our avatar.

Our avatar looks and sounds like us, but it's not really us—it's the persona we adopt in any sort of public sphere, which now includes your "followers" on Twitter and Instagram, and thousands of friends on Facebook. And since bad things go viral, everyone fears any misstep that could cause America's pearl-clutchers to point and scream at you like it's the end of *Invasion of the Body Snatchers*.

Think of all the people who've lost job offers because there's a picture that got posted of them holding a bong or having a dick drawn on their face when they were passed out. Which I think should get you *more* job offers, because being passed out tells employers, "When I do something, I do it 110 percent."

Americans today crave any kind of authenticity because our avatars are just so full of shit. Trump's enduring popularity with his fans is largely because Americans are so sick of politicians who are "inauthentic"—who, essentially, are *all* avatar. Isn't that what people hated about Hillary?

But then *we* became the politicians. Everyone's social media persona now is like a candidate running for office: phony photo ops and making sure every statement is carefully sanded down so as to not upset anyone. Facebook should be called "*Two*FacedBook."

It's funny, in movies avatars are the more interesting versions of the characters, flying around doing whatever they want. But your avatar on Facebook isn't stronger or faster than you are. It's just prissier. Its great superpower is remembering birthdays.

If you want to know who someone *really* is, ignore their avatar and check out their web browser history. There's a book out called *Everybody Lies* that's about what we search for on Google, and according to the author, "thirty percent of people exclusively watch stuff that you would find disgusting." Look at a list of popular porn categories: cuckold, cheerleader, stepmom, double penetration, creampie, tentacle sex—it sounds like we're playing *Password* for perverts.

On Facebook, women's top terms for describing husbands are "the best," "my best friend" and "amazing," but when you type in "my husband is" on Google, the top three results are "mean," "annoying" and "gay." You have to wonder if the more bland we make our public avatars, the more weird we want to be at home.

THE NARC AGES

America is Snitch Nation now. Being a snitch used to be a bad thing.

"Nobody likes a tattletale" is one of the first things we used to teach children. But now virtually any public accomplishment comes with the obligatory follow-up snitch story a few days later.

Like what happened with that poor schmuck who was supposed to host *Jeopardy!*, but fortunately the honor of game shows was preserved when Squeal Team Six went through his old podcasts and found he once used the term "booth slut"—whatever the hell that means. Sorry, buddy, but we, the perfect people who have never made a mistake, just can't let society be sullied with *horrible* people like you. Buh-bye.

Fans of cable news might remember the rising journalist Alexi McCammond, who was appointed editor of *Teen Vogue* but then had to resign before her first day when some of her high school tweets suddenly became too much to bear—tweets like "now googling how to not wake up with swollen, Asian eyes" and "hahahahah you're so gay lmao."

Oh, the inhumanity. Her resignation was endorsed by the hierarchy of the magazine, including the senior social media manager, Christine Davitt. Good for you, Christine, you helped catch the Zodiac Killer. Oh, no, you just ruined someone's career for no reason—same diff.

Funny end to the story: after Alexi McCammond resigned for her innocuous tweets, someone went through Christine Davitt's old high school tweets, and—oops, it seems she tweeted the N-word twice to a white friend in 2009. Buh-bye.

This is why I'm a little hopeful this purity purge may end: because it's starting to eat its own.

ESPN reporter Rachel Nichols was a feminist success story, but when she complained in a private telephone call about ESPN's "crappy longtime record on diversity" and expressed her view that she felt like she was being sacrificed by the network so that they could make up for that crappy record, the call was leaked and she was toast.

Now, in addition to the fact that a person shouldn't have to love getting fired even if it does achieve more "equity," this was a *private call*. Does "private" mean anything anymore? Apparently not. Even sadder, this love of snitching seems to be one of the few areas now that is truly bipartisan.

Snitch Nation isn't about what side you're on, it's about this mindset where everyone is an amateur secret policeman and tattling is a virtue. The woke side of the Internet thinks going through someone's old MySpace account makes them part of the resistance, and Republicans lately have been sponsoring a new reality show: *Texas Zygote Hunters*.

Yes, Texas's abortion law includes the idea that anyone even helping a woman get an abortion, like the Uber driver who takes her to the clinic, can be sued by some random Citizen Snitch for up to $10,000. Finally a way to tap into that vast reserve of Uber-driver wealth.

When did West Texas become East Germany? Even if you hate sluts and love money, you have to admit bounty-hunting people who help pregnant women is a little un-American. Also—you're working too hard, Texas! This is 2024—you don't have to pay people to snitch.

Conservatives also have been encouraging college students to whip out their phones to record and report professors who espouse leftist ideas—which is all of them, so good luck with that.

As always, the snowflakes fall just as hard on the right as they do on the left.

Colleges pride themselves on being "safe spaces." But not for professors, at least not any who might want to stretch young minds to get them to think differently or try on new ideas. Do that at your peril. Same with comedy clubs, where ever since smartphones came out, comics have been complaining about snitches in the audience who'll rat them out for "crossing the line"—which is practically the job description of a comedian.

Comics are joking constantly—even some people who aren't comics do that, and if you're lucky enough in life to be around people like that, I'm sure you know: they can't all be gems. Sometimes you get "the twisties" and the joke doesn't land just right. Exposing that doesn't make you noble.

You're not David Kaczynski, the brother of the Unabomber, who turned in his own brother lest any more mail bombs go off—that was noble. Because it was about bombs, not bombing.

There's a real difference between the Unabomber and the editor of *Teen Vogue*. For one thing, the Unabomber made some good points.

Or think of Edward Snowden, enduring exile in Russia so he could expose unlawful government snooping: noble. Or Colonel Alexander Vindman, exposing Trump's Ukrainian blackmail fiasco: noble. That's not you taking down the host of the Ice Capades. You're a loser with Wi-Fi and all the time in the world to listen to long-forgotten podcasts. You're not a journalist, you're just a creepy little rat. Go to Texas and catch a runaway embryo. What, you dug up a letter where JFK once said "Indian giver"? Great, now we can tear down the Kennedy Center.

BANISH INQUISITION

Lately, Republicans have been trying to appropriate the term "cancel culture" to describe what happens to them when they get a just comeuppance for actual crimes—and this muddying of the water is unfortunate because cancel culture is real, it's insane and it's growing exponentially.

And it's coming to a neighborhood near you. If you think it's just for celebrities, think again. In an era where everyone is online, everyone is a "public figure." It's like we're all trapped in a show called *The Hills Have Eyes . . . and Wi-Fi*.

Take Mr. Emmanuel Cafferty. He was a San Diego Gas & Electric worker, but he got fired because someone reported him making a "white supremacist hand gesture" outside the window of his truck. But he's not a white supremacist; he's Latino. And he wasn't making a hand gesture, he was probably just flicking a booger.

Is this really who we want to become—a society of clenched-assholed phonies, walking on eggshells, always looking over our shoulder about getting ratted out for something that actually has nothing to do with our character or morals?

Think about everything you've ever texted, emailed, searched for, tweeted, blogged or said in passing—or now even just witnessed! Someone had a Confederate flag in their dorm room in 1990 and *you didn't doooo something*? You laughed at a Woody Allen movie?

Andy Warhol was wrong: in the future, everyone will experience not fifteen minutes of fame but fifteen minutes of *shame*.

Sixty-two percent of Americans say they have opinions they're afraid to share. In a 2019 poll, 80 percent of Americans said they find political correctness to be a problem, including 75 percent of African-Americans, 74 percent of Americans under thirty, 82 percent of Asians, 87 percent of Hispanics and 88 percent of Native Americans. If you're not a statistician, let me break those numbers down: nobody likes you! Including the so-called marginalized groups whose feelings you decided need protecting.

And that's the problem with today's wokeness: everybody hates it, and no one stands up to it. It's always the safe thing to swallow what you really think and just join the mob, because no one ever gets canceled for being *too* woke.

MIRTH IN THE BALANCE

And I want to know: who are these people who say cancel culture isn't a real thing? Just among comedians who got fired and lost gigs for exercising their freedom of expression, the toll is high. Gilbert Gottfried and Norm Macdonald were tasteless—yes, that's why we liked them. Comedians are the ones testing where the line is—we can't always be perfect any more than Patrick Mahomes will never throw an interception.

Louis CK and Dave Chappelle lost distribution for movies they made, and Sarah Silverman was fired from a film over an old sketch where she wore blackface to make fun of racism. Roseanne lost the TV show she created with her name on it over tweets that were offensive, but it was not at all clear Roseanne knew them to be. She is crazy, and I say that as a friend. All comedians are a little crazy. You need crazy on that wall.

Nimesh Patel was literally pulled offstage during a performance at Columbia University for a joke about how hard it is to be gay *and* Black. Not an antigay joke, mind you, a pro-gay joke. One of the event organizers walked onstage and said, "I don't think you're entitled to certain jokes you're making."

A sense of entitlement certainly comes into play here, but not on the part of the comedian. And that's the thing: the people who can't take a joke now aren't old ladies in the Bible Belt—they're Gen Z at elite colleges. Colleges, where comedy goes to die. Kids used to go to college and lose their virginity—now they go and lose their sense of humor.

Comedians as varied as Chris Rock, Jerry Seinfeld and Larry the Cable Guy have all in recent years stopped playing colleges. That's right, a Jew, a Black man and a redneck walk into a college campus and they all can't wait to get the hell out.

Vice interviewed college bookers who revealed that before a comedian even takes the stage they're asked to edit out anything from their act that may cause offense, leaving a world where more and more topics are off-limits and soon there'll be nothing left to joke about except airplane food and Starbucks getting your name wrong.

George Carlin is the owner of the most famous 180 in comedy history, when he turned his back on a lucrative career in nightclubs in order to let his hair down and be himself in front of a younger crowd who welcomed irreverence. In 1990, George said, "I got to go to colleges . . . I belong with people who are open and will let me be myself and experiment."

Oh, George, it's a good thing you're dead. Because today the seven words you can't say on TV are "Jada, can't wait for *GI Jane 2*."

For all those who are constantly demanding an apology for jokes: Maybe it's you who should apologize to us. For all the great jokes that we never got to hear. For all the brilliant thoughts that never got uttered. Those are the invisible scars of cancel culture. Let's have a moment of silence for that, and a spot in every awards show's "In Memoriam" package for all the viable jokes that could have lived but were aborted because a voice in someone's head said, "Are you *sure* you want to risk saying that?"

The Mandalorian's Gina Carano is a person I'd never heard of, and I resent that I have now. She's some conservative MMA chick who kicks ass on a show I wouldn't watch if I was in prison. And she made a Nazi analogy—who doesn't these days? "You're like the Nazis" is the new "I don't like you," and it's always OK when Trump is the Nazi.

But of course that disqualified her from marching around Planet Who-Gives-a-Shit in a helmet.

By the way, "You can't work in Hollywood if you don't believe what we believe" . . . in the 1950s, that's exactly what the Left complained *they* were being told.

Chris Harrison was the host of *The Bachelor* and had to "step away" to educate himself "on a more profound and productive level than ever before." Oh good, because all my life I've looked up to the host of the "fuck a stranger" show, and if I thought I couldn't count on *The Bachelor* for moral guidance, I don't know if I could go on.

And Chris didn't "step away" because he's the host of a televised snake pit where thirty-two female contestants are trapped in the sorority house from hell—it was because he wouldn't throw one of the contestants under the bus when it came to light that in college she attended a Dress Up Like We're in the Old South party.

Granted, this is not a type of party we should be throwing anymore in that it winks at a civilization built on slavery—but apparently in 2018, millions of people were still doing it, because mature people understand humans are continually evolving, as opposed to the citizens of Wokeville, where they're always shocked we didn't emerge enlightened from the primordial ooze. What was Chris Harrison supposed to do, build a time machine, go back to 1859 and knock the mint juleps out of their hands?

Maybe while he's time traveling, he can have a word with Abraham Lincoln, who had his name taken off high schools in San Francisco and Illinois. Yes, the Land of Lincoln canceled Lincoln. Memo to social justice warriors: when what you're doing sounds like a headline in *The Onion*, stop.

THE SCORN IDENTITY

There are too many people in this country who are motivated not by what they really believe, but by what will get Twitter to give them "likes" and retweets. This is called bad faith. And it's why Matt Damon is always in trouble. Some recent headlines tell the story:

USA Today: "I Wish I Could Cancel Matt Damon."

Washington Post: "Matt Damon Has More Damonsplaining to Do!"

Daily Beast: "Shut Up, Matt Damon."

Vox: "Matt Damon Isn't a Terrible Person, He's Just Ignorant."

Really? That bad, is he? We're talking about Matt Damon? I don't know, he's got a clean-water charity and delivers food to Haiti—what have *you* done, Vox headline writer? And yet, he is always getting pulled over by the Woke Police for something. It's a phenomenon that truly fascinates me—that every couple years, Matt Damon, one of the most likable guys in Hollywood, with impeccable liberal credentials, is flailing around in cancel culture quicksand.

On the reboot of the *Project Greenlight* series, Matt was booked on obstruction of social justice for maintaining that a director should be chosen on merit first. But "merit first" is not synonymous with racism. *Thinking* that it is—that's kind of racist.

In 2015 Damon did hard time in Twitter jail on two counts of accessory to homophobia for saying that actors do well when they keep their private lives private so that audiences can watch the character on the screen without thinking about the caricature from the tabloids, and that includes your sexuality. But in Wokeville, somehow that became "gay actors should go back in the closet." Which is not what he said, but the verdict was in and he was sentenced to apologize on *Ellen*. But here's how un-homophobic Matt Damon is: he played the guy who fucked Liberace!

In 2016, the movie *The Great Wall* opened, and Damon was brought up on charges of whitewashing in the third degree—whitewashing being when filmmakers cast white actors for parts meant for people of color. Which is exactly what he was *not* doing. His role was never meant for a Chinese actor. In fact, it was a Chinese-made movie targeted primarily to the Chinese audience that was purposefully using his white ass so the movie would have crossover appeal *here*.

Nevertheless, when I heard about this, I immediately replaced Matt's poster over my bed with Chris Evans.

And then there was what happened in 2017. In the early days of the Me Too movement, Damon was locked up in Wokeatraz on a charge of aggravated mansplaining during a reckoning and was sentenced to not less than one year of having to shut the fuck up.

During an interview where Damon called the Me Too movement "wonderful" and a "watershed moment," he added that sexual misconduct involved "a spectrum of behavior" and that there was "a difference between patting someone on the butt and rape."

True . . . undeniable . . . and unforgivable! Even though the legal system has always differentiated degrees for all crimes, even murder. Oh, Matt—always getting in trouble for saying perfectly reasonable things.

In 2021 it happened again when Matt broke Liam's Law, the law that refers to the time actor Liam Neeson recounted a story of personal growth involving having racist thoughts as a young man but then realizing the error of his ways and expunging the racist element from his anger. Matt Damon revealed in 2021 that he too had committed the crime of not always being the person he would become. Damon admitted that in his youth, he often used a gay slur. I won't say the word, but it's the one your teenage son greets his friends with when they meet up at Dave & Buster's.

Damon owned up, saying that while coming of age in Boston in the seventies and eighties, that word was thrown around without any thought put into it, and now . . . he's put some thought into it. And he's going to stop using it. One might say he became "woke."

But of course in so doing, he committed the cardinal sin of admitting he was not born perfect and did not emerge from the womb completely enlightened. OK, he was late to the party—to which we could say, "Welcome, glad you made it!" Or we could say, "You came later than I did, DIE!"

I'm so tired of bad-faith arguments, and it's all we do now, on both sides of our divide. In the summer of 2021, Nancy Pelosi called Republican House leader Kevin McCarthy a moron. That's not the bad-faith part of the story, that's true. But a few days later McCarthy was speaking to a group of Republicans and said, describing the Republicans' possibly taking the House in 2022, "I want you to watch Nancy Pelosi hand me that gavel. It will be hard not to hit her with it."

Pelosi's office called it "a threat of violence." Hakeem Jeffries said, "Violence against women is no laughing matter." And Eric Swalwell said McCarthy was "a would-be assailant" who must "resign."

This is what bad faith is: you don't really think it was a threat of violence, or that anyone thinks such violence would be a laughing matter, or that Kevin McCarthy is a would-be assailant—any more than anyone thinks Matt Damon's a homophobe. You just know you can get away with pretending you think that. Because, again, no one ever gets canceled for being too woke. Maybe they should.

And, Matt, my advice to you: stop hunting for goodwill, you're not gonna find much in this country.

LEGEND OF THE BALLS

A few years ago, I was asked to moderate a discussion at the home of a very prominent Hollywood producer, and the attendees that night were a who's who of A-listers and stars. If a bomb had gone off in that room, there'd have been nothing on TV next year but . . . well, let's just say it would have been a great year for Kevin Sorbo. I can't say exactly who was there, but if there really is a Jewish space laser, these guys have the codes.

Anyway, the subject we all wanted to talk about that night was cancel culture. Now, if this had been ten years ago, we all would have been talking about censorship from the Right. Back then it was the Jerry Falwells and Pat Robertsons, the Bill Bennetts and Rush Limbaughs, who kept us up at night—I mean, besides the cocaine. The book banners and boycotters then were Republicans, like the ones that got me fired after 9/11—but that's in the past now. And by "the past," I mean Florida.

And of course, not just Florida—today's Republicans have shown that when it comes to canceling, they're still more than capable. They canceled Colin Kaepernick for taking a knee, Liz Cheney for defying Trump and Kathy Griffin for performance art.

The Redneck Royalty of the music world—Travis Tritt, John Rich and Kid Rock—threw a hissy fit in 2023 because they thought Anheuser-Busch was trying to turn their beer gay.

But there's no getting around the fact that what was on the mind of the liberals that night in Brentwood—or wherever we may have been—was that the most powerful witch hunters now were coming from Twitter, the Ivy League and the "progressive" Left. J. K. Rowling used to be a villain to the Right because she wrote books about witchcraft; now she's a villain to the Left because she has this crazy belief that there's more to being a woman than pronouns and lipstick.

So that was the point of the evening: How do we take a stand against cancel culture? And I suggested, since we were mostly all in show business, that we start an awards show to honor the brave people who *have* fought back. The idea was met with great enthusiasm by everyone, and in short order different people were suggesting the ways that their varied talents could be put to use.

And then of course, this being Hollywood, nothing happened. But I never forgot it, and so in 2023 presented on *Real Time* the first annual Cojones Awards, honoring outstanding achievement in growing a pair. And these were the first year's winners:

Martha Pollack, the president of my alma mater, Cornell University, where students recently demanded trigger warnings before all lectures, in case any of the adult subjects *you specifically went to college to learn about* came up . . . and Martha said, "Yeah, no—we're not doing that."

She didn't cave in or hire a new dean of sensitivity, she just said nope, college is for introducing you to new ideas, not for kissing your ass and making you feel wonderful and always right—you're thinking of brunch with your parents. I'm amazed at how this generation can simultaneously be too sensitive for anything distasteful and somehow also so into eating ass.

The second award went to the place where many Cornell grads will be working next year, Trader Joe's—who for years have been selling a line of ethnically themed products "trading" on the name Joe. For example, they have Trader José's beer. So of course one teenager on Twitter heard the word "José" and said it was racist, and then there was a petition, and then Trader Joe's management did the right thing: they burned down all their stores and killed themselves.

No, they didn't. They said, "Fuck off, you oversensitive little shits, get a life and a sense of humor," and released this statement: "We disagree that any of these labels are racist and we do not make decisions based on petitions." You see how easy it is?

The next Cojone went to a man who's dear to comedians' hearts for standing up for stand-up. When dozens of Netflix employees walked out over Dave Chappelle's reckless decision to perform comedy on his comedy special, CEO Ted Sarandos could have pulled the special and replaced it with more episodes of *Who Wants to Watch Koreans Get Killed?*

But instead he reminded his Netflix employees that comedy "exists to push boundaries" and told them, "If you'd find it hard to support our content breadth, Netflix may not be the best place for you." For making the phrase "Don't let the door hit you in the ass" never sound better, Ted Sarandos earned himself a Cojone.

And finally, when movie lovers get together these days, one phrase comes up a lot and always makes me sad: "You couldn't make that one today." Top of that list is the great *Tropic Thunder*, which the scolds have been after for years. But *Tropic Thunder* creator Ben Stiller tweeted: "I make no apologies for Tropic Thunder. It's always been a controversial movie since when we opened. Proud of it and the work everyone did on it."

Again . . . it's not. That. Hard.

If you stand up to the mob for just a day or two, their shallow, impatient, immature, smartphone-driven gerbil minds will forget about it and go on to the next nothing burger—and you, you will still have your cojones!

10

COPS

UNREST ASSURED

There's a general feeling these days that the social order is breaking down—that there are no more safe spaces anywhere. Street crime, home invasions, carjackings, porch pirates . . . medical staff attacked at hospitals, incivility at sports arenas. On airplanes now the in-flight entertainment is a fistfight. And I think the Grubhub driver is eating my French fries.

Last year the LA city council voted that every homeless tent had to be removed from dozens of locations—yet every freeway overpass still looks like history's saddest Coachella. The homeless are both preyed upon and, frankly, a concern that they will do who knows what.

Los Angeles is also pioneering the new phenomenon of "follow-home robberies," where gang members stake out nice restaurants and then follow home the people who leave in expensive cars and force their way into their houses. It's why Lady Gaga now drives a 2009 PT Cruiser and eats at Sbarro.

It's all too easy to find videos of the latest smash-and-grab robbery, where thieves in broad daylight just smash the front windows of ritzy stores and take all the jewelry they can carry.

And when did they legalize shoplifting? There used to be shame in shoplifting—or at least some skill needed. Now criminals just brazenly walk out of Walgreens—again, in broad daylight—with a trash bag full of aisle three, while the security guard just watches. They have to keep even the most mundane products all caged up; CVS isn't a store, it's a zoo for teeth-whitening strips.

San Francisco in the last few years has seen store after store just give up and close locations because that town seems simply beyond the law. Which is heartbreaking, because I, like so many people, love that city—and I don't think it's corny to admit that, yes, I left my heart in San Francisco. Also my wallet and iPhone.

Bay Area citizens have been complaining in recent years about all the human feces in the streets, but now the streets are full of something else—they call it "San Francisco snow." It's piles of broken glass from car windows that were shattered, and it's so routine to have this happen to any parked car that people purposefully leave the windows down and the glove compartment open so thieves can see there's nothing of value. Or they leave a note on the car politely assuring the thief that there's nothing worth stealing, so please don't break the windows:

"Dear Mr. Criminal, I hope this note finds you well. Please don't break my window—thanks, you're the best. PS: There's a Rite Aid around the corner, if you want to hit that."

Democrats can tell voters it's not so bad, or that they're stupid and racist and we don't want their votes anyway, but Trump's message of "This American carnage stops now" is a powerful campaign theme when there's that feeling that things are descending into every-man-for-himself lawlessness.

New York was like that in the Son of Sam seventies, which may be why the vigilante movie was birthed in that era—films like *Death Wish* and *Dirty Harry* and *Taxi Driver*, about guys who took it upon themselves to fight back against crime. But we don't have Taxi Driver now—we have Uber Driver, and he doesn't kill pimps, he has a podcast called *Are You Talking to Me?*

Democrats like to point out that crime has actually been worse before. Yes, true, and also: Who gives a fuck? I'm not living "before," I'm living now.

In 2020, America experienced its largest annual increase in homicides ever. Assaults are up. Mass shootings are up. Voters' focus is, unsurprisingly, on safe streets, not making women's swimming safe for men.

And what's so disturbing *now* is not just the amount of crime and mayhem but the audacity of it—like there are no lines anymore that can't be crossed.

And this is where the tricky issue of the police comes in. Proper policing will always be one of the hardest balances to find, especially in a country with as many guns and as many nuts as this one has. How do you allow the cops to do the often impossible job they have to do without also empowering them to abuse their monopoly on violence?

First, let's live in the year we're living in. Let's acknowledge that things have changed—I'm sure not enough, but they have undeniably changed.

During the George Floyd social justice protests in 2020, police chiefs from across the country knelt and marched with the protesters—in Miami-Dade County, and New York City, and Santa Cruz, California, and Flint, Michigan. Houston police chief Art Acevedo even said he was outraged at Americans who "*don't* see a problem."

This is new. Not that long ago, police never admitted they ever did anything wrong. No matter what they did, they always would say it was "by the book."

"Put six slugs into an unarmed man from the seat of your car? By the book." "Strangle a handcuffed guy to death? By the book." "Kill a twelve-year-old who had a toy gun? By the book."

Who wrote this book, George Zimmerman?

And no cops, no matter what they did, ever suffered any legal ramifications for their actions. But in the last decade, dozens have gone to jail for murderous behavior.

Police sergeant Howard Banks of Omaha said, "It's all of us versus bad people and bad cops—and we want to get them out of the line of duty and police work."

Yes, that is certainly what many people have been demanding for a long time. But wanting it and doing it are two different things. People like to say, "Most cops are good," like we know that to be true. I *hope* it's true, but I need some actual evidence. Unlike cops. The bad ones, not the good ones.

Forever, we've been talking about "bad cops"—you know, a few "bad apples." But we do have to allow for the possibility that it's the orchard that's the problem. I have to ask, if most cops are good, why are there so many videos of them being bad? Really, there's a lot of videos. Of guys who barely exist, doing shit that hardly ever happens.

And this is often while they know they're being filmed: someone has to explain to America's police that the purpose of the body cam isn't so you can upload your beatings onto YouTube. When did punching someone in the head become a law enforcement technique? The cops need to make up their minds: they do a Riverdance on your skull and then when they're putting you in the car they say, "Watch your head."

They're always "reviewing" these videos, as if they're ghost hunters looking for signs of a poltergeist. It could be a baby holding a rattle and they'd say, "The baby did point the rattle at the officer and crawled toward him in a menacing way. Babies have to understand—when the officer tells you to drop the binkie, drop the damn binkie."

The only thing they need to "review" is their hiring practices. We need better psychological screening to weed out the people who become cops as payback for a time in their life when other people were pushing *them* around. "How much of high school did you spend stuffed inside a locker?" should be question number one on the psych evaluation.

We need to ask the question: Are the wrong type of people becoming cops? It's a fair question because the police attract bullies like the priest-hood attracts pedophiles. Like carnivals attract meth addicts.

There's obviously a lot of rage that police work brings out in a person, and I don't doubt for a moment there are parts of police work that I can't imagine that bring out that rage, and we need to do more to help officers find better ways to channel it. But we also have to call men who whale on the defenseless while their buddies hold 'em down what they are: cowards.

Eighty-four percent of cops say they've directly witnessed a fellow officer using excessive force, and 61 percent say they don't always report serious abuse. It can't be the duty of every American to say something if they see something except for the people whose job it is to do something. You can't get away with crimes on account of being the people who are supposed to stop crimes. When cops ask minorities why they don't snitch on their own, minorities have every right to say "You first."

I've known quite a few cops in my day, and others I've met for briefer conversations on the side of the road, and it seems they are mostly not that guy. But that guy is who we have to weed out.

Instead of police departments making the psych eval the *last* step in joining the force, make it the first, so meatheads with a chip on their shoulder aren't given a license to perform urban executions. Because that's always the real crime with bad cops, isn't it? Attitude. Not being instantly deferential.

Look, I know there are good cops—I know some personally. I used to buy drugs off one; great guy. I know that many do their jobs like total pros. And it's true, there are no viral videos of an officer putting his life on the line with utter professionalism every day for years.

And I get why cops are so often ready to explode—America is a nation that current statistics show is 3.6 percent scumbag. OK, that's not a real statistic, but whatever it is, that's who cops deal with every day: thieves, pimps, road ragers, gangbangers, people who lock their kids in cars and perverts jerking off in bookstores.

But if you don't want to deal with dregs, don't be a cop! Be a Mountie.

If our deal with the police is we have to constantly reassure them how much we love them or else they throw a tantrum, then we're not supporting them; we're dating them. Because right now, honey—I mean Officer—I'm confused. Yes, you have a tough, dirty job, but you volunteered for it. It's like a proctologist coming home every night and saying, "I can't believe I have to look at assholes all day."

I support the police, and I understand, their job *is* looking at assholes all day. But the sign on the car that says "Protect and Serve" refers to *us*. The citizens. This emptying of the whole clip any time something makes you nervous, that has to stop. The cops have a saying: "Better to be judged by twelve than carried out by six."

Better for who?

In 2015, when Bill de Blasio was mayor of New York, he said, "There are . . . many families in this city who [ask] every night, is my child safe? And not just from . . . crime and violence . . . but . . . from the very people they want to have faith in as their protectors." And the cops basically stopped working.

I know, how dare he spread a myth that is only corroborated by every single Black person ever. But you can't stop doing your job just because you feel unloved. Cops are the badasses who deal with the rabble in an ugly business, but if cops want us to give them a little extra room to be tough because they've got a bad, dangerous job, then they have to *do* the bad, dangerous job.

One New York detective said, "Cops have feelings too," and another complained, "There are people out there who don't like us."

Yes, because you choke them to death. Probably not you, specifically, and I'm sure not most cops, but you can't anymore get away with "This one is the bad cop," and any cops who aren't actually *committing* the crime but just watching are good. No, if your partner is doing something horrendous, you can't just watch and do nothing like the husband in a cuck video.

And that is part of what is changing. The cops who watched George Floyd get killed learned that the hard way.

Right now, it's easy to spot the toughest police officers: they're the ones telling their fellow cops to stop this shit. A crack has been made in the blue wall of silence—please, let it break down altogether, or else we're gonna be in the streets again and again, all the time. And in LA, that doesn't work, because, you know, we're not really a "walking" town.

There's a meme that says, "Nobody hates bad cops worse than good cops." OK, if you hate them so much, turn them in. Because let's be real: if there weren't video of the Floyd murder, how do you think those other cops would have described that encounter? It'd be, "We found Mr. Floyd unresponsive, so we administered CPR, lie lie lie."

Lately, I feel we're getting the worst of both worlds: the abusive-policing part is still with us, like the brutal murder of Tyre Nichols in Memphis in 2023, while the law-and-order part seems to be on the decline. Police feel like they can't do their jobs anymore without being castigated for it, and that we in the peanut gallery have no idea what it takes to keep the shit to shoe level. And I'm sure they're at least partly right about both.

Police reform is still needed, but we also can't just allow cops to be hunted and targeted for assassination, as happened over a hundred times in 2021.

I've said many times in discussing the police that civilization is a mile wide and an inch thick, so when people say, "Cops are all that stands between civilization and chaos," I agree.

I try to understand as much as I can without *being* a cop that it's not like the jobs most people have, and it's not: when a voice on the radio says, "Man with machete on Fifteenth and Main," you're the one who has to *go* to Fifteenth and Main.

And I'm guessing if you're a cop, you rarely get called out to a redneck's front porch because some guy wants to tell you how *well* the marriage is going.

11

SCAMERICA

SEISMIC GRIFT

It's time to admit that here in America, there really is such a thing as the "deep state." But it's not the one MAGA Nation is freaked out about. The FBI is not a bunch of closet radicals, it's a bunch of guys who iron their underwear. Washington *is* a city of big stone buildings full of bureaucrats, but they're not plotting against "real" Americans. They're issuing passports, cutting Social Security checks, running the census, updating maps, buying bullets for Ukraine, inspecting dog food, ordering plastic gloves for the TSA and measuring the methane in cow farts.

But there *is* a deep state, which is the bureaucratic class that justifies its existence by making up new rules—and that's my job. It's the vast network of regulators, administrators, inspectors, contract reviewers, project managers, fee assessors, special commissioners, zoning officers and consultants whose job seems to be to make sure nothing ever happens and then charge you for it. The people who answer the phone "Permit office, how may I hinder you?"

Fourteen percent of workers in America work for the government. That's twenty million people, with one shared vision: to fine you if your mailbox is too big. They say a conservative is a liberal who just got mugged—but it could also be a liberal who just got cockblocked trying to remodel a porch. Or got a parking ticket because their car was facing out instead of in.

In 2022, Wyoming began construction on the largest wind farm in North America, which will power two million homes in Arizona, Nevada and California. And to think, it only took eighteen years. Not to build it. To approve it. Eighteen backlogged, knuckle-dragging, pencil-pushing, thumb-twiddling, ball-scratching years to finally get to "yes." When they started doing the paperwork, Leonardo DiCaprio's girlfriend wasn't even born.

And how ironic—with all the talk about the urgency of switching to green energy, our deep state of petty tyrants wasted almost two decades on permitting and nitpicking over the environmental impacts and "social effects" of the very thing that would most positively impact the environment. *Semafor* estimates that if the red tape could be cut on everything that's currently stuck in the renewable queue, the United States could be 80 percent zero-carbon in six years. The enemy of clean air isn't just Big Oil. It's Big Permitting. It's not that America isn't able to get anything done anymore—it's that we're not allowed to.

Of course there should be consideration of the environment on everything we build, but as so often happens on the left, they seem to have no ability to recognize when they've taken a concept way too far and are in fact hurting their own cause. America has become Gulliver, the giant that got tied down with a thousand tiny ropes by Lilliputians, the horde of little people who do big damage. "Build back better"—it sounds good. So does "shovel-ready jobs." But as Barack Obama said, one of the biggest lessons he learned as president was "there's no such thing as shovel-ready projects."

Environmental impact statements used to be a few pages long. Now they're thousands of pages of legalistic nonsense and take an average of

4.5 years to complete, with thousands of bureaucrats filling out millions of paper forms that kill hundreds of forests to answer the question "Is this good for the environment?"

In San Francisco, the city so nice you'll step in poop twice, there's an area where homeless people were urinating and defecating, and it was starting to annoy the people breaking into cars. So the city tried to build a public toilet last year, but then gave up when the cost hit $1.7 million. Not $1.7 million for a public toilet system—$1.7 million for one toilet. And this wasn't some magic toilet that catches your phone when you drop it.

So then a private company took pity on San Francisco and offered to build them their one toilet for free, but after, quote, "project management, construction management, architecture and engineering fees, permits, civic design review, surveys, contract preparation and cost estimation," the "free" toilet was still going to cost $1.2 million. You know, if you tack on fees like that, you're not a city, you're an airline. It feels like San Francisco is actually *proud* of being impossible. Asked about the toilet, a spokesperson for San Francisco Public Works said: "We are a city of public input." Fine. But I'm stepping in public *output*.

Meanwhile, the median time to get approval to build a house there is 627 days. That's 217 days longer than it took to build the Empire State Building. You need 87 permits: 15 from the Planning Commission, 26 from the Public Utilities Commission and the Fire Department, 19 from the building inspectors, 17 from the Public Works department, 10 related to public spaces and one from a guy in a T-shirt that says "Federal Boob Inspector." No wonder in 2021 San Francisco issued only 2,000 permits for new homes. Sure, there are people living in the streets, but that's because we want to make sure the apartments they *don't* live in are perfect. I don't fear AI anymore because it couldn't possibly be any more robotic than the humans who run things now.

Not that there was ever any real reason to build it in the first place . . . and not that there would be any reason to do it again . . . but just as an exercise in realizing how far we've regressed as the can-do people, I think we should all try to imagine how it would go down if we tried to sculpt Mount Rushmore today.

First, we'd have to make the mountain handicap-accessible so we could hire handicapped people to work on the side of a mountain. Then there'd be a ten-year delay while we studied the effect of construction noise on the mating habits of woodchucks. Then another ten years to bring the dynamiting up to code, and another two years to apologize for being on Indian land. And finally, after fifty years and a cost that had ballooned to a hundred billion dollars, we'd have half a nostril. And it wouldn't be Lincoln, it'd be Che Guevara.

TO LEECH HIS OWN

There's a breaking point in an economy when the scam parasites kill the host. And we're coming up to that point.

A vial of insulin costs about $12 to produce and is sold for over $500. Why? For the same reason it costs twelve bucks to get Pringles out of the minibar—because they *can*. Why, if at one Philadelphia clinic they can do a colonoscopy for a grand, does another one in the same city charge four grand? Because the price comes out of *their* ass.

How it is that, for most consumer products, there's such stiff competition that a common sales pitch is "If you find this item at a lower price, come on in and we'll beat it"—but a knee replacement can cost $17,000 in one hospital and sixty-one grand in another, *in the same city!*

With most products, there's no possible way to gouge you like that; that's how capitalism is supposed to work: a weirdo in a bad suit pledging he'll kill his whole family before he's undersold. But that doesn't apply to the big-ticket items, like the Pentagon and hospitals and infrastructure, where everyone gets to wet their beak before anything gets done, and that's why nothing ever does get done.

Why can't we help the homeless? If you look around any big American city lately you probably are saying to yourself, "Either the homeless problem is getting worse or camping isn't what it used to be."

After World War II, there was a huge housing shortage when all the vets returned home and had nowhere to live. So the government found some empty space and in a matter of months built Quonset huts for six thousand people, all for a total cost of what in today's dollars would be less than eighteen million.

Well, that was then. In the bond measure LA passed in 2016 to build housing for the homeless, each unit was projected to cost $140,000. Which at that time was more than the asking price for a four-bedroom Dutch Colonial in Little Falls, New York. And after LA actually started building these apartments, the cost for each unit rose to $531,000. How is that possible? you may ask. Do they each come with a shark tank and an infinity pool?

Of course, they still make those Quonset huts, and one today would cost about eight grand. But it's hard to skim money off eight grand. But $531,000? Sure. About 40 percent of that cost goes to something the city calls "soft costs" and I call "bullshit costs." Layer upon layer of middlemen, inspectors, contractors, lawyers, lobbyists and labor unions. And my favorite, "consulting."

Lot of consulting going on in America these days. Everyone seems to need consulting. Apparently nobody in America anymore knows what the fuck they're doing, so we need consultants to come in and be paid to tell you how to do the job you're supposed to do.

RESERVOIR HOGS

There's something else besides high levels of homelessness that California has accepted as the new normal in recent years: never-ending, life-threatening drought and wildfires—and that's not just California, that's all through the West. Meanwhile, in the East, the opposite: that's the "extreme rainfall" area—what I call the Cardi B region, because if you live there, your ass is going to be wet.

This isn't an imponderable quandary, like cold fusion. As the general manager of the Southern Nevada Water Authority once said, "One man's flood control is another man's water supply." Does anyone see where I'm going with this? That it would be a giant win-win if we just built pipelines from where the water *is* to where the water *isn't*? I'm not a civil engineer, but if we can extract shale oil from tar sands two miles below the frozen surface of Canada and pipe it to Louisiana, why not water? Water is a lot easier to get than oil—I've heard there are places where it literally falls from the sky.

Now, in the past when I've brought up the idea of a water pipeline, I was deterred from pressing the point by the conventional wisdom that this has been proposed and studied and it's just not feasible. But I looked into the details and I'd like to call bullshit on that. What's not feasible is *us*. This idea is only a "nonstarter" because of petty political squabbles and insane levels of graft and red tape. It's completely doable, and in fact has been proposed many times by serious people.

Availability of water is not the problem. To the east, flooding, to the west, a giant reservoir called the Pacific Ocean—oh yes, the ocean. Did you know that Israel gets most of its water from desalinization? Why can't we do desalinization if Israel does? We have Jews here—I'm sure they can figure it out. We have lots of smart people. The problem isn't one of know-how—it's will. And selfishness. And greed.

Think about it logically: Why would it really be harder to get water through a pipe than oil? The US already has 2.6 million miles of pipelines. To transport oil. And natural gas, and hazardous liquids—are they all really easier to move than water? Is a water pipeline really more of an engineering challenge than when we built railroads through the Rocky Mountains, or laid the transatlantic cable, or dug the Panama Canal?

Or put a man on the moon, which, even if you think it was faked, you have to admit: pulling off a prank like that would in itself be quite a remarkable achievement.

Moving water is not impossible. It can be done. Others have done it: the Romans did it with first-century technology and some of their aqueducts are still in use. The Incas, the Minoans, the Egyptians—lots of ancient people did it. And let's not forget Moses parting the Red Sea.

China does it now. Beijing depends on water that is provided by their massive South–North Water Transfer Project, which was begun in December 2002 and, of course, this being China, completed the next day.

In two generations, China has built five hundred entire cities from scratch, moved the majority of their huge population from poverty to the middle class and mostly cornered the market in 5G and rare earth minerals. Oh, and they bought Africa. Their New Silk Road initiative is the biggest infrastructure project in history, indebting not just that continent but large parts of Asia, Europe and the Middle East to the people who built their roads, bridges and ports. If you want to go anywhere in the world these days, you better have a yen for travel.

In China alone, they have forty thousand kilometers of high-speed rail. America has . . . none. Our fastest train is the tram that goes around the zoo. California tried to build high-speed rail connecting the entire state but finally gave up after spending billions just trying to finish the track connecting the vital hubs of Bakersfield and Merced. Because it was costing two hundred million dollars per mile, as opposed to in France, where building high-speed rail costs thirteen million per mile. And it's not like France is cheap or doesn't have labor unions. France is nothing *but* labor unions. They have strikes like we have mass shootings. But what they don't have is this level of systematic graft and greed.

China sees a problem, and they fix it. They build a dam, we debate what to rename one. That's why their airports look modern and ours look like bus stations. The Big Dig, a tunnel in Boston, took sixteen years. China once put up a fifty-seven-story skyscraper in nineteen days; they demolished and rebuilt the Sanyuan Bridge in Beijing in forty-three hours. We binge-watch, they binge-build.

Now, I fully understand a big reason why China is able to do this is because they're a dictatorship, and we don't want to emulate that—but there's got to be something between authoritarian government that tells everyone what to do and a representative government that can't do anything at all.

Even when we all agree on something in America, the inertia, the ass-covering, the graft, the lawyers, the cowardice: nothing ever moves in this impacted colon of a country. We see a problem and we ignore it, lie about it, fight about it, endlessly litigate it, sunset-clause it, kick it down the road and then write a bill where a half-assed solution doesn't take effect for ten years.

I mean, we can't even get rid of the penny.

Big projects just don't get done in this country because so much bullshit is built into everything that it's a boondoggle before it starts. This is our tragic flaw: the ever-ballooning costs, the inflated contracts, the back-scratching, the kickbacks, the private contractors, the padded expense accounts, the permits, the fees, the lawsuits, the lawyers, the lobbyists . . . graft on a scale untamable.

But seventy-eight million people live in the West. What do we do in the not-so-distant future when they're all water refugees? The Colorado River supplies forty million people with the water they need to live, and it's drying up—those people can't all get in covered wagons, head east and move back in with their parents.

And even though California has spent the last two decades in perpetual drought, there isn't, even with the drought, really a water *shortage* problem—it's more a "where the water is going" problem. California agriculture accounts for 80 percent of the state's water use even though California agriculture is less than 2 percent of its economy. Cali actually has enough water—it's just that it's given away to farmers, who get *their* water subsidized by the government, because we still act like it's 1890 and farmers are small and independent, when really they're mostly part of Big Ag. Old MacDonald is now EIEIO Incorporated.

Almond farms in California have doubled in this century—despite the fact that almond production alone uses more water than all the humans and businesses of San Francisco and Los Angeles combined. Even on days when your teenage son spends two hours "showering."

Oranges, tomatoes, strawberries: all take around eleven gallons of water to make one pound. Almonds? Nineteen hundred gallons! There simply isn't enough water to go around. And we have to make a painful choice: getting it in the people or getting it in the nuts.

I don't have some personal vendetta against almonds—they're just not more important than the entire ecosystem of California. So when I hear that my state grows 81 percent of the whole world's almonds, the world's thirstiest crop, while we sweat out droughts and giant fires burn out of control, I have a few questions. Starting with "What the fuck?"

This is life-and-death, and almonds are just not crucial. No one has a T-shirt that says "Don't talk to me until I've had my almonds." There will still be almonds in the world even if they're not grown in places that never get rain. But if we can direct coal miners in West Virginia to another line of work because coal is killing us, we should be able to tell almond farmers you can't grow almonds where they don't grow anymore: you're bogarting the water.

Because it's not like California doesn't know how to regulate. California's got rules about every nitpicky thing you can imagine, and if you don't believe me, try parking in Santa Monica. Or starting a business. Or getting your solar power hooked up.

You can't fly a kite in a park in Beverly Hills or ride a bicycle or climb a tree, and yet for thirty years Nestlé took water out of the San Bernardino National Forest under a permit that expired in 1988, and Coca-Cola is somehow allowed to take water from municipal water supplies, stick it in bottles and sell it back to the taxpayers who own the water to begin with.

California is a blue state that is completely held together by red tape—395,000 regulations. But somehow *that* one slipped through the cracks?

Where *is* the heavy hand of government when you need it? Californians can live without nuts but not water. California should stop thinking about how to get water on almonds and start thinking about how to get it on fires. It's basic logic that the more water we don't waste by giving it to Nestlé or using it to grow trail mix, the more we'll have for the important stuff.

I wish we still lived in an era where the water flowed like . . . water. I like green lawns and big fountains, and while I don't play golf, I always liked golf *courses* because they keep douchey white people off the street. But global warming isn't in the future: it happened, and now I want government to deal with it. Because my house is one gender-reveal party away from burning down while I sleep.

AMERICAN SWIPER

If brazen larceny is concerning to you, then you might want to take a look at how much of the trillions of dollars in free government Covid relief money was just flat-out stolen. Warning: What you're about to read may be triggering. And if it's not, it should be.

Let's start with what we spent—the checks the government sent out to get America through the pandemic. There was the Families First Coronavirus Response Act for $192 billion, the Paycheck Protection Program for $464 billion, the Consolidated Appropriations Act for $800 billion, the American Rescue Plan for $1.9 trillion and the CARES Act for $2.2 trillion—although for how much of that money actually made it into employees' pockets, they should have called it the WHO CARES Act. All told, $5.6 trillion laid out.

Now, certainly some large amount of spending was necessary to avert catastrophes like hospitals being overrun or the country falling into a depression, so we can argue another day if that 5.6 trill was the right amount—but for today, let's just look at what happened after the Forever Flu hit America and Washington's answer was a mountain of money and a sign that said "Come Steal It."

$872 billion went out to unemployment assistance. You know how much of it went to improper payments and fraud? Well, they don't have a solid figure; that would require accounting. But the low-end estimates are $163 billion in fraud. The inspector general says, "It's likely higher than that," and ID.me, an identity authentication service, estimates that the number is closer to $400 billion. That's almost half of it. In one instance, $2 million in unemployment checks got sent to one address. What was the job that guy was out of?

In Arizona, scammers got nearly 30 percent of the benefits. And that's Arizona, where the most "fiscally conservative," penny-pinching Republicans used to live. Republicans at least used to pretend to be the mean old man who watched your money, but now nobody, from either party, even pretends to. Defunding the police? Yes, that's a bad idea—but so is de-policing the funds.

Palm Beach, which has 160 golf courses, got Covid money—what did they do with it? They built another golf course. Several nonprofits, overseen by an organization called Feeding Our Future, got $65 million to feed needy children during the pandemic, but it was actually a "massive fraud," and the FBI says "almost none of this money was used to feed children." That's like something Trump would do. Even the kids were like, "If we wanted to get fucked that bad, we could've gone to church."

The Paycheck Protection Program was designed to help small businesses pay their laid-off employees, but hundreds of loans went to fake farms in areas where farming isn't even done. You know that saying "Don't have a cow"? They literally didn't have a cow. The government sent $1.4 billion in stimulus payments to a million dead people. One woman used Covid cash to hire a hit man. And I assume the guy who got whacked then got a check.

The Shuttered Venue Operators Grant program gave out $10 million to Broadway's *West Side Story*—no wonder they're singing, "I want to live in America." And *Harry Potter and the Cursed Child* also got $10 million. Because otherwise J. K. Rowling would be living in her car.

There's an old adage that government cannot transfer money except by means of a leaky bucket—and I get that; some amount of leaking is inevitable. But when it's all holes, it's not a bucket anymore—what you have there is a handle.

A January *New York Times* article about the effectiveness of the PPP included these quotes: "overall the PPP was extremely inefficient" and "only about a quarter of the money spent by the program paid wages that would have otherwise been lost," and the money "didn't primarily go to workers who would have lost jobs" and "was effectively a windfall for business owners—on the whole a wealthy group."

Shouldn't liberal Democrats be the ones who are most upset about this? Who do you think is getting fucked the worst by all this graft and thievery? If I say, "They take our money and waste it," people say, "You sound like a conservative."

But I haven't changed my politics: the hole-to-bucket ratio has changed. Should I never notice that to keep my progressive card? Should I stay supportive of government transfers of money until the percentage that's stolen is . . . unlimited? What if they start to shoot money out of a T-shirt cannon; still good?

12

DRUGS

YOU'VE GOT ALE

In Ken Burns's great documentary *Prohibition*, the first episode is called *A Nation of Drunkards*. It describes how on farms in the nineteenth century, there was a barrel of hard cider by the door, which you dipped into every time you came and went.

"Americans routinely drank at every meal, including breakfast. In many towns, a bell rang twice a day to signal what was called 'grog time' so that men could stop whatever they were doing in factories and offices, mills and farm fields, and drink."

Well, here in the now times, we seem to be heading back in that direction. Yes, America has a drinking problem.

I can't believe we'd ever be so stupid as to outlaw booze again, but that doesn't mean we shouldn't take notice when the nation goes through one of its periodic binge-drinking phases like we are now. Since the turn of the millennium, alcohol consumption in this country has risen steadily and alcohol-related deaths have doubled. Even millennials, who used to be the more sober generation, are now dying of cirrhosis of the liver at record rates.

And that was before Covid hit, when Lockdown Nation really hit the bottle. The pandemic was an excuse for people to drink more, drink during the day and drink alone—a condition psychologists call "Melania." Restaurants were delivering meals, but also cocktails with hard liquor. I know this because they were delivering them to my house. Because as long as I had liquor, I didn't care that there was no toilet paper.

But as a historical trend, this can't be good. There's a word for when everyone in society gets drunk just to get through the day. And that word is: "Russia."

And I do mean "through the day," because even before Covid, we started putting liquor everywhere. Every month you could see some viral video of an all-out brawl at a Chuck E. Cheese because even a children's restaurant serves beer now. Alcohol is also everywhere on TV: hosts of the *Today* show have it on their desk, and, of course, stars of *The Real Housewives* have it on their faces. The flight crews of all the major airlines are constantly having to treat drunken, unruly passengers like children now: "I will turn this plane around and *no one* will go to Dallas–Fort Worth!"

Grocery stores now serve beer on tap—for the first time ever, husbands are asking, "Honey, you need me to pick up anything at the market?" Supermarkets also invite customers to "shop 'n' sip" from their open wine bars: belly up, Mom, leave your troubles in the produce department. And your baby in the car. But hey, if you get drunk at Whole Foods, please: remember to vomit in a reusable bag.

Movie theaters now also serve beer and wine, and sometimes hard liquor. So do Taco Bell and Disneyland. And Starbucks. You thought they had trouble spelling your name on the cup before!

And of course, what's the point of living large if you can't get offered a drink when you shop and get your hair done? Book clubs have long been just an excuse to guzzle wine, the way fishing is really just drinking on a boat, hunting is drinking in the woods and bowling is drinking with rented shoes on.

Aquariums serve alcohol now, and zoos. Zoos? Who gets shitfaced at the zoo? When did people start saying, "If I'm going to stare at a polar bear taking a nap, I'm going to need a couple of stiff ones"?

Maybe you recognize yourself in some of this. Ask yourself, "Do I drink in the morning? Do I drink alone? Do I receive 'mystery' packages from Amazon that make me ask, 'When did I order snowshoes?'"

And while the Covid pandemic may be over, the epidemic that preceded it—the anxiety epidemic—is not, and usually when people drink, it's to alleviate some form of anxiety. We're using liquor as a crutch for our pandemic-exacerbated problem of being socially impaired. We call it "social" media, but really it's the opposite of social, and our increasing detachment from one another in real life and dependence on screens and online relationships makes us ever more vulnerable to the lure of liquid courage when it comes to really interacting.

But drinking is not the answer. OK, it's part of the answer. Taking the edge off a bit, yes—I myself have a long history of using liquor to take the edge off. Usually off some other drug, but still . . .

But not at two in the afternoon. Not at the Ralphs. And definitely not at the zoo. We have got to get a handle on our anxiety, and it can't be through the bottle. Everybody just needs to get a grip.

PILLBILLIES

So much of the rot in our society stems from our modern-day version of Prohibition. The people massing at our border to escape the violence in Central America? That's the Drug War. The record-shattering amount of incarceration this country does, with all its implications for racial injustice, wasted lives and skewed elections because so many felons can't vote—that's the Drug War.

Other people get it: Mexico legalized weed in 2021, and Canada did it in 2018. Why are we always last at everything? Portugal ran this experiment—they decriminalized all drugs ten years ago, and they had less than one hundred overdose deaths in 2018. We had eighty-one thousand. The war is over. West Virginia lost. And it lost big: it was Trump's best state in two elections, but folks there have downed more hydrocodone and oxycodone pills than anywhere else in the country. West Virginia's mascot is a dilated pupil.

In Wisconsin, another key Trump state, between 2008 and 2014, heroin deaths nearly quadrupled. I never thought I'd hear myself say this, but, kids: don't do heroin! It's a gateway to being a Republican.

Of the fourteen states with the highest number of painkiller prescriptions per person, they all went for Trump in 2016. Trump won 80 percent of the states that have the biggest heroin problem, and the counties that he won in Ohio and Pennsylvania that went for Obama in 2012 are the ones that are racked by opiate abuse. So let's stop calling Trump voters idiots and fools, and call them what they are: drug addicts.

And the thing that sticks in my craw about this is: for decades it was liberals who were accused of "destroying the fabric of society" with drug use. In 1968, Merle Haggard had a big country hit with an anthem called "Okie from Muskogee" that put the counterculture in its place:

"We don't smoke marijuana in Muskogee / We don't take no trips on LSD."

Today, Muskogee, population 36,700, has seven drug treatment centers. They should change the lyrics to "We don't share our needles in Muskogee / We don't mix our smack with PCP . . ."

Somewhere along the line, things changed for the "real Americans" in the heartland who were always chastising liberals for undermining patriotism by being stoned all the time. Well, who's stoned all the time now?

Liberals moved on to kale smoothies and an occasional craft beer. Meanwhile, "heartlanders" have meth mouth and are taking their dog's arthritis pills. "Live Free or Die"? More like "Press Down and Twist."

The good news is, if the problem is drugs, that's something I can help with—if there's one thing I know, it's how to manage a high. So if you're new to drugs, let me share a lifetime of wisdom and experience in getting fucked up. Things like:

Don't mix pills and alcohol—but if you do, oxycodone goes with white wine, and hydrocodone goes with red.

Don't drive on pills: call Uber or Lyft, and have someone on pills drive *you*.

Ignore the asshole across the bar who keeps staring at you—that's a mirror.

Always have a wingman. Someone to say "Cool it" or "You shouldn't drive" or "Don't put that in your mouth." Willie Nelson once pulled me away from a long conversation with a Christmas tree that I swore was Jared Leto.

And most important: you're doing the wrong drugs. Stick to the stuff that comes out of the ground. Christ, 90 percent of you are farmers—you grow, fertilize, harvest, eat and for all I know fuck your own crops; you never once thought to *smoke* them?!?

GRASS WARFARE

4/20 is the holiday where stoners everywhere smoke weed to celebrate smoking weed every other day of the year, and to celebrate it in 2018, the aforementioned John Boehner—the weepy, chain-smoking, chamber of commerce golf course drunk who used to be Republican speaker of the House, and who used to say he was "unalterably opposed" to decriminalizing pot—announced that he had "evolved" and accepted a position on the board of directors of Acreage Holdings, one of the largest legal pot growers in the country.

You think Boehner cried a lot before? Wait till he gets stoned and sees a sunset.

It's also a Republican, not a Democrat, who has introduced the most sweeping federal legalization bill ever in Congress. Democrats are going to lose this issue if they're not careful, because now Republicans smell the money. Which would be a shame, because pot could be for Democrats what guns have always been for Republicans: the issue that gets enough of their base to the polls to swing elections.

Every election, Republicans run on "They're comin' for your guns!" If Democrats talked about weed that way, they could turn potheads into single-issue voters too. And it should be easy, because nobody's really coming for your guns, but Joe Biden and Chris Christie really do want to take away your pot, for which there is no protection like the Second Amendment.

Democratic politicians can talk all they want about "making college more affordable," but weed is what makes it *bearable*. We can bring those jobs back from China, but they're still going to suck. You're in an Amazon warehouse for eight hours with no one to talk to but robots, you're going to want that vape pen.

This should be an especially potent issue for the youngest voters, the ones Democrats are so desperate to get to the polls. Many of them are the type who say they're coming out to vote for gun control—maybe, but being against guns is not a lifestyle.

Guns is a lifestyle. And *weed* is a lifestyle. It's not just something people have an opinion on—it's in your home. It's a passion. You like touching it.

Gun nuts have magazines, and so do stoners. They have gun shops, we have dispensaries. They know the difference between automatic and semiautomatic; we know the difference between indica and sativa.

I tend to think guys who need a fifty-caliber rifle that can shoot through Iron Man are crazy, but then I remember I once paid three grand for a device called the Mothership. It heated hash oil to exactly 462 degrees and had a spherical donut chamber with detachable bubbler and dual-wax ceramic coil, and a seventy-two-hole percolator with matching showerhead ash-catcher. Did it make getting high any better than using an apple? No. Because that's the thing about hobbies—they don't have to make sense. It's just about doing what you love.

PUFF LOVE

I could go on and on about the benefits of weed: increased focus, less anxiety, better sleep . . . it makes food taste better, music sound better, bad dates more tolerable . . . good for migraines, glaucoma, and the nausea associated with making small talk at the dog park. Yes, you're doing a heckuva job, brownie. But even though we've come a long way, please remember that legalizing pot is still far from being a done deal.

I know, you're tired—I am too—of making the same old obvious arguments, like how pot is less dangerous than other legal adult activities, but somehow you can legally drink alcohol, smoke cigarettes and do that thing where you cut off your oxygen with a belt and masturbate. Which is not only dangerous, but take it from me, it'll get you kicked out of Macy's menswear in a heartbeat.

Everybody seems 100 percent certain that a completely weed-legal America, on the model of gay marriage, is right around the corner. "Yes," the pot lovers say, "sure it's still not fully legal in twenty-seven states, but the rest are going to fall like dominoes!"

I hear it all the time: "They'll fall like dominoes . . . dominoes . . . hey, let's order from Domino's!"

Hippies, you need to get your head out of your grass; progress doesn't just automatically snowball. Think of other rights we never thought would be rolled back. Look at what's happened with abortion. Somehow every far-left, ultra-woke idea is now on the table, but when it comes time for Congress to make pot fully legal nationally, it's like smoking a joint with Woody Harrelson: they just won't pass it.

Because pot is not like gay marriage; with gay marriage, no one stood to lose money if the law changed. But the War on Drugs keeps billions flowing to DEA agents and police and prisons, and legal weed would mean Americans had an alternative to altering their mood by downing oxycontin and Budweiser, or as Rush Limbaugh used to call it, "lunch."

Raymond Schwab is a Gulf War veteran who wanted to move to Colorado when it became the first state to legalize pot, to treat his chronic pain and PTSD, because, while the VA gave him lots of prescription drugs, for him, pot was the only thing that actually worked. So Raymond thought moving to Colorado was a great idea.

But Kansas, his home state, got wind of the move and took away his five children. Now, I'm not a big fan of children, but I believe if you like yours you should get to keep them. Maybe that's my "New York values" talking.

But this is what happens when pot is legal in some states, sort of legal in others and completely *illegal* in places like Kansas, where, frankly, they could use some. We can't leave this up to the states, because "states' rights" is always code for taking away rights.

And since liberals have never accepted "states' rights" as an excuse to deny Black people education or voting, or outlaw gay marriage or abortion, why do they accept it with this? When only some people have it and some don't, that's not equality—that's Wi-Fi.

I can't think of another example of a drug that's legal in one state but not in another. It's not a tenable situation. Because when I leave Colorado, Oregon, Washington or Alaska, my back pain doesn't go away. Or whatever it is I have. I'm kidding, I use medical marijuana because my third eye has glaucoma.

13

RELIGION

GOD MAN OUT

Conservatives who constantly whine that Christianity is under attack from liberals have to explain: Why are there over three hundred thousand churches in the US, but only five hundred Whole Foods? Clearly, your side is winning.

Now, I get it, Christians love to feel persecuted—it's part of their origin story. But it's been a long time since anyone was getting eaten by lions in the Colosseum. Sixty-four percent of the country is Christian, not to mention every president we've ever had, so please tell me, in what universe does it makes sense when Sean Hannity says, "The liberal media's war against religion is alive and well."

Really? Tell me exactly who that is. Michael Moore? He's the liberal Republicans hate the most, but . . . nope, he's Catholic. Stephen Colbert is so Catholic he teaches Sunday school. On Sunday. In the morning. When normal people are just getting in from an after-party.

Is it the other late-night guys? Because I never hear any of them do it. And we know it's not Oprah. When she considered running for president, she said, "God, if you think I'm supposed to run, you gotta tell me and it has to be so clear that not even I can miss it." (Humblebrag!)

Scott Walker said, "I am certain this is God's plan for me." Something God also told Rick Perry, Rick Santorum, Ben Carson, Michele Bachmann, Herman Cain and Sarah Palin.

God's a nice guy, but he doesn't follow politics.

Where is religion belittled in the liberal world? The *New York Times* editorial page? No. The op-ed page? No. *Any* newspaper's *any* page? No. *Newsweek* and *Time*? They put Jesus on the cover more often than *Cat Fancy* puts a cat.

Athletes? If they so much as fart on the field they point to the sky and give God credit. So who? Counterculture types, like devilish musicians? Have you ever watched an awards show? Every speech is "I want to thank Jesus, without whom I could never have written 'Face Down, Ass Up.'"

This idea that everybody on the left is plotting against Christianity and wants to wipe out religion is offensive. To me.

Because I'm the only live-action television figure who consistently puts religion "under attack," and I'll be damned if the credit's going to go to the entire Left when I've been doing all the heavy lifting.

HEATHEN SENT

Here's a new rule I'm 100 percent serious about: you shouldn't be able to talk about diversity, equity and inclusion anymore in America without including atheists. Atheists and agnostics are approaching a third of the population now, and so it becomes ever more outrageous that there are this many of us and we still have zero representation in government.

Congress has 535 members and only a handful who will even sheepishly admit they're "religiously unaffiliated."

The Supreme Court is two Protestants, one Jew and six people more Catholic than the Pope. Even an intellectual president like Obama, who admits to being a "secular humanist" (wink wink—atheist), had to pretend to be religious. No one has been able to admit their shameful secret: "I don't believe in ghosts."

There's now a movement for schools to officially recognize Ramadan, the Muslim month of fasting, and I'm all for it—anything to get our fat kids to eat less. But while approximately three million Americans celebrate Ramadan, almost one hundred million say they have no religion at all. Where's our day?

Is it really so much to ask that this many people get one day a year—Atheists Day!—when we recommit ourselves to observable reality? One day with no atonement, no corpse reanimation, no fasting, no tree in your house, no big rock to circle, no dirt on your forehead, no candles to light and please, God, no fruitcakes—just an annual three-day weekend to celebrate our deeply held belief that with Monday off, you can drink on Sunday night.

And get to sleep in. Because there *is* no place to get up and go to and gather to affirm we all believe the same shit. We know what we believe and what we don't believe; we don't need to rub elbows with other people who don't believe it too.

And we don't need to commercialize our holiday, like other religions do. Atheists Day is about *not* buying something. Like virgin birth: I'm not buying it.

We have the numbers. We can do this. I used to be a lonely pioneer calling religious thinking a neurological disorder, but now it's like anal—everyone's doing it. The fastest-growing religious group in the United States is "nones": people who, when asked how much they want to be involved with a religion, say "none."

The unaffiliated share of the population, consisting of people who describe their religious identity as atheist, agnostic or "nothing in particular," has risen from 5 percent in 1972 to 15 percent in 2005 to 32 percent today. You're welcome.

And lest you think it's only young, educated, white liberals—no, just about everybody is losing their religion. Or as I call it, "holy ghosting."

The average age of a "none" is now forty-three; a third are people of color, and a quarter voted for Trump. Seventy percent don't have a four-year college degree.

Millennials lead the way: they're the first generation to be less than majority Christian—their idea of hell is a coffee shop with no Wi-Fi. When asked how often they go to church, 34 percent of younger millennials answered "seldom/never" or "don't know." *Don't know?* Hey, kids, going to church is like having an orgasm—if you don't know if you did, you didn't.

And just like you don't have to be Christian to enjoy Christmas, you don't have to be an atheist to celebrate Atheists Day. I'd like it to be the one day a year that the devout can get a little taste of what it's like to live your life without some mythical daddy figure judging you and condemning you for being the exact person *He* made you!

Atheists Day should be a day for believers to stop and ask themselves . . . why? Why make up a being who's constantly disappointed in you? You don't need it. You've got your spouse. And your parents. Your siblings. Your coworkers. Your trainer, when you *don't give 110 percent!*

There are plenty of people right here on Earth who will gladly make you feel like a lame, incompetent fuckup—why make up one more? It's like adding an extra mother-in-law. Wouldn't you like for there to be one goddamn day in the year when for twenty-four hours you can tell your God to climb down off your ass? Why always be tormented by "I better not make Baby Jesus cry"? Why? Is he sitting behind you on a plane?

And until someone sees Christopher Hitchens's face in a tree stump, religious people must stop making the ridiculous claim that "atheism is just another religion." Yes, except for one little difference: religion is defined as "the belief in and worship of a superhuman controlling power," and atheism is . . . precisely not that. Atheism is a religion like abstinence is a sex position.

The "college" that Jerry Falwell started, Liberty University, isn't really a college—because it teaches "creation science." Which is the opposite of science, even though they have an actual Center for Creation

Studies, complete with some bones and a guy with a lab coat. Suck on that, Smithsonian Institution! And they teach that the Earth is five thousand years old and dinosaur fossils washed up in Noah's flood. This is a school you flunk out of when you get the answers *right*.

Problem is, if you start thinking "creationism" is science, then it's a shorter leap to "Christian Science" is medicine and "gay aversion therapy" is psychology and "praying away hurricanes" is meteorology. It'd be like teaching American history by saying the Declaration of Independence and the Constitution were written by God. And even the world's most ridiculous imbecile wouldn't say that. Oh wait, Glenn Beck did: "God's finger . . . wrote the Declaration of Independence and the Constitution."

Conservatives often say that gay marriage "cheapens" their marriage. I think a "diploma" from Liberty University cheapens my degree from a real school. I worked really hard for four years and sold a lot of drugs to get that thing. If you want to go someplace that teaches that the Bible is literally true and the Earth was created last Tuesday when God got into gardening, that's fine, but you can't call it a university. Target has pizza; that doesn't make it a restaurant.

I'd say we should take away Liberty's accreditation, but it's a private college and they can teach whatever they want. But at the very least, diplomas from Liberty should come with a huge asterisk next to your name, and at the bottom it should say, "This institution teaches superstitious nonsense. Hire at your own risk."

Religions, ironically, do not fight in good faith. Not only do they claim adherents that don't exist, they also accuse secularists of secretly being like them.

There's a disturbing new trend of labeling any ideology, no matter how evidence based, a "religion" simply because you don't like it and want to create a false equivalency. I've heard conservatives say that belief in man-made climate change is a religion, and Darwinism is a religion, and atheism, the total lack of religion, is somehow a religion too. According to the always reliable *Encyclopedia Moronica*.

It's a dodge, of course, straight out of the grand intellectual tradition of "I know you are but what am I?" It's a way of saying, "Hey, we all believe in some sort of faith-based malarkey, so let's call it a push."

Sorry, no—we're not two sides of the same coin, and you don't get to put your unreason up on the same shelf with my reason. Your stuff has to go over there on the shelf with Zeus, Thor and the kraken. With the stuff that is *not* evidence based. Stuff that religious people never change their mind about, no matter what happens. That's not atheism. I'm open to anything for which there's evidence.

Show me a god, and I'll believe in Him. If Jesus Christ comes down from the sky during the next Super Bowl and turns all the nachos into loaves and fishes, I'll think two things: "How dare He interrupt Harry Styles's Gender-Fluid Halftime Show," and "Oh, look at that, I was wrong. There He is. My bad. Praise the Lord."

I don't begrudge religious people claiming the majority of humans on Earth who legitimately and voluntarily desire to be "people of faith"— but it's a little greedy to also claim those who don't.

Some years ago, Mitt Romney's father-in-law, Edward Davies, an enthusiastically antireligious scientist who called organized faith "hogwash," was posthumously baptized, in the Mormon tradition, fourteen months after he died. They tried to do it sooner, but he wouldn't stop spinning in his grave. This is just wrong. And so I give you history's first *un*-baptism ceremony for the late Edward Davies:

Dearly beloved, we are gathered here today, in the presence of math, gravity, evolution and electricity, to honor Brother Edward, and to send the powers of SEAL Team 666 to rescue him from Planet Kolob so that he may spend eternity with the kind of freethinkers he chose to hang out with on Earth. So by the power granted to me by the Blair Witch . . . schlemiel, schlimazel, e pluribus mumbo jumbo expecto-patronum su su sudio yo mama! I call upon the Mormon spirits to leave your body the fuck alone!

One last myth about atheism to shoot down: every time you blame religion for so much of the world's misery, religious people will come back with "But, Bill, the godless cultures like Hitler's Germany and Stalin's Russia and Mao's China were the worst, and they had *no* religion!"

But here's the thing about Nazism, Maoism and Stalinism: Those *were* religions. State religions. These dictators didn't get rid of God because they hated religion, they got rid of God because they hated competition.

Same with North Korea today: they claim to be godless communists, but their calendar begins on the day the country's founder, Kim Il Sung, came to Earth from heaven. His son, the next ruler, Kim Jong Il, is believed by North Koreans to have started walking at three weeks old and talking at eight weeks. When he was born, winter turned to spring. He can make it rain based on his mood. He never used a toilet because his body was so well calibrated he didn't need to defecate. His first time golfing, he shot a thirty-eight under par with eleven holes-in-one. He wrote fifteen hundred books in three years, narrowly beating out James Patterson.

Kim also invented the hamburger. I'm not making that up; *they're* making that up. Talk about a whopper. This is not an atheist nation. I've heard of people who claim their shit don't stink, but only a god will say they don't shit at all.

State religion: I try not to have all roads lead to Donald Trump . . . but this one really does.

BULLY IDOL

We need to stop pretending there's no way we'll ever understand why the Trump mob believes in him. It's because they're religious and they've already made space in their heads for shit that doesn't make sense. When you're a QAnon fanatic, you're also a fundamentalist Christian—they just go together, like macaroni and cheese. Or chardonnay and Valium.

The Capitol insurrection looked like a revival meeting, with people praying around wooden crosses, waving the Christian flag and "Jesus Saves" signs, and yelling "Jesus is my savior, Trump is my president." A "Jesus 2020" banner hung near the gallows that was erected for Mike Pence, who is Judas in this version of the story.

It's not a coincidence that every senator who objected to certifying the Electoral College vote in Arizona is an Evangelical Christian. When Ted Cruz defended his vote to overturn a legitimate election, he said: "Recent polling shows that thirty-nine percent of Americans believe the election that just occurred . . . was rigged. You may not agree with that assessment. But it is nonetheless a reality for nearly half the country."

In other words, "We have no proof the election was stolen, and you may have verifiable evidence that it wasn't, but that doesn't matter—*it only matters that we believe it.*"

The events of January 6 were a faith-based initiative. And Trumpism is a Christian nationalist movement that believes Trump was literally sent from heaven to save them.

There's a lot of talk in liberal quarters about how Republicans should tell their base—who still believe the election was rigged—that they need to grow up and move on and stop asking the rest of us to respect their mass delusion. And, of course, it is a mass delusion.

But the inconvenient truth here is that if you accord religious faith the kind of exalted respect we do here in America, you've already lost the argument that mass delusion is bad.

It's fun to laugh at QAnon, with the baby-eating lizard people and the pedophile pizza parlors—but have you ever read the Book of Revelation? That's your holy book, Christians, and they've got seven-headed dragons, and locusts that have the face of men and the teeth of lions. And other stuff you only see after the guy in the park sells you bad mushrooms.

Marjorie Taylor Greene believes in Jewish space lasers, but Revelation will tell you exactly where the world ends: Megiddo, Israel. I've been there. I don't know if the world ends there, but we used it as the setting for the end of *Religulous*, and for that it was actually pretty cool. Because it's where the Bible says that all the armies of the world will gather and Jesus will come down on a flying horse, shooting swords out of his mouth—Jesus, not the horse—and have a thousand-year cosmic "boss battle" with Satan, the Beast *and* the Antichrist. It's like ten Avengers movies plus ten Hobbit movies times a night out with Cocaine Bear.

Spoiler alert: Jesus wins. After which he will rapture up all the good souls, plus 144,000 Jews who were grandfathered in. By Oskar Schindler. But space lasers?! Hahaha!

Magical religious thinking is a virus, and QAnon is just its current mutation. That's why megachurches play QAnon videos: it's the same basic plot. Q is a prophet, Trump is the messiah and there's an apocalyptic event looming: "the Storm." There's a titanic struggle of good vs. evil, and if you want good to win, just keep those checks coming in.

The reason Donald Trump has an easy sell with Evangelicals is because they're hardwired to put faith over reason.

Well, that and the fact that Trump is the spitting image of the religious con men they grew up with on TV: he's got Jim Bakker's hair and Tammy Faye's makeup, he's immune to sex scandals, he had a sham university and he doesn't pay taxes. And he personifies that "prosperity gospel" bullshit they all spin: the more money I have, the happier *you* are.

The Ten Commandments is the list of the ten worst things you can do but manages to leave off torture, rape, child abuse, incest, cannibalism and slavery. The top four are all variations of "stroke my ego and kiss my ass." There are only two people I can think of who would sign on to that: God and Donald Trump.

Commandment One: "Thou shalt have no other gods—other gods are fake news! I'm the greatest god in history, with the best brain."

Commandment Two: "Only make statues of *me*. I am the only bronze-colored thing you should bow to. And don't make the hands small. Because they're not, and neither is something else, I guarantee."

Commandment Three: "When you say bad things about me, it's very unfair, and no other god has accomplished what I have in just six days, that I will tell you."

Commandment Four: "You must spend one day a week not doing anything but talking about how great I am. Let me help you: God deserves an A-plus."

So yes, Evangelicals have always needed to solve this little problem they had with wanting to support the Republican but this particular one happening to be the least Christian person ever. A man who loves flesh-peddling, coveting, cursing, cheating, bullying, bragging, sloth, adultery and ripping off charities, and who lies more frequently than the rest of us pee. The type of man who could go into a confessional booth and never come out. How to square that circle?

Mike Lindell, the MyPillow guy, said: "I see the greatest president in history. Of course he is, he was chosen by God." Yes, Mike's pillows are made from foam, but his head is stuffed with feathers.

But Mike's belief is not unique: a significant portion of our population believes that God put Donald Trump in office. And I was giving all the credit to Putin. And if you watch *The 700 Club* regularly like I do, you know that Evangelicals have lined up behind the idea that Trump's myriad sins can be forgiven because he's a modern-day version of King Cyrus in the Bible.

And who is King Cyrus? He's the ancient king of Persia who conquered Babylon, where the Jews were living in captivity—this is before Miami. Now, Cyrus didn't do it for the Jews—he did it for Persia, his country—but it had the happy side effect of allowing the Jews to return home to Israel. So Cyrus, you see, is an unwitting conduit—a "vessel" for God's will.

Except Trump isn't a vessel for God's will; he's a vessel for fried chicken.

And the analogy on which the whole thing rests is shit.

For one thing, Cyrus wasn't a fat, orange, conscienceless scumbag; he just wasn't Jewish. But nothing in the Bible says he was the antithesis of what the Jews believed in, the way Trump is the antithesis of what Christians are supposed to believe. Cyrus wasn't a notorious sinner. He wasn't a pathological liar. He didn't call scribes "the enemy of the people." He never paid a concubine hush money. And Cyrus wasn't the leader of the Jews. If Trump equals Cyrus, he would have to be a foreign leader who "unwittingly" helps America—we're the Jews in this analogy!

But the Evangelicals don't care. The *essence* of religion is: the more it doesn't make sense, the more we like it, because it proves your faith.

So when the name Cyrus comes up among Chreeestians, they all nod approvingly. They're down with the code, like when potheads hear "420."

They also believe it's significant that the chapter in the Bible that mentions Cyrus is Isaiah 45, and Trump was the forty-fifth president. You can't argue with science.

Frankly, I don't believe anyone even checks biblical passages anymore—you say a biblical-sounding phrase with a couple numbers after it and religious nuts will crochet it and hang it up in the kitchen.

But here's the scariest thing about Evangelicals, or any truly faith-filled person who takes this shit literally: they're not necessarily rooting for life on Earth to continue. A majority of Evangelicals say Jesus Christ will either probably or definitely return to Earth by 2050. Depending on his schedule.

Take the Seventh-day Adventists—please. This is a religion founded in the nineteenth century on Pastor William Miller's guarantee that Jesus would return to Earth on October 22, 1844. I don't remember everything that happened that day, but I know Jesus didn't come back to Earth; he totally flaked and never showed up. Which you'd think would have made the followers say, "Well, I guess that was a bunch of bullshit." It's like believing in the Wizard of Oz after Toto pulls back the curtain.

But no, that's logical, and this is religion. Seventh-day Adventists are obsessed with the world ending and refer to the world *not* ending in 1844 as the "Great Disappointment." They're *disappointed* that the world still exists.

You know what my Great Disappointment is? That I live in a country where four out of ten people believe we're living in the End Times, and that the media never asks Jesus freaks running for office two questions: Do you believe the world is ending soon? And is that a bad thing?

Because I'm the opposite of an end-timer; I'm a spend-timer. I don't have to agree with a politician on everything—we can disagree on abortion, entitlements, paid sick leave, the earned income tax credit—but the Earth staying put is kind of a deal-breaker for me.

PRAYA HATER

One more thing about Trump and religion: he did do one positive thing in this arena. He ruined the phrase "thoughts and prayers" forever. Of course, the problem with "thoughts and prayers" has always been that thoughts are the opposite of prayers: one is from the Enlightenment, and one is from *The Exorcist*. But it wasn't until Trump tweeted *his* "thoughts and prayers" after the Parkland shooting and one of the survivors tweeted back, "I don't want you condolences you fucking piece of shit . . . prayers won't fix this," that prayer officially became an eye-roll.

Yes, America is finally getting it: prayer doesn't work, because if it did, every drug test would come back clean and there'd be no need for the morning-after pill.

PLACING AMY

The Supreme Court of the United States really needs to take a case about taxing churches, because it hasn't done that since 1970, and since religion has become so much less popular since then, it means about a quarter of us are being forced to subsidize a myth that we're not buying into.

But I doubt that's going to happen. Democrats keep threatening to "pack the court," but I got news for them: it's already packed—with Catholics: Chief Justice Roberts, Clarence Thomas, Samuel Alito, Brett Kavanaugh, Sonia Sotomayor and Amy Coney Barrett are all Catholics, and Neil Gorsuch is really one too since he was raised Catholic and is now Episcopalian, which is just a Catholic who flunked Latin.

I have nothing against Catholics, except my entire upbringing—but they are only 20 percent of the population. If seven out of nine justices were Jews or Muslims or Buddhists, would that be OK? And if faith is this super-important element of life, as Barrett and her Republican supporters say it is, shouldn't we have a healthier balance on our highest court?

Not to mention, atheists actually make better judges, because we don't have to work to separate church and state. We're not torn between rational decision-making and what it says in the Old Book of Jewish Fairy Tales.

In 2006 Barrett told a graduating class of law students: "Keep in mind that your legal career is but a means to an end . . . that end is building the kingdom of God."

No, it's not. That shouldn't be the point of a legal career in a secular democracy, but Barrett was groomed since birth to overturn *Roe v. Wade*. She's like the Terminator, a robot programmed to fulfill one task, except she wasn't sent from the future, she was sent from the past.

Because here's the truth about Catholics in America: there's two types, scary and not scary. The vast majority? Not scary, not doctrinaire. In fact they're famous for ignoring everything the Pope tells them not to do: they masturbate, they divorce, they use contraception, they have premarital sex, they have anal sex—sometimes all in one night.

My question for these Catholics is: If you're "Catholic" but you don't follow anything the Church says, what are you staying for? The stained glass windows? It's OK to let go. No one can fault you for losing faith in an organization that won't even allow women priests, because, the reasoning goes, Jesus didn't have any female apostles. You remember the Last Supper, it was a total sausage party.

But there's another strain of Catholic who is uber conservative, has an agenda and has enormous and growing influence to achieve it. American politics includes a long line of these Republican Catholic moralizers who pine for a return to the Middle Ages, when the church *was* the state. Bill Bennett, with his sanctimonious *Book of Virtues*; Rick Santorum, who predicted gay marriage would lead to man-dog marriage . . . Pat Buchanan, Robert Bork, Newt Gingrich, Sean Hannity, Bill O'Reilly—the list goes on. Or as they're known in Hollywood: *Law & Order: Special Virgins Unit*.

Antonin Scalia was "Mel Gibson's dad"–level hard-core: he advised people to be "fools for Christ" and said, "If it were up to me, I would put in jail every sandal-wearing, scruffy-bearded weirdo who burns the American flag." Hmmm . . . sandal-wearing, scruffy beard . . . who does that remind me of . . . who? Who??

William Barr, in 1995, wrote, "We have lived through thirty years of permissiveness, the sexual revolution, and the drug culture . . . The greatest threat to free government, the Founders believed, was not governmental tyranny, but personal licentiousness." You see? It's not about tyranny; it's about tits.

Barr once wrote in *Catholic Lawyer* magazine—worst swimsuit issue ever—"The Founders believed the choice was clear. We could govern ourselves guided by religion and morality, or we could lose our liberty altogether."

Yes, they believed it so strongly they wrote it down *nowhere*. There is *nothing* about morality in the Constitution.

"Permissiveness" . . . "licentiousness" . . . "drug culture"—I've heard these words and listened to this same horseshit my whole life. This creepy substrain of Catholic conservatives who think "limited government" means government should put a limit on people's sex lives. Brett Kavanaugh was a significant contributor to the Starr Report, and he *wanted* it to be about Clinton's cock. He said Clinton had "disgraced his office, the legal system and the American people by having sex with a 22-year-old . . . it is our job to make his pattern of revolting behavior clear—piece by painful piece."

These people are not just mad they weren't invited to the party— they're mad there *is* a party.

And these old-school Catholics play the long game. Amy Barrett had been on their radar since forever because she was raised in an extremist Catholic community called People of Praise, where they speak in tongues, otherwise known as babbling, and believe "a husband's responsibilities [include] 'correcting' his wife should she stray from the proper path," and where women are called "handmaids."

Handmaids? On-the-nose much?

These are the folks who make Jehovah's Witnesses go, "Shhh, don't answer the door." It's not wrong to call something nuts when it's nuts.

In 2013, Cardinal Ratzinger, a.k.a. Pope Benedict, was in his last year of wearing the pointy hat, and he shocked the world by telling Vatican Radio—you know, Vatican Radio, playing the hits from the eighth century, the ninth century and today—that he was going to resign, because the Church needed a fresh, young face. Somewhere other than a priest's lap.

But that decision might have been because he knew he was becoming too crazy even for the Church. After he retired and became the spare-parts Pope, the only one ever to collect a pension, Benedict wrote a letter for the world to enjoy where he decried the loss of morality beginning in the 1960s.

He wrote: "Standards regarding sexuality collapsed entirely . . . that is why sex films were no longer allowed on airplanes, because violence would break out among the small community of passengers."

OK, one, what airline do you fly? And two, what the fuck?! Yeah, I think we all remember those days in air travel when there was more legroom, and they'd also show porn on the flight until you got so horny you'd punch the guy in 32B.

Benedict also wrote that "because of the 'Revolution of '68'"—whatever that was—"pedophilia was then . . . diagnosed as allowed and appropriate."

Is that what the Who meant by "the kids are alright"?

You know, before anyone at the Vatican starts calling anyone else a pedophile, you might want to check the color of your kettle, because we traced the call, and it's coming from inside the belfry.

Amy Barrett said during her confirmation hearings that she had no strong feelings about climate change but was very concerned about large belt buckles. During these same hearings, Chuck Schumer said Democrats wouldn't make Barrett's religion an issue—but they should have. Because being nuts is relevant.

FATE FATE . . . DON'T TELL ME!

There's no such thing as karma. Sorry, but life is random—the only word to describe it when a big-game hunter gets trampled by an elephant and then eaten by lions is "hilarious."

Karma, as Americans understand it, is nothing more than an extension of the common logical fallacy called *post hoc, ergo propter hoc,* which means "after this, therefore because of this." It's the fallacy that happens when someone assumes that if one thing follows another thing, then the first thing must have *caused* the second thing.

People make this mistake all the time, but honestly, washing your car doesn't really make it rain. If it did, we would have tried it in California already.

This is how Americans see karma—but karma is not a system of reward and punishment. That's Catholicism. *Karma* is a Sanskrit word meaning "action"—it's about making the conscious choice to put good out into the world. Karma is the memory of our souls, the sum of a person's actions in previous states of existence that decide their fate in future existences.

Now, of course, all that's bullshit too. Reincarnation? If that was real, wouldn't we have some evidence by now, like a raccoon spelling out in acorns: "Help me! My name is Herb Zoller, and I got trapped in this raccoon body! I have a meeting next week, and I can't show up as a raccoon!"

So yes, the Buddhist version of karma is certainly unprovable, but at least it's a beautiful, positive thought.

But what Americans did was take karma and, like everything else in this hateful, spiteful country, turn it into something bitter and nasty. We use it to mean: "You took the last cupcake and God will have my revenge!"

"Ellen was mean to her staffers and then she lost her show—karma!"

"You stole the parking spot I was waiting for at Trader Joe's? Enjoy your early-onset dementia!"

"You voted for Trump and then you got Covid? Ha, karma! Now, die!"

We took something that was meant to be gentle, kind and hopeful and turned it into a Tarantino movie. Someone did you wrong, and then sometime later, something bad happened to *them*. Karma, bitch! No, something bad was bound to happen to them at some point because they're alive. If you keep living, something bad will happen—only in this dumb country do we make it all about us and connect the two and call it karma.

But your old high school boyfriend didn't wind up a janitor because he dumped you a week before the prom, he's a janitor because he got 600 on his SATs. What Americans really mean when we say "karma"—the foreign word that really describes our feeling—is found not in Sanskrit but in German: "schadenfreude"—getting pleasure out of someone else's misfortune.

The real essence of karma is nonattachment: letting shit go. It's very Zen. Which, by the way, no one knows what that means either.

REASON'S GREETINGS

When I was a kid, one of the songs that played throughout the house during the Christmas season was Andy Williams's "The Most Wonderful Time of the Year." But if it is, then why in recent years have there been so many books with titles like *How to Survive Christmas*, *Christmas Sucks* and *Skipping Christmas*? Why a movie called *Surviving Christmas*? And what do people say when Christmas is over? "Did you make it through the holidays?" Christmas shouldn't be something you "make it through," like basic training or a colonoscopy or a stretch in the hole. Which is my nickname for a colonoscopy. You shouldn't be looking at the open oven and thinking, "Should I take the sugar cookies out or stick my head in?"

I know I might seem like the last person you'd suspect of wanting to save Christmas, but I actually do. Because while it's obviously for many people a religious holiday to which I don't subscribe, it's also a national holiday and a year-end celebration replete with irreplaceable family memories for me.

So I ask the question: What can we do to rehabilitate Christmas? To get its poll numbers back up? Well, here's my three-point plan:

First we gotta shorten the season. Christmas really now starts in October, so let's just combine all the end-of-the-year holidays into one big one called Thanks-hallow-istmas. A day when the whole family gets together, in costumes, and gives thanks for a big meal of turkey and candy, and then gathers around a tree covered in toilet paper to exchange presents and sing ghost carols.

Second, we must recognize that, although stress from seeing family has always been there, it's gotten worse, because thanks to the Internet and Fox News, half your family is now full-on insane and impossible to talk to. Therefore, we need to start a tradition that all conversation around the table be restricted to: the weather, the big game, whether Gene Hackman is still alive, what the dog looks like he's thinking and when you're going to have that thing looked at.

Subjects that should be off-limits include: politics, child-rearing advice, weight gain, "good things" Hitler did and whether the "carpet matches the drapes." Oh, and FYI, the kids and their cousins didn't "go for a walk." They're in the garage getting high.

And finally, if we really want to get rid of the Christmas stress, we gotta get rid of the gift-giving. Spending money you don't have to give people you don't like stuff they don't want—that must stop. All that anxiety over what to get, how much to spend, if I buy something for this one do I have to buy something for that one, the parking, the shopping, the returning—yikes! I don't know how my assistant does it!

14

MONEY

COMMON CENTS

If there's one place God shouldn't be, it's on money. Why? Because one is a supreme, all-powerful entity that Americans worship above all else. And the other is God.

Speaking as America's favorite celebrity atheist, here's the thing America is going to be learning as more and more people abandon religion: it's not that atheists are militant, it's that we don't give a shit. God on money? I don't really care on which of your treasured totems you scrawl the name of your myth—put Hello Kitty on the flag, knock yourself out. If the fifty says, "Kneel Before Allah, White Devil," but they still take it down at the dispensary, I'm good.

Mitt Romney once told a crowd in Virginia, "I will not take God off our coins!" staking out a bold and unwavering stand against something no one has ever asked anyone to do. Other things Mitt won't do with currency no matter how much you threaten or plead include nailing a silver dollar to his forehead and shoving a roll of dimes up his ass.

But it is kind of funny to put God on money. This is the same God who sent his son down to beat up the money changers? If Jesus got angry and kicked the money changers out of the temple, imagine how apeshit he would have gone at Goldman Sachs.

The silliest part about putting "God" on money is it's redundant. Because our god *is* money. It's like Victoria's Secret embroidering the word "tits" on a push-up bra. Worshipping money is how we let things like our wars and our prisons and our health care turn into for-profit business endeavors.

Is the War on Drugs ever going to end? Of course not, because it's making billions for the private prison, alcohol and prescription drug industries, all of whom sniffed out a source of cash like a pig on a truffle. And they'll never let it go. Will we ever scale back the Department of Homeland Security, a bloated federal monstrosity that eats our wealth and lives beyond our reproach—er, I mean safeguards our freedom?

Of course not. Because "free" is only the first part of "freedom." The other part is "dumb."

You can tell there's an income inequality problem in this country because the stores like Sears and Penney's that used to cater to the middle market have all died. But you know who's doing great? Neiman's and Gucci for the Marie Antoinette crowd, and the Dollar Store for people who don't see a problem with Halloween candy in June.

Just think of how many "dollar" places there are now: The Dollar Store. Dollar Tree. Dollar General. Giant Dollar. Family Dollar. The 99-Cent Store. The 98-Cent Store. Where does it end? Just a homeless guy handing out expired toothpaste for free?

But that's our economy now: you're buying either Rembrandts or Chinese cosmetics made from dirt. But in the middle? Restaurants like Chili's, Outback Steakhouse and TGI Fridays are also struggling because they've lost their best customers: people with a little money who fill up on bread. They're the restaurants that say, "I still love you, baby, but just barely."

Fifty years ago, America's biggest employer was General Motors, where workers made the modern equivalent of $50 an hour. Today, America's biggest employer is Walmart, where the average wage is $17 an hour, which means you can share a room in a transient hotel with a drifter who cuts his toenails with a machete.

When Walmart released their annual report a few years ago it was revealed that most of what Walmart sells is food, and most of their customers need food *stamps* to pay for it. Meanwhile, Walmart's owners are so absurdly rich that one of them, Alice Walton, spent almost a billion dollars for an art museum in Bentonville, Arkansas, five hundred miles away from the nearest person who would ever want to look at art, and she said about it, "For years I've been thinking about what we could do as a family that could really make a difference."

How about giving your employees a raise, you deluded nitwit?

Some years ago the Olsen twins were sued by forty unpaid interns who were just trying to get minimum wage, and who pointed out how wrong that seemed at a time when the Olsens were selling a $55,000 handbag made from the hides of other, less successful child stars.

But in America, outrageous income inequality has always been accepted, even by most of the people getting fucked by it. And that's how we got what economists now call the "sharing economy." We used to have stores that provided jobs; then commerce went online, and now we just have apps.

There are apps now that connect you with people who will buy your groceries or park your car, and on Etsy, you can sell your handmade crafts without the middleman of a store—how liberating! Now you're the guy on Venice Beach with a little stand and a fold-out chair—but virtually!

Oh, and by the way, I'm not planning on wearing pants tomorrow, so if anyone needs pants but can't afford the long-term investment, head over to TrouserDeal.com.

TrouserDeal, where you can rent my pants for just $5.95 a day!

I think anyone who during this pandemic repeated the mantra "We're all in it together" should now have to work a shift at DoorDash. Because the truth is, half the country sat home in their comfy clothes ordering takeout while the other half was out in the cold delivering it—so stop with the "in it together" bullshit. "We're in it together" was just a new version of "Thank you for your service": the thing to say to the people doing the dirty work from the people who weren't doing any of it.

And even before the pandemic hit, America was already well into being this "gig economy," which *sounds* kind of hip, like you're in a rock band. Except you're not in a rock band, you're delivering hot chicken, and it doesn't cover your rent. Even "side hustle" sounds kind of cool—but you're not a private eye who runs drugs, you're an Uber driver who also makes jewelry out of seashells.

You can call it "remote work," but what's really remote is any chance of getting health insurance. What are Uber and Lyft but Americanized rickshaws? It's not like it's what anyone *wants* to do. No one ever had a friend throw up in their backseat and said, "Gosh, I hope someday I can make a career out of this."

But in the gig economy, everyone is a freelancer, and finding work is the virtual equivalent of hanging out in the parking lot at Home Depot. Have a spare room you don't mind strangers fucking in? Rent it on Airbnb. Does anybody really want to have total strangers living in their apartment for a week? "Oh, look! Someone else's pubes on my soap—I'm living the dream!"

Got some old *Star Trek* stuff from your childhood? Sell it on eBay and ship it to some forty-five-year-old guy's mom's house. Even famous people are not above scrounging for cash on the site Cameo, where you can get D-list celebrities to wish you a happy birthday or tell you to get well soon or tell you a joke.

And then there's OnlyFans, which in 2021 swelled from twelve million users to eighty-five million. And if you're a little behind and don't know what OnlyFans is, don't worry, it's the side hustle your daughter is using to pay off her college debt. It's just a platform where you can share recipes, or maybe your poetry.

Yeah, you *can* do that on OnlyFans, but no one does. It's women showing their vaginas to a webcam so men can masturbate. I'm sorry,

I'm being crude—what I meant to say was, OnlyFans is a "social media" site where over a million "creators" provide "exclusive content" to eighty-five million "subscribers."

Who are masturbating.

Because apparently that's what our economy revolves around now—losers in their underwear paying poor, desperate web girlfriends to fake an orgasm while a toddler cries in the next room. According to the website Stripchat, this kind of thing has become so routine that now there's actually a most popular time of day to take a break from your busy schedule and rub one out, and that's between three and four in the afternoon—what I call "fappy hour."

Remember Belle Knox, the Duke University freshman who was outed as a porn star? She doesn't have the typical porn star biography—abused by an uncle, addicted to coke, locked in a closet by Charlie Sheen. She was a levelheaded, articulate eighteen-year-old majoring in women's studies. Just like I did.

So why the porn? Because Duke costs sixty-three grand a year! Since 1980, college tuition has increased 600 percent above the inflation rate—I'm surprised they're not *all* doing porn. This is not, for the most part, a country of lazy people and good people so much as it's a country of rich people and desperate people. Do you know how much Americans owe in student loans? One point seven trillion dollars. We're gonna have to sell a lot of ass to pay that tab.

I'm looking forward to the day when OnlyFans merges with Cameo to become OnlyCameo, where you can order those has-been celebs to do freaky shit—that's when we'll know our economy has hit Peak Gig: when you can make Ian Ziering open a bottle of beer with his asshole. And he does it, because, "Hey, anything for a fan."

How did America spend sixty years fighting communism and end up in a barter economy on Craigslist? The Trumps of the world would like to blame it all on Mexico and China, but actually, the soulless workers coming to take your job aren't being smuggled across the Rio Grande; they're robots being built in Palo Alto. And that's not counting the next big thing—driverless cars, and I don't just mean the people texting be-hind the wheel.

But robots and cars didn't do this—we did it to ourselves. As usual, by worshipping greed. From replacing people with robots to exploiting interns, from the slave labor we use overseas to the music everybody steals at home . . . we've all become so good at scheming, cheating, in-venting, raiding, gouging and just plain fucking each other that we woke up one day with this "sharing" economy, where the one thing we're not sharing is the profits. Somehow they forgot to create an app for that.

SERFIN' USA

American workers really should get at least as much paid vacation as the Chinese slaves who make their phones. Did you know that 176 countries mandate vacation time by law? But one of them isn't the Republic of "Here." In England you get 28 paid vacation days a year. In Switzerland you get 20. In Sweden you get 25. In Greece you get infinity.

So maybe we should take a minute to reflect on how it's possible that a nation so lazy that we invented the heated automobile seat—because who has the energy to make body heat come out of their ass?—can also be the only real country where no one ever gets a day off.

Here's something I've noticed when I've visited our national parks: *Everyone there is German.* Or Canadian. Or Japanese. Because they have the time to go to our parks, and we don't. Because our government re-quires zero paid vacation days.

In France, they get a minimum of thirty. Which is why French men always look like they've just been blown. Even tiny, impoverished, war-torn Sri Lanka guarantees fourteen vacation days. Don't Americans de-serve a shot at the Sri Lankan dream? China gets ten days—the people who make everything sold at Walmart while a soldier pokes them in the back with a bayonet and screams, "Faster! Faster!" treats its workers to more time off than we do.

Have you ever been to Europe in the summer around lunchtime and suddenly you look around and think, "Wait a minute . . . where the fuck did everybody go?"

"Sorry, American, it's siesta time! Now, excuse me while our entire nation has sex in the afternoon." And Americans look at this and think it's weird without realizing *we're the weird ones*. But the Declaration of Independence says "life, liberty and the pursuit of happiness," not "work, consumerism and the pursuit of quarterly profits." And if we're the greatest, most exceptional country in the world, how come *we're* not having sex in the afternoon?

Because that's not how we roll. Many Americans get two weeks' vacation, unpaid, which they often don't even take because they're too afraid their job won't be there when they get back. Our politicians love to brag, "The American worker is the most productive worker in the world"— yeah, because they work scared.

That's why a majority don't even take all of the few vacation days they get, because you don't want to seem less valuable to your boss, especially since we live in the only big-boy country where losing your job often means losing your health care. And then you won't be able to get the Prozac that helps you forget how depressed you are about having no free time. For God's sake, having to cram an entire year's worth of relaxing into two weeks is more stressful than your job! You might as well stay home, sit in the baby pool and snort bath salts.

PRIME BOSS

The problem with the free market today is it's neither free nor much of a market. That's because big business *is* the new big government: the massive, unwieldy bureaucracy that just doesn't work. JPMorgan Chase may be too big to fail, but the phone company, the credit card company, the mortgage company, the insurance company—they're too big to care.

Everyone bitches about the post office, but at least there are people behind the counter there, which is more than I can say for Duane Reade. I wandered around there for thirty minutes the other night looking for someone to pay for my cough syrup—it's a good thing I didn't have a cough.

My friends on the right have this unshakable idea that the free market is always perfect because it lets consumers find the best product at the best price. And that's a nice idea for business school, or at the Rand Paul Bootstraps Club, but here in Realityville, what happens is, you get cable from the one cable company in your city, and you sign a piece of paper and then Rumpelstiltskin comes to your house and sodomizes you and laughs.

I'm kidding. He doesn't come to your house, you have to call.

Elizabeth Warren once had a plan to break up Amazon—and I say let's go for it. Senator Warren says, "I'm a capitalist to my core," and so am I, but when a company gets so big it smothers all competitors in the crib, that's *anti*-capitalist.

Like when Amazon destroyed the startup Diapers.com by cutting Amazon's own diaper prices below cost. By one estimate, this cost Jeff Bezos $200 million in his quest to corner the online diaper market—but he owns it now. Which raises the question: What is wrong with this man? OK, you had one brilliant idea—that when people get drunk at home, they'll go online and buy shit they don't need. Great, congratulations, you won, you're the best at making money. But one of the rules of the game of capitalism is: you can win big, but not so big there is no game.

There was a famous folk song from the 1940s called "Sixteen Tons," and, like all folk songs, it was horrible. But it did raise awareness about a certain problem we also have today: having just one store. The song was about the old mining towns where the workers only had the one company store, and at least back then we seemed to understand that getting everything from one store was a *bad* thing. But that was BP—"Before Prime."

We now live in an age not of innovation but of domination, and in the online marketplace, Amazon has become the company sto'. And that was *before* an event happened that made everyone stay home and order everything online. Predictably, once Covid hit and America locked itself upstairs like a babysitter hiding from a slasher, the rest of the economy cratered—but Amazon's stock price went up 25 percent. And if we don't do something soon, we're going to discover that there's only one store. And it knows where you live.

We've been through this before. A century ago, John D. Rockefeller was personally worth 2 percent of America's GDP, and his Standard Oil Company became such an overwhelming monopoly that government had to eventually address the issue of monopolies. But Rockefeller had only one product—oil. Amazon sells 350 million different items. And when one supplier brings you everything, you're not a customer, you're a dependent.

STUCK IN THE MIDDLE WITH FEW

In 2019, when Amazon announced it was going to open two enormous processing centers somewhere in the United States, a fierce competition broke out all over the country to compete for them. Two hundred thirty-eight cities and regions submitted proposals to Amazon for the company to locate in their area, all desperate for jobs that don't involve guarding prisoners or murdering chickens. And after much deliberation, Amazon picked two places that didn't need them at all. Places where prosperity already was. Which was a shame, because Amazon could have helped one of the many areas in this country that are dying economically to come back to life.

I know this sounds like a pipe dream—and it's true, I was smoking a pipe when I dreamed it—but if liberals are serious about winning elections, they have to start recolonizing the parts of the country they've abandoned.

We have a problem in America experts call "spatial geographic inequality," which means that the most affluent and educated people are clustered in just a few cities. Hillary Clinton said after her 2016 defeat, "I won the places that represent two-thirds of America's gross domestic product . . . I won the places that are optimistic, diverse, dynamic, moving forward." Yes, you did, and maybe that has something to do with why Trump voters are obsessed with "owning the libs"? Because the libs own everything else.

The blue parts of America are having a big prosperity party, while that big sea of red feels like their invitation got lost in the mail. And they still use the mail. They turn on the TV and all the shows take place in a few hip cities—there's no *Real Housewives of Toledo* or *CSI: Lubbock*. There are no red carpets in Wyoming, and no one ever asks you, "Who are you wearing?" Because the answer is always "Target."

The flyover states have become the passed-over states—that's why red-state voters are so pissed off. They don't hate us—they want to be us. They want to go to the party.

There *are* two Americas, and it seems like one is where all the cool jobs are, where people drive Teslas and eat artisanal ice cream. We have orchestras, theater districts, world-class shopping and Chef Wolfgang Puck; they have Chef Boyardee. Our roofs have solar panels; theirs have last year's Christmas lights. We've got legal bud, they've got Bud Light. Well, not anymore.

Mississippi is the poorest state in the country—Amazon could buy the whole state and rename it Amazippi. If we keep leaving the red states behind they're going to keep getting angrier and crazier, because if you're not invited to the party, the next best thing is to throw a turd in the punch bowl.

As opposed to what would happen if Amazon moved to West Virginia: people get better jobs that don't give them black lung; the locals meet people of different races and backgrounds and sexual orientations, none of whom kill them; they find out gays don't ruin anyone's marriage, but they do improve the karaoke scene; a yoga studio opens up, then an art gallery, then one of those trendy bars where the inside looks like outside; Asians come and open a Chinese restaurant, then Jews come because there's a Chinese restaurant.

If Bugsy Siegel could invent Las Vegas out of a desert stopover for GIs, Amazon can turn Nebraska into the next Silicon Valley.

LAND OF THE FEE

When did the American business model switch from honestly selling you a product to tricking the consumer who doesn't read the fine print? Late fees, rebooking fees, restocking fees, roaming fees, overdraft fees, cancellation fees, fees because you forgot to say "Simon says." My credit card has a maintenance fee—for what? It's a piece of plastic in my wallet, it's not like someone from Citibank comes by once a month to water it.

You ever wonder, "Why is my cell phone contract longer than a CVS receipt?" If you forget to turn off "data roaming" and you go to Vancouver for the weekend, Verizon gets to keep your children. This is the new way we do business, and it's all based on the cynical premise of you fucking up: that they can wear you down, confuse you or count on you to forget.

Take something as simple as gift cards. They look like an easy and convenient way to say, "I wanted to buy you something, but I just barely give a shit." But almost a third of the people who receive gift cards never use them. It's a bet between you and Long John Silver's that even when it's free, you still don't want to eat at Long John Silver's.

Same thing with gym memberships: only 18 percent of Americans who join a gym wind up actually using it; the rest go twice a year, the way Catholics go to mass. And again, it's a bet between consumers of gym memberships, who are saying, "This is the year I get off my butt and get in shape, I know I can do it!" and the owner of the gym, who's saying, "Well I know you can't, you lazy loser, you'll come here three times in January and then I'm done with you for the rest of the year, thanks for the free money, enjoy your Cinnabon."

Because in America, a fuckup is our best customer.

Credit card companies are based wholly on the premise that you the consumer want something *now*—some crazy impulse purchase like "gas"—and you think you'll be able to pay for it before the interest kicks in.

And for people who want to get screwed even harder than the credit card companies do it, there are payday loans, where the average interest rate they can charge is sometimes over 100 percent. If an actual loan shark charged you that much, you'd break *his* legs.

But hey, don't worry, payday loan victims, as soon as Congress passes "tax reform," you'll be cashing your checks at a casino in Monte Carlo!

I'm kidding, you'll be cashing them *outside* a casino *in* a Monte Carlo.

And if twenty-first-century America really is a service economy—and I guess it is, since 80 percent of American jobs are in the service industry—someone has to tell me: Why does the service here suck so bad? If we're the service people, why am I still on hold with Pan Am?

There was a recording that went viral about ten years ago of a Comcast customer service rep arguing endlessly with a customer who just wanted to cancel his service. It was eighteen minutes of a guy saying, "I'd like to cancel," followed by . . .

"Why?"

"Doesn't matter, just want to."

"Why?"

"Please, I'm just looking to terminate."

"Why?"

I'm no business expert, but I don't think your customer service experience is supposed to feel like a car ride with a four-year-old.

Comcast later apologized and said, "This is not how we train our customer service representatives." Except for one tiny detail: it's exactly how they train them. They're not in the service industry—they're in the small-print industry, and this is the new business model in America: annoying you out of your money. Wearing you down until you're too weak to complain, and then when you just can't go on, and die, charging you for early cancellation.

Or just make something up and put it on a bill and hope no one notices. What the hell is a "resort fee" at a hotel? Resort fee? I went straight to my room, rubbed one out and went to bed. When was I resorting? Why, because you have a treadmill? It's like going to a restaurant and being charged extra because they have a candle on the table. Why not just have the maid take a couple twenties out of my wallet when she's in the room? We'll call it "an undocumented surcharge."

Or how about the surcharge the airlines tack on for the privilege of bringing luggage on a trip? The airlines, always bitching about *their* costs—the price of jet fuel and unions and planes—as a justification for their fees. You know, if I want to hear a crying baby never shut up, I'll fly your shitty airline. Where you charge me a fee for checking my luggage now . . . and another one if it weighs too much and a fee for wanting to talk to a human on the phone. You want a blanket? Fee! You want to fly *inside* the plane? Fee! If Sully landed on the Hudson today, they'd charge a life vest fee. It can cost two hundred dollars just to change your ticket. Multiply that by the number of sad sacks too hungover to make their flight out of Vegas, and you see how in America now, there's no margin for fucking up.

Why? Because they can. Because mergers and consolidation and no options are great for business. The flight attendant always says, "We know you have many choices in airlines . . ." And I always think, "Come on, that line is older than you."

Back in the day, flying was a joy. The seats were roomy, the chicken looked like something that was once a chicken and the bathrooms were large enough to *enjoy* the mile-high club. The seat in front of you could recline without starting a fight.

I remember the first time I flew first class, and it blew my mind: they were literally carving a roast on the cart in the aisle like it was friggin' Thanksgiving up there.

Contrast that with today, where there's first class, business class, premium economy, economy and fuck you.

And just like with the economy writ large, they squeezed incrementally. First they took away the pillows, then the free booze, the free headset, the free luggage allowance, legroom, the whole can of Coke, even the blankets, putting an end to in-flight masturbation.

On the upside, the flight safety films are "funny" now, so porn parodies have something to look down on.

But here's the thing about squeezing people and keeping them insecure: it virtually ensures that our long-term, major problems never get fixed. Because reducing the debt or repairing infrastructure or reversing climate change are things that require long-term thinking, which is something you can't really do when the wolf is always at the door.

Bangladesh will be underwater in twenty years? I'm underwater *today*.

Vulture capitalism has done to our middle class what the airlines did to their customers—because we didn't lose the comforts of being middle class all at once. They took them away from us an inch at a time, just like the legroom on a plane.

When I was a kid, being a middle-class family meant only one breadwinner, two cars, a vacation and a paneled basement that smelled like cigarettes. College was affordable, getting sick didn't mean going bankrupt and you could go out to dinner once a week. You could have a dog, and when he got older, your parents could afford to send him to live on a farm where he was, um, happier.

But, little by little, the middle class got squeezed. Now "middle-class" means two breadwinners and one car, and the only reason your daughter can afford college at all is Sugardaddies.com.

Our economy no longer creates a middle class, it sucks it dry. Sometimes "middle-class" just means you're poor but you don't do meth. And remember, *this is the good economy*, where 40 percent of Americans can't afford a $400 emergency expense and fifty million have nothing saved for retirement. Sorry, but it's not middle-class when your retirement plan is a lotto ticket.

Americans keep asking, "Why doesn't our economy work for people like me?"

Because it's not designed to. Because somewhere along the way, we bought into this insane idea that everything always has to get bigger. Economic performance is always about one thing: growth. Having a really good year and then just repeating it? Not good enough! In corporate America, where the stock market is the tail that wags the dog, growth is the only thing that matters. *Better* than last quarter. *Beat* expectations. Eat *more* hamburgers.

Next time Apple wants to really "think different," they should try *not* releasing a new phone every year. Because somebody should teach Americans that we don't always have to have something newer and better every year. Or, in the case of our upside-down economic system, every quarter. The only people who really need you to get a new phone every year are the shareholders.

But just because they need to sell it so they can jerk off the stock price, it doesn't mean you have to stand in that nerd line and buy it. You're not "early adopting." In fact, quite the opposite; you're taking too long to catch on.

And I know what the people on that line are thinking: "Oh, Bill, the old phone had an A9 processor and a camera with an aperture of 2.2, and the new one has an A10 and a 1.8! And the old phone weighed 143 grams, the new one 138! I guess you *could* keep lugging around a 143-gram phone in your pocket if you want your ass to stick out!"

OK, but you've already got in your hand a device that has all your email, all your music, the Internet and GPS, and takes pictures, gets you laid, gets you a car and a driver when you're drunk, films cops when they shoot you and oh yeah, it's a phone. It does everything but scratch your nuts for you, and I'm sure there's an app for that. It has Pokémon Go *and* Grindr, an app that enables guys to poke-a-man and go.

So why is the financial section always blaring headlines like "Why Apple Needs a New Hit" or "Is a New iPhone Enough to Snap Apple's Sales Slump?" Sales slump? Since 2007, that phone has made over 1.6 *trillion* dollars. To put that into perspective, take the amount of money Donald Trump has given to charity . . . and add 1.6 trillion dollars.

For Apple, revolutionizing the world wasn't enough—that was *last* quarter!

And it's not just Apple, it's every company. Did you ever wonder, for example, why shaving needs to keep reinventing itself? Men used to shave with a sharp rock. Then there was the straight razor. The single-blade razor, the double-blade razor, the three-blade razor and now the Quattro.

Let me tell you something—if you've got something on your face that doesn't come off after three blades, that's not a whisker, that's a tumor.

THE REAM TEAM

One of the casualties in the January 6 attack on the Capitol was Ashli Babbitt, a Trump-loving small-business owner who had a pool-cleaning company in San Diego. She was an air force vet who served in Iraq and Afghanistan, and she lost her life trying to prevent Biden from becoming president, even though she had voted for the Obama/Biden ticket not that long ago.

The tragedy of the modern Republican voter is they never learned to stop hating the underprivileged and start hating the overprivileged. The greatest con Republicans ever pulled off was convincing the working class that it was immigrant dreamers and single moms on food stamps who were blocking them from the American Dream. They're pissed off at the greed and corruption that, yes, has squeezed the middle class hard, but always coming up with the wrong answer to the question "Who is doing the squeezing?"

Ashli Babbitt was in financial trouble because, in order to keep her business afloat, she resorted to a short-term loan with an interest rate of 169 percent. That's right, she was being charged 169 percent interest and went to Washington so she could chant, "Stop the steal."

She died for a second Trump term, even though that would have solved exactly none of her problems—the same mistake made by all of her friends in the Let's-Go-Brandon Brigade. They thought Trump was going to be their bull in the china shop. He was, but they didn't realize: they *were* the china. And they were smearing feces on the wrong walls.

I'm certainly not shy in calling out the many flaws of the Democrats, but if economic exploitation is your issue, I have to ask these people: Which party do you think would be more likely to help with that? Let me give you a hint: it's the one with Elizabeth Warren in it, not the one with Jared Kushner. Who once said, "The problem is people who don't work hard enough." Exactly, Jared! People who are too lazy to roll up their sleeves and inherit their own money.

Of course, Ashli lived in California, a state that's run entirely by Democrats and that also did exactly nothing to stop the charging of 169 percent interest on a loan. So you couldn't blame her for thinking, yes, California is a place that cares more about your toxic whiteness than your toxic brokeness.

This country is in quite a pickle. Conservatives govern without shame, and liberals shame without governing. It shouldn't be that surprising that America is full of fed-up, unhappy people who just want to break shit.

MARX MADNESS

America has a problem with socialism. Or actually, many problems: we don't know what it is, we don't know we already have it and we want either too much of it or not enough.

Conservatives say they hate socialism, but when it comes to Social Security, Medicare, unemployment, disability, Fannie Mae and Freddie Mac, corporate welfare, bailouts and farm subsidies—what they're really saying to socialism is, "I can't quit you."

One of the iconic lines in modern American history was delivered by an angry protester at a town hall in 2009: "Keep your government hands off my Medicare!" And that guy is not alone: in one survey, 40 percent of people who get Medicare say they have not used a government program. Who do you think paid for that hip replacement, a secret benefactor?

The actor and not very bright person Craig T. Nelson once said about hitting some rough spots in his life, "I've been on welfare and food stamps. Anybody help me out? No."

And that's what's so hard about being a closeted lover of big government—you have to lie to yourself. But here's a message to all of you deniers: It gets better. Or at least it could.

Every modern democracy is a hybrid of capitalism and socialism—as it should be. You think you can't make big money in Finland or Sweden? Tell that to the billionaires who run Spotify and Nokia. Of course, the difference between American socialism and European socialism is European socialism works. For their tax dollars, Europeans get full health care coverage, a generous pension, day care, long paid vacations, maternity leave, free college and public transportation that doesn't smell like pee.

Whereas our tax dollars go toward military bases in Germany, subsidies to oil companies, wars and building bridges to nowhere. And yes, this being the human race, some percentage goes to grifters and fakers. (See chapter 11.) But Europeans get universal health care; we get a Blue Angels flyover at the Fiesta Bowl. They've got Airbus. We've got *the* bus.

And I still don't hear Democrats explaining that the programs that *do* work, like Medicare and Social Security and the Obamacare ban on denying coverage for preexisting conditions, *are* socialism.

Trump once gave farmers a $12 billion bailout to make up for his stupid tariffs, which meant we took tax money from some people—mostly in New York and California—and gave it to farmers. That's socialism.

Socialism is the reason you don't have to bring your own highway when you want to drive somewhere. The US military builds weapons that even the Pentagon says it doesn't want—that's a jobs program. Someone needs to explain to the "Free Market Solves Everything" crowd that when it comes to socialism, you're soaking in it.

Florida's Senator Marco Rubio says, "If you want to live in a socialist country, why not move to a socialist country?" You mean like Florida, where half the population is on Social Security? Yes, so many Americans hate the word "socialism" but love the concept. Forget the transgender debate, what America really needs is a separate bathroom for welfare queens.

In 1961 Ronald Reagan said if we passed Medicare we'd wind up telling our children "what it once was like in America when men were free." Thanks, Nostradumbass. Republicans always think if you allow a little socialism it'll spread out of control—but actually, it's capitalism that has spread to places it never should be, like our health care system, our prison system and our news media.

I'm not arguing against the free market—just not for *everything*. Socialism as an economic model replacing capitalism is a terrible idea, but socialism as a *supplement* to capitalism is good. Kind of like how gin and tonic are terrible by themselves, but mixed together: delightful.

Republicans think socialism is a one-way ticket to becoming the nightmare of Venezuela—they have a hard time understanding that done right, you don't get "long lines for bread" socialism, you get "you don't have to win the lotto to afford brain surgery" socialism.

That's the form of socialism that a lot of the happiest countries in the world embrace. There's a reason the UN World Happiness rankings consistently list socialism-friendly places like Finland, Norway, Denmark, Iceland, Switzerland, Sweden, the Netherlands and Canada near the top.

Because happiness isn't only about what you have. It's also about what you don't have to worry *about*. All the countries on the list are ones with some form of universal health care. All have free or almost free higher education. All have strong pensions and social safety nets. Turns out, freedom from the fear of ending up in a tent below the overpass is a really great freedom too. It's called peace of mind.

Conservatives push the canard that unfettered capitalism makes you more free; but the right kind of socialism can make you the most free. In fact, let's not even call it socialism. Call it "capitalism plus." Because that's what it is. It's a plus when you get sick and you can focus on getting better instead of not going broke. It's a plus when you get pregnant and can think of anything besides "What's this little shit gonna cost me?"

Bernie Sanders tweeted that in the US it costs $12,000 to have a baby, while in Finland it costs $60, and supposedly smart Republican presidential wannabe Nikki Haley responded with: "Comparing us to Finland is ridiculous. Ask them how their health care is. You won't like the answer." Actually, it's Nikki Haley who didn't like the answer, because it turns out they have Twitter in Finland too, and a lot of Finns gave testimony about how much they like their health care.

For example, in the US, the maternal death rate is almost seven times what it is in Finland. Isn't that odd? They only pay sixty bucks to have a baby, yet they don't die. It's almost as if our system kind of sucks. You know why we can't have nice things like Finland has? Because we're ruled by corporatist nincompoops like Nikki Haley who write books with titles like *Can't Is Not an Option*. When in America, "can't" is not only an option, it's often the only option.

We look at the rankings of the happy nations and see we're getting our ass kicked by people in wooden shoes. Christ, there's no sun half the year in a lot of these places, and they're still in a better mood—how can that be? You mean the average Norwegian guy is happier than us? His car is a bicycle and his dinner is canned fish *again*. The women in his country look like Tilda Swinton, and the men in his country also look like Tilda Swinton. But he's happy because he's not constantly sweating a mountain of student debt or gallbladder surgery.

Socialism is needed to curtail capitalism, like a raging river needs the occasional dam, because the profit motive creates horrible incentives that must be curbed. Like treating bullshit as "breaking news."

But let's also not romanticize socialism the way conservatives romanticize capitalism. These are economic systems, not your first kiss.

It's funny; older people think socialism is capitalism's enemy, and younger people think it's capitalism's replacement, but they're both wrong: socialism is capitalism's Lap-Band—something to prevent it from eating everything.

If you say the word "socialism" to people under forty, the reaction is night and day from that of baby boomers, for whom socialism has always been seen as communism's gay cousin. But for millennials, the word "socialism" doesn't conjure up images of Stalin and Castro; it conjures up images of naked Danish people on a monthlong paid vacation. Millennials and Gen Z don't remember a threatening Soviet Union or *any* Soviet

Union—the only time they've ever had to crouch under a desk was to go down on their teacher.

So the new generations are ready for socialism—problem is, they may be ready for a little too *much* socialism. To bail ourselves out of the Great Depression, America spent 6 percent of our gross domestic product over a decade. To get out of Covid, we spent, in one year, 26 percent of GDP. The way we handed out money, you'd think it had an expiration date on it. Defeating the combined fascist powers of Nazi Germany and Italy and imperial Japan—otherwise known as World War II—cost $4 trillion in today's dollars. Covid cost $6 trillion. That's nutty.

In 2008, when the global economy was on the edge of collapse, Congress passed what was then considered a massive bailout of $700 billion—so massive, over a hundred protests broke out across the country. The Occupy Wall Street movement was born. Now? The word "billion" is so two thousand *late*.

Bernie Sanders was adored by young voters because he promised free college and free universal health coverage for no more than an extra thousand dollars in taxes, even though that's not really socialism—that's Santa-ism. And look, no one's arguing that millennials haven't gotten a rotten deal in this economy, but they've also gotten too used to getting shit for free, from being able to sit in Starbucks all day for the price of a scone to free music and Wi-Fi and birth control.

We've accepted that the new normal in America is people in their twenties and even thirties still on their parents' cell phone plans and health care plans, Mom and Dad still paying their car insurance and almost a third of them still living at home. If you're under forty, you may never have known the concept of paying for certain things that all of us used to pay for.

I'm a baby boomer—I think the natural order of things is to pay for music I like. To do less doesn't make you a revolutionary, it makes you the person who goes to the bathroom when the check comes.

And it's not just music—what about what stealing someone's work has done to pornography? I was still in my prime masturbating years when porn became free, and I saw how it decimated a proud industry that once produced full-length features with plots and pubic hair.

Just like with musicians, the men and women of the adult industry who entertain and divert and, yes, release millions of Americans every day deserve to be paid for what they do. Porn doesn't just happen, people—locations must be scouted, sets must be built and wood must be maintained. Think about the long hours put in by horny housewives and naughty secretaries, and the hardworking, shaven-headed, dead-eyed meth addicts plowing them. They're not doing it for shits and giggles. That costs extra. When I hear about people stealing porn, I have one question: Where do you get off?

BEING FOR THE BENEFIT OF MR. BYTE

Nothing with "crypto" in the title ever turns out good, and that includes cryptocurrency.

One in ten Americans used their Covid stimulus checks to invest in one of thousands of cryptocurrencies in existence, Bitcoin being the most famous. But there's also Ethereum, Tether and even one called CumRocket. There's also one called Dogecoin that someone started "as a joke," but as far as I can tell, it's exactly the same as all the other cryptocurrencies, because the whole thing is a joke.

I understand that our financial system isn't perfect, but at least it's real. Nike stock is worth money because Nike makes sneakers that give jobs to Vietnamese teenagers. But Dogecoin at one point rallied to be worth more than the market cap of Ford and Kraft Foods, and it has no product and no workers—it's just Easter Bunny cartoon cash.

I've read articles about cryptocurrency, had it explained to me, and I still don't get it—and neither do you or anyone else.

I'll explain why. OK, there's these things called "nerds." And in 2008, one of them—we don't know who, because this person or group of persons is still anonymous—made up Bitcoin out of thin air using the fake name Satoshi Nakamoto, which I think are the Japanese words for "Monopoly Money."

Now, capitalism, of course, has always contained an element where, instead of actually making something or providing a service for money, you could make money in the exciting field *of* money. But we knew money had to originate from, and be generated by, something real somewhere—to which cryptocurrency says, "No it doesn't."

Maybe this is why Warren Buffett said, "Cryptocurrencies basically have no value and they don't produce anything . . . What you hope is that somebody else comes along and pays you more money for them later on, but then that person's got the problem. In terms of value: zero." Or to put it another way: it's a Ponzi scheme. It's like having an imaginary best friend who's also a banker.

This is how the world economy crashed in 2009—it wasn't the lost value in actual houses that sank us, it was this "virtual market" that required inventing algorithms to bet on how much houses might be worth in a virtual scenario. But then the landlord called in the bill for this virtual market, because, in Adult Land, it turns out the landlord is always real.

Our problem here is, at root, not economic but psychological: people who have been raised in a virtual world are starting to believe they can really live in it. Much of warfare is a video game now; why not base our economy the same way?

And cryptocurrency is literally a game. Bitcoins are created by what they call "mining"—but not the kind of mining that's done by seven dwarfs who share a woman. This kind of mining involves using rooms full of supercomputers to make something that is purposefully arbitrary: essentially, one computer thinks of a number between one and infinity and other computers take trillions of guesses at what it is. It's the old game of "I'm thinking of a number between one and ten" except times a gazillion, and the guy guessing the number lives in China and the guy who knows the number lives in the Matrix. Take that, work.

Do I need to spell this out? There's something inherently not credible about creating trillions in virtual wealth with nothing ever actually being accomplished and no actual product made or service rendered. It's like Tinker Bell's light—its power source is based solely on enough children believing in it.

Unfortunately, what is real is the unfathomable amount of electricity that those massive supercomputers suck up for their "mining." The power being used right now to guess numbers and win imaginary prizes is the same as all the electricity needed to light all of New York City.

Bill Gates said, "Bitcoin uses more electricity per transaction than any other method known to mankind." Just one uses more energy than a million Visa transactions and has the same carbon footprint as eighty-five thousand hours of watching YouTube—or what a fifteen-year-old calls "the weekend."

Almost all the people who tout Bitcoin and deal in Bitcoin and who won't shut the fuck up about Bitcoin—the millennials, the Gen Z–ers, the Silicon Valley types—are the same people who see themselves as hip and progressive and big environmentalists.

Bullshit. You're money-hungry opportunists and you're not allowed to pretend you care about the environment. According to the journal *Nature*, Bitcoin's growth could single-handedly push global temperatures above the tipping point of two degrees Celsius. Because it's a Beanie Baby that runs on coal. I know, melting ice caps can wait, *your* green new deal involves cash. Social scientists call this "cognitive dissonance"—a disconnect between who you think you are and what you actually do. I call it "being full of shit."

RANKS FOR EVERYTHING

Someone has to tell me, when did America decide to redesign its entire economy based on everyone rating everyone else? Does every interaction have to be followed by a survey? Let's bring back "I give you money, you give me lightbulbs and we both go on with our lives."

Enough with the "Was it good for you too?" Look, I just want to fuck, I don't want to talk about your good qualities and where you can improve—because you're not my girlfriend, you're Roto-Rooter. Snake my drain and move on. Amazon doesn't need to do a follow-up on every purchase: "How did you like that shower curtain?"

Great. It blew my mind.

Or when they ask, "Would you be willing to share your experience?" Yes, let me get right on that. I was gonna screw the wife after dinner, but let me sit down and type out a three-hundred-word story about how much I liked your fucking cookie.

How many times when you're on hold have they asked you to "stay on the line after the call to answer a survey"? Why would I want to stay on the line *after* the call when I couldn't get someone on the line *during* it? "How would you rate your customer satisfaction?" Oh, definitely a four. As in "for fuck's sake, leave me alone."

When did American business get so insecure? I was even asked recently to rate my "experience" in the airport bathroom. Which was poor. I didn't meet a single Republican congressman. But come on, it's an airport bathroom—what do you want me to say? "Of all the urinal cakes I've ever pissed on, LaGuardia's are the finest." Why does *Denny's* need to be on Yelp? There's already a way to tell if Denny's sucks: there's a sign out front that says "Denny's."

How about this: If you didn't like the way a company conducted its business, stop using it. This seemed to work for the first million years of commerce: the practice of either rewarding a company with repeat business or going somewhere else.

People's jobs shouldn't depend on some rando judging them, and I don't want to be the one narcing on hardworking people in shit jobs. If the waiter forgets my salad, I get over it. I don't whip out my phone: "Bitch, you're going down!"

And stop rating *me*! I don't want to have to be "on" all the time. When I get into an Uber, I just want to chill out and enjoy the Armenian disco music. I'd give ten stars for just one honest Uber ride: "Hi, I'm your Uber, Dan. I hate my life." "I'm your ride, Bill. I'm hungover. So, shut the fuck up."

It's not a good mental space to be in to constantly be asked to "rate" each other. We're supposed to be the "freedom" people, but we're always being watched, tracked and rated—on camera at traffic lights, ringing doorbells, at the ATM; being watched at gas stations, in elevators and parking lots. Married people complain they can't cheat anymore because cell phones and cars are now tracking devices. It's impossible to have an affair because Siri can't keep her big mouth shut.

I don't want to become China, where they have a "social credit system" where you get brownie points—or demerits—for your behavior as it's observed by cameras and by your fellow citizens, almost like a financial credit score, except it's on *you*, a human being who sometimes has a bad day. But you can't ever have one now. Let's not go there.

Which is why I've created a new site called Rotten-*er* Tomatoes—where you can review the reviews of other reviewers. I came up with that stoned. And I'm going to give that weed a nice review.

15

GUNS

WHO'S YOUR SADDY

America needs to ask itself this question: What do we do about the easy access to firearms by young men who simply feel like shit?

There's no shortage of reasons offered as to why America has a gun violence problem, but isn't a lot of it because America is an every-man-for-himself, winner-take-all culture that chews up and spits out people who don't keep up? You can fly as high as you want here, but if you fall by the wayside our response is: Sucks to be you. Unfollow. You want a friend? Get a gun.

About one-third of the people in America make less than $15 an hour—how much of a life can you really have on that budget? What is an American mass shooter, really, but a suicide bomber wearing Axe body spray? The NRA should change its slogan to "Guns don't kill people, seething loners who can't get laid kill people."

Yes, we have too many guns, but there are other reasons in the mix as to why America has an epidemic of gun violence, and one of them is because it has an epidemic of guys who were picked last in gym. Forget "red flags"—just find the guys who cut their own bangs. I know profiling is wrong, but if a guy takes his mother to the prom, he goes on the list. Does your fondest sexual memory involve two other people you heard through a wall? You've been selected for extra screening.

"Armed and lonely" is not a good combination—and America has a loneliness crisis. Twenty-two percent of millennials say they don't have any friends. Twenty-five percent say they don't even have an acquaintance. Ten percent didn't know that pizza comes in slices so someone else can have some.

Mass killers are always male, and almost always woman repellent. And what must make it even worse for them is in America, it just looks like everyone else is getting laid constantly. Every billboard, perfume ad and movie trailer is practically soft-core porn, and every corner of social media is full of bragging studs and sexy selfies.

Before Instagram, you could be a loser but not feel it, because the winners weren't always in your face. But now even the most mundane post of avocado toast in a hipster coffee shop sends the message "I'm having fun and you're not. Enjoy your Cup O' Noodles, loser." Social media tells you everyone is having *more* fun with *more* toys and *more* friends than you. They're always in Saint Kitts having mai tais at sunset, while you're in Canoga Park selling your plasma at dusk. YOLO!

We used to wake up, read the paper, see all the terrible things in the world and say, "Well, at least my life is better than those poor slobs'"—but now it's the opposite.

This is how the Internet gets you coming and going: guys watch the "haves" on Instagram and then go over to sites like 8chan to brood with the "have-nots." Being a loser used to just mean that you stayed home on Friday nights to get a head start on your Star Wars fan fiction—sure, you had a hard dick and no social skills, but it wasn't a *movement*.

But now, with sites like 8chan, it is. 8chan is where mass shooters post their "manifestos." It's where QAnon got started. 8chan is to lonely white men what the Hometown Buffet is to gastric bypass patients: both dangerous and inescapable.

In 2015, a good-looking young man who drove a Mercedes and attended the University of California at Santa Barbara took out his frustrations on several women at the campus and left us with these words: "I've been forced to endure an existence of . . . unfulfilled desires all because girls have never been attracted to me . . . I've never even kissed a girl, and I will punish you all for it."

Which is either a cry for help or the worst eHarmony profile I've ever heard.

The Virginia Tech shooter was accused of following and harassing female students. Timothy McVeigh famously never had a date and almost certainly died a virgin. The Sandy Hook killer left a document on his computer explaining "why females are inherently selfish." Plainly, because they won't give it up to a real catch like him.

I don't know for a fact that no man in history has ever said, "Sex, sex, sex, that's all I ever do—where's my gun, I'm mad at the world!"—I just know it's true. Unrealized adolescent sexuality can be a very dangerous thing—just ask my hand.

This is why people need real friends—not chat room friends, not Facebook friends, not fellow paranoids feeding each other misinformation on a screen, but real, human friends. People who can look you in the eye and tell you your theories about the coming race war are horseshit. And who can tell you that social media isn't real, so stop comparing yourself to a fantasy. No one is having *that* much fun, they're just distorting reality to big themselves up. And if you knew how much everybody else is faking it, you wouldn't want to join them anyway.

LAND OF THE SPREE

Now that we live in an age of uber corporate responsibility, where every large company in America bends over backward to get on the politically correct side of every issue, Hollywood has to tell us: Why doesn't that include gun violence?

When liberals scream "Do something!" after a mass shooting, why aren't we also dealing with the fact that the average American kid sees two hundred thousand acts of violence on screens before the age of eighteen, and that according to the FBI, one of the warning signs of a potential school shooter is a fascination with violence-filled entertainment?

It's funny, Hollywood is the wokest place on Earth in every other area of social responsibility: they have intimacy coordinators on set to chaperone sex scenes, they hire sensitivity readers to go through and edit scripts, Disney stood up to the "don't say gay" law and another studio spent $10 million to digitally remove Kevin Spacey from a movie.

But when it comes to the unbridled romanticization of gun violence: crickets. Weird, the only thing we don't call a "trigger" is the one that actually has a trigger. If you make a movie today, you can't show bullying, fat shaming, slut shaming, girl chasing, gay baiting, ethnic stereotypes or underage hookups where drinking is involved—you know, what we used to call "comedies." Those things are bad, and everyone knows you can't "platform" bad things.

But you know what you can still platform? One guy—who's *the hero*—getting over a grudge by mowing down a multitude of human beings.

Now, am I saying don't make these movies? Not at all, I'm never for censorship or organizing society around what crazy people might do. But don't look me in the eye and tell me this isn't a big part of the problem. Every bad idea a kid can get about how to handle feeling abused and disrespected is in all these movies.

Now, the usual suspects on the Far Left will say that this is some sort of "conservative" rant, or that I'm undermining gun control, but it's neither; it's just what's real. There's a few reasons why mass shootings happen and we don't exactly know how much each of the pieces is responsible for, but the major ones are: mental health—that is, broken young men who feel like losers and want the world to hurt like they do; easy access to guns; kids having smartphones, which make losers feel even worse because of the bullying and all the fake lives that look better than theirs; and, yes, crazy amounts of gun violence in movies and TV.

We don't show movie characters smoking anymore because it might look cool and influence children, so please don't tell me cool-looking dudes shooting guns don't influence them.

And it's not just the idea presented over and over again that guns are the best solution to life's problems—it's *why* the hero is using a gun. They call them "action movies," but they should be called "revenge movies." Because that's the plot of every one of them.

Here's a list of just the action movies that have vengeance *in the title*: *Blind Vengeance. Bitter Vengeance. Cry Vengeance. Sweet Vengeance. Dark Vengeance. Fast Vengeance. Blue Vengeance. Forced Vengeance. Heated Vengeance. Naked Vengeance. Acts of Vengeance. Deadly Vengeance. Out for Vengeance. Bound to Vengeance. Fistful of Vengeance. Streets of Vengeance. Angel of Vengeance. Ministry of Vengeance. With a Vengeance. Code Name: Vengeance. Fort Vengeance. Kickboxer: Vengeance. Ninja Vengeance.*

And *The Taste of Vengeance*, my least-favorite Chinese restaurant. Vengeance has been in more movies than pets in sunglasses.

There's even a movie called *I Am Vengeance: Retaliation*, even though "retaliation" *means* "vengeance." It's like calling your movie *I Am Pregnant: Expecting.*

Getting revenge on them that wronged ya is what happens—it's *all* that happens—in movies that are made for, and loved by, young men. It's the male version of getting your groove back or Meryl Streep getting a big kitchen. Like every school shooter, our movie heroes are grievance collectors, and when it comes to "action" movies, there's one story: "He was a nice guy, but they pushed him too far and now it's on."

"They took my daughter!" (*Taken.*) "They killed my father!" (*The Northman.*)

"They killed my fiancé!" (*Kill Bill.*) "They killed my family!" (*Death Wish.*)

"They killed my family again!" (*Peppermint.*) "They killed my puppy!" (*John Wick.*)

All of which creates not just a culture of violence but a culture of *justified* violence. Liberals hated Kyle Rittenhouse, but somehow the liberal capital of the world is OK with making five hundred movies about vigilantes. They hate it when gun people say, "It takes a good guy with a gun to stop a bad guy with a gun," but then they endlessly produce movies with *that exact plot.*

16

TIME

THE PAST AND THE FURIOUS

You can get creative with a novel, a TV show or a movie, but history books? That's not supposed to be fan fiction. How we teach our kids history has become a big controversy these days, with liberals accusing conservatives of wanting to whitewash the past—and sometimes that's true.

But the woke want to abuse history to control the present, and in 2022 a scholar named James Sweet caught hell for calling them out for doing just that. He criticized a phenomenon known as "presentism," which means judging everyone in the past by the standards of the present; it's the belief that people who lived a hundred or five hundred or a thousand years ago really should have known better.

Which is so stupid—it's like getting mad at yourself today for not knowing what you know now when you were ten. Stupid me, spending all that time raising Sea-Monkeys and playing with slot cars and ogling old *Playboy*s in the woods behind my house.

Who doesn't have moments from your past that make you cringe?

Who hasn't said "I can't believe I said that, I can't believe I thought that, I can't believe I did that . . ." You ate dirt, you wanted to be a Ghostbuster, you shoplifted gum, you tried to be a white breakdancer. You wanted to marry Scott Baio.

I did incredibly stupid things that of course I regret. I smoked. I was into numerology. And astrology. And Christianity. I read Hemingway.

Yes, because we hadn't yet grown into the persons we would become—and humanity writ large is just the collective version of that.

Did Columbus commit atrocities? Of course. But people back then were generally atrocious. Everybody who could afford one had a slave, including people of color in other parts of the world.

The way people talk about slavery these days, you'd think it was a uniquely American thing that we invented in 1619. But slavery throughout history has been the rule, not the exception: the Sumerians, the Egyptians, the Greeks, the Romans, the Arabs, the British, the early Americans—all the way up through R. Kelly.

The Holy Bible is practically an owner's manual for slaveholders. The word "slave" comes from "Slav," because so many Slavic people were enslaved, and they're as white as the Hallmark Channel. Who do you think gathered the slaves from the interior of Africa to sell to slave traders? Africans, who also kept their own slaves. Humans are not good people. We're a species prone to making others of our species our bitch. And the capacity for cruelty is a human thing, not a white thing, even though that doesn't jibe with the current narrative.

But in today's world, when truth conflicts with narrative, it's the truth that has to apologize.

Being woke is like a magic moral time machine, where you judge everybody against what you imagine you would have done in 1066, and you always win. Professor Sweet is right about presentism: it's just a way to congratulate yourself about being better than George Washington because you have a gay friend, and he didn't. But if he were alive today, he would, and if you were alive then, you wouldn't.

Portland Public Schools teach kids that the idea of gender being mainly binary was brought here by white colonizers. The curriculum guide says, "When the United States was colonized by white settlers, their views around gender were forced upon the people already living here."

Not even *Star Trek* would try that story, where they discover a planet and give them separate bathrooms. It's like they finally discovered a Unified Theory of Wokeness, incorporating all their ideas about race, gender and colonizers. Like the New World was a great big diverse dance club and the Pilgrims were the bridge-and-tunnel crowd who came in and ruined everything.

The play *I, Joan* was presented in London recently, written by Charlie Josephine, who identifies as nonbinary and uses they/them pronouns. The play portrays Joan of Arc as—surprise—nonbinary with they/them pronouns. Which, if you think about it, makes even less sense because Joan, being French, spoke a language where every noun is masculine or feminine. Joan says in the play, "I'm not a girl. I don't fit that word," as if she's a character on *Euphoria*.

And while it's true Joan did wear pants, that's what the soldiers wore—and she was soldiering. But in the retelling, Joan would rather die than stop wearing men's clothing. But Joan of Arc wasn't executed by the fashion police—her trial went on for over two months, we have the transcript—and not once did she complain about being misgendered.

Which is not to say there isn't truth to the old rubric that history is written by the winners, and it is subjective. Napoleon said history is just a fable we all agree on. And he should know, because he was a deaf woman named Diane.

But it's also true that much of history is indisputably factual, because we have artifacts and coins and birth records and archaeology and somebody in Mesopotamia kept a record of how much grain they ate. It's not all up in the air to change or delete or reinvent based on what makes you feel better today.

A couple of years ago they made a movie called *The Aeronauts* about the scientists who broke the record for the highest altitude reached in a balloon. In fact, they were both men, but the movie made one of them a woman because, as the director explained, "representation is important." So true. Women never get enough credit for the things they didn't do. Meryl Streep should play Seabiscuit, so every girl will know she too can grow up to be a racehorse.

OK, GLOOMER

Presentism has a companion disease, and it's called progressophobia. That's the term coined by Steven Pinker to describe a brain disorder that makes people, usually liberals, incapable of recognizing progress. It's like situational blindness, only what you can't see is that your dorm in 2024 is better than the South before the Civil War. If you think America is more racist now than ever, more sexist than before women could vote and more homophobic than when blow jobs were a felony, you are suffering from progressophobia.

Before 2012, every time gay marriage was put before a state's voters, it lost: *thirty-five times in a row.* Now it's the law of the land in every state. Even half of Republicans are for it; the other half are for closeted gay sex.

The chant from gay protesters used to be "We're here, we're queer, get used to it." Well, we did. Pride Month is not even a big deal anymore: thirty days of parades and festivals celebrating a cause that was once so divisive Ellen pretended to be straight. You literally can't find a major American corporation that doesn't do something for Pride Month. NASCAR does it. Raytheon, maker of high-tech, lethal weaponry that kills people from the sky, does it. Next year they're going to paint "You go, girl!" on the side of their missiles.

Statehouses fly pride flags now. Disney celebrates it. By federal law, every single TV show must include a storyline about lesbians having a baby. If someone announces they're gay on TV, it's met with thunderous applause.

My *accountant* says "Yas queen."

Not that long ago, I knew people who went to prison for growing pot; today you can legally smoke it for fun in 46 percent of the country, and I will.

Even something like bullying—it still happens, but being outwardly cruel to people who are different is no longer acceptable. That's progress, and acknowledging progress isn't saying, "We're done," or "We don't need more." And being gloomier doesn't make you a better person.

In 1958, only 4 percent of Americans approved of interracial marriage. Now Gallup doesn't even bother asking—the last time they did, in 2013, 87 percent approved. An overwhelming majority of Americans now say they *want* to live in a multiracial neighborhood—that's a sea change from when I was a kid. Employees of color make up 53 percent of Microsoft, 53 percent of Target and 56 percent of The Gap, as companies become desperate to look like their TV commercials.

Old sitcoms like *Friends* look weird now because if you even suggested a show today about six people, all of whom were straight and white, the network would laugh you out of the room.

And yet there is a recurrent theme on the far left that things have never been worse. Kevin Hart expressed a view many hold when he told the *New York Times*, "You're witnessing white power and white privilege at an all-time high."

This is one of the big problems with wokeness: That what you say doesn't have to make any sense. Or jibe with the facts. Or ever be challenged, lest the challenge itself be conflated with racism.

But saying white power and privilege are at an all-time high is just ridiculous. Higher than in 1921, the year of the Tulsa race massacre? Higher than the years when the KKK rode unchecked and Jim Crow went unchallenged? Higher than the 1960s, when the Supremes and Willie Mays still couldn't stay in the same hotel as the white people with whom they were working? Higher than during slavery? And I mean *actual* slavery, not Prince-doesn't-like-his-record-contract slavery.

Racism is unfortunately still with us—we have the footage. In policing, housing, job discrimination, segregated schools and wealth inequality, the legacy of injustice sadly lives on and demands remedial action. I try to understand, as best I can, how racism singes a person's soul so much that they see it everywhere.

But seeing clearly is necessary for actually fixing problems, and clearly racism is simply no longer everywhere. It's not in my house, and it probably isn't in yours. For most of the country, the most unhip thing you could ever be today is a racist. The cops who were responsible for killing George Floyd were not backed up by their fellow officers, and that never used to happen.

The low point of race relations wasn't a white girl wearing cornrows, even though it happened on Snapchat and George Wallace standing in a doorway didn't. Because here's the thing, kids: there actually was a world before you got here. We date human events AD and BC, but we need a third marker for millennials and Gen Z, BY: before you.

It's telling that in a recent Harvard Youth Poll of Americans between eighteen and twenty-nine, 72 percent of Black respondents said they were hopeful about the future of America, as compared to only 46 percent of white respondents. I'm not surprised. There are a hell of a lot of Americans trying really hard these days to embrace a new spirit of inclusion and self-reflection.

This progressive allergy to acknowledging societal advances is self-defeating, because progress, and the hope that we can achieve it, is the product progressives are selling. And having a warped view of reality leads to policies that are warped: Black-only dorms and graduation ceremonies; a growing belief in "whiteness" as a malady and white people as irredeemable; giving up on a colorblind society. Only if you believe we've made no progress does any of this make sense.

I can name some things that actually *are* worse than they've ever been, like the health of the oceans and homelessness and the prospects for maintaining an actual democracy in America. But where progress has been made, it's not a sin, and it's certainly not inaccurate, to say *we've come a long way, baby*. Not "mission accomplished." Just a long way.

THE EVOLUTION WILL NOT BE TELEVISED

The woke are funny—they believe in evolution, except when it comes to people.

Kamala Harris ran for attorney general in California in 2010, and I contributed to her campaign, even though I was disappointed when she opposed legalizing marijuana.

But then she changed her mind and now she's for it. That's all that matters. We don't need to beat her up about 2010. That's called "learning." We used to want that in a leader. Obama was against gay marriage when he became president, as was most of the country. But then he said he was "going through an evolution on this issue."

Humans evolve. You could be against gender-inclusive bathrooms and then one day change your mind because you have to take a wicked piss.

The new trick in Democratic politics is to dig up something your opponent said decades ago that looks bad by today's standards and then pretend that it's mic-drop evidence of your awesome moral superiority.

The woke need to stop pretending that if they were alive back then, they wouldn't have been the same asshole as everyone else. Yes you would. I know your parents told you that you were exceptional, but not to the point of seeing the future. Stop flattering yourself that you're Nostradamus and would have foreseen, had you been around *then*, everything that's unacceptable *now*.

You would have driven without seat belts and drunk when you were pregnant and hit your kids and hit your neighbor's kids. Because wokesight is not 20/20 and you don't have ESPCP—"extra-sensory politically correct perception."

If you were around in the 1980s, you would have worn the giant shoulder pads, and if you were around in the 1780s and were rich and white, you likely would have had slaves or had no problem with those who did.

The first abolition society in America was founded in 1775. It had twenty-four members. Twenty-four people in the whole country thought slavery was wrong the year before we declared independence. Stop being surprised we used to be dumber than we are now.

You're not morally better than your grandparents, you just came later. You're the iPhone 14.

It's funny, nobody has trouble grasping technological evolution. Nobody writing a love note with a quill ever said, "Why can't I send a dick pic?" Nobody in 1975 asked, "Why isn't my TV flat?" or "Why is my eight-track not satellite radio?"

Nobody speaking into the first cell phone, which looked like a Kleenex box, was mad at it because it wasn't a smartphone yet. Things get obsolete because we grow and improve, including us. Can we please stop pointing out people breaking rules that didn't exist yet and just grandfather in the shit *you* would have done if *you* were alive then?

A GRIEF HISTORY OF TIME

I think we should all listen to Lisa Simpson, who spoke for millions when she addressed the controversy some years ago around Apu, an Indian character on *The Simpsons* who runs a convenience store and speaks with an accent:

"Something that started decades ago and was applauded and inoffensive is now politically incorrect . . . What can you do?"

Twenty years ago, the jokes on old sitcoms were just funny. Now some younger viewers find the jokes sexist, transphobic and fat shaming. OK, but if you spend time combing through old TV shows to identify stuff that by today's standards looks bad, you're not "woke," you're just a douchebag with too much time on your hands.

Molly Ringwald got a lot of attention a few years ago when she "revisited" *The Breakfast Club* and her other eighties movies and found them "troubling" in the age of Me Too. She said she was "taken aback by the scope of the ugliness." Oh please, they were teen comedies, not snuff films.

Ringwald said, "It's hard for me to understand how John Hughes was able to write with so much sensitivity, and also have such a glaring blind spot." Should we dig him up and yell at him? You can't blame someone for not being "woke" thirty years before "woke" was a thing. I remember the eighties: "being woke" meant you'd had too much cocaine.

Enough with "revisiting" things. Stop being surprised every time you watch an old movie or TV show and find some of the ideas in it didn't age well.

You can't enjoy music, movies or TV from *any* era without hearing or seeing something we just don't do anymore. But aren't we adult enough to separate what we like about an old movie from what we don't? We can watch *Big* as a movie about a kid who becomes an adult and not as a movie about a grown woman who fucks a twelve-year-old.

The most beloved and wholesome act in history is the Beatles, but even they wrote, "She was just seventeen. You know what I mean," which today sounds a little "Prince Andrew on Epstein Island." They also sang, "I'd rather see you dead, little girl, than to be with another man," and "I used to be cruel to my woman, I beat her." Jeez, if all you need is love, how come they keep threatening everybody?

But that last lyric is from the song "Getting Better," which is what we've been doing. It's all you *can* do. Because every generation could be called the "What Were You Thinking?" Generation.

In the early 1900s heroin was in children's cough medicine. In the fifties amphetamines were sold to housewives as diet pills. We used to drive without seat belts and drink while we were pregnant and litter indiscriminately—just throw shit out the car window.

We smoked on airplanes! We'd board an enclosed aluminum tube with old people and children and asthmatics *and light up a Chesterfield.* We had pageants where we paraded women in swimsuits and judged them on their appearance . . . Oh, wait, we still do that?

And that's the point—we're never finished evolving. I hate to break it to you, but no matter how woke you think you are, you're tolerating things right now that will make you cringe in twenty-five years. Beauty pageants, mass incarceration, putting our parents in old-age homes, how we treat animals . . . The humans of tomorrow will be horrified by *us*. They won't believe we used to sexualize people during sex.

Millennials seem to think they came along right as society met perfection. As if future generations will look at man buns and the giant, stupid lobe-stretching earrings and say, "That was the moment civilization peaked, we can add nothing more."

No, actually, one day your kids will grow up and ask, "What's TikTok and why were you on it all day?" "What's a 'reality TV star' and how did one become president?"

You can't believe people in old movies smoked? They won't believe you put the cell phone in your pocket next to your nuts.

I have a feeling young people look at the clothes we wore in the late eighties with the giant shoulder pads and think, "They had to be doing it as a goof." No, we thought we looked good. We all did it, we walked the streets every day with giant shoulder pads, and it went on for years and years and no one said anything . . . we turned away and we let it happen because we wanted our shoulders to look really, really big!

So let's chill out on busting balls for breaking rules that didn't exist at the time. The arc of history is long, but it bends away from Hammer pants.

17

EARTH

SMOTHER NATURE

You remember the Zombie Lie, right? Talking points that were either never right, like "tax cuts pay for themselves," or were proven wrong, like "in-person voter-fraud is rampant," or became wrong when things changed—and yet people refused to stop telling them. Well, there needs to be a subcategory: Zombie Lie, Environmental Edition. And, Republicans, you have to own it, because they all came from you. Starting with . . .

"I don't believe man-made global warming is settled in science," because that feeds the "needs more study" myth. Of course, scientific fact is never unanimous; there will always be some mountain man somewhere with a PhD in birdcalls who says temperature spikes are caused by God farts. However, in 2013 an MIT professor studied almost eleven thousand peer-reviewed articles about climate change and there were only *two* dissenters.

So yes, there is a scientific community that doubts climate change— but it could fit on a motorcycle.

236

Or how about this one: "Let's not panic about the Earth warming, because in the seventies, everyone was told global cooling was a really big problem."

No, not everyone, really just one article in *Newsweek* that for the deniers is the "Dewey Defeats Truman" of science: the one time a newspaper, in 1948 Chicago, got an election result wrong, and it proved that journalism is a hoax and "Chicago" is just a theory.

But here's the thing about that *Newsweek* story: it didn't say an overwhelming consensus of scientists thought the Earth was cooling; it said a few were floating that theory. Or as Mike Huckabee remembered it: "When I was in college, all the literature at that time from the scientific community said that we were going to freeze to death." And again, by "all the literature," he means one *Newsweek* article.

Just for context, *Newsweek* also predicted that M. Night Shyamalan would be the next Steven Spielberg; he wasn't even the next Murray Spielberg.

There are so many eco Zombie Lies, like "carbon is good for you," "the climate is always changing" and "I just made a snowball."

And who could forget "Al Gore has a big house."

But my favorite is the one that says even though there may be a scientific consensus, consensuses have been wrong before. Ted Cruz once said, "Just look at Galileo." Ted, I worked with Galileo. Galileo was a friend of mine. You, sir, are no Galileo. But as long as you want to look at Galileo, the consensus he disproved was that the sun orbits the Earth, which wasn't a *scientific* consensus, it was a Bible myth from cavemen. *He* was the scientist!

And of course, that's the Republican politicians' longtime favorite dodge when it comes to the climate, the one they all say all the time: "I'm not a scientist . . ."

No, you're a legislator, which means you have to vote on things like building new highways. Even though you're not a dump truck.

FOSSIL FOOLS

If insanity is defined as doing the same thing over and over expecting a different result, we have to stop being insane in our approach to fixing the environment and try something new.

I don't know what will work, but I know what *didn't* work: Asking people to be good. Trying to convince our own citizens, and other countries, to use less, pollute less and sacrifice more. When you tell humans, "If you do these environmentally friendly things, we all can continue to live," their response is: "What's in it for me?"

To be clear: I believe more than ever that climate change is an emergency, but I don't think we're going to win this by grocery shopping with a laundry bag, or banning gas stoves, or imagining a human can really drink a milkshake through a paper straw. Scrolling on your phone can use more energy in a day than the refrigerator, but no one's ever going to give that up; we'd have to go back to having sex with people we know. And we all must be aware what buying everything from Amazon does to the environment, but do we stop?

It's just not in us. Including me. And I'd like to come clean: my name is Bill, and I fly private.

And so does every other person who calls themselves an "environmentalist" who *can*. It's not hard to find pictures of all your favorite stars and politicians who speak about the need to reduce our carbon footprint getting on a private plane. All the "environmentalists" of Hollywood and Washington do it. Their position on climate change is: "We must do more to stop pouring carbon into the air . . . except for me when I want to go somewhere. And then I take a private jet."

It turns out there's one thing in this world that is completely impossible to resist, and this is it. It's like heroin: if you do it once, you'll never stop. There are two kinds of people in the world: those who fly private, and those who would if they could.

A third category, those who could but do not . . . does not exist, except for Ed Begley Jr. and Greta Thunberg, and that's why you never see a picture of Greta smiling. Ed and Greta—that's who walks the walk. Everyone else is full of shit, and I'm done being full of shit. I can take being called a bad environmentalist, because almost all of us are, but I can't take being a hypocrite.

Now, I always justified renting a plane because I only used it for work and literally couldn't get to most of my stand-up gigs on time any other way—how do you think I did it all those years when I said good night on the set of *Real Time* in LA at eight p.m. and was onstage in Las Vegas at ten?

And don't tell me "the younger generation is better"—they're not, they're just poorer. They're actually worse: the family they look up to is the Kardashians, where everyone has their own private jet. And kids love Bitcoin, which takes an amount of computer processing that uses more electricity than some whole countries. Kids could have rejected that, but they didn't, they love it. Why? Because they want to be rich. *Why?* So they can *fly private*!

No one can resist: John Kerry is our climate czar and he uses a private jet. It's like if the secretary of Homeland Security smuggled drugs in his butt. People take private jets to environmental conferences—if you could run TED Talks on hypocrisy, you wouldn't need coal.

But sorry, not sorry. I tried to do my part for the environment: I never had kids, the one thing worse for the planet than private jets. I had the first-generation Prius in 2001, which looked like a Tylenol gelcap. I was always handing my keys to valets who were driving a better car than me. I had the first Tesla in 2010—and honestly, both these cars sucked. The Tesla came up to about my waist. If I had a hard-on I couldn't fit in this thing.

But both times I said to myself: OK, I'll take one for the team, because I have a platform, so I'll do the right thing and then everybody will follow. That's it, people will . . . they'll surely . . .

Nobody followed. In 2021, 80 percent of new vehicles weren't electric. They weren't even hybrid. They weren't even *cars*. They were SUVs and trucks. In 1973, the share of global electricity generated by coal was

38 percent. You know what it was forty-six years later in 2019 after all the talk and all the trying? Thirty-seven percent.

Do you know what percentage of plastic gets recycled? Five percent. Those blue bins that are everywhere? They're not full of bottles, they're full of shit. Can you blame us for being a little cynical when we find out that all the plastic that we've been painstakingly separating out for the last twenty years all goes to the same damn place anyway?

So, yes, it's fun to laugh at powerful people—that's how I can afford to fly private. But we need to get serious: More nuclear? Moving way more money into research and development? I don't know, but something serious. Because the real technological problem is the way people are wired. I know, it's easier to just blame Taylor Swift's plane. But honestly: Do you really want to be stuck on Southwest with a pissed-off Taylor Swift?

SHOP MAKING SENSE

Since America is such an incredibly fucked-up place right now, let's scale back our goal of making it great again and settle for making the mall great again. Just start with that, and get a W—and I'll tell you why it's actually a bigger win than you might think: because online shopping is killing us, psychologically and environmentally.

Did you ever wonder why shopping through the mail didn't become so big until this century? Of course, the Internet and smartphones made it easier, but the Sears catalog was founded in 1888. It *was* Amazon—just Amazon that never grew. People could have been getting everything in the mail a century and a half ago, and often with better reason to: before there were cars that made going to a store so easy. Why didn't they?

I don't know, but lately I've been seeing a lot of stories about how isolated and lonely people are—maybe it has something to do with that.

In the golden age of the mall, it was often called America's town hall, as marketplaces have always been the center of society. OK, ours was a little tacky, but it was better than ordering everything online, which is way more eco-unfriendly than driving to the store ever was.

And how could it not be, considering that Americans now shop by the most inefficient means humanly possible? Since we can't get off our asses to go try something on and see how it actually fits and looks and feels, we order nine of them and send eight back. Do you have any idea of the ecological shitshow that's caused just by making people chauffeur your pants all over town?

And look, I use Amazon, and love it like everyone else; I'm not saying Amazon is pure, unadulterated evil. That's Wells Fargo. But Amazon preys upon the Achilles' heel of the American character: we will sell our soul for convenience.

Back when people still went out, before brick-and-mortar stores were just for shoplifting, people didn't shop every day. They made these things called shopping "lists"—words that corresponded to items they needed—and then they went to the store or mall and gathered all the items on the "list" at one time.

As opposed to how we do it now, where robots, and humans who are treated like robots, pack your little bag of scrunchies in a box the size of a doghouse and deliver it to your home along with three other giant boxes, each containing one item. They ship a disposable razor in a box the size of a coffin and in enough plastic to choke a whale—which it eventually does.

Does anyone really need a grill cover to get to you overnight and in a separate box from something you ordered the day before from the same warehouse?

When I was a kid, getting a package was a rare event—now kids think the UPS man is their dad. Why do socks need a protective air cushion? I'm going to shove my foot in it and stomp on it all day. How can Amazon have a thousand types of shoehorns but only three sizes of box to send them in?

Where do we think all that packaging goes? We stuff it in blue bins like it's a portal to plastic heaven, but only 5 percent of it is actually recycled. The rest goes into landfills, incinerators and the ocean.

In 2009 America's most successful investor, Warren Buffett, went big on railroads, and everyone said, "Warren, you senile old coot, come on, we're living in the age of streaming and AI and Google glasses and robot dogs—railroads?! Hahaha!"

And Warren said, "Yeah, but after all of you are done clicking to get your Garden Weasels and avocado slicers, something has to actually get it to your door. For some reason, people just don't trust a condom made by a 3D printer. Good luck with Dogecoin."

There's a vaping device for pot that I—I mean a friend of mine—uses that has a feature that allows you to turn it on from an app on your phone—even though it has a button right on the side that works just as well.

Anyone under thirty who sees the app feature thinks it's the eighth wonder of the world because it doesn't work the old-timey way by pushing a button. It's so cool cuz it's on the *phone*!

Hey, kids, get a fucking clue: just because it's on the phone doesn't make it cool. We think we're super technologically advanced when we push a button, but every time you click "Buy It Now," a tree gets its wings. I know, we don't want to think about the kids who make it, or the truck that brings it, or the landfill where it ends up. We just want that T-shirt that says "Mindful."

It's all so easy: you clicked on the picture of the hot dog toaster and it appeared at your door, ready for you to toss in the garage. But it didn't come without a cost. It came across the Pacific on a diesel-powered cargo monster spewing sulfur.

The most downloaded shopping app in the US is for a Chinese company called Shein, which produces six thousand new styles a day and ships them direct from their warehouse in Guangdong to the twenty-four-year-old living in his old room who thinks he's an influencer.

Shein is part of a new industry called "fast fashion," which specializes in clothing that will absolutely, positively fall apart if you so much as look at it wrong. And that's deliberate. These clothes are made cheap—real cheap, out of the flimsiest materials possible—because apparently now

Gen Z and millennials like to buy clothes, wear them once and throw them away.

The average US consumer now throws out eighty pounds of clothing *each year*. I hear a lot about how my generation has ruined the environment—I don't think it's my generation that's doing this. And for what? So you can hear someone say "Nice dress—is that paper?"

BEEFER MADNESS

If the pandemic lockdowns taught us anything, it's that if you keep animals in cages, be they tigers or turkeys . . . it's humans who wind up being the prisoner.

Most infectious diseases are "zoonotic," meaning they start in animals and jump to humans. AIDS likely came from primates—someone butchered a monkey, or fucked one, or did something they shouldn't have been doing with a monkey. Mad cow came from cattle eating cattle, which is like feeding a chicken an omelet.

To thwart the coronavirus, we were told to create distance, avoid others who are sick, lower our stress and exercise. Are you surprised that diseases flourish among animals when they're forced to live in conditions that are the complete opposite of all that? They're on top of each other, they can't move, they're stressed out—I've seen airports treat luggage better than we treat animals. Egg-laying hens are starved and given no water for weeks to shock their bodies into molting. Beaks of chickens are removed. Have you ever driven by a high-density feedlot? To get relief from the stench you have to stick your nose in an egg salad sandwich.

Torturing animals is what got us into this mess. That's the lesson we keep refusing to learn: that you can't trash the environment—including animals—and not have it come back and kill *you*.

America's factory farming is just as despicable as a wet market and just as problematic for our health. Factory farms have a lot more lobbyists, but ecological time bombs tick the same. Americans should not get too high and mighty about wet markets while we're doing worse.

Eighty percent of pigs have pneumonia when they're slaughtered. Because we make them live in conditions that would make a zombie vomit. And then, so they don't die before we kill them, we pump them full of antibiotics, which in turn get passed on to humans, which leads to antibiotic-resistant diseases. It's Six Degrees of Tainted Bacon.

We're on the cusp of returning to a pre-antibiotic era where strep throat was a death sentence. Let me put it as basically as I can: if we keep producing food the way we do, you're going to get sick with something medicine can't fix. You don't have to care for the sake of the animals; I wouldn't want to mess with anyone's reputation as a heartless asshole. Do it because animal cruelty leads to human catastrophe.

The food supply is not what it appears to be. I hate to break it to you haute cuisiners, but did you know that your Chilean sea bass is neither Chilean nor bass nor from the sea? It's koi from the pond out front that the valet guys piss in. And your mahi mahi is really made of mercury-drenched bottom-feeders like tilefish that squirm along the ocean floor, eat feces and occasionally provide legal representation for Donald Trump.

And if you like sushi, you really don't know what you're eating, because those fish are mislabeled 74 percent of the time—which is really scary, because I can deal if the tuna in my tuna roll isn't tuna, but what the fuck is the eel?

And then there's IKEA. I didn't know you could eat there, but you can, and it turns out that in 2013 we found out their Swedish meatballs are a little too Seabiscuit-y—challenging all of our cherished notions about the integrity of food served at furniture stores. Sure, I was here buying a prefabricated bookshelf made of compressed sawdust and vinyl, but I didn't think they'd try to sell me something cheap!

If you think the wet market in Wuhan is gross, you should visit one of our giant poultry processing factories, but of course you can't because we have "ag gag" laws that make it a crime to report the crime—and it is a crime—of animal abuse that goes on in our food industry.

Because we're the United States of You Don't Wanna Know. Seven states have laws making it a crime to film inside a slaughterhouse.

Because when someone did that, and people saw cows too sick to stand being pushed into the food supply with a forklift, it resulted in the largest meat recall in history. So naturally, the answer to that problem was *ban the filming*.

It's weird; in America, everyone is under constant surveillance. Except livestock. They apparently need total privacy. You never see a chicken on TMZ.

A few years ago, a chart made the rounds on the Internet showing how big the chickens we eat have gotten, and some people wanted to know why. Well, it turned out to be the same reason the baseball players got big for a while. And again, the solution we decided on was "Maybe you should stop being so nosy and just relax."

Because when consumers know things, they tend to make informed choices, and that could affect corporate profits . . . so I'm sorry, but your right to know something is always gonna be outweighed by their right to hide it from you. Because in America, you can be armed—just not with the facts.

If the beef lobby had its way, there'd be nothing on the label but a picture of a cow killing itself. The label usually says something like "Product of Australia, USA, Nicaragua, and New Zealand." Come on, no cow is that well traveled! But a single hamburger today can contain "meat" from a hundred cows, so it's more than just delicious; it's like a beef-based gangbang in your mouth.

All of which made me think about how Californians—the health-nuttiest people on Earth—rejected the GMO labeling law the last time they had a chance to vote on it. Not banning, just labeling—just a law that said if food was genetically modified, it should just say so on the label. To which the people said, "Hell *no*, we don't want to know! GMO? More like TMI!"

Sixty-five countries label GMOs. China does it, a country that puts melamine, a chemical fire retardant, in their baby formula. Which *sounds* irresponsible, but come on—when's the last time you saw a Chinese baby catch on fire?

Saudi Arabia does it: they cover women from head to toe, but *everybody* wants to see what's in their food.

This is why I find it so strange that the idea of eating horse meat is freaking people out—it's not as if horses are more cuddly than cows. True, they'll let you sit on their backs, but cows allow you to yank on their titties. I'm just saying, if you're willing to eat an animal that'll let you get to second base, you'll eat anything.

But hey, let's look at the silver lining: it's actually a good thing Americans don't care what they put in their mouth, because in the future, thanks to overpopulation, overfishing and global warming, we're running out of the food we *do* like to eat. One reason why there is so much fish mislabeling now is because they don't have the heart to tell you the fish you like are gone. Eighty-five percent of the world's fisheries are either fully exploited, overexploited or collapsed. You know where fishermen can no longer find cod? Off of Cape Cod. That's like going to Hooters and finding out all the waitresses are flat-chested.

If we don't fix how we grow food, and don't stop turning the oceans into a carbon sink for coal, we're going to have to learn to eat the few gnarly, maggoty things that can survive mankind. Your grandkids will grow up *dreaming* of getting some horse meat while they sadly munch down their McPlankton sandwich. Run home, Anthony, it's Wednesday, and everybody knows Wednesday is algae and caterpillar/synthetic meat day!

So enjoy eating your chemically processed crap now, America, because it won't be long before lunch is dung beetles and moss. And when all that runs out, I'm afraid it's Papa John's.

NEVER HUMPERS

Every week it seems there's a new study about how little sex the younger two generations are having, and I'd like to be the first to say thank you! Less sex means less babies, and that's what this planet desperately needs.

Masturbation, not procreation. The best thing you can do for the Earth is to not have kids, die and stay dead.

Researchers at the Nunya Business Institute have found that people between the ages of eighteen and thirty just don't fuck like they used to due to financial constraints, career aspirations and, mostly, an unwillingness to put down the phone.

Also, more young adults are living at home, and it's just awkward to say, "Dad, can I borrow the bed tonight?"

But instead of asking why America's young people are having less sex, let's just be glad they are. I can't think of a better gift to our planet than pumping out fewer humans to destroy it. People talk a lot about using paper straws and composting and driving electric, but the great underdiscussed factor in the climate crisis is there are just too many of us, and we use too much shit.

The population of planet Earth reaching eight billion in 2022 was not good news. And those who regard it as such should be treated for TikTok Brain.

The secretary general of the United Nations, of all people, said that welcoming our eight billionth person was "an occasion to celebrate our diversity"—yes, what a comfort that people of all races will be contributing to an already unsustainable carbon footprint and choking and starving equally.

Have you seen what's been happening with the climate in recent years? Our farmland is shrinking due to scorching temperatures and drought. One out of four people on Earth is food insecure—what we used to call "hungry"—and billions face some form of water scarcity. And water is hardly the only thing we're running out of: clean air, quality soil, rainforests, wetlands. The precious metals that make our phones work. We're even running out of sand. Which may not seem important, but without it you can't make concrete or glass. Like for windows, so you can look outside and see the world ending.

All of this is not unrelated to there being ever more people on Earth. Who tend to use things. Tracy Stone-Manning, director of the Bureau of

Land Management, said, "If there were fewer of us, we would have less impact. We must consume less, and more importantly, we must breed fewer consuming humans."

Yes. I thought this was a "duh." And until very recently, it was. But now there's a growing movement of people more worried about population decline—which is the thing we should be *celebrating*! Elon Musk says, "The biggest problem the world will face in twenty years is population collapse."

Oh come on, of all the excuses not to wear a condom, that one takes the cake. Population collapse? Has he been to Disney World on a Saturday? The only thing that's collapsing is the Dumbo ride under the weight of all the obese eight-year-olds.

I'm not worried about the population collapsing, I'm worried about the glaciers collapsing, and the food chain and the electrical grid. I have no idea what Musk is talking about when he says, "Earth could sustain many times its current human population and the ecosystem would be fine." It's not fine now!

Nature World News reported an unprecedented global extinction crisis with more than a million species expected to die off in the next few decades. The bees are dying. And the coral reefs. Fish populations in the ocean are collapsing. What are these people talking about?

America's population is now approaching 350 million, and there's an allegedly smart guy named Matthew Yglesias who wrote a book called *One Billion Americans*, arguing that there should be a billion Americans. Insert your own traffic-on-the freeway joke here.

His argument is basically that the country with the most people has the most power, and that should be us. And why not, we have plenty of space! Yes, we do have space. Point conceded. Climate deniers like to say, "There's no population problem, just look out the window of an airplane, it's nothing but empty space down there."

But it's not about space. It's about resources. Humans are already using 1.7 times the resources the planet can support.

You can make a billion Americans, but they're still not going to want to live in North Dakota—and even if they did, what are all these new residents of the Greater Bismarck Metro Area going to eat, Soylent Green?

The famous theory put forth in 1798 by Thomas Malthus, that population grows exponentially but water and food do *not* . . . that has not changed. We've improved food-growing ability, yes, but it's still finite. And you can't grow water.

Scientists say it would require almost an entire other Earth to produce the resources we need to sustain the population we have *now*, and it would take *five* Earths to support the population if everyone consumed like the average American. Which most of the world wants to do. To deny these facts makes you—I don't know, kind of a flat-Earther of population science.

There just is no "there" there to the argument that we can keep adding people with no consequences. The "argument," as far as I can tell, is the same one people use for Bitcoin: We haven't thought it through, but who cares. It seems like it'd be good for business.

And business *is* affected by declining birth rates; Japan is often cited as a frightful harbinger of things to come in other countries. You see, for reasons perhaps better left unexplored, some years ago in Japan the men decided to stop having sex and just masturbate on the subway. The ensuing decline in birth rates was routinely called a "population crisis," but a) it's not a crisis, Japan is doing fine, and b) the "crisis" is really just one of GDP growth.

Yes, a falling birth rate does cause some problems because we need fresh, new participants entering the workforce to fund the retirements of the previous generation of workers. And yes, if birth rates decline too much and people keep living longer, the result is a society of the aged and enfeebled—or as it's known today, Congress.

But isn't running out of water an even bigger problem? Finite-ness as a concept has not been repealed. We've forced upon ourselves an economic model where businesses need ever more customers, but more customers means more carbon, more waste, more plastic in the ocean, more mouths to feed.

Let's figure out a way to be happy without always having to grow and grow and grow and always keep growing—what are we, an alien on a spaceship? Even more than needing smaller carbon footprints, we need fewer feet.

Utah's Republican senator Mike Lee once said, "Climate change is an engineering problem . . . and problems of human imagination are not solved by more laws, but by more humans." Which is easy for Mike Lee to say, he's a Mormon. When he dies, he gets his own planet.

Mike also says, "The solution to so many of our problems, at all times and in all places: fall in love, get married and have some kids." Eww. Sounds like something Colin Firth says at the end of a rom-com. But again, remember: Mike Lee belongs to a cult that believes all sorts of fantastical nonsense—it's called the Republican Party.

But liberals are also at fault on this issue: I've never heard a liberal say that falling birth rates are a good thing—which they are. Everyone talks about a falling birth rate like it means there's something desperately wrong with a country: they're depressed, they're not fucking enough!

Whatever problems are caused by falling birth rates aren't nearly as dire as the ones brought on by overpopulation. In 1900, there were less than two billion people on Earth; now it's over eight. We can't keep going on like this—the world is just too crowded. When was the last time you sat comfortably in an airplane?

Wouldn't it be nicer to just have fewer people around? It's no secret that there are a lot of Jewish people in show business, so on Jewish holidays in Hollywood the traffic is . . . delightful! That's what we should be shooting for: to make every day look like a Jewish holiday in Los Angeles.

RED ERRING

In 2019 there was big news about Mars from a NASA robot called the "*Curiosity* rover," which sounds like your Tinder profile if you only do anal out of town. Anyway, the Rover found methane up there, and there was a lot of high-fiving from nerds at mission control, followed by a lot of talk lately about space forces and manned missions and going back to the moon and on to Mars and . . . please.

Have you flown coach lately? We can barely put a man on the surface of O'Hare. I don't know if Mars is full of methane, but we're full of shit. We're not going anywhere.

America can't maintain our infrastructure, can't update our power grid, can't get off oil—and we're going to fly thirty-five million miles to Mars? Have you looked at our math scores? Forget the launch, we can't even do the countdown. You want to find water on Mars—how about first we find it in Flint, Michigan? I'm sorry, but we're not the "We'll race you to the moon!" country anymore. We're the "I've fallen and I can't get up" country.

And as far as this argument goes that we need to get back to the moon to use it as a launching pad to get to Mars, where we really need to get to because we're trashing this place so bad we need a backup planet . . . here's an idea: instead of going to Mars, how about we just stop treating Earth the way Led Zeppelin treated hotel rooms?

Everyone has to just shut up about Mars and how cool it would be to live there and start over someplace new—like we're the Chinese moving to Vancouver. This is a dangerous idea that our culture is already too taken with: that we can keep on trashing Earth because we got Mars, this fun, new, happening spot.

"C'mon, Bill, don't be a stick-in-the-solar-system. Red is the new green! It's the party planet right next door! Mars? More like Mars-a-Lago!" It's practically Eden, if you don't mind growing dinner in Matt Damon's poop.

Well, I do mind. We need to quash this stupid fantasy that Mars is a perfectly reasonable planetary backup. Movies, TV shows, articles and memes—there's this constant drumbeat to get to Mars, explore Mars, colonize Mars. To paraphrase Jan Brady: "Martians, Martians, Martians . . ."

Budweiser announced in 2021 that they were investigating how to brew quality beer on Mars, something they can't even do here.

Billionaires talk about Mars like it's Margaritaville. Jeff Bezos wants to go, and so does Elon Musk, who wants us to have a million people living there in fifty years. Richard Branson says, "I'm determined to be a part of starting a population on Mars."

Even Donald Trump, who isn't a real billionaire but played one on TV, signed a bill when he was president calling for a manned mission to Mars by 2033, which NASA estimated would cost four hundred fifty billion dollars. Just stop. If we're going to take up the challenge to overhaul a planet, let's do *the one we're already on*!

Let me spell this out in terms simple enough for Steve Doocy to understand, so he can explain it to Mr. Trump: Mars is an airless, lifeless, freezing shithole. It's Antarctica crossed with Casey Anthony's trunk. If we're going to spend the time, effort and money to make an entire planet sustainable for human life, why not the one that already has air and water and the right temperature and, oh yeah . . . *we're already here*!

Of course, this position is deemed completely unacceptable by a number of experts who went to Space Camp, who say it's "anti-science." I'm not anti-science—I'm just a big fan of oxygen. It's my second-favorite thing to inhale. This is kind of a "must" with me when I book travel. They almost always throw in oxygen. Which Mars has none of.

It's easy to list what Mars *does* offer by just taking everything humans need and adding "no." No air. No surface water. No heat. No natural resources. I'd say let's colonize Mars if we didn't know what was up there, but we do know what's up there: nothing.

And if your space suit gets a small rip in it? Carbon dioxide will mix with the oxygen you brought up there with you, causing your skin to dry up, your brain to shrink, your hair to whiten and your eyes to sink into your skull. You'll look like Mike Pence. Your eardrums will rupture and the water in your eyes will dissolve. So will the water in your mouth, when you open it to say, "Oww, my eyes." The temperature at night runs from a balmy 76 below to a quite chilly minus 225. So remember to bring a sweater.

You want to explore something cold and hard? How about the *facts*. Facts that confirm climate change is killing us, but figuring out how to survive it on Earth is still way more practical than living on Mars.

We hear a lot about putting America first—let's put Earth first. Millions of years of evolution shaped us to thrive here and only here. Earth is essential. Would you go see a band called Wind and Fire?

And even if it comes to that, and we do someday need a side-piece space rock, why not the moon instead of going all the way to Mars? Why travel tens of millions of miles when we have our own desolate, lifeless shithole only 250,000 miles away? I have more frequent flyer miles with Delta.

It takes six months to get to Mars, and Mars and Earth are rarely aligned for travel, so missions can only happen during a two-week window every two years. If you get in trouble on Mars, you're on your own. Like living in Puerto Rico when Trump was president. But we can get to the moon in three days—Amazon will be delivering there.

"Oh, but, Bill . . ." I know. I know, nerds, I know the argument you're gonna say: "But a Mars day is close in length to our Earth day, whereas a moon day can last twenty-eight Earth days!" So true. And also, who gives a shit if you have to live underground or in a dome the whole time?! How badly would we have to rat-fuck the Earth before living like that was preferable? It's not easy to live in the Sahara or the North Pole, or Phoenix in July, but it still beats Mars.

Mars is a mirage, not an oasis. To sum up:

Mars: no air; Earth: air. Earth: food; Mars: Matt Damon's shit potatoes. Earth: mostly water; Mars: maybe a little water far below the surface, or maybe not. In any event, don't bother waiting for a busboy to fill your glass.

Mars: eight months away by spaceship. Earth: You're here. You're home.

Stop looking for the Goldilocks planet. This is it. Mars doesn't have cool breezes, or trees, or mangos, or butterflies. There's no kale for liberals, no opioids for conservatives. No waterfalls, no hot springs, no rainforests, no rainbows. As the Eagles once sang, "there is no more new frontier, we have got to make it here."

TROUBLE VISION

On the other hand, blowing up the world is something that could actually happen.

If you don't think so, you haven't seen enough movies. Movies always foresee the future: flip phones in *Star Trek*; touch screens in *Minority Report*; iPads in *2001*; Black presidents in a million movies before Obama; spectacular terrorist attacks on American soil before 9/11.

Network, in 1976, predicted Fox News and reality TV, and *Blade Runner* showed a future Los Angeles where life is bleak, overcrowded and dehumanizing—and that was just on the 405. And of course *Forrest Gump* came out in 1994, years before we elected George W. Bush.

And what scenario has Hollywood envisioned endlessly in the last few decades? Earth after an apocalypse.

The Hunger Games, Divergent, Mad Max, V for Vendetta, Maze Runner, The Matrix, Interstellar, The Postman, The Book of Eli, The Road and even little *WALL-E*, to name but a few.

And how did Earth reach this point? Always, because we did it to ourselves. In *The Day the Earth Stood Still*, Keanu Reeves plays an alien sent to Earth to exterminate mankind because stupid, selfish humans are destroying a perfectly good planet. He gets talked out of it, but it's not like he didn't have a point.

In most of these movies, it starts with, "After humanity destroyed itself in the great war, what was left of government decided human passions needed to be controlled."

By Kate Winslet in *Divergent*. Julianne Moore in *The Hunger Games*. Jodie Foster in *Elysium*. Tilda Swinton in *Snowpiercer*.

Meryl Streep, in *The Giver*, says: "When people have the freedom to choose, they choose wrong."

Plainly the problem is white ladies in pantsuits.

18

RACE

PANDA EXCESS

At the 2022 Winter Olympics in Beijing, Eileen Gu, a model, influencer and gold-medal-winning skier who was born and raised here in America, chose to compete in the games for China, and many people in the American press thought that was cool.

Is it? Is that cool now? To choose to represent a totalitarian police state over America?

The Olympics pretends to only be about sports, but of course the games have always been a bit of a proxy war for which country has the best system, and by choosing Team China, Eileen Gu became a living symbol of China's "triumph over the West." Which wouldn't bother me so much if I thought China had triumphed over us in the ways that really matter, but they haven't.

We *do* have human rights issues right here at home—but we're still, at least until Trump takes over again, a democracy based on freedom, and they are an authoritarian surveillance state based on "How'd ya like to disappear for a few months?" Like tennis player Peng Shuai, who vanished for a while in 2021 after she said she'd been raped by a government official.

We have a horrendous history of throwing undeserving Black people in jail, but perspective matters: China has basically put an entire ethnic minority, the Uyghurs, into concentration camps, a situation both the Trump and Biden administrations called a genocide. That's an exaggeration, but it's still a cynical dodge to pretend that China's sins should be overlooked because "we all do it."

In 1997 Britain returned Hong Kong to China with an agreement from Beijing that Hong Kong could retain its free press, honest courts and democratic government. They lied. Democracy and freedom are being crushed there, and China doesn't want anyone to talk about it. And because so much money is involved, almost no one does.

When the general manager of the Houston Rockets, Daryl Morey, tweeted, "Fight for Freedom. Stand with Hong Kong," in 2020, *he* was forced to apologize. In America, we're supposed to root for democratic government, not apologize for it. But the NBA has a television deal with China worth a billion and a half dollars, so LeBron James said Morey needed to be "educated on the situation." The situation being, "I've got shoes to sell."

"Kowtow" is a Chinese word, but Americans have sure gotten good at it. For years, Google proudly refused to kowtow to Chinese censors, adopting the slogan "Don't Be Evil." But the Chinese market proved too lucrative so, well, OK, a little evil. That's the deal China offers American companies and celebrities: we'll give you access to our billion-plus consumers, as long as you shut up about the whole "police state" thing.

John Cena took that deal. China accounts for a big chunk of global box office, and he's a movie star now . . . so, like the Uyghurs, he learned he needed to get some "reeducation." His sin? Referring to Taiwan as a "country," as if it were a separate country from China.

Which it is! But China would like to do to Taiwan what it did to Tibet and what it's now doing to Hong Kong—so we were treated to Cena not only apologizing but doing it in Mandarin! And I thought *steroids* shrunk your balls. When a country can make your big, muscly macho-man action stars grovel in their language, you know you're somebody's bitch.

In the original *Top Gun*, Tom Cruise wore a bomber jacket with the flags of several of our Asian ally countries sewn on the back—but in *Top Gun: Maverick*, the flag for Taiwan magically disappeared. Well, he used to be a Maverick. Now he does whatever China says.

So can you blame Eileen Gu, who's already made over $31 million as the face of twenty-three products in China, for following in the footsteps of other American celebrities?

Some of Gu's defenders say it's racist to ask if she's still an American citizen, and she herself won't say. Why is that racist?

Why was it racist to think that Covid might have originated from a lab leak as opposed to from eating bats? Besides the fact that the idea that Covid came from eating weird, gross food seems way more racist than the idea it came from a high-tech lab, the definition of "woke" was supposed to be "being alert to injustice in society."

But because the woke now see race first and everything else never, fear of being accused of racism has given a free pass on human rights abuses to China and any other places perceived as nonwhite. China is the new Islam.

If China were in Europe, would they get away with having concen-tration camps without more of an outcry from America? If men were forcing women to wear burkas in, say, Massachusetts, would that go as unremarked on as it does? The Chinese classify transgender as a mental illness and edited *Friends* episodes so that Ross's wife is definitely *not* a lesbian. How would that go over here?

Didn't Martin Luther King say, "Injustice anywhere is a threat to justice everywhere"?

In 2020, NBA players wore jerseys that said "Freedom," "Speak Up" and "Justice," but I guess those things only matter for home games. Sorry, Uyghurs. Someone has to tell me where we got this rule that you can't criticize China. Because I suspect we got it from China. It's where we get everything else they sell at Walmart.

THE NAMING OF THE FLU

In 2020, Congressman Ted Lieu tweeted against calling Covid the Wuhan virus: "The virus is not constrained by country or race. Be just as stupid to call it the Milan Virus." No, that would be way stupider, because it didn't come from Milan, and if it did I guarantee we'd be calling it the Milan virus.

Scientists have been naming diseases after the places they come from for a very long time. Zika is from the Zika Forest, Ebola from the Ebola River, hantavirus from the Hantan River. There's the West Nile virus and Guinea worm and Rocky Mountain spotted fever and, of course, the Spanish flu. "MERS" stands for "Middle East respiratory syndrome"— it's plastered all over airports and no one blogs about it. So why should China get a pass?

When they named Lyme disease after the town of Lyme in Connecticut, the locals didn't get all ticked off. Can't we even have a *pandemic* without getting offended?

This isn't about vilifying a culture—this is about facts. Barely four months into the pandemic, the wet markets in China—the ones where exotic animals are sold and consumed, which may have been the origin of the virus—started to reopen, and the PC police said it was racist to attack any cultural practice different from our own.

I say liberalism lost its way when it started thinking like that and pretended that gender apartheid in the Muslim world was just "different" instead of an abhorrent human rights violation.

To those who said during the crisis, "What if people hear 'Chinese virus' and blame China?" the answer is: we *should* blame China. Not Chinese-Americans, but we can't stop telling the truth because racists get the wrong idea. Sorry, Americans, we're going to have to ask you to keep two ideas in your head at the same time: Covid had nothing to do with Asian-Americans, and it has everything to do with China. And it's not the first time.

SARS came from China, and the bird flu, the Hong Kong flu and the Asian flu. Viruses come from China like shortstops come from the Dominican Republic. If they were selling nuclear suitcases at wet markets, would we be so nonjudgmental? And the next one could be worse.

And China can do it. As I've noted, China once built a fifty-seven-story skyscraper in nineteen days; there's been a pothole on my street for nineteen *years*. They're not like us, they can actually get shit done. This is a dictatorship that for decades enforced a one-child-per-family policy, under penalty of forced sterilization. But they can't close down the farmers market from hell?

RATIONAL ANTHEM

In the wake of the social justice protests in 2020, the NFL added "Lift Every Voice and Sing," commonly known as the Black national anthem, to "The Star-Spangled Banner" before games. Now, I don't believe we should enforce patriotism by singing *anything*. And if there's one thing I hate more than groupthink, it's audience participation. But I am what you might call an old-school liberal who was brought up with the crazy idea that segregating by race is bad.

The only time there should be two national anthems played at a sporting event is when the other team is from Canada.

When it comes to an anthem, it doesn't have to be the one we currently use—but it has to be just one. You know, because it's a *national* anthem. And symbols of unity matter. And purposefully fragmenting things by race reinforces a terrible message—that we are two nations, hopelessly drifting apart from each other.

That's not where we were even ten years ago, and it's not where we should be now. A young politician named Barack Obama scored pretty good at the Democratic National Convention in 2004 when he said: "There's not a Black America and white America and Latino America and Asian America; there's the *United States* of America."

An African-American professor at Clark Atlanta University named Timothy Askew wrote an entire book about "Lift Every Voice and Sing," and he said, "To sing the 'black national anthem' suggests that black people are separatist and want to have their own nation. This means that everything Martin Luther King Jr. believed about being one nation gets thrown out the window."

He's right. If we have two anthems, why not three? Or five? Why not a women's anthem, a Latino anthem, a gay, trans, Indigenous people's or Asian/Pacific Islander anthem?

Because "I'm not dealing with you, I'm not speaking to you" is not a way you can run a country. And most people of all backgrounds understand that and don't even want to try it that way. I'm not out of step— believing in "separate but equal": that's out of step. By seventy years. It was 1954 when the Supreme Court handed down their landmark *Brown vs. Board of Education* ruling, which said separate but equal isn't what we do here. We decided we're going to try to make this work. Together.

And yet a survey of 173 colleges in 2021 found that 42 percent offer segregated residences, 46 percent offer segregated orientation programs and 72 percent offer segregated graduation ceremonies. Congratulations, liberal parents, you just paid a hundred grand for your kid to move to Biloxi, Mississippi, in 1948. I thought the whole point of going off to college was to be exposed to people from different backgrounds, people who may not share all your opinions, but somehow you find a way to get high with them.

We're a nation that professes diversity as our strength, but now half the kids' dorm rooms are determined by racial purity? The University of Michigan–Dearborn thought it would be super progressive to set up one virtual café for people of color and a separate one for white people. This is what it means to become so woke you come back out the racist side.

The University of Ohio suggested a gym for minorities only. I have a hard time believing that the vast majority of African-Americans care. That in private conversations they're saying, "Oooh, I just can't stand doing squats in front of white people!" Really—we can't even go to the gym together?

Because what's next? What follows separate dorms, anthems, ceremonies, cafés and gyms—separate neighborhoods? That was redlining. They wouldn't let Black people live in the town where I grew up. Then they did. The word for that is "progress." It's where the term "progressive" comes from.

Most Americans, including nearly 80 percent of African-Americans, want to live in racially diverse neighborhoods. The Black silent majority seems to be behind the idea that you can't have a melting pot with two pots. Yes, America was born from the original sin of slavery, and redress for that is certainly still in order—but not at the cost of destroying a country that most Black people now also have found a decent life in, with a relatively high standard of living, and don't want to lose. And balkanizing our nation will certainly cause us to lose it.

BRIDE AND PREJUDICE

In 2020 Ryan Reynolds and Blake Lively apologized for having their wedding eight years earlier at a plantation in South Carolina. And while I'm sure we could all do better in being aware of the presence of racism, including in the past, if this is the new rule, it's going to be hard to visit a lot of places in the South. It was kind of one big plantation.

And not just the South. The stock exchange is two blocks from New York's first slave market. In 1991, construction on a new building in lower Manhattan unearthed a massive slave burial ground from the seventeenth century. Among the businesses that stand over that ground today are a dance studio and a ballet academy, so people are literally dancing on those graves.

Because America *is Poltergeist*. We're *all* Six Degrees from Genocidal Assholes. If we start turning history into a big game of guilt by association, it never ends. Are we really going to make everyone apologize for standing somewhere that humans used to stand when they were more barbaric than they are now?

Ryan Reynolds said of his wedding, "It's something we'll always be deeply and unreservedly sorry for," and it was "a giant fucking mistake." OK, *The Green Lantern* was a giant fucking mistake. This was you getting married at a beautiful venue you saw on Pinterest. Look, every wedding, funeral and Slip 'N Slide on this blood-soaked land is inappropriate; the country itself is named after a slave trader named Amerigo.

But we can't just pack up our government and pretend none of this country ever happened. Here's a crazy idea—let's live in the present and make the future better. Of course, tear down statues of Confederate traitors, but in San Francisco protesters tore down one of Ulysses S. Grant because Grant was once gifted a slave, who he later freed.

OK, not a perfect score, but Grant was the guy who kicked the asses of the other statues you've been taking down. You know, while they were alive and could fight back.

There was a drive to remove a statue of Lincoln at the University of Wisconsin, because, as one student put it: "I just think he did, you know, some good things . . . [but] the bad things he's done definitely outweighs them."

Gosh, I wish I had been raised with the kind of self-esteem parents give their kids these days, where you can think that when it comes to accomplishments in racial justice you're just a little better than Abraham Lincoln.

Washington and Jefferson are also always up for cancellation because they owned slaves, and being a product of your time isn't an excuse anymore. But if that's the case, what about Jesus? And his dad, God? Neither one of them had any problem whatsoever with slavery.

The Confederacy used the Bible to justify their cause because it has plenty of passages from both testaments to back them up: "Slaves, obey your earthly masters," says Colossians 3:22. "Slaves, be obedient to your human masters," says Ephesians 6:5. "Slaves, submit yourself to your masters," says Peter 2:18. You see a pattern? If we're going to be consistent, I think we're going to have to cancel God.

Jesus himself says, "The servant who knows the master's will . . . and does not do what the master wants will be beaten with many blows." Thanks, son of God! A question for the woke: Would you let those words slide if it was in somebody's tweet today?

Jesus did heal a slave once—but not to free him, to get him back working. Because this is how slavery was back then: they didn't see it as a problem, because no one did, and if you had been there back then, you wouldn't have either.

But Jesus—being God—really should have known better, so when he comes back to judge the living and the dead, he's got a lot of explaining to do. Like: "Hey, you were always performing miracles—instead of bar tricks with loaves and wine, why didn't you zap the chains off a slave? With all the sermons and parables, why not one time throw in a little, 'Oh, and this whole people-owning-people thing—that's not right.'" Nada. On the subject of slavery, Jesus says sweet fucketh-all.

So first thing when Jesus returns is, we're going to need an apology. And I mean a *real* apology, not any of this "I'm sorry if my condoning of slavery caused offense." And then I think rehab would be in order, and sensitivity training. And he can forget about hosting *SNL*.

STATUE OF LIMITATIONS

In 2020 the Oscars announced a new set of requirements for Best Picture nominees that are based on fulfilling diversity quotas. And look, I'm all for inclusion—I don't know anyone in Hollywood who isn't. OK, Mel Gibson. But in general Hollywood is a liberal industry in a liberal town in a state that's bluer than the Pope's balls.

Have you watched the Oscars this century? Because this really seems like a case of washing a glass that's already been through the dishwasher. The Academy is not exactly unknown for rewarding liberal virtue—they should call "Best Picture" "Most Worthy."

Contenders and winners in recent years have been dominated not by their popularity with audiences but by their diversity and virtue signaling: *Green Book, Parasite, The Shape of Water, Boys Don't Cry, A Beautiful Mind, Moonlight, Frida, Fences, Precious, Dallas Buyers Club, 12 Years a Slave, Roma, The Hours, Brokeback Mountain, Call Me by Your Name*—and many more, some very fine movies—but getting super-liberals to be more liberal is not exactly the heavy lifting in the fight against racism.

What the new rules say is: to be eligible to compete for Best Picture, a film must meet the standards of two of four new inclusion groups. They are: a storyline that centers on—or a star that represents—an underrepresented identity group, or 30 percent of minor roles from two underrepresented identity groups, which include Asian, Hispanic/Latinx, Black/African-American, Indigenous/Native American/Alaskan Native, Middle Eastern/North African, Native Hawaiian or other Pacific Islander, women, LGBTQ+ people and people with cognitive or physical disabilities, or who are deaf or hard of hearing.

Wouldn't it be easier just to say "not Chris Pine"?

And that's only Group A. Then there's stuff, worthy goals I'm sure, about diversity in the production company, the studio and the crew—all I know is, if in the interest of diversity they make a straight guy cut my hair, I'm fucked. Diversity is important, but it needs to be said: It's not the only thing that's important. It's also important that we don't wind up with artists guided less by a creative vision and more by a to-do list.

Cameron Diaz is Cuban on her grandfather's side; is that Latina enough? Clint Eastwood is two hundred years old—does that count as a handicap? Darth Vader is voiced by a Black man, but when they took off his helmet, the character was white—how many points is that? I want to know, so I can be good. Because we are talking about a world where, if you want to make the next *Schindler's List*, the first thing you'll need to do is give a racial breakdown of all your employees. Does anyone see the irony in that?

Kirstie Alley did; she tweeted: "Can you imagine telling Picasso what

had to be in his fucking paintings. You people have lost your minds. . . .
OSCAR ORWELL."

You know Hollywood is in trouble when the voice of sanity is a Scientologist. But she was right—art and coercion is a bad combination. Some of the best movies ever made were by refugees from communist and fascist countries who got out because they didn't like being told what art was "acceptable." They didn't want to make a movie called *Natasha Gets a Tractor.* We're supposed to be the free country where artists can do what they want without having to show their paperwork to prove they know where everyone comes from, who they fuck and if they can hear.

Given that the industry is reeling as it is, and given that so much creativity and originality has already been sucked out of movies by sequels, blockbusters and comic-book franchises, maybe this isn't the wisest move.

And at the end of the day, people don't want to be hired because they fill a quota; they want to be hired because they're good.

INHERIT THE WIN

A new term has entered the lexicon in the last few years: "nepo baby." It means a celebrity who's the spawn of another celebrity, and there's a lot of them.

It doesn't make them bad people or untalented, but let's also admit that they weren't the only ones who could have gotten the job they got: when it's between a few good people, and one of them is going to get you the kind of publicity you get from being a nepo baby, who do you think lands the part?

So enjoy the good life, nepos—just don't say you didn't have a huge advantage, or it didn't matter that much who your parents are, or "it just got my foot in the door." In show business getting your foot in the door is 80 percent of it!

Yes, there are difficult roles that require acting only the great ones can do, but most acting . . . ? Please. Vin Diesel can do it. Bodybuilders can do it. Children can do it. Steven Seagal can do it. I did it. Reality TV is acting: acting like you don't know a glass of wine is about to be thrown in your face.

This is one reason why, of the top-rated telecasts on television, sports now accounts for over ninety of the top one hundred. Because it's the last refuge of meritocracy in America. Show business is full of nepo babies. Politics is full of nepo babies. Even modeling, which used to require the integrity to find a freakishly perfect fourteen-year-old in a small Slovenian village, has fallen to nepotism.

But in sports, there are no nepo babies. There are the sons and daughters of former players, but it's not *why* they play. Laila Ali didn't knock out twenty-one opponents by smacking them with her birth certificate. Sports is the last place where it doesn't matter who you are or where you're from, just what you do. No one gets hired either because it would make the team "look like America" or because their rich white daddy pulled strings.

I don't trust the government, media, churches, judges, juries, banks, Jiffy Lube or anyone on a dating app covering their chin with their hand. But I do trust that the 450 players in the NBA are the absolute best 450 players the teams could find anywhere in the world.

The fact that Bronny James's future in the NBA is not assured is very assuring to me. Everyone wants to see LeBron James's son play on the same team with his father: there hasn't been a feel-good story that feel-good since Macaulay Culkin escaped from Neverland. But just because we want to see it, that's not going to make it happen—only Bronny James himself can do that. Doc Rivers's kid plays, but not because "his father played and so it's a great story."

In sports, they don't tell each other stories. They perform.

Maybe that's why sports looks to me—at least on TV—like a place that has really good race relations. On the field or court, it's just about "Who can get me the ball? Who can score for our *team* when we need it?" They earn each other's respect, and the love follows. You can see it when they slap each other's butts.

So why does America have that in sports—something that is, after all, just a diversion—but not for stuff that really matters? Forty-two percent of private colleges admit applicants based almost entirely on the fact that their parents are alumni. You get in if you work hard and your dad bought a building. These are called legacy admissions, although I'll also accept "entitled fuckface."

But it also must be said that, in the interest of righting historical wrongs and evening out our despicable past, the concept of merit itself is now under attack everywhere but in sports. Instead of getting the kids who lag behind up to higher standards, schools all over are eliminating honors classes.

Eighty percent of four-year colleges no longer require any standardized tests for admissions. San Francisco's top-rated Lowell High School replaced merit-based admissions with a lottery in 2021, and the result was a threefold increase in D's and F's. Turns out, getting rid of merit admissions just made kids feel worse about themselves—and that's what Instagram is for.

At least sixteen schools in Virginia are under investigation for failing to give students their National Merit Scholarship awards, which are a big deal: they can open a lot of doors academically, and get you laid at math camp. The Republican governor there called it a "maniacal focus on equal outcomes for all students at all costs." You may not like him, but that accusation strikes a lot of people as true, and this is a bad issue for Democrats.

Because most Americans seem to agree: If they're on an airplane, they want a cockpit that looks like America. But they'd also like someone up there who knows how to fly the plane.

CULTURE FLUB

Black people really should demand that white people stop culturally appropriating how mad they are about racism. It's great that Caucasians have finally joined the fight for racial justice in unprecedented numbers, but hating racism the *most*? You can't steal that. Elvis taking Little Richard's act was bad enough.

Victor Sengbe is an African-American Oakland resident who put up small loops for footholds on trees in a local park for "exercise and games." He said: "Out of the dozens and hundreds and thousands of people that have walked by, no one has thought that it looked any way close to a noose."

But Oakland's mayor Libby Schaaf wasn't going to let all that cheat her out of a chance to signal her virtue. She said, "These incidents will be investigated as a hate crime." My question: Why is this white woman seeing racism where a Black man isn't?

The mayor also said, "Intentions don't matter." But they do matter. And white people need to stop trying to cancel other white people whose heart is in the right place but don't get it exactly right on the first try.

During the 2020 social justice protests after the George Floyd murder, when everyone was posting a black square on Instagram, BuzzFeed wrote, "Influencers: It's a Privilege to Post a Black Square and Then Go Back to Your Usual Content." As opposed to what, abandoning your life and just posting a black square *every* day? People got called out for *not* posting the square, then for *just* posting it without speaking out, and then for posting it and speaking out but not voicing their support in the exact way that was set in the new decoder ring. They were helping wrong!

Ellen DeGeneres felt enough pressure that she erased a tweet that said, "People of color in this country have faced injustice for far too long." That may not be exactly "Black Lives Matter," but it's also very true, and pretty close to what we're trying to get everyone to understand. Liberalism should be about lifting people up, and you don't do that by slapping down people who are trying to say, "I'm on your side."

No wonder white people right now are acting like a nervous waiter on their first day, so scared of making a mistake that they put a fork in your iced tea and a straw in your salad. We don't want to chant the wrong chant or hold the wrong sign. Please, it's all we can do to clap on the right beat.

You want to be a good ally—but careful, not too good or you're being a white savior! Use your voice—but don't make it about yourself! But you must speak up! Unless it's your time to just listen! But then silence is violence . . .

Even though sometimes silence just means someone works two jobs and has three kids. They have baby food on their shirt, not hate in their heart.

The *New York Post* printed this letter in 2020: "I am a senior-level leader in an organization and feel compelled to speak up about racial injustice, but I'm afraid to . . . as a white man, I'm afraid that I will say something that will be misinterpreted and I will do more harm than good—for my career too. Staying silent seems wrong but safer. Am I alone in this?"

Unfortunately, no. There was a sports announcer in Sacramento who tweeted, "All Lives Matter," and immediately got fired, even though he apologized and said he just didn't understand; what he said came from a place of ignorance, not racism. That difference is important. Someone could have just explained to him why there's a deservedly special reason we single out Black lives for protection. But now instead of a possible ally, we create a bitter unemployed person.

I worry that the kind of tension that the Guardians of Gotcha are creating is going to make people afraid to mingle at all, and thrust us back toward a re-segregation of sorts where instead of just seeing a person and *not* a color, now we're *only* seeing color.

I guess this is old-school liberalism talking, but I don't think that's the way to go. Let's hang out, and if I fuck up, tell me *why*, not "goodbye."

BEIGE AGAINST THE MACHINE

White people have to find some middle ground between racists and people who see racism everywhere. Because at this point, I can't tell who is more annoying: the type of conservative who doesn't care about anyone who isn't white, or the liberals who hate themselves because they *are* white. There's got to be a sweet spot somewhere between the PC police and the Memphis police.

I don't know how we got to this place where Caucasians are either nonstop apologizing for the unbearable whiteness of their being, or they're Trump voters who somehow convinced themselves that it's white folks who can't catch a break in America.

These are both stupid positions—but let me address the liberals for a minute: Attention, Whole Foods shoppers. Put the kale down, we need to have a talk. Because this idea that being white automatically equals lame is getting out of hand.

You know who I'm talking about. The kind of person who goes away to some exclusive vacation spot and comes back and says, "It was nice, but soooo many white people."

What's with the "I'm embarrassed to be white" subgenre of the Internet? The tweets that say, "I'm finding myself constantly embarrassed to be white," "I'm watching 'Emily in Paris' and I've never been so embarrassed to be white," "Retweet if you're embarrassed . . ."

Rosanna Arquette once tweeted, "I'm sorry I was born white and privileged. It disgusts me. And I feel so much shame."

Exactly. You think it's hard being a Black man in a white man's world? Try being a white woman who feels bad about you being a Black man in a white man's world.

I know, you're trying to demonstrate to minorities that you're a sympathetic ally by dumping on your own whiteness, but most minority folks couldn't give a shit—they think it's ridiculous, you, pretending you're making a difference when you're just making *yourself* feel better. It's so . . . white.

White liberals have to start listening to me when I tell them, "You can't be more offended than the victim." There was a study done in 2018 where people were asked to rate their feelings about various races and white liberals were the only group that had a *bias against themselves.* They want to hang out only with people who are *not them.* That's like your mother preferring the neighbor's kids.

There's a weird self-loathing going on among white liberals, and it's not helping anyone. Lifting up those who society has cheated or forsaken: that's liberalism; hating all things white is just tedious virtue signaling. The answer to mass incarceration is to stop putting undeserving Black people in prison, not to put more white people in Twitter jail.

It seems like every thought that's uttered nowadays needs a disclaimer—the other day I heard a guy say, "I realize I'm speaking only as a white male and I acknowledge our tragic history of oppression . . . but you left your lights on."

Yes, you have some advantages for being white. But you have some disadvantages too. Many white people were born with a terrible personality—you don't need to advertise it. And constantly crapping on yourself doesn't fix anything. In fact, it's a perverse sort of narcissism: the more I hate on my own whiteness, the better a person I am!

I hear it all the time: "Check your white male privilege!" OK, I checked. Now what? Should I tweet an apology to Kendrick Lamar and lop off my cock?

Look, none of us chose to be born white, not even Ed Sheeran. So just stop—because you know what might be the worst part of white shame? You bore the fuck out of Black people at parties. You meet Black people and say things like "*Black Panther* was so meaningful to me." Ew. No it wasn't. It wasn't a cultural milestone for you.

I've taken an informal sampling among some Black folks I know, and the consensus seems to be: awareness is great—white people certainly should acknowledge a history of overwhelming favoritism—but Black folks are not asking whites to always be flagellating themselves. Because it makes everything awkward. It puts the burden on Black people to absolve you.

It's really asking Black people to, again, do something for you: Forgive me. Absolve me. Recognize that I'm one of the good white people— Jesus, haven't Black people suffered enough? Slavery, Jim Crow and now I gotta make some yuppie feel better about himself? As a Black friend of mine said, and I quote, "I'm doing a'ight, I don't need your pity."

And if you really feel this bad about the whole race thing, if being white is really this toxic for society, let's tax it. Let's tax whiteness. A Honky Tax. We'll do it like carbon offsets: we'll calculate your exact level of white lameness and then charge you a Caucasian offset fee, based on a mean percentage of household income indexed to the net, not gross, national product and averaged with the consumer price index. We will come up with just the right dollar figure to offset the exact amount of you being a fucking loser. A lame, white fucking loser.

Now, pay up, asshole. You fucking white piece of shit. Fucking worm.

I mean, that's what you want to hear, isn't it? Isn't it, maggot? You fuck. You want to be told what a disgusting piece of white shit you are, you white piece of shit.

Look, America has done a lot of good things, and a lot of bad ones, and the number one bad one, with no close second, is racism—it's a sorry history, and we're not done with it. And yet, Black and white increasingly intermingle. We get to the finish line on race by just being with each other more. We don't need awkward. We need laughing with each other, finding out what's good about each other, befriending, intermarrying—enjoying someone's company without thinking every minute, "I'm with a person of color."

You're with a person. You are not uncool just because you're white, and it is not a crime to know all the words to "Sweet Caroline."

19

IMMIGRATION

SCORN IN THE USA

There's an oft repeated moment in political debates where the moderator says to the two candidates, "Say something nice about your opponent."

It's always awkward, because the candidates just spent an hour describing how America would be an out-of-control dumpster fire if the other guy won the election, but they try. But I think that in future debates, the moderator needs to frame that question a little differently: "Say something about *America* that you like."

Because honestly, I don't know why the people who are fighting for this country so hard even want it anymore.

What do Republicans like about America? It's not democracy. They mostly stand with a president who tried to pull off a coup! And at least a dozen Republican nominees for Senate and governor in the 2022 midterms said they absolutely would not commit to accepting the results. "Elections only count when we win them"—that's what America is to you now? That shows more disrespect for the flag than any kneeling football player ever could.

In 2022, at least twenty-seven states introduced or enacted laws that restricted voting. If you say you love America, don't you also have to love the idea of everyone getting to vote? Don't you have to love the peaceful transfer of power? Republicans are like the trophy hunters who say they love wildlife. Then why do you shoot it?

Republicans used to be the rule-of-law people and lionized the officers who upheld it—but when rioters stormed the citadel and symbol of America on January 6, most Republicans took their side, and not the side of the police, over a hundred of whom were wounded. "Fuck the police"—that's the clarion call of the Republican Party now? When did the GOP become NWA?

And then there's the FBI. Steve Bannon says they're the gestapo, Marjorie Taylor Greene says they should be defunded, and Congressman Paul Gosar said, "We must destroy the FBI." The FBI is not American now? FBI agents are so square they yell fore when they ejaculate. They think matching windbreakers are cool. Their flag pins have flag pins.

The military used to be in the same category—the bedrock of the super-patriot crowd. But Trump began his first campaign by doing something that up till then was unthinkable: he mocked John McCain, a Republican war hero, and it was not a bridge too far for Republicans; they shrugged and walked across it. As they did when Trump called the joint chiefs "losers" and our soldiers who died in World War I "losers."

So, I ask again: If you don't like democracy, voting, the FBI, the military and cops . . . what about America *do* you like? Oh, I know: the Constitution. But Congresswoman Lauren Boebert said, "I'm tired of this separation of church and state junk that's not in the Constitution."

But it *is* in the Constitution, and it's another one of those pillars of this country that, if you don't believe in it, it makes me wonder why you're fighting so hard for this place at all.

And that's what's so odd about this time we're living in: for all the talk about fighting for the soul of America, nobody seems to like it very much.

Too many liberals give the impression that to them, America is just a big "ugh." The red, white and eww. A country that started out bad and will always be bad, founded on an unrelenting history of sucking and unable to change.

Congresswoman Cori Bush tweeted, "This land is stolen land and Black people still aren't free"—and this was on the Fourth of July. Not that I care about the Fourth of July—but I do care about perspective, and that's what too much of the Left has lost.

The truth is, we *have* changed. A lot. And as far as the land goes, yes, I guess we could change the name of Captain America to Captain StolenLand. But to all the people who start every public event now with one of those "land acknowledgments" where they say, "I'm standing on land that was stolen from the proud Indigenous people of the Chumash Tribe," I say: either give it back or shut the fuck up.

AOC says, "So many people in this country hate women." That's a pro-choice talking point that they just completely made up. Pro-lifers do not hate women, they just think abortion is murder. And it kind of is. I'm just OK with that.

Congressman Jamaal Bowman says capitalism is "slavery by another name." Not only is it not slavery, it's the thing that has given more people, including millions of African-Americans, more prosperity and hope than any other system, flawed though it surely is. And again, something like the free market is kind of synonymous with America, and if you don't like it I don't know how you can say you love *this* country.

You know who loves *this* country? You know who's not constantly complaining about what happened two hundred years ago, and who's not obsessed with seeing America through shit-colored glasses and shaking off the stench of what irredeemable, privileged assholes we are? Immigrants. Ask any of them why they came here, and they'll all tell you the same thing: Ron DeSantis put me on a plane.

But they'll also tell you that America, for all that's so crummy about it right now, is still the last, best hope, and almost always way better than where they came from. Blind hatred of America is just as blinkered as blind love. And we Americans should really get some perspective about where we live.

Every conversation I've ever had with an immigrant included the notion: "Oh, you people have no idea. All you do is bitch about and bad-mouth your own country, but if you knew about the country I came from, you'd stop shitting on yours."

Now, I've never been a rah-rah-America type, and as you may have noticed, I take joy in mocking the Republicans' dewy-eyed, sloppy-drunk love for their country, which often renders them incapable of acknowl-edging its problems. That's how we got the 2013 Supreme Court ruling gutting the Voting Rights Act—not because John Roberts is a monster, but because people like him tend to over-romanticize America. He thought the South was ready for the honor system; they weren't.

But liberals, as usual in this era, have now gone too far in the other direction. They under-romanticize America. They have no perspective.

As Afghanistan was slipping away in 2021, the Taliban murdered a comedian. His name was Nazar Mohammad, and he made up funny songs on TikTok. They forced him into a car, tortured him and then ex-ecuted him. A comedian.

A thing like that hits a little close to home for me. I've had two presi-dents up my ass: one, Donald Trump, sued me over a joke, and then as president called me every name in the book for the crime of predicting he'd do exactly what he did, refusing to concede an election; and another, George W. Bush, had a press secretary, Ari Fleischer, who warned me to stop speaking my mind.

Neither experience was pleasant, but I never had to worry about being dragged until I was dead behind a Toyota Tacoma.

There was a "draw the prophet" contest in Garland, Texas, a few years ago—provocative, yes, but either you believe in free speech or you don't. This is America; we're supposed to.

Unfortunately, a couple of Muslims didn't, and attacked, and when they got shot, a local Muslim resident named Mohammed Jetpuri said: "The extremists got what's coming to them. You don't just shoot people . . . I'm glad they got killed." Mr. Jetpuri may be Muslim, but he's a real Texan.

Any American Muslim I've ever talked to has basically told me the same thing every immigrant says: that they're glad they left the old country behind and came to a place that's better, freer, less beholden to . . . "traditions."

There was a meme going around for International Women's Day that said, "A woman should be . . . whatever the fuck she wants." Liberals can either applaud that or they can pretend that a woman in a burka is just a fashion trend—but you can't do both.

Have a little perspective about the stuff we howl about here. I'm sorry your professor said something you didn't like—that won't be a problem with the Taliban, because you're not allowed to go to school. In Saudi Arabia, grown women can be jailed for doing the kinds of things we think of as routine without the permission of a male guardian. China rounds you up if you're the wrong religion and puts you in camps. More children in Burkina Faso work than are in school.

Only 5 percent of Burundians have electricity. The homicide rate in Honduras is eight times what it is here. The inflation rate in Venezuela tops 2,000 percent. The Philippines under their former president Duterte put to death twenty-seven thousand low-level drug dealers. In North Korea, people starve to death.

America has its problems but the only people who starve here are doing it for a movie.

If you think America is incorrigible, turn on the news. Or get a passport and a ticket on one of those sketchy airlines that puts its web address on the plane. During the Afghanistan pullout, there was a reason mothers were handing their babies *to* us.

And we should take them. Americans should take in Afghan refugees, into their homes and into their neighborhoods, and I'm sure many people reading this are thinking the same thing: "Yes! Someone who isn't me should definitely do that!"

We made a lot of mistakes in Afghanistan, but that doesn't make us the bad guys. Oppression is what we were trying to stop there. We failed, but any immigrant will tell you, we've largely succeeded here.

And yet the overriding thrust of current woke ideology is that America is rotten to the core. Hopelessly racist from the moment it was founded, and so oppressive, sexist and homophobic it took a year to find a host for *Jeopardy!* And this is where your new Afghani roommates—and most other immigrants—will prove so valuable, because they'll turn to you and say:

"Have you people lost your fucking minds? Have you ever heard of honor killings? Public beheadings? Throwing gay men off of roofs? Purposefully blinding slumdogs so they're more valuable as beggars? Arranged marriages with minors? State-sanctioned wife beating? Female genital mutilation? Marriage by capture? Because we have."

Maybe the lesson of Afghanistan is that everyone from the giant dorm-room bitch session that is the Internet should take a good look at what real oppression looks like.

Ask your maid. Ask your Uber driver. Ask the Asian woman giving you a "massage." She'll tell you, "This place is Shangri-la." And not just because she works in a place called Shangri-la. America may not be the country of your faculty lounge and Twitter dreams, but no one here tries to escape by hanging on to a plane.

No, we wait until we're *inside* the plane to fight, and then only because they cut off the beverage service.

KANGAROO COURTING

While conservatives here remain apoplectic about Mexicans crossing the Rio Grande, and Europe freaks out about refugees flooding in from the Middle East, no one is paying attention to the ethnic group that's taking over this country while we blithely do nothing: Australians!

It can't just be me who's noticed that every single bartender in LA is suddenly some six-foot-four Australian dude with a great personality who's generous with the free drinks—and *we're just letting it happen.*

Wake up, people: you can't swing a dead wallaby these days without hitting an Australian—and it's not just bartenders. Australians now make up 30 percent of America's surfing instructors, and an alarming 65 percent of our ski bums.

And I'm sorry to have to say this, but Australia is not sending us its best people. They're bringing drugs—yes, enough for everybody, but still. They're rapists—OK, not rapists, but they do a lot of fucking. And some, I assume, are good people.

How do Australians get here? No one really knows. Some say the jet stream carries them over. But we do know this: you meet one and have a few beers, next thing you know he's sleeping on your couch, borrowing your car and fucking your girlfriend—and somehow you're OK with it! It's like getting a golden retriever, if golden retrievers fucked your girlfriend.

Did you know that in the whole history of the world, there are only three inventions Australians can claim: the disposable syringe, the long-wearing contact lens, and penicillin—all created so they could party longer.

We used to think oceans could protect us from Australians, because oceans are full of sharks, and sharks eat a lot of Australians. But now sharks are endangered—and that's the tough situation we now face: not enough sharks, and too many Hemsworths.

Does anyone remember when American movies were cast with *American* actors? That seems like a long time ago—have we become so weak and effete that no defense is mounted against this Aussie horde that flawlessly mimics our American accent and then takes jobs that rightfully belong to Billy Bob Thornton?! Does America really need Simon Baker when Patrick Dempsey is sitting by the phone?

I partly blame myself. First, the Australians came for parts in our cop movies, but I wasn't an actor, so I didn't speak out. Then they came for our action movie blockbusters, but I wasn't a soulless studio chief, so I didn't speak out. Then they came for the Tony Awards—but I'm not gay, so I didn't speak out. But I'm speaking now.

Because I don't really hate Australians, but I am an American, and it's in our tradition to hate *someone* and blame them for all our problems. In the mid-nineteenth century it was my people, the Irish. Then it was the Chinese, the Italians, the Mexicans, the Jews, the Swedes, the Japanese, the Russians and now the Mexicans again.

If Donald Trump really wanted to make America great again, he wouldn't build a wall, he'd build a mirror.

MIGRANT HEADACHE

Trump fans want a wall because a wall represents an impregnable barrier that keeps out not just Mexicans but everything that makes them feel antsy about the old America slipping away. The wall is like one of those prescription drugs that "blocks the causes of your discomfort."

"Yes, now there's Mexiplan! Mexiplan has been clinically proven to reduce the pain caused by foreigners entering the country illegally. Mexiplan works with your natural gullibility to construct a wall that keeps immigrants from shithole countries out, and good-paying jobs in, so you can get back to cleaning your guns and sending out Facebook memes of Hillary getting hit with a golf ball."

Except, it doesn't work that way. Most illegals don't even cross the border. They come here the same way you came back from Cabo: they catch a flight. And then they just stay. Like the Australian on your couch.

Even Trump once admitted the wall was bogus when he was caught on tape in a call to Mexico's president saying the wall "is the least important thing we are talking about." It was always just an applause line that got out of hand.

So there you have it: the wall will not help with employment, it's not feasible to build and even Trump knew it was bullshit. And may I add to Trumpsters: You don't need it! Because everything that wall represents—the bigotry, the racism, the ignorance, the paranoia—is already in your heart. The wall has been inside you the whole time. Trump just brought it out. Because he's the jackass whisperer. But you don't need it.

Every time you feel rage because a voice recording says, "For Spanish, press two," the wall is there.

It's there whenever you begin a Facebook post with "I'm not racist, but . . . ," and it's there every time a unisex bathroom makes you hold it till you get home.

It's there when snow makes you deny global warming, and it's there at the ball game when two gays on the kiss cam make you throw up in your mouth.

It's there when you use "Jew" as a verb, and it's there every time you're Tucker Carlson.

20

SHOWBIZ

WHO'LL STOP THE VAIN

Someone needs to be honest with the never-ending line of celebrities who think they can run the country: you're not good enough, you're not smart enough, and doggone it, it completely doesn't matter that people like you.

They like you now because you're an entertainer, and thus largely uncontroversial—but governing is the opposite.

Celebrities as diverse as the Rock, Caitlyn Jenner, Matthew McConaughey and Randy Quaid have all in the last few years teased out the idea that when it comes to running their state—or the entire country—they have what it takes. And they do: malignant narcissism.

The Rock says he might be the right man for the job because he believes he can unite the country. I'm sure the Rock is a good guy, but frankly, the fact that he thinks he can step into the single hardest job in the world with no preparation tells me one thing for sure about his judgment: it's terrible.

Did we all not just witness the cautionary tale named Donald Trump? The years 2017–2020 were a warning, not an inspiration. You were supposed to see that and think, "I guess high-level government jobs should go to people who've trained for it and know what they're doing."

When he was running against Obama, John McCain said of him, "He's the biggest celebrity in the world. But is he ready to lead?"

Turns out, he was ready to lead. Because he wasn't Black Justin Bieber, he was a brilliant academic, former law professor and statesman. Government was his skill, his life and his calling. Like the Kennedys before him, he *was* a star—but a star because of what he accomplished *in office*.

Yes, Obama enjoyed his TV time, but he did it to sell policy, not to do "robot voice." Republicans elect a celebrity who becomes a politician; Democrats, at their best, elect a politician who's so good at public service they become a celebrity.

Look, I understand the temptation to pick a celebrity. After all, Trump started with a big advantage, because he was a household name, like Preparation H. And in today's political atmosphere, where substance makes you an elitist and experience means you're part of "the swamp," it's as if the whole country just said, "Fuck it, the government can't do anything. Which candidate will give us the most laughs?"

But when the prime directive for government goes from "keep us safe" to "keep us entertained," that's bread and circuses, end-of-the-empire stuff.

Matthew McConaughey is a lovely person and a talented actor, but when he says he's considering a run for governor in Texas I must say that is not all right, all right, all right.

I'm sure Caitlyn Jenner is a nice person, but as California governor she would be in charge of the world's fifth-largest economy, based on her qualifications of being a background character in a reality show not about her.

Randy Quaid, who you'll remember as Cousin Eddie in the *National*

Lampoon's Vacation movies, and as "guy rooting through your recycling bin" in real life, also says he might want to run Cali. Probably into the ground.

And then there are people who are actually excited about Kanye West in politics. These people are called morons.

I'm not saying that these celebrities haven't led lifetimes of glorious achievement: the Rock proved once and for all that weight lifters can drive, and Matthew introduced Lincolns to stoners, and Caitlyn married the woman who married the guy who defended O. J. And the problem isn't that they *are* actors—it's that they're *not professionals in this other field.* Called government.

When did governing become the safety school for when the guest spots on *Chicago Fire* dry up? We treat government like the lowest rung of celebrity: rock stars, movie stars, TV stars, *Dancing with the Stars*, magicians . . . congresspeople.

Governing is a difficult, nuanced job with people's lives and livelihoods at stake. To be president and do it right, there are a thousand things you have to know *before* taking office.

Do we imagine that our celebrity friends could, on day one, tell us—oh, I don't know: What is budget reconciliation? What are the three legs of our nuclear triad? What's the TPP? What does the Fed do? Where's Chad? What agency is responsible for our nuclear weapons? What does the Fourteenth Amendment say? Who's the prime minister of India? In the event of another nuclear standoff with Russia or China, describe Kennedy's strategy that got us out of the Cuban Missile Crisis.

Governing is not a job you can pick up on the afternoon of the inauguration. You can't learn it on the fly. You can't fix it in post. Putin's not on a green screen, and he doesn't care about your million-dollar smile. If he tells you at a summit that he'd like to take Belarus now, you have to know that's a country and not his lunch order.

No one has to tell Joe Biden what's in the Constitution. Because he was in the room when it was written.

STAR JONESING

We need affirmative action for Republicans in show business. They're not good enough to make it on their own, but if we give them a leg up, maybe they won't take their rejection out on the whole country.

I say this because it's obvious that conservatives have a chip on their shoulder about celebrities. The party that endlessly proclaims its disdain for Hollywood will run literally any "celebrity" who's a conservative. They pretend to hate it when celebrities give their political opinions even though they're the party that made Reagan and game show host Donald Trump president!

It's not liberals' fault that conservative celebrities are usually D-list losers.

At Obama's first inauguration gala, he had Beyoncé, Springsteen, Sheryl Crow, Bon Jovi, John Mellencamp, Usher, Stevie Wonder, Garth Brooks, Tom Hanks, Denzel Washington and U2. Trump's inauguration had Jackie Evancho and the rock band 3 Doors Down—as in three doors down from fame.

Antonio Sabato Jr. ran for Congress, but before that he was an underwear model who all the other underwear models referred to as "the dumb one."

And after he spoke at the last Republican convention, he claimed he was "blacklisted in Hollywood." Blacklisted? Blacklisting would be an upgrade. He wasn't on *any* list. He'd be lucky to get on a Do Not Call list. You'd have to run him *into* show business.

James Woods's last "credit" was on a Mastercard bill.

And then there's Dana Loesch, who America has come to know as the fiery voice of the NRA.

What you may not know about Dana Loesch is that before her job as NRA spokesmodel, she was a show business wannabe: a homemaker in St. Louis with a mommy blog and a radio show and dreams of TV stardom. *NCIS* producer Paul Guyot says that Dana pitched him a sitcom starring herself as "a hot young mom who does a far-right radio show." Think *Frasier* meets . . . awful. And if only they'd made that sitcom, today she might be a completely normal person.

The same thing happened to both the founder of the right-wing Breitbart website Andrew Breitbart, who admits he came to Hollywood "with the hope that [he'd] eventually become a comedy writer," and to his successor there, Steve Bannon, also a showbiz reject who didn't have the talent to cut it here, and so spent the rest of his life hating Hollywood, and by extension liberals.

In his memoir, Breitbart mentions Reagan six times and me thirty-four times. He called celebrities "elitist pestilence" with their cocktail parties on the Westside: "God, I fucking hate them," he said.

Which is funny, because for years, whenever I'd see Andrew Breitbart out, you know where it was? At a cocktail party on the Westside. Oh, he hated Hollywood—hated, hated, hated it! Mostly from his home in America's heartland, Brentwood.

As for Bannon, George Clooney remembers him as "a schmuck who literally tried everything he could to sell scripts." Including a rap musical of Shakespeare's *Coriolanus*—think *Hamilton*, but instead of Founding Fathers, Romans, and instead of a cultural phenomenon, a piece of shit. Bannon lost his shirt on that deal, but luckily he was wearing three more.

But if Bannon could have sold a screenplay, or Breitbart a sitcom, they wouldn't have ended up ranting and raving about cocktail parties on the Westside, they'd have been attending them. And in Bannon's case, finishing the drinks people left on the table.

And that's why I implore all Hollywood execs: next time a conservative comes to you with a really dumb idea for a movie or a TV show, just fucking do it so we all don't have to live with the consequences.

DREAD CARPET

Oscar-nominated movies lately are like the menu at a trendy restaurant where all the choices are very impressive, but there's not one thing I actually want to eat. Where's the comfort food? I don't have to leave the theater whistling, but would it kill Hollywood to once in a while make a movie that doesn't make me want to take a bath with the toaster?

Virtue signaling has already ruined most of the Internet, the *New York Times* and all of the colleges where football isn't a priority—please, leave us the movies. Because in all honesty, I have to ask: If your movie is so woke, how come I'm falling asleep?

What happened to *show* business? Did they all decide to quit cocaine at the same time? Did they forget that Hollywood is still the number one place to go if you're an egomaniac looking to fill that hole from your childhood with applause?

They forgot how to help people escape from their problems, and then they wonder why they're losing audience in droves. Of course! If you keep offering up *The Immigrant Who Shit in a Coffee Can*, at some point the crowd is going to say, "Oh fuck it, just give me the Netflix movie of Mötley Crüe taking drugs and getting blown."

Academy nominations used to say, "Look what great movies we make." Now they say, "Look what good people we are." It's not about entertainment—it's about suffering. Specifically, yours.

It's not two hours to forget your troubles; it's traffic school at the Holocaust Museum. Today if you're at the movies and wondering, "Which one is the bad guy?" it's you. Because you have indoor plumbing, and the characters the nominees are playing don't.

After the Covid lockdown, the first movie to get people back to the theater was *Godzilla vs. Kong*. Because it was *Godzilla vs. Kong*, not *Godzilla vs. Kong and His Crippling Battle with Depression*. Not that I want to see *Godzilla vs. Kong* either!

Hollywood used to know how to make a movie that was about something—a movie for adults—that was also entertaining and not just depressing. There was already a category for that: Best Documentary. Important filmmaking about the conflict in Yemen or the plight of hot dog stand owners. You know, the part of the Oscar show where you got up and went to the bathroom.

But now that's the whole show. The funniest part of the whole night is the "In Memoriam" segment.

It's such an odd psychological quirk—I keep asking myself, why do so many liberals have this seeming desire to be sad? Could it be because being sad allows you to feel like you're doing something about a problem without actually having to do anything?

Like the poor lady living in her van in *Nomadland*. There is a solution to homelessness: building affordable housing, possibly in your neighborhood. But do people, including liberals, vote for that? No—they fight it. But it does make them sad. Without affecting home values.

In the future, if the Oscars are going to keep on this path, they should change their name to the Debbies. As in Debbie Downer.

"Welcome to the eighty-first Academy Awards! Brought to you by razor blades, Kleenex and rope! Now, please welcome your host, the Sad Emoji!!"

DECRYING INDIAN

And if you want to know when this trend started . . . it was farther back than you might think.

In 1973, an activist for Native American causes named Sacheen Littlefeather was the first person in Oscar history to walk onstage and say, "I know this award is for acting, but I'm going to bore you with my politics anyway," transforming the Oscar telecast into what it is today: a four-hour lecture on how bad most people have it, by the people who have it the best.

You see, 1973 was the year Marlon Brando won Best Actor for *The Godfather*, and instead of accepting the award himself, he sent Ms. Littlefeather onstage in his place to voice what truly was, and is, an important cause.

And a little context: Brando had just made one of the all-time great comebacks by playing Don Corleone, and anyone else would have eagerly shown up to the ceremony for their victory lap. But Brando chose to stay home for two reasons: to draw attention to Native American rights, and because, like 2022's Oscar favorite *The Whale*, he was stuck in his chair.

But it's how Ms. Littlefeather was greeted by the Hollywood crowd that night that interests me—and the picture of "liberal Hollywood" that night is best captured in the title of another Oscar winner: *The Way We Were*.

Here's how the *New York Times* described it in Sacheen Littlefeather's recent obituary:

". . . at the podium [she] endured a chorus of boos . . . drawing jeers onstage . . . she said that some audience members did the . . . 'tomahawk chop.' . . . A producer for the Oscars . . . told her that she would be arrested if her comments lasted more than 60 seconds. The actor John Wayne was so unsettled that a show producer said security guards had to restrain him so that he would not storm the stage."

And this was back when storming the stage to assault someone was frowned upon.

The obituary also said that Littlefeather "recalled that while she was giving the speech . . . she had 'focused in on the mouths and jaws that were dropping open in the audience, and there were quite a few.'"

Now, come on, if Sacheen Littlefeather had made that same speech talking about the plight of Native Americans at last year's Oscars, she would have gotten a standing ovation, and there would have been no shocked looks on faces—and that is because of progress!

And also Botox. But let's talk about the progress part, because people today don't have a realistic view of how progress works.

For example, do you know who *Time* magazine's Man of the Year was in 1973? Me neither; the point is, *Time* magazine was still calling their award the *MAN* of the Year! *Time* magazine, another pillar of liberal enlightenment, like the Oscars—but it only changed the name to "Person of the Year" in 1999.

I don't know if everything happens everywhere all at once, but I do know that everyone is late on everything. Because that's what it is to be human.

Ronald Reagan was very late on doing something about AIDS—but the liberals aren't on time either. Obama was late on gay marriage, JFK was late on civil rights, Bill Clinton was late on not having the interns blow you.

Biden is currently, as we speak, late on pot, and it's going to look bad in the future. The difference is, the next Democrat *will* legalize pot. The liberals are late—like all people are—but they do tend to keep going until we get there.

I'm constantly amazed when I rewatch movies from only a decade or so ago, and they were made in a way that today would get you burned at the Twitter stake. *It's Complicated*, from 2009—to name just one of many I could choose—was made by a who's who of the most blue-ribbon-certified Hollywood liberals, woke approved and Democratic Party contributing, from the stars to the producers to the director, but it apparently occurred to none of them to have any kind of minority in the cast. You would need a divining rod to find a person of color within five hundred feet of this movie set. But if they made it today, they'd do it better.

When it comes to social justice, liberals are still the tip of the spear, but even that spear comes up short a lot. They were dicks to an Indian in 1973, and they were still blind to diversity in 2009, but along the way Hollywood also moved the country forward by opening people's eyes to a host of worthy causes: racism, antisemitism, AIDS, disabilities, the environment, addiction, LGBT rights . . . and yes, the plight of the American Indian.

MO FUNNY MO PROBLEMS

One of my favorite recurring bits we've done over the years on *Real Time* has been the one called "Explaining Jokes to Idiots," where we explain to idiots jokes they missed, because they're idiots.

When Amy Schumer's 2018 film *I Feel Pretty* debuted, the professionally offended decided that, even though it was a movie by women filmmakers presenting a pro-woman message, it was helping wrong! Even though Amy really just remade *The Nutty Professor*, where someone not thin and not cool magically sees themselves as better looking and gains confidence. Except when Eddie Murphy did it, he didn't have the purity police up his ass.

The *Hollywood Reporter* wrote an article titled "Dissecting *I Feel Pretty* and Its Questionable Message of Empowerment." *Rolling Stone* called it "fat shaming." The *Independent*, reviewing the trailer—because why wait for the actual movie when you can start hating something two months early—wrote that *I Feel Pretty* "seems so offensive it's frankly exhausting."

Exhausted by a movie trailer—I think we've achieved peak snowflake.

The *Los Angeles Times* asked, "Wouldn't a bolder, more progressive version of this story have cast . . . a woman of color?" Oh, for Christ's sake. Can't it just be funny? Can't we just sit in a movie theater, unclench our assholes for two hours and laugh at what it is, instead of "dissecting" it for what it's not?

Movie reviews aren't even reviews anymore, they're just "How come you made the movie you made, and not the one I would have made? If I had talent, which I don't."

Some reviews noted that casting Amy as "the ugly fat" person undermined truly ugly fat people—bad Amy, not fat enough. Others asked why her self-esteem had to be linked to her physical appearance. And yes, why *wasn't* the role given to a woman of color? I don't know, maybe because they thought since it's an Amy Schumer movie they ought to have Amy Schumer in it?

Who wound up, by the way, apologizing for appearing in her own movie. On *The View* she said, "I recognize that I'm Caucasian . . . I would love if this movie were starring a woman of color who's had it way harder than me." Because all goofy comedies should also address the Black experience. Like that one where Jennifer Garner grew up overnight—you remember that one, *13 Going on 30 Years a Slave*?

Life is too complicated to reduce everything to "real problems" on one side and "white problems" on the other—but being white is hardly the only thing Amy did wrong.

The *New York Post* says the film is "tone-deaf" for casting a "straight, white, able-bodied blonde," and the *Independent* concurs, noting the film was flawed because Amy was "still blonde, able-bodied, and well-dressed, with all the trappings of Western beauty standards." Yes, she's a traitor to feminism because she wears clothes, has all her limbs and is hotter than Predator.

Comedian Sofie Hagen also noted Amy's able-bodiedness, adding that she's "femme, and yes, thin. She *is* society's beauty ideal." No, she's precisely *not that*. That's her act, you idiots!

But you know who *is* society's beauty ideal? Wonder Woman, Gal Gadot—the one feminists love more than life itself, starring a six-foot supermodel in hot pants. News flash: people just like the physically attractive better—the taller candidate usually wins the election, and studies show the better-looking person, other things being equal, usually gets the job. Even babies prefer to look at attractive faces. Wait until you see the blog I'm going to post tearing *them* a new asshole!

Models are tall and thin because that's what sells clothes. The answer isn't to insist that everyone in society love you exactly the way you are, it's to learn to tell the ones who don't that you don't need them. Which is exactly what Amy learns in the movie, just the way at the end of *The Wizard of Oz* Dorothy realizes she didn't have to go on that big acid trip to appreciate what she had at home.

JINGO UNCHAINED

Someone has to tell me why the same film critics who find every movie somehow lacking in woke credentials absolutely loved *Top Gun: Maverick*, a two-hour propaganda ad for defense contractors, militaristic jingoism and bombing foreigners.

Every other movie that comes out falls short: if the movie is about poverty, the director didn't grow up poor enough to understand it; if it's about being gay, it's not gay enough; Asian, not Asian enough; female, not enough agency. Race? Don't even try: sidelining, whitewashing, colorism, white saviorism. No amount of virtue signaling is ever virtuous enough.

But somehow 96 percent of film critics loved *Top Gun* like a Catholic priest loves sleepaway camp. I liked it too—it was fun and nostalgic, and Tom Cruise has been such an ageless, reliably entertaining movie star for so long it sometimes makes me think, "Maybe there is something to Scientology."

But if you're a critic and you've been making it your life's mission to root out the insufficiently liberal in cinema, did you not notice that *Top Gun: Maverick* was a lot about making warmongering sexy again? The weapons porn, the endless money shots of engines burning jet fuel, the big dick energy, the aircraft carriers dancing in the sumptuous, oily haze, all to the manly, macho, masculine sounds of . . . Kenny Loggins?

Did you know that if the US military were a country, its fuel usage alone would make it the forty-seventh-largest emitter of greenhouse gases in the world?

It spews so much smog you can barely see the highway to the danger zone.

The defense budget in the year *Top Gun: Maverick* came out was $801 billion, more than the next nine countries combined. In 2003, it was $378 billion. Somehow we took two wars off the books but now need to spend more than twice as much?

And to fight exactly *who*? In *Top Gun: Maverick*, the enemy is just called "the enemy." We don't name them, we never see their faces, we don't hear them talk—who are they?

That's not important. We don't know who we're bombing, and we don't care. We're bombing someone? Awesome! You had me at "America, fuck yeah"! Whose ass we're kicking is on a need-to-know basis. God bless America and death to . . . to whom it may concern. Sorry, "enemy," it's not about you, it's about us. We have Tom Cruise and you don't. This is a dick-measuring contest and it doesn't really matter who owns the other dick as long as ours is longer.

It's so ridiculous: "the enemy"—it's like having a movie called *Godzilla vs. None of Your Business.*

And that's on purpose. The people who made this movie understood that we as a nation right now are just too fractured to even have a common enemy we can agree on. It used to be Russia, and still could be—but Republicans did a 180 on the Evil Empire and now they like it.

And for liberals, you couldn't have "the enemy" be an Arab country (that would be Islamophobic), and it couldn't be an Asian country (that would be racist). So they left it up to our imagination: Who do you hate? Put 'em in there!

The old cliché has always been that if Martians attacked, it would unite all the nations of the world against this common outside enemy. Now I don't think it would even bring *Americans* together. The Martians could blow up the White House like in *Independence Day*, and half the country would be cheering in the streets. And when they said, "Take us to your leader," 70 percent of Republicans would drive them to Mar-a-Lago.

Giant, robotic tripods could be vaporizing New Jersey and Republicans would say, "This is what happens in Biden's America . . . it never happened when Trump was in office." Democrats would point out how the death lasers were disproportionately affecting low-income communities and people of color, and AOC would tweet, "Stop demonizing the Martianx community." Alex Jones would call it a "false flag operation" and accuse the people whose heads were melted off of being crisis actors, Marjorie Taylor Greene would criticize the Jews for not using their space lasers on the Martians and Lindsey Graham would volunteer for the anal probe.

21

HEALTH

PEE-WEE VERMIN

Isn't it interesting that so many of the health food pioneers of years past are—how should I put this? Dead. And not just dead, but they didn't even live as long as the average life span.

Euell Gibbons swore he'd live forever thanks to a diet of wild plants, and now he's a diet *for* wild plants—dead at sixty-four. Adelle Davis, who was so ahead of her time in saying we should avoid starchy foods like white bread, is, ironically, toast—dead at seventy. Nathan Pritikin, of the Pritikin diet—dead at sixty-nine; Clive McCay thought the path to living past one hundred was severe caloric restriction—dead at sixty-nine, last words: "I'm fucking starving." Michel Montignac sold seventeen million copies of *Eat Yourself Slim* and died at sixty-five, just before finishing his next book, *Drink Yourself Erect*. Jim Fixx wrote *The Complete Book of Running*, which his heart stopped doing at fifty-two.

Meanwhile, Keith Richards is fine.

This made me think about author Pagan Kennedy's 2018 think piece that made the point that when it comes to staying healthy, "it's the decisions that we make as a collective that matter more than any choice we make on our own." In other words, no matter how much you do for yourself, how right you eat, if the air is full of lead and the bug populations are out of control and your city is underwater, it doesn't matter. You can eat kale till it comes out your ears, stay hydrated, slather on sunscreen, steam your vagina, eat your placenta, work at a standing desk and put a healing crystal up your ass, but there's no escaping the environment we all live in.

In Los Angeles, hardly anyone smokes anymore. But we are all still breathing smog. You hear it all the time: "I eat paleo," "I eat organic," "I do a juice cleanse—ten days of nothing but cayenne and papaya!" OK, but aren't we expecting a little too much from the papaya? The poor papaya is saying, "Isn't it enough I'm delicious? Now I gotta clean your colon too?"

In the 1970s, when America passed a law to get the lead out of gasoline, the lead levels in our blood dropped by more than 80 percent. In the eighties, when fluorocarbons were destroying the ozone layer, we banned them, and the hole closed up.

But that was back when "Scientific American" was the name of a magazine. Now it's a contradiction in terms. This battle will not be won in the checkout line at Whole Foods. To address a problem of this scale, we need governments, preferably ones that don't employ former oil lobbyists at the EPA.

Tick-borne Lyme disease has become alarmingly common in the last decade because global warming isn't just about souped-up hurricanes and yearlong fire seasons and inundated cities. Rising temperatures have caused the creepy-crawly population to breed out of control because their season is longer and their range is farther; what used to only live in the tropics is now coming north. Forget the border wall— we need a border net. *These* are the migrants we should be worried about.

And since it's still mysterious to most Americans, let me explain ticks in terms my politically savvy readers can appreciate: like Rudy Giuliani, they latch on, suck blood and sicken everyone around them; like Trump, they're very hard to remove; like Chris Christie, they gorge themselves until they nearly explode; and like Matt Gaetz, they just make you want to squeeze their head until it pops.

Contrary to popular belief, ticks are not insects—they're tiny arachnids, more closely related to spiders. And they're very, very tough. Simply removing one requires a magnifying glass and tweezers, like when Stormy Daniels gave Trump a hand job.

And it's not just ticks anymore that can bring the pain: mosquitos are in more places now, because more places are warmer now, and they can carry the Zika virus, yellow fever, West Nile and malaria. Thirty years ago this wasn't a problem because we had a very, very powerful pesticide. It was called "winter."

GERM LIMITS

The next time we have a worldwide pandemic, we have to come up with a better solution than "Everyone becomes Howie Mandel."

Howie is one of the great comics and great guys in this world, and he's also the world's most famous germophobe; he was social distancing before it was cool. But he'd be the first to tell you he has a disease that fucks up your life. He can't touch a doorknob or wear shoes with laces, because they might touch the ground. When he excuses himself to go to the bathroom, it's to clean it. No wonder he says, "It has always been a curse. That behavior didn't allow me to date or go out with anybody when I was young—or really even have friends," and "I'm always on the verge of death in my head."

I worry that two years of quarantine gave too many people the idea that the way for humans to win our million-year war with microbes is to avoid them completely, and I must tell you: you can't. The best way to beat almost any pathogen isn't dining through glass, or never going to a concert or ball game again. It's your immune system.

You hear people say, "Covid-19 is a new virus, so the immune system doesn't know how to handle it." Of course it does—that's why the vast majority of people who got it either recovered or didn't even know they had it. What do you think did that? The human immune system.

Now, there are people with immune systems that can't do the job, and we should make it a priority to protect those people. But compulsively dousing your hands in antibiotic gels is counterproductive; exposure to the trillions of germs and viruses in the atmosphere is not only unavoidable but necessary to stay healthy. In his later years, when he was peeing into jars and wearing Kleenex boxes for shoes, we pitied Howard Hughes—because it's pitiful!

Microbes are ubiquitous. You can keep discovering new things to scare people into buying protection for, but we're solving the problem from the wrong end. We can't sanitize the universe.

We've all read the articles: Your sink has 500,000 bacteria per square inch, your toothbrush has feces on it, E. coli's been found in makeup. Carpets, bedding, the remote, cutting boards . . . the average pillow has 350,000 bacteria colonies—they're filled with more shit than the guy selling them. Your phone has ten times the bacteria of your toilet, which your dog drinks out of and then licks you.

My dogs lie down on the driveway, where cars, with God knows what on their tires, pull in, and then they roll in it. Sometimes, I see a dead mouse in the driveway. I don't have a cat. *Something* here killed it. I'm not pointing fingers, but there are only the three of us. God knows what is all over your pets, and in their mouths, and then you invite them on the bed and they try to French-kiss you. And sometimes succeed. Some people don't even fight it. Because what's the point of a pet if you're not going to pet it? And what's the point of life if you can't live it?

Have you ever had sex in a hotel? Did you wash your hands first? Well, the last couple didn't either. And yet you're still alive, because your immune system said, "We got this."

Because at the end of the day, you can't keep all the pathogens out. It would be as silly as thinking you could stop immigration with a wall.

WORST RESPONDERS

Why is bombing the only thing America can do with precision?

We can send a laser-guided missile down an ISIS tunnel from a drone at twenty-five thousand feet, put one through a window without even rustling the curtains. When it comes to killing machines, we're an atomic clock. For everything else, we're a sundial in the fog.

After 9/11, we could have done what Israel would have done: hunted down the people actually involved and reinforced the cockpit doors on planes. Precision. Done. Who wants ice cream?

But no, we spent trillions attacking the wrong country and creating a giant "homeland security" bureaucracy. We've now spent decades in airport lines taking off our shoes while TSA agents pat down babies and grandmas. They say, "If you see something, say something." I see us afraid to identify threats by likelihood and bleeding ourselves dry just like bin Laden wanted us to.

When people asked me during Covid, "Why are you so skeptical of what the medical establishment tells us?" I said, "Because I've seen them react to a virus before."

By 1987, CDC officials pretty much knew how HIV was spreading and who was in danger. Now, of course, there's no moral dimension to this, despite what Pat Robertson used to say—gay sex is just as loving and natural as the other kind. But AIDS infects someone through the bloodstream, and that is simply more likely from anal sex; that's just science. But instead of being precise and focusing on who should be protected, we launched a fear campaign about how AIDS was going to explode into the heterosexual community.

Oprah Winfrey summed up what people were hearing when she said, "Research studies now project one in five . . . heterosexuals could be dead from AIDS . . . by 1990." But that didn't happen, and the upshot of bad information was that in the late eighties, low-risk Americans were swamping testing facilities and diverting our energy away from the truly at-risk.

New York in 2020 learned the hard way how much better precision would have been in prioritizing protecting the nursing homes. Contrary to popular lore, Covid is not Russian roulette. Of course, any virus—any *thing*—can kill anyone at any time. But we know who Covid kills: 75 percent of the deaths are people sixty-five and older; 98 to 99 percent are unvaccinated; over 70 percent who've died or been hospitalized were overweight.

If you're obese and unvaccinated, or eighty-five and still crowd-surfing at music festivals, yes, Covid would likely go badly for you—but at some point that has to stop being my responsibility.

Wouldn't it have made more sense to focus on helping the vulnerable stay safe and let the rest of us go back to living normal lives? And sadly, there are always going to be some people who want to go on forever in permanent, hair-on-fire, cancel-Christmas, hand-jobs–through–a–hazmat-suit, freak-the-fuck-out mode.

What we did to kids was unnecessary and horrible—and I don't even like kids. But making kids, who have a Covid survivability rate of 99.98 percent, mask up like bandits? Unfortunately, what got stolen was their education, their sanity and their social skills.

I'm not saying the medical establishment isn't trying to figure shit out, or that they're corrupt—although there is that too. But how about just *wrong a lot*. Wrong about HIV, wrong about lockdowns, wrong about kids, wrong about how you couldn't get it—or pass it—if you were vaccinated and how you could from walking alone outside. Or not washing your packages. To say nothing of the studies that are coming out now revealing what little effect lockdowns and masking had.

So much of what we did was theater. Watching athletes mix it up on the court and then mask on the sidelines; not being able to touch a menu but then seeing the people in the kitchen touch my food; maskless at dinner while sitting, but put it on to walk to the bathroom. And by the way, if Applebee's really cared about our health, they would make us cover our mouths *after* the food arrives.

I'm just asking, how much wrong do you get to own while still holding the default setting for people who represent "THE science"? Eat eggs, then don't, then do; take aspirin, then don't, then do. The food pyramid—really? Bread and milk every day? OK, you do you.

Thirty years ago they were recommending trans fats—now they're illegal. Just like hundreds of prescription drugs that were once called "safe and effective" and then yanked off the market, or pulled before they were about to be. It reminds me of how the Republicans are constantly doing traitorous things like trying to steal elections and inviting the Russians into the Oval Office and somehow are still known as the party of patriotism.

We've had this problem in medicine for a long time. Somehow, the number one piece of advice they offer if you're sick is "get a second opinion"—but not when it comes to public debate. Even though, plainly, the medical-industrial complex has not earned the right to claim monopoly status on information about Covid, or medicine in general.

Yes, free speech has allowed people to hear misinformation sometimes—and a lot of it was theirs.

MEDI-SCARE

Don't spin me when it comes to my health. The Covid pandemic prompted the medical establishment, the media and the government to take a *Scared Straight!* approach to getting the public to comply with their recommendations. Well, I'm from a different school: "Give it to me straight, Doc." Because in the long run, that always works better than "You can't handle the truth."

Now, I get it, doctors tell people lies because they don't trust you to finish the antibiotics after it stops hurting when you pee. And media? Well, I think we all know "if it bleeds, it leads." The more they can get you to stay inside and watch their panic porn, the higher the ratings.

Researchers at Dartmouth built a database in 2021 that monitored the Covid coverage of the major news outlets across the world and found that while other countries mixed the good news in with the bad, the US national media reported almost 90 percent bad news. Even as things were getting better, the reporting remained negative.

And politicians? They lie because it's their nature to cover their ass so they don't get blamed if things go badly. And also to keep in practice.

But when all our sources for medical information have an agenda to spin us, you wind up with a badly misinformed population, including on the left. Liberals often mock the Republican misinformation bubble, which, of course, is very real—ask anyone who works at Hillary's pizza parlor. And we do know conservatives had some loopy ideas about Covid, like "Bill Gates put a microchip in there!" As if Bill Gates cares about tracking your gullible ass to the Piggly Wiggly.

But what about liberals—you know, the high-information, by-the-science people?

In a 2021 Gallup survey, Democrats did much worse than Republicans in getting the right answer to the fundamental question: "What are the chances that someone who gets COVID will need to be hospitalized?" The answer is between 1 and 5 percent—but 41 percent of Democrats thought it was over 50 percent!

Another 28 percent put the chances at "20 to 49" percent. So almost 70 percent of Democrats were wildly off on this key question, and also had a greatly exaggerated view of the danger of Covid to, and mortality rate among, children. If the right-wing media bubble has to own things like climate change denial, shouldn't liberal media have to answer for: how did *your* audience wind up believing such a bunch of crap about Covid?

An article in the *Atlantic* reported that the media wouldn't stop putting pictures of the beach in stories about Covid, even though it was becoming increasingly apparent that the beach was the best place to *avoid* it; sunlight *is* the best disinfectant, and vitamin D is the key to a robust immune system. When Texas lifted its Covid restrictions in 2021, their infection rates went *down*, in part because of people getting outside to let the sun and wind do their thing.

But to many liberals, that couldn't be right, because Texas and beach-loving Florida had Republican governors.

But life is complicated. I know it's counterintuitive, but apparently the governor of Florida reads. I know we like to think of Florida as only middle school teachers on bath salts having sex with their students in front of an alligator, but apparently the governor is also a voracious consumer of the scientific literature, and maybe that's why he protected his most vulnerable population, the elderly, way better than did the governor of New York. Those are just facts. I know it's irresponsible of me to say them.

I don't want politics mixed in with my medical decisions—and now that *everything* is politics, that's all we do. If one side said Covid was nothing, the other side had to say it was everything. Trump said it would go away "like a miracle" and liberals said it was World War Z. Trump said we should ingest household disinfectants, and we laughed, of course—and then it turned out 19 percent of America was literally drenching the fruit in Clorox.

And then we found out that all the paranoia about surfaces was bullshit anyway, even though we spent six months washing every piece of mail like it was a stool sample from Chernobyl.

If you lie to people, even for a very good cause, you lose their trust. I think a lot of people died because of Trump's incompetence, and I think a lot died because talking about obesity had become a third rail in America.

FEAST MODE

America's top health officials should find the courage to do what the health officials in Huntington, New York, did in 2020: they told the entire town of two hundred thousand to go on a diet because, as the head of the program put it, "[with] COVID-19, you're twice as likely to have a poor outcome if you're obese."

Actually, it's worse than that: Public Health England found that people with a body mass index of 35–40 have a 40 percent greater risk of dying from Covid, and over 40 it's a 90 percent greater risk. Even being mildly obese makes it five times more likely that catching the virus will land you in the ICU.

And yet, during the pandemic, people *gained* weight. Weird, I remember when plagues had a slimming effect on people.

I don't think it's a coincidence that the countries with the lowest rates of obesity generally wound up with the fewest Covid deaths. Maybe China wasn't hiding all their deaths; maybe their "secret" is that their obesity rate is 6 percent and ours is 42 percent.

And pointing all this out doesn't make me a dick—in fact, the shame is on everyone in media and government who is too cowardly to emphasize how important an issue this is. Obesity was already killing us slowly, but mix it with Covid and it kills you fast.

No one deserves to die because of their weight, and we should spare no expense protecting vulnerable people no matter why they're vulnerable—but make no mistake, America went into the Covid fight like a boxer who was out of shape and took a beating for it.

Every day during the crisis, we heard the same warnings about fighting the virus: wear a mask, wash your hands . . . have sex through a glory hole. But the people in charge of health during a health crisis never mentioned the one major thing most people could do to ensure a better outcome should they get it.

And what a great time it would have been to start a campaign to get decent food into poor neighborhoods. Or a national campaign to get in shape, which would have dramatically improved our chances against the virus and made us feel better about ourselves to boot. But it was never even mentioned in a country that loves "challenges"—the ice bucket challenge, the "this will make you puke" challenge, the condoms-up-your-nose challenge . . . why couldn't they have gotten behind a real challenge, like the "getting healthy so the virus doesn't kill you" challenge?

But as Michelle Obama found out, just trying to give sound nutritional advice gets you vilified in America; it makes you a health "nut"— that's what is said about people who merely eat right: they're "nuts." Into weird, hippie shit, like vegetables.

Yes, the Right sure was infuriated back when First Lady Michelle was trying to impose her radical Black Panther agenda of encouraging kids to eat healthy. Sarah Palin went so far as to defiantly show up at a school with plates of sugar cookies—that'll teach you kids to eat a carrot! How did vegetables get to be un-American? OK, super-patriots, eat what you want, but let's get real about one thing: these colors don't run because these colors *can't* run.

But the rotund Right isn't alone in promoting tolerance of a national health crisis. During the Trump administration, Steve Bannon was once asked why Sean Spicer was spending less time in front of the cameras, and he joked, "Sean got fatter." OK, not the greatest joke ever, but it was *a joke.*

Not to Chelsea Clinton. She tweeted, "Fat shaming isn't a joke I find funny. Ever." Christ, even your mom knew when to fake a laugh.

And that's what's so depressing about this debate: there is no debate. Keeping people unhealthy is our most successful bipartisan enterprise. To conservatives, any attempt to even offer guidelines smells like social engineering, as opposed to freedom, which smells like bacon. And in liberal circles the worst thing anyone can ever do is even bring up the subject, because that's fat shaming.

But shame isn't ridicule or prejudice—it's the beginning of where we look at ourselves and say "I could do better." As opposed to "I'm always perfect the way I am, how dare you?" Americans felt no guilt about shaming people out of smoking and into wearing seat belts. We shamed them out of littering. And most of them out of racism.

Back when I drank too much, sometimes someone would say, "You know that's not great for your health, Bill, maybe you should slow down a little, you went kind of hard last night" . . . and I'd say, "Yeah, I know, I'm gonna start next week." And then of course I didn't. But I didn't say, "How dare you drink-shame me! Being blotto is beautiful!" Of course I didn't say that. I was focusing on the road.

Fat activist Ted Kyle, founder of ConscienHealth, says, "The media and public needs to stop catastrophizing obesity." Actually, they should be catastrophizing it more, because it's a full-blown catastrophe. The *New York Times* stated it succinctly: "Poor diet is the leading cause of mortality in the United States." So when folks say to me, "Do we have to talk about this subject?" . . . yeah, we kind of do.

We've gone to this weird place where fat is good, and pointing out that fat is unhealthy—*that's* what's bad. Fat shame? We *fit* shame now; you hear it all the time. Someone sees a merely trim person and says, "You should eat something!" Or maybe *you* should *not* eat something. Weight Watchers had to literally take the words "weight" and "watchers" out of their name—it's now "WW"—because merely the idea of watching your weight is now bullying. If people can face shame campaigns for *losing* weight, what's next, banning scales?

Well, yes. There's a card now that you can give your doctor, and it says, "Please don't weigh me unless it's really medically necessary." *It's always necessary!* This is like asking your dentist not to look at your teeth.

We rewrite science now to fit ideology, or just to fit what we merely *want* reality to be. The fashionable term now is "body positivity," and it is utterly Orwellian, used to describe as healthy what is precisely not healthy. "Healthy at any weight" is another in-vogue term that is an unchallenged lie. Honestly, have you ever seen a fat ninety-year-old?

At some point, acceptance becomes enabling—and if you're in any way participating in this joyful celebration of gluttony that goes on today, you have blood on your hands, full stop. You can make believe you're fighting some great social justice battle for a besieged minority, but what you're really doing is enabling addicts, which I thought we decided was bad.

There's a popular T-shirt that says, "I Don't Owe No Man a Flat Stomach." OK, no one said you did. You do you. But you're not a freedom fighter because you want to keep eating donuts.

People say to me, "Oh, come on, Bill, people struggle with this." Of course they struggle with it—everything's a struggle, life's a struggle! But somehow fifty years ago humans in this country looked entirely different. You don't think it was a struggle for them? You think cake wasn't delicious in 1969? The problem is, we look at fried chicken now and think: "That's a good start, but put it on a bun. And add bacon. And cheese. And something no one even thought to put on it. Make my mouth *cum*."

We scream at Congress to find a way to pay for our medical bills, but it wouldn't be nearly the issue it is if the average citizen didn't eat like Caligula. All the candidates always talk about their health plans, but no one ever mentions the key factor: the citizens don't lift a finger to help. They discuss preexisting conditions but never ask, "Why do people have so many preexisting conditions?" Being fat isn't a birth defect; nobody comes out of the womb needing to buy two seats on the airplane. We can keep pretending that health care is solely an issue between you and the government, but it's really between you and the waitress.

USA Today actually wrote the sentence, "Science hasn't yet figured out how to solve obesity," and Ted Kyle concurs, saying, "We don't know how to blunt the rise in obesity because we don't know precisely what the factors are that are causing it."

Yes, what could it be . . . *what could it be?*

22

LOVE

NERD IMMUNITY

Someone has to tell me why we keep allowing social media, and our very lives as social creatures, to be dictated by Mark Zuckerberg, the most socially awkward person in history.

When Facebook announced a few years ago that the name of the parent company would change to Meta, it was to better reflect Zuckerberg's new master plan for what he has called "an embodied internet, where instead of viewing content, you are in it."

Because why spend hours typing on Facebook to argue with your brother-in-law about ivermectin when your avatar can yell at his avatar in person! Well, not in person, of course—in the Matrix, where Mark wants us all to live.

Mark says anything you do in real life can be done in this new metaverse: playing cards, sitting in a park . . . getting a bad haircut. It's easy, you just put on goggles, gloves and, I don't know, suction cups on your balls, and now you're in the magical land of the metaverse. Because everyone looks so cool with shit strapped to their head.

In the metaverse, you can tour the pyramids or have a sword fight with a duck, all without having to leave the comfort of your parents' basement. We've all seen this depicted in movies like *Ready Player One*, where an elaborate metaverse serves as a retreat for people to escape the misery of existence. Something I always felt was better handled by weed.

But I'm not a visionary like Mark Zuckerberg. I tried virtual reality once: I put on the goggles and suddenly I was in a hot-air balloon over France, and then I was riding a broomstick around Hogwarts, and then I was in the bathroom throwing up. It was like getting roofied by Walt Disney.

Mark's vision is that two friends can attend a concert together when in reality—I mean, the old reality—both are really sitting at home. What great fun, especially for the band playing to an empty stadium. That's right, a concert where no one has to actually be at the concert. Or as Travis Scott said, "Now you tell me."

But I'm worried that if we get ourselves too far away from reality, we won't be able to find our way back. Phony used to be a bad thing, and "keeping it real" was good. That's why I named my show *Real Time* and not *Avatar Time*. We just went through a pandemic—the last thing I want is more virtual, and that's what the metaverse sounds like it's going to be: the pandemic year, except forever.

You have to ask yourself, why does Mark Zuckerberg think living in a metaverse would be so much better? Because look at him: the dead eyes, the lack of recognizable human features, the painted-on hair: he's already an avatar! I'm pretty sure the person we think is Zuckerberg is a Sim, while the real one lives on a yacht staffed by a hundred beautiful women. Who he ignores while he plays Minecraft all day. I'm just saying, this is the worst kind of person to make the overlord of a new universe.

Even before the pandemic, nearly three in ten American males between eighteen and thirty weren't having sex—almost triple what that number was ten years earlier. The closest they come to talking to a girl is Alexa. And spending so much time on screens has a lot to do with that. This is the phenomenon known as "incels," which is short for "involuntarily celibate," and it's not harmless. It never is when any society, for whatever reason, creates men who are cut off from women.

Incels have become a toxic subculture of angry, misogynistic digital eunuchs—and the metaverse is only going to make it meta worse.

Because it's a vicious cycle: the more time you spend in the virtual world, the more you suck at engaging in the real world, so the more you retreat into the virtual, which further atrophies your real social skills, including, and most important, getting laid. You've heard of the cycle of life? This is the cycle of "get a life." Of men with no game who, ironically, immerse themselves in games. And other substitutes for female companionship. Like superhero movies. They all want to be a hero so badly—all the movies are about how "a hero will rise."

You want to be a hero? Rise from the couch. Lose the cargo shorts, get a shirt with a collar, brush the crumbs off your beard and get it through your head that women still need to be, and want to be, courted. Earn being heroic by taking that long, brave walk across a room to ask someone out. The vast majority of men don't have to fight wars anymore or hunt for food, and Lord knows, there aren't any real Lokis or Green Goblins to fight. The one place you can step up and show courage is this.

The good news is that after years of being conditioned to search out prospective mates by swiping our phones, it seems in-person meetups are finally making a comeback. At the upscale grocery chain here in LA called Erewhon, also known as Shop and Shag, it's said that they purposefully make the aisles narrow so that "as you squeeze by, you feel people's energy." In-person energy? So retro.

Apparently, even Home Depot has become quite the pickup place. The Home Depot Dating trend on TikTok has 3.6 billion views by women who regard it as the perfect venue to find eligible men willing to work with their hands—who cares if they're mostly illegal aliens!

As one woman wrote, "I'm headed to Home Depot to 'look confused'" in the lumber aisle." Ah, a damsel in distressed jeans . . . and why not? Even a not terribly bright guy can figure out how to respond when a woman—or a gay man—says, "Excuse me, I'm looking to get some wood—can you help me?"

But I have a little life tip for men. If you want to get with a woman, try this trick: Talk to her. In person.

Because what happened in the last ten years is, the phone ruined dating and porn ruined sex, and women have been left with men who don't know how to actually talk to a woman anymore, and who think first base is anal and second base is choking.

So it's not surprising that women are finally revolting against the superficial scroll-and-swipe form of dating that, of course, works for men, who are oversexed and disgusting and biologically designed to seek the maximum orgasms for the minimal amount of work.

Dating apps took the worst inherent traits of men and exacerbated them by a magnitude of infinity: "Let's see, I'm horny, I'm lazy, I'm a coward, and I suck at honest communication—is there a way I could have an electronic harem right in my hand where the only answers are 'Yes' and 'Next'?"

As far as effort goes, it's one notch above sticking your dick in the vacuum cleaner.

Don't get me wrong, technology is a wonderful thing—I was just saying that the other day to my Japanese sex robot, R2-MeToo. But just because something is on your phone doesn't mean it's better, and that's the lesson women should take away from all this. Dating from the phone took away any incentive for men to cough up the two things women want most from them: courage and communication.

The courage to step to her for real and demonstrate you desire her enough to risk rejection . . . and communication. Women are communicative creatures—even when they're breaking up with you they say, "We need to talk."

We're endlessly hearing about "girl power" and being a "girlboss"—please, ladies, you let the technology play you and you got punked by your phone. Of course Tinder is every guy's dream: a hookup Rolodex. But it's the opposite of what you want: intimacy, emotional availability and being seen as a full human being.

I know we're all fluid now, and nonbinary and totally free and super brave, but here's the thing: We're not. Not mostly. Women haven't changed that much. You know how I know? Because *The Bachelor* is still on. And so is *The Bachelorette, Bachelor in Paradise, The Golden Bachelor, Are You the One?, Perfect Match, Cosmic Love, Love in the Jungle, Love on the Spectrum, Love Is Blind, Love Island, Temptation Island* and *MILF Manor.*

OK, not *MILF Manor*, take that one off the list, that's some sick shit. But the other thousand shows where women still want the roses, the romance and the commitment should tell you something. They don't want an eggplant emoji and a text at one in the morning: "Wassup?" They want you to compliment their hair, notice what they're wearing and hear about their day.

I know, it's a fucking nightmare. But it's still better than the incel life of having a fake girlfriend on OnlyFans and paying rent to your mom. So let's build on this budding trend of doing it in person. Let's harken back to that time when the mirror wasn't just for selfies, but to make sure you didn't look like shit when you left the house.

BACK TO THE GRIND

And given that there are only a few places where Americans meet each other in person anymore, it's long overdue that America had a review of our war on office romance.

Does anyone really think that swiping right on some rando because he has nice hair and is posing in front of a Dodge Challenger is a better way to meet someone than at the office?

And while it's true that in a workplace setting a power imbalance can be abused, a policy of denying two humans who are anxious for each other the chance to find love in the same office is now an anachronism.

This is no longer the *Mad Men* days, where there was no HR, there were no yearly mandatory sexual harassment seminars and the Me Too movement hadn't happened. Almost all businesses now have serious protocols in place where employees can report and get relief from being harassed.

And yet nearly a quarter of employers require all employee relationships, of any kind, to be disclosed. God forbid grown-ups start making decisions about their own bodies without getting corporate involved. And when it comes to managers and subordinates, the majority of companies don't allow any relationship at all.

But love is the last mystery. And where and when it might happen is serendipity. Also, when you're doing someone at the office, you at least know they can hold down a job.

Under current guidelines, Michelle Robinson could never have dated Barack Obama, who was a summer associate at her law firm when they met. She was literally fucking the intern.

In 2019 the CEO of McDonald's had to step down after it was discovered that he was having a consensual relationship with an employee. I know, gross—who would date someone who works at McDonald's? I remember reading the article about this "scandal" and wondering where the scandal was: there was no harassment, no off-color texts, no dick-rubbing against underlings.

We all know that "no" doesn't mean "yes"—but now "yes" doesn't mean "yes"? What happened to "my body, my choice"?

Same thing happened to the CEO of Priceline, forced out because he had a relationship with an employee. But come on, it's hard not to have an affair or two when you're getting such a bargain on hotel rooms.

But this is how it works now. The rule is, if I want to have sex with another willing adult, but we both work for Hyundai, we need permission from Hyundai. And we just accept that. Like taking our shoes off at the airport.

Former CNN president Jeff Zucker is another executive who was forced to resign after he admitted he kills hookers in a van. Wait, no, that's not what happened—he had consensual sex with a forty-nine-year-old

CNN executive, who did not complain then and does not now. She said they were in "a relationship." Sure. Like a forty-nine-year-old executive knows better than we do about whether or not she's a victim.

I have to ask: Who are we protecting here? Exactly who at CNN would have been traumatized by this unauthorized boning—the war correspondents?

And what about all the directors and actors who've gotten together over the years—Tim Burton, James Cameron, Joel Coen, Taylor Hackford, Darren Aronofsky, Steven Spielberg, and Noah Baumbach, to name but a few, all married or began serious relationships with a star they were directing.

Was there a power imbalance? Of course—on a movie set, the director is God. But sometimes people fall in love with God; it's a very attractive position. Who are we to tell two people they can't have love because when they met they weren't exactly coequal? People are not always attracted to their coequals—we're not robots.

Although . . .

TECHMATE

I keep reading about an increasing number of people who identify as "digisexuals" or "robosexuals": humans who prefer to have relationships with, and even have sex with, a robot. Or their phone. Or a doll.

A guy in China couldn't find a wife, so he built one. In France, there's a woman with a similar story, who says she isn't attracted to human men, only male robots, so she made one with a 3D printer and now they're engaged. She says she simply dislikes "physical contact with human flesh."

A German woman named Michèle Köbke claims she's erotically in love with a Boeing 737. And planes *are* sexy, I can see falling in love with one—but a Boeing?

There's a guy in Japan who married a hologram—which is great unless the electricity goes out. He says to judge him by human standards is "simply not right . . . it's as if you were trying to talk a gay man into dating a woman."

This is a movement now. They're here, they've got gears, get used to it.

This is the latest emerging sexual orientation demanding equality: people who don't need people and feel that makes them the luckiest people in the world.

There's also an app now for kissing someone virtually, using a pair of wax lips affixed to your phone. But no tongue—that would be weird!

But has no one noticed that in all the movies with human-machine interaction, it never ends well for the humans? *Ex Machina, Lars and the Real Girl, AI, Westworld, Blade Runner 2049, Her*—all of them feature hookups that violate my number one rule in relationships: never make love to someone you have to unplug to clean.

But maybe we're at the point where every couple should ask themselves: Do you already have an unhealthy relationship with technology? When you wake up, do you turn toward your partner first, or do you pick up your phone first?

Because I don't think we need AI to figure out where the trend is going. From the beginning of time to 1937, there were zero instances of any kind of hanky-panky with machines. Then came the first in-home washing machines, followed by the first housewives sitting on them.

Then in 1968, the Hitachi Magic Wand made men obsolete. In 1998, the first webcam girls allowed interpersonal relationships to happen in real time through your computer. And with the advent of the iPhone in 2007, sexting, Tinder, Grindr and dick pics quickly became mainstream.

Five years ago, a shockingly realistic sex doll called RealDoll X came on the market. Gone are the days when having a sex doll meant fucking an air mattress with rouge on it. Not only are these dolls made from high-end silicone and sculpted to perfection, like the Real Housewives, but they're actually part robot now, so they can simulate orgasms—just like a real woman!

And this stuff isn't just for men anymore. They're working on a male companion to the female robot, a male sex-bot named Henry with a huge bionic dick that ejaculates face moisturizer from Sephora. How are we supposed to compete with that?

THERE WILL BE STUD

And then there's this: since the 1980s, American men have literally been losing their testosterone, with average levels declining by about 1 percent per year, along with declining sperm counts.

Researchers have found that Americans across the board are at a thirty-year low for sex, one in four American adults has not had any sex in the past year and half of Americans don't even have it once a month. Forty-four percent of adolescent *males* say they don't even masturbate! What, are they afraid to touch their own dicks because a gym sock can't give consent?

The question is why—why this sex drought? I think the answer might be that American men are often such pussies now that actual pussies want nothing to do with them. It's the result of having it drilled into us in recent years that masculinity is itself toxic and scary and un-evolved, and women don't like it.

And the ones who think they do? They really don't. And if you think you do? You're wrong too. What do you know about you? I think you're probably committing a microaggression against yourself right now and you owe you an apology!

Even the act of just asking a girl out is now seen by many younger people as overly aggressive. There's a feeling that the attributes tradi-tionally characteristic of men are inherently problematic. Which sounds a lot like "men are born wrong." Type the phrase "men are trash" into Etsy and you can purchase a slew of swag with that phrase on it.

Women have come a long way, baby, and the vast majority of that has been long overdue and very, very positive. But maybe in this one way, women have become victims of their own success. You can win the battle and lose the war if you harangue men into becoming less like us and more like you, and end up with someone you have absolutely no desire to fuck. And that's not good for any of the seventy-one genders we have now.

Maybe what we need these days is more sex and less gender. Women aren't attracted to these girly-men they've created. The guy you whipped into total sensitivity isn't sexy to you anymore, no matter how many gummies you eat before bed. There's a special place in a woman's heart for a man who learns to suppress his masculinity—it's called "the friend zone."

Could it be that, as much as women may want to create the perfect man, there's always going to be a little bit of toxic mixed in with our masculinity and no amount of training will turn us into your favorite *Twilight* character?

Masculinity is like coffee: even when you decaffeinate it, there's still a little caffeine in there.

There's certainly no denying there has been a lot of toxicity associated with men throughout history—oceans of brutality, all of which is horrible. And some of which is why our species still exists on Earth. There are brave women fighting in Ukraine, but the images of people I've seen on the news fleeing all seem to be women and children, while every able-bodied man in Ukraine is sticking around to fight and maybe die. It's not always a great advantage being a man. And toxic though we may be, we do sometimes come in handy.

As much as you may not want to admit it, there's a direct correlation between the fact that the Internet is filled with posts like "Every woman in your life now has at least a small crush on Volodymyr Zelenskyy and there's absolutely nothing you can do about it," and the fact that he's what people used to call a "man's man." He can't "share" right now, he's killing Russians. Turns out, after two hundred thousand years, there's still a lot of "another tribe is coming to kill us," and when that happens, you want some big dick energy.

This guy gets women hot—so maybe now would be a good time for relationship gurus to stop saying women just want a man who'll listen. Because Zelenskyy, he's not just listening—he's fixing the problem.

This is something I've heard for years: women just want a man who listens, don't try to fix their problems! Put that to the test sometime. Go over to her house tomorrow and fix her radiator. I bet she loves it.

GEAR AND LOATHING

I recently caught up with the movie *Baby Driver*, because the critics loved it and I had forgotten that critics are stupid. Turns out it's just one more in a long line of movies like the *Transporter* series and *Fast and Furious* parts one to infinity, and *Wheelman* and *Gone in 60 Seconds* and *Driven*, and *Drive* and *The Driver* and *Drive Angry*, and ten others all with the exact same plot: when there's a tough job, or even an impossible mission, the key to it is a guy who possesses the *elite, mind-blowing skill of driving*.

Something we let sixteen-year-olds do. What does it say about our psyche that Hollywood can always count on men to plunk down ten bucks to watch another man make a motor go vroom vroom?

If *Baby Driver* were about an actual *baby* who could drive, that would be impressive—but it's not, it's about a *man* driving a car, which isn't impressive because *I'm a man who drives a car*. Practically every day. And rarely as I'm turning left onto La Cienega do I think, "This would make a terrific movie." Because driving is not that hard! If Baby Driver is unavailable, you know who else can pick you up after you pull a job? Your mom.

Driving is so easy that cars can now drive themselves, in the same way that vacuum cleaners now vacuum by themselves. But there's never been a movie about vacuuming. There *was* a movie called *Eat My Dust!*, but it was about driving.

And yet, every day on the street, I see some guy in a muscle car waiting at the light for the chance to peel out and burn rubber and tear ass down the street like we should all be impressed that he can do this with his foot. But you know who you never see doing that? A woman.

ALONG FOR THE PRIDE

If something about the human race is changing at a previously unprecedented rate, we have to at least discuss it, and that includes the fact that the LGBT population of America seems to be now roughly doubling every generation. According to a recent Gallup poll, less than 1 percent of Americans born before 1946—Joe Biden's generation—identify that way. Two point six percent of boomers do, 4.2 percent of Gen X, 10.5 percent of millennials and 20.8 percent of Gen Z. Which means if we follow this trajectory, we will all be gay by 2054.

I'm just saying that when things change this much this fast, people are allowed to ask: What's up with that? All the babies are in the wrong bodies now? Was there a mix-up at the plant? Like with Cap'n Crunch's Oops All Berries?

It wasn't that long ago that when adults asked a kid, "What do you want to be when you grow up?" they meant "What profession?"

Just before the Supreme Court struck down *Roe v. Wade* in 2022 and made abortion once again illegal in many states, the ACLU tweeted a list of those groups who would be "disproportionately harmed" by this. You'd think "women" might top that list—but no, it wasn't even on the list.

Second on the list was LGBT people. Really? Abortion rights affect gay and trans people more than, you know . . . traditional "breeders"?

I'm happy for trans folks that we now live in an age where they can live their authentic lives openly, and we should always be mindful of respecting and protecting them—but someone needs to say it: not everything's about you. And it's OK to ask questions about something that's very new and involves children. The answer can't always be that anyone from a "marginalized" community is automatically right, trump card, mic drop, end of discussion. Because we're literally experimenting on children.

Maybe that's why most European countries have stopped giving puberty blockers to kids—because we just don't know that much about the long-term effects, although common sense should tell you that when you reverse the course of "raging" hormones, there are going to be problems. We do know it hinders the development of bone density, which is kind of important if you like having a skeleton. Fertility and the ability to have an orgasm also seem to be affected.

This isn't just a lifestyle decision: it's medical. Weighing trade-offs is not bigotry. Yet when Abigail Shrier released her book *Irreversible Damage*, questioning the sudden uptick in transitioning children, a trans lawyer with the ACLU named Chase Strangio tweeted, "Stopping the circulation of this book and these ideas is 100% a hill I will die on."

How very civil liberties of him. Chase, by the way, was named one of the grand marshals of the 2022 New York City Pride March, along with three other trans people and a lesbian. Hmm, what's missing . . . oh right, a gay man. That's where we are: gay men aren't hip enough for the gay pride parade anymore. Compared to trans, gay is practically cis, and cis is practically Mormon.

And this is a phenomenon we need to take into account when we look at this issue: yes, part of the rise in LGBT numbers is from people finally feeling free enough now to tell it to a pollster, and their family, and that's all to the good. But some of it is simply that it's trendy. Some of it is a TikTok challenge that got out of hand. "Penis equals man? OK, boomer!"

Remember, the prime directive of every teen is: do anything to shock and challenge the squares who brought you up. It's why nobody gets a nose ring at fifty-six. And if you haven't noticed that, with kids, doing something "for the likes" is more important than their own genitals, you haven't been paying attention.

Dr. Erica Anderson is a prominent seventy-one-year-old clinical psychologist who is herself transgender and who now says, "I think it's gone too far . . ." As the *Los Angeles Times* summarizes it, she's "come to believe that some children identifying as trans are falling under the influence of their peers and social media."

If you attend a small dinner party of typically very liberal, upper-income Angelinos, it would not be uncommon for half the parents there to have a trans kid; what are the odds of that happening in Youngstown, Ohio? If this spike in trans children is all natural, why is it regional? It's like that day we suddenly needed bottled water all the time. Either Ohio is shaming them or California is creating them—and the honest answer is, it's probably a bit of both.

But if we can't admit that in certain enclaves there is some level of trendiness to the idea of being anything other than straight, then this is not a serious, science-based discussion—it's a blow being struck in the culture wars using children as cannon fodder. I don't understand parents who won't let their nine-year-old walk to the corner without a helmet, an EpiPen and a GPS tracker, and God forbid their lips touch dairy—but hormone blockers and genital surgery? Fine. Talk about a nut allergy.

And never forget, children are impressionable and very, very stupid. Kids don't know why Mom drinks every day or why Dad has two cell phones. Maybe the boy who thinks he's a girl is just gay. Or whatever Frasier was. Maybe the girl who hates "girly stuff" just needs to learn that being female doesn't mean you have to act like Megan Fox. Maybe childhood makes you sad sometimes and there are other solutions besides "hand me the dick saw."

And while I'm sure the vast majority of parents do not take this lightly, it's also very hard to know when something is real or just a phase. And I understand being trans is different, it's innate—but kids do also have phases.

They're kids; it's *all* phases. The dinosaur phase, the Hello Kitty phase—one day they want to be an astronaut, the next day you can't get them to leave their room. Gender-fluid? Kids are fluid about everything. If kids knew what they wanted to be at age eight, the world would be filled with cowboys and princesses. I wanted to be a pirate; thank God nobody took me seriously and scheduled me for eye removal and peg leg surgery.

SEX AND BALANCES

Twenty seventeen was a great year for women, because finally men were put on notice: harassment of any kind is going to be noted now, so you're going to have to think of another way to meet women. All men are playing with five fouls now, as they should. The Me Too movement was a landmark civil rights advancement, long overdue and overwhelmingly positive.

It's also true that Democrats woke themselves into a corner when they adopted "Believe Women" as their slogan, when it should always have been "Take All Accusations Seriously."

Me Too? Yes. Me-Carthyism? No. I knew something was way off when Senator Kirsten Gillibrand went unchallenged after saying, "When we start having to talk about the differences between sexual harassment and sexual assault and unwanted groping, you are having the wrong conversation."

Can't we just be having an additional conversation? We can only have one thought now? Is that why Al Franken had to become roadkill on the Zero-Tolerance Highway—a highway, it seems, only Democrats have to drive on? Do liberals really want to become the distinction deniers? The people who can't tell, or don't want to see, a difference between assault in a van and a back rub by the water cooler?

Masturbation is normal and healthy, but not in the park. Giving up on the idea that even bad things have degrees is as dumb as embracing "alternative facts." Justice requires weighing things. That's why Lady Justice is holding a scale and not a sawed-off shotgun.

Senator Gillibrand also said, "You need to draw a line in the sand and say none of it is OK." Agreed, but we can't walk and chew gum anymore? We can't agree that groping and rape are both unacceptable, *and* one is worse?

When Matt Damon said, "There's a difference between . . . patting someone on the butt and rape or child molestation, right?" Minnie Driver responded by saying, "You don't get to tell women that because some guy only showed them their penis their pain isn't as great as a woman who was raped."

What? This is crazy. No woman in the world, if she actually had to pick, would choose rape over merely seeing a penis, so why did we all have to pretend Minnie Driver's statement is noble and Matt Damon is crazy?

We're losing the thread back to thinking itself. The Declaration of Independence begins with the words "We hold these truths to be self-evident"—*self*-evident, as in, some things are such obvious, indisputable no-brainers that we start from that point, assuming we're all generally on the page that shit is measurably, chemically different from Shinola.

But now basic building blocks of thought, like "there are facts" and "things have degrees," are being tossed aside. Kirsten Gillibrand said of the Al Franken allegations, "The women who came forward felt it was sexual harassment. So it was."

That was never tenable, because believing everything doesn't make you noble—it makes you gullible. And leaves us with a world where Republicans don't care about this stuff, so it's just a unilateral weapon that is used only against Democrats. Trump rides the bus with Billy Bush, and we throw Al Franken under it.

We can have Me Too and Al Franken too—they're not mutually exclusive.

America always overreacts and then has buyer's remorse: we did it with 9/11 and Janet Jackson's nipple and Covid and Bill Clinton's blow job. And certainly, one of the all-time overreactions was "Al Franken, sex predator."

Let's review what Al did. It started with a gag picture from a USO tour of him pretending to feel—but not actually touching—the breasts of a pretty D-list celebrity on the tour, Leeann Tweeden. Al apologized for the picture, and no one died.

Then there's the sketch Al wrote to perform for the troops with Tweeden. She says, "Franken had written a moment when his character comes at me for a 'kiss.' I suspected what he was after."

Well, he'd performed that same sketch many times before with other women and there were no complaints, and it seems what he was after was a big laugh from the soldiers in the audience, because the payoff is one of their own winds up getting the girl.

Also what got lost in this is Al saying that he hoped by resigning he didn't give people the "false impression that [he] was admitting to doing things that, in fact, [he hadn't] done." He was careful to always say women should be heard, but he never said, "Yeah, I did it."

I believe Al. I think that's still my right as an American. Yes, women should be heard, always, and we should always keep in mind the vast majority of women reporting serious abuse are truthful—but women also didn't completely lose the ability to lie in 2017.

I find it very curious that in Leeann's two decades in Hollywood— including parties at the Playboy Mansion and popularity in the world of sports—the only guy who ever got out of line was Al Franken.

Leeann Tweeden was long a staunch conservative, a favorite guest of Sean Hannity and a Donald Trump Jr. Twitter pal, and somehow Roger Stone knew it was "Al Franken's time in the barrel" right before she made her allegations public.

Seven other women, four anonymous, accused Al of mostly hand-drifting while taking pictures. Does it matter that at least two of these are ridiculous?

Was it really wise for Democrats to permanently send away one of their ablest warriors for an accusation of touching a woman's waist wrong while taking a photo? I don't know what happened that day, and neither do you. It's possible he was being deliberately handsy, and it's possible it was innocent. But he didn't drive her off a bridge and leave her to drown.

Can we get some perspective? Does every infraction, no matter how small, have to be rehashed for an entire lifetime? That's not politics— that's marriage.

ROM DOM

Trying to micromanage every possible human interaction is never going to be the answer, especially when it comes to the imprecise, inexact science of initiating a romance. The movement falters if it thinks we can make pain-free the often messy transition from two people *not* in a romantic relationship to two people who *are*.

Sometimes people at work fall in love. Sometimes people try something new in bed without having a pre-production meeting about it. Not every guy who makes a woman uncomfortable did it because he's an asshole.

A Harris poll says 38 percent of Americans have dated a coworker and 31 percent of office romances have led to marriage. The rest ended happily. And yet, Meta, Google, Netflix, Airbnb and others all have policies where you can only ask a coworker out once: if she or he or they say no, you can't ask again. Right, because feelings in human beings never change.

But what about rom-coms? Women like them precisely because the men *do* change! In *Fifty Shades of Grey*, Christian Grey starts out as a sadist, and by the end he's traded in his butt plug for a heated toilet seat.

In romantic comedies there are only three plots: "She married her boss," "Stalking is romantic" and "I hate you and then I love you."

Now, it's true that men made most of these movies—but women bought most of the tickets. I sure wasn't the one who wanted to go see *Failure to Launch*. And *Fifty Shades of Grey* was written, directed and devoured by women.

Because people are complicated. That's why there's a relationship status category called "It's Complicated."

We don't know why we're attracted to a woman, or a man, or, if you've seen *The Shape of Water*, a fish. Yes, that movie is about a cleaning woman at a secret government lab who takes the Creature from the Black Lagoon home and bangs it in the bathtub. If that's not workplace sex, it's certainly "stealing office supplies."

Love Actually is somehow a lot of people's favorite movie, but if it were made today it would have to be called *Inappropriate Actually*. It's nothing but men hitting on their underlings, and one character is such a stalker he shows up at the door of his married crush, who winds up chasing him down the street and kissing him! Most women today call the police if you leave a note on their car.

I'm not saying men act the way they do primarily because of movies, but they have been getting the message for a long time that this is what women want. And it *is* what women want—the catch being, *only from the men they want it from.*

The problem is, we don't know which one we are until we try. I wouldn't try the "throwing a chair through the window" move used by William Hurt in *Body Heat*, but it totally worked for Kathleen Turner. In *Jerry McGuire*, the hero barges uninvited into the home of the assistant he's hired and had sex with and says, "I'm not letting you get rid of me, how about that?"—and it's adorable, because it's Tom Cruise!

Ted Cruz, not so much.

John Cusack? Always cute—even when he shows up uninvited outside his ex's house playing the music *they used to have sex to.* In the movie, she loves it. In real life, the cops arrive, mistake the boom box for a gun and shoot him fifty-seven times.

NONE IN THE OVEN

In the last fifty years, the share of Americans who live alone has doubled, which begs the question: if single people are such a large part of this country now, why do our political and economic policies always still revolve around families? Just one time I'd like to hear a politician say, "I'm Congressman Harry Spooner and I'm not for working families. I'm for people whose babies ended up in the reservoir tip."

As a lifelong single person, I have always stood up for the person who chooses to remain single—and although we've come a long way in terms of respect, there's still a ways to go.

Everyone is so used to "married with children" being the norm that nobody noticed that single people are now nearly half the population. And yet, we still remain a somewhat suspect group. Somehow, in the eyes of many . . . incomplete.

Jennifer Aniston told *People* magazine that she's been "shamed" as a "sad, childless human." Yeah, like she's the pathetic freak, as opposed to those pillars of the community the Duggars, with their litter of nineteen children. Call me antifamily, but I say you're overdoing it when your wife has to say, "Not tonight, honey, I'm giving birth."

Having kids or not having kids: there should be no moral dimension to it. It's just your taste. I don't have kids for the same reason you do: because that's what each of us wants. Although, I must say, no one in the world ever looked happier than the people Maury Povich used to tell, "You are *not* the father."

Whenever single people are at a party, married folks always feel free to tell us how good it would be to get married and have a kid. But somehow it's rude if I say, "And you guys should totally get divorced!" And it's always OK for married people to ask the single person about their sex life, but we can't say to them, "Boy, I bet it's been a long time since you guys did it!"

When you're childless, people love to tell you: "You *have* to have a baby!" But you don't *have* to. You *have* to have car insurance.

Remaining single isn't for everyone, but it's a perfectly rational decision. The science is in: singles exercise more than married people do, single women have better overall health and single men have lower rates of heart disease. Singles actually have stronger social ties and less debt, and are more likely to volunteer for civic organizations.

Now, of course, a lot of this is to get laid. But not all of it. So stop asking a woman why she isn't married or why she doesn't have children. She doesn't owe you an explanation. You owe her nine thousand tons of carbon.

That's right, you can drive a hybrid, recycle and not throw batteries in the trash, and it all adds up to a fraction of the good it would do to have just one fewer child, because that child increases your carbon legacy by over nine thousand tons. And since there's literally nothing you can do that's better for the environment than to *not* produce another resource-sucking, waste-making human being, there really should be, along with Mother's Day and Father's Day, one day a year that's set aside as Singles' Day.

We don't have a day. Only happy hour. We've spent a lifetime being the cool aunts and uncles, but while we celebrate everybody else, no-body ever celebrates us. And they really should. Because you know what Mother Nature loves even more than electric cars? Condoms.

I *didn't* bring a kid into the world to consume valuable resources—where's *my* breakfast in bed? Where's *my* coupon "good for one foot rub"? Where's my greeting card that says: "Roses are red. Violets are blue. You helped the Earth by keeping a lid on your goo?"

And remember, every time a single person does something to pre-vent pregnancy, they're creating more slots on college campuses for your kid.

Hallmark needs a card that says, "It's not that you're gay, it's not that you're lesbian. But because you didn't have kids, mine got into Wesleyan."

23

TRUMP

There has been no figure in the time I've been doing television who has dominated our attention quite like Donald Trump—and, America, don't take this the wrong way, but I don't mean that as a compliment.

Of course, we did dozens of editorials about him on *Real Time*—and there may have even been a few jokes about him in the previous pages. But I'm not going to let Donald Trump have the satisfaction of dominating this book. We know him only *too* well—so let's just play the greatest hits and call it a day.

DONNIE DORKO

The first example of our "Explaining Jokes to Idiots" bit came in 2013, after Donald Trump sued me. Here's how I explained it in February 2013:

Now that Donald Trump is suing me for five million dollars because he says he's proved that he is *not* the love child of an orangutan, Donald Trump must learn two things: what a joke is, and what a contract is.

Let me catch you up on how all this got started: During the last week of the presidential campaign last year, Donald Trump, who previously had been a one-issue candidate obsessed with Obama's birth certificate, announced that he would give five million dollars to charity if Obama produced his college records—because, come on, a Black guy getting into college? Something fishy there.

So, playing on the fact that the only other thing in nature with the same color hair as Trump's is the orange-haired orangutan, I demanded that Donald Trump show me *his* birth certificate to prove *he* wasn't hiding a bad secret about *his* birth—this is known as "parody," and it's a form of something we in the comedy business call a "joke."

Naturally, I also "aped," if you will, Trump's offer of money to a charity of his choosing, which I identified as the Hair Club for Men. This upset the Donald so much they could barely get him to stop flinging his feces.

Now, public figures of course don't always like everything that's said about them—but that's how we roll here in America; just like how we're the "gun country," we're also the "joke country." We're not England, where it's easy to win a libel suit. We love our free speech, and we love celebrities getting taken down a peg. And if you're lucky enough to be one, you just have to suck it up like everyone else does.

But not Trump. His lawyer sent me a letter that says: "Attached hereto is a copy of Mr. Trump's birth certificate, demonstrating that he is the son of Fred Trump, and not an orangutan." Do these morons even know it's impossible for people and apes to produce offspring?

So, I ignored the letter like I ignore all letters I get from crazy people, and I forgot about the whole thing until this week, when Trump actually sued me for the five million.

And don't forget, this is not a libel case. No, this is an attempt to set a bold new precedent in American jurisprudence: that jokes about public figures on television shows are now legally binding agreements between the comedian and the person they're making fun of.

EGO-WARRIOR

In 2019, I thought I might be able to take advantage of the ultimate blind spot in Trump's psyche by flattering him into becoming an eco-warrior. I offered him my vote if he would just get religion on one issue: the environment. Here was my plea:

Sir, at one of your recent rallies, you called me a "serious person," and I appreciate that. You also called me "third-rate" and a "so-called comedian." And then a "respected" comedian. You also said I was "wacky," which isn't really that big an insult for a comedian.

But I'm not here to fight—I'm here to offer my vote. And so, Mr. President, Your Excellency, least racist person in the world, let me address you directly and try to win you over with logic, because I know flattery simply will not work. You're impervious to it—bounces off you like bullets from Superman's chest.

So I'm not gonna try that—not on a man as great as you. I'm not that wacky! I'd look foolish trying, and you'd see through it right away, because you're a stable genius. And did I mention handsome? When I see you and Melania together I always think, "Which one was the model?"

But, sir, picture this headline: "Trump Saves Earth." Feels right, doesn't it? And all it would take is for you to undergo a sudden, profound change, like the Grinch when he saved Christmas. How befitting for a man of such power, intellect and a large, completely un-mushroom-like penis. Someone with the most beautiful words and a slavish devotion to the truth.

I bet if you devote yourself to solving the climate crisis, the people will put your face on the $100 bill, combining your two great loves: money and you. And then they will put you on Mount Rushmore. That'd be a switch, huh? Someone chiseling *you*.

Wait, I was kidding—I'm sorry—please, Mr. President, before you change the channel and go back to your chess game . . .

I know we've tangled in the past: you sued me once, and we both have said some things. You called me "stupid," "not considered smart," "a dummy," "not a smart guy," "the dumbest man on television," "fired like a dog," "very sad . . . pathetic, bloated and gone," "dumbass," "a rather dumb guy," "a lowlife dummy," "dopey," "dumb as a rock," "moron," "stupid guy," "a very dumb guy," "failing comedian" and most hurtful of all, "smokes too much pot."

And I called you a whiny little bitch.

But I'm just gonna admit it right now: I was jealous. Always have been. I mean, who's kidding who? We both know you have the best brain, and everything you take on is an incredible success. You won the trade war, you built the wall, you effortlessly solved the Middle East and Stormy Daniels is still basking in the afterglow of your incredible lovemaking. Women want to be with you, and men want to be like you. I know I do: as a tribute to you, I've even taken to wearing toilet paper on my shoe.

And I'm sure many would follow: if you would just embrace the environment as a cause, think about all the A-listers who overnight would become your biggest fans. Brad, Matt, Clooney . . . the White House would be like *Ocean's Eleven*!

Taylor Swift will be begging you to follow her on Instagram. DiCaprio will love you. Gisele will love you. Ivanka will get invited to parties again! You'll be a big hero in her eyes, and we know you love her—in a completely appropriate way.

Look, you're already the greatest president ever—we know that's a fact because "people are saying it." So I can see why you might be thinking, "Why do I need to gild the lily? I've already saved mankind from extinction once, after Obama—do I have to do it twice?"

Yes, sir, I'm afraid you do. Please, lend your giant brain to work with the other, lesser brains in the scientific community. If you save the planet, billions of children will be grateful—and one of them could be your next wife!

Remember my pledge: Become a pit bull for planet Earth and you won't need Russia to hack my polling place. I will vote for you. I will gladly take my paper ballot and put my prick next to your face!

BOB COST US

Here's our editorial from April 2019 after the Mueller report came out:

Just because you have a stone face doesn't mean you belong on Mount Rushmore. For over two years, America has had a crazy person in the White House, and for over two years the Democrats have done fuck-all about it, because they were waiting for the report from yet another Republican We Can Count On, Robert Mueller. We all sat around waiting for Prosecutor Jesus to turn in his big report, and he came back with "Ask someone else."

We needed Superman and we got Clark *Can't*.

Trump calls the Mueller report "the crazy Mueller report," and in a way he's right, because it's over four hundred pages detailing terrible crimes by a corrupt president, yet Mueller doesn't prosecute. If Dostoevsky had written this report, it would be called "Crime and *No* Punishment."

Mueller's report is full of "but"s. Don Jr. met with the Russians, *but* . . . Manafort gave internal polling data to a Russian, *but* . . . Trump obstructed justice every day, *but* . . .

Robert Mueller: he loves big buts, and he cannot lie.

Preet Bharara was on *Real Time* the week the Barr summary came out, and I had one burning question: Could a different prosecutor have reached a completely different conclusion? And he said . . . yeah.

That's all I need to know. I get it, Mueller's a Boy Scout, a straight arrow—he played it by the book. But you may have noticed, for the past three years, we've kinda been *off book*. And greatness sometimes means *not* doing everything by the book.

Thomas Jefferson made the Louisiana Purchase in 1803, doubling the size of the United States—without any authority to do so. But history called his name, and it said, "Take the shot, Mav."

That's what Spielberg's movie *Lincoln* is about. Even after the Emancipation Proclamation, Black people were not free—that required a constitutional amendment initiated in Congress. And to make that happen—while he had a window to make it happen—Lincoln lied, bribed, freed prisoners, even fast-tracked an entire new state into the Union.

None of which Mueller would have had to do to reach a satisfactory end to his two years of work. All he had to do is what people in the justice system do every day: *use* the law to come to justice, not be so restricted by technicalities that the bad guys win.

There's a reason Clint Eastwood never made a movie called *Clean Harry*. Sometimes it comes down to you. In America today, the attorney general is corrupt and the Congress is dysfunctional, so what good is leaving a "road map for impeachment" if you know a tribal, party-before-country Republican Senate will never remove the president?

Bob, your trail of breadcrumbs isn't good enough—we're not that smart anymore. America is like an aging shortstop: you have to hit it right at us.

To me, this report is summed up in the words "Donald Trump Jr. declined to be voluntarily interviewed."

So make him! Was he too busy? You couldn't work around his tweeting schedule? And you, tough guy, couldn't get the president's taxes? You didn't "follow the money"?

You didn't interview Trump, we're told, because he couldn't possibly testify under oath without perjuring himself. And that's *our* problem? It's one feckless punt after another.

Rudy Giuliani said this week, "There's nothing wrong with taking information from Russians." That's where we are now. I lay that on Mueller. From now on, you can meet with foreign governments, invite them to hack your opponents, and break campaign finance laws as long as it's by reason of "Duh, I'm plausibly too dumb to know what I was doing."

For a guy who didn't want to break precedent by indicting a president, Mueller sure created a lot of new precedents. Because that's what law is: new precedents, always evolving.

And most infuriating of all, "You can't indict a sitting president" isn't in the Constitution; it's not even a law. It's a *guideline*, like drinking white wine with fish or not fucking your cousin. It's a fucking memo.

In Watergate, the special prosecutor Leon Jaworski faced a very similar guideline, but he understood the big picture, and his role in history, and sued a sitting president anyway. Mueller could have done that, and the headline the next day would have been "Mueller Breaks with Precedent, Indicts Trump," and then that would be our new reality.

A better reality, because now Trump goes into the 2020 election as a vindicated martyr. Maybe we should have brought back Ken Starr as prosecutor. At least he knew how to go after a dick in the Oval Office.

WELCOME BACK, PLOTTER

As of the time this was printed, Donald Trump's fate in his many indictments and trials was as yet unknown—but here was the view after the first Stormy Daniels one:

This whole "going after the president for fucking around" thing? I've seen this movie before. It was called *Kill Bill*. And America didn't like it the first time, in the nineties, when President Bill Clinton had a fling with a White House intern named Monica Lewinsky, and the Republicans exposed him as a dirty, filthy, disgusting sex-doer. And when they were done with him, he had an approval rating of 73 percent. This despite every Republican on every TV station for two years saying, "What do we tell the children?" And those children are today's millennials, who, according to polls, don't know anything about it and don't care—so I guess you didn't tell them anything! Good job, parents! Funny how the Republicans NOW don't care at all when their kid asks, "Mommy, what's up with Trump and the lady who starred in *Titsicle*?"

As I watch the circus around our latest horny ex-president who loves fast food and hung out with Jeffrey Epstein, it seems worth asking the Democrats: Having gone through this yourselves, what don't you get about "sex scandals don't work on presidents"? Because no matter what the legal reasons are underpinning a sex scandal, to the average person, it's just always going to be about sex. Nothing can compete; law is boring. It's the constitutional equivalent of golf.

I remember what people were talking about during the Clinton scandal, and it wasn't the finer points of perjury law. It was about how one of his blowies happened during a phone call with congressional leaders, and how he came in the sink, and how they did it on Easter, and that thing he did with the cigar. Yeah, if you're too young to know, don't ask.

Same thing with Trump today: Joe Sixpack is not going to take the time to wrap his head around how the statute of limitations applies to a misdemeanor of falsifying business records if it involves a violation of state election law in a second crime involving a federal campaign, conditional on the residential status of the defendant. My head hurts just reading it.

There's a reason every news outlet in the country recently ran the headline "How Strong Is the Case Against Trump?" It's their way of saying, "Don't get your hopes up." Yes, Trump fucked Stormy Daniels at a charity golf event while his wife was home with their newborn—the kind of thing we all *assumed* Trump was doing. What's your next bombshell—that his hair is a comb-over? The shocking part wasn't the sex, it was that he was involved in a legitimate charity.

To half the country it looks like: You tried to get him on Russia, and you tried to get him on Ukraine, and you tried to get him on classified documents, and you didn't, so now you went for the old reliable. Congratulations, you found out powerful men have an Achilles' heel—their balls.

It was the same thing with Clinton back in '98, with the positions reversed: an Arkansas land deal called Whitewater became something-something Paula Jones became "Why is the president testifying about what the definition of sex is?" Oh yeah, because sex is fun. And it works. So don't come on my dress and tell me it's raining.

Back then, Republicans were always telling us how much they hated, just hated, having to investigate Clinton's sex life, but their hands were tied by the "rule of law . . . oh, it's a sad day for America, but for the sake of the Constitution and the honored dead of Gettysburg my conscience leaves me no choice." And like Monica, most people found all that a little hard to swallow.

Of course, Clinton's situation and Trump's have important differences: Clinton was in office, and Trump is not. Trump's case hinges on an NDA, and Clinton's was more about DNA. One involved a naïve young ingénue who had genuine feelings, the other an older, more sexually experienced bottle blond with big tits: Donald Trump.

But there are also important similarities: Monica was an intern, and Stormy wanted to be an apprentice. Neither wife could stand to hold her husband's hand. And both men claimed they lied to protect the person they really loved—in Clinton's case, Hillary, and in Trump's case, him.

But the element that most vitally sets these two cases apart is this: Republicans went after Clinton on sex because they didn't have anything else; they had combed through his life like a school nurse looking for head lice and all they could ever come up with was the blow job. But Democrats didn't have to do this: Trump commits real crimes. He commits them on TV. He obstructed justice, such as when he fired James Comey; he pressured state election officials to fix an election in Georgia—on tape; he asked another country to interfere in our elections *publicly*; he sides with our enemies. He refuses to concede elections and thereby incites insurrection.

Look, I understand how cathartic, bordering on ecstatic, it is to see Donald Trump get hauled from his retirement home to stand trial with his meathead goombah lawyers like the slumlord from Queens that he is. It just *feels right.* But unfortunately, now we're so used to seeing Trump hauled into court that it's no big whoop. Just like how we got used to watching him get impeached. And that's a real shame, because I was saving my good drugs for the coup trial.

NOCTURNAL OMISSION

Someone needs to explain to me how there have been over twelve hundred books written about the Trump presidency, books that were mostly competing to reveal every detail of his life, and not one of them tells me the one thing I'm most curious about: Who is Donald Trump fucking?

He's fucking somebody, and it's not Melania, and it's not nobody—he's a dog and always has been, and I doubt that went away after he became the most powerful man in the world.

How is it possible I don't have the answer to this question: who is blowing Donald Trump? How could it be that if you read every page of *Fire and Fury, Confidence Man, Team of Vipers, A Very Stable Genius, Betrayal, Disloyal, Revenge, Unhinged, Rage, Fear, Peril, Blitz, Full Disclosure, The Divider,* and *The Room Where It Happened,* you'd still have no idea what happened in the room?

We know everything else about the guy down to the most minute detail because everyone around him has the loyalty of a pet scorpion. All White Houses are a bit of a sieve, but the Trump White House leaked more than Nick Cannon's condoms.

We know he cuts his own hair with giant scissors and listens to show tunes to calm down. We know how he gets two scoops of ice cream when everyone else gets one. We know he tweets *on* the toilet and throws documents *down* the toilet. We know he cheats at golf, was once caught eating paper, doesn't like dogs, is a germaphobe, uses a tanning bed, once cashed a check for thirteen cents, has his pants steamed while wearing them, sleeps four hours a night and hesitated to give Don Jr. his name because "what if he's a loser?"

We even know that his penis is shaped like a mushroom. How is it possible we don't know who is servicing it?

And don't tell me it's nobody! He's on tape bragging that when you're a star you can do anything you want—that guy didn't just go away. Alpha dogs never die. Anthony Quinn had a baby out of wedlock at seventy-eight. His wife was very mad at him—and then he did it again at eighty-one. Italy's lecherous old prime minister Silvio Berlusconi was having bunga-bunga parties in his seventies. Do you think Donald Trump just one day said, "Yeah, sex was fun but I think I'll switch to building ships in a bottle"?

And again, we know it's not Melania. Please—it's just not. She won't even give him hand. She hates him, and he's made it plain he's not into women her age. To him, she's a MILD: a mom I'd like to divorce. Do they even live together? Is she alive? He seems to live completely as a single man—still alpha, still crazy and I bet still horny.

It doesn't add up. Someone—or some team of people; Lindsey Graham could be involved, possibly Hannity—is blowing Donald Trump, and it's a scandal that we don't know what the scandal is.

We certainly know all about his *past* sex life—the cheating, the groping, the walking into the dressing room at beauty pageants. Hot for daughter. Telling ten-year-olds he'll be dating them in ten years. The parties with Epstein, the grabbing pussies, the porn star mistress—everything. And then the historical record goes blank. What happened? Why can't we unearth his bone?

Not even anything from the post-presidency years at Mar-a-Lago? He lives at a country club! With hundreds of people coming and going—you wouldn't even have to fake how the groupies get in. And they must get in; he's a man who lives to be adored, and Florida is full of thousands of unhinged MAGA sluts who see him as sent by God to save America—and it's well known Evangelical chicks are the freakiest.

Cult leaders get laid. There's no way this is not happening.

Who is blowing Donald Trump?! I have to know this. I have a right to know this. It's not like these are the days of JFK, when the media covered up indiscretions for the sake of the country. Please, like the media has too much class to blab? Hahahaha. This would get the most clicks ever. Twitter would be so lit up Elon would have to hire back all the employees.

I don't count on the news media for much anymore—but I do expect them to tell me who's fucking who.

Unless the answer is he just can't. We all remember that debate where he said, "I guarantee there's no problem."

Well, maybe there is. Maybe there is a problem—in which case I feel for him. Look, I'm not trying to bait Donald Trump into a response to prove his dick still works, the way I got him to produce his birth certificate. Probably his dick doesn't work. But maybe it does. I mean, it's possible theoretically.

Although there's really no other explanation for how a cult leader with hundreds of willing groupies who's not restrained by his wife, by his options or by morals could not be having sex with anyone. In fact, I wouldn't be surprised if Trump nicknamed his penis "Mike Pence" because it's not hung like it should be.

CASKET CASE

In the later years of the second decade of the twenty-first century, America was able to achieve a rare bipartisan uniformity on one single issue: no one wanted Donald Trump at their funeral. When John McCain, Barbara Bush, Elijah Cummings, John Dingell and John Lewis died, their families all had the same reaction: "Our loved one is dead, don't ruin it."

Yes, it seems Donald Trump is about as welcome at a funeral as the Gypsy woman who wanders into restaurants and sells you roses at a business dinner. And this is even when he was the president! That's like a children's hospital turning down Spider-Man. What kind of spectacular prick do you have to be that everyone's last request is "Make sure that asshole isn't at my funeral"?

But then I remembered how, in *The Adventures of Tom Sawyer*, Tom and Huckleberry Finn get to attend their own funeral—and from doing so, they learn a lot about themselves. And I thought, "If Trump could hear what a eulogy for *him* might sound like, maybe that would give him some insight into himself." So in 2020 I prepared a modest example.

Dear family and frenemies of Donald Trump. Some men look at the world and ask, "Why?" Donald looked at the world and asked, "What's in it for me?" His generosity knew only limits, and he never once failed to put himself before others. He was a devoted father who every day tried to teach his children the wrong lessons of life: be quick to anger, never let go of a grudge, see the worst in people and treat them all equally, based strictly on how much money they make and what they look like.

So many wanted to speak here today but couldn't break their non-disclosure agreements. And our hearts go out to Melania, who RSVP'd "maybe." Donald always said he knew she was the one the moment he saw her and said those three little words: "Add to cart."

Donald loved so many things: money, golf, lawsuits, porn stars, dictators, organized crime and the 35 percent of the American people who liked him. The other 65 percent could go fuck themselves. He once said that the experience of not being in Vietnam taught him the most important lesson of all: that there's no problem so big you can't lie your way out of it.

When it came to flouting the law, he was a "criminal's criminal." And intellectually, a midget among giants. A man of few words. About a hundred. Mostly "tremendous," "disgusting," "strongly" and "shithole."

Donald Trump never met a man he liked—and yet he always suffered fools: you could tell him anything, and he'd believe it. It's painful to think he could still be with us if only his personal physician wasn't that lady who believed medicine came from outer space.

Donald's greatest hero, Winston Churchill, said of his own mortality, "I'm ready to meet my Maker. Whether my Maker is prepared for the great ordeal of meeting me is another matter."

Well, God: Trump's your problem now. As for me personally, I guess what I'll miss most about Don is his dull wit. He was never laughing. And when he made you laugh, it was always unintentional. But as a walking parody of himself, he was a challenge to satirize and made me a better comedian for it.

He died as he lived—wearing makeup and lying in front of all of us. So fly free, whiny little bitch, fly free. May you find the peace your Twitter thumbs never could.

24

CIVIL WAR

DIVISIONIST HISTORY

I love historians. I watch the History Channel like most guys watch Pornhub. In college, I majored in history. And who didn't love high school history? There was always a 50 percent chance the teacher would be hungover and just show a movie. But this stance that historians are always selling on cable news that "America's like a cat—it always lands on its feet"—I don't buy it.

I don't buy that just because something didn't happen before, it can't happen now. Rome didn't fall and didn't fall and didn't fall—and then it fell. Gonorrhea has been around for a long time and we could always kill it with penicillin, but now there's drug-resistant super gonorrhea and we can't.

Was incivility bad at other times in our history? I'm sure it was; I've heard the anecdotes. I know that during a brawl in the House chamber in 1798, Congressman Matthew Lyon of Vermont tried to beat Roger Griswold of Connecticut with a pair of iron tongs. I don't care; what's going on in America lately isn't two gentlemen slapping each other in the face with gloves.

George W. Bush may not have been my favorite, but he believed in democracy. So much so he tried to export it to Iraq. Whereas Trump believes in oligarchy so much he tried to import it from Russia. That's not just a difference in degree but a difference in kind. Previous presidents declared war—but never on reality. You gotta admit, that was kinda new.

To paraphrase the Farmers Insurance guy, "I know a thing or two because I've seen a thing or two." And—to paraphrase the Allstate guy—we're *not* in good hands. Marjorie Taylor Greene didn't invent our country's polarization any more than she can spell it, but she's playing with fire when she says, "We need a national divorce. We need to separate by red states and blue states . . . we are done . . ."

And then she threw Biden's things out onto the lawn and said, "I'll be at my mother's."

Ben Shapiro has also floated the idea that our "best hope" now is a "friendly separation" of states. Sounds crazy, but a full third of likely voters agree with them, and approve of a national divorce, with Texas the most enthusiastic: in a 2022 poll, 66 percent of all voters there said they were ready to split, including 59 percent of Democrats.

I'd like to remind them of one thing: America is a family. And the definition of "family" is "people who hate each other without resorting to violence." Never forget the single shining truth about democracy: it means sharing a country with assholes you can't stand.

I've preached that you can hate Trump but not all the people who like him. If we want to simply exist, we're going to have to find a way to work together. Like the Rolling Stones. A lot like the Rolling Stones, because we also need a comeback tour to pay our bills.

People keep sending me these maps showing how red states and blue states should just go our separate ways. "We'll get New York, they'll get Texas." Take it from someone who's traveled this country my whole life: there *are no* red states or blue states. They call toss-up states "purple states," but in reality all the states are purple states. If you win an election in America sixty to forty, it's considered a landslide.

We're among each other now, all swirled together and marbled in. We can't have a second civil war because the two sides aren't neatly separated like they were for the first one. The Mason-Dixon Line of today would cut through states, cities, streets—even bedrooms. There are 3.8 million Biden voters in Texas and 4.5 million Trump voters in California. We can't go to war because I think my dry cleaners might be behind enemy lines. I don't want to fight the Battle of Trader Joe's.

Donald Trump's middle name might as well be "existential threat"—and I have not been shy about calling him that myself. But the other side sees Democratic control of government in exactly the same way, and it's unfortunately no longer the case that they're completely wrong about that. And when both sides believe the other guy taking over means the end of the world—yes, you can have a civil war.

So let's not have one. We're no good at war, and they're no good at being civil. Like 'em or not, neither side is going anywhere. The only people who ever threaten to leave the country are rich celebrities, and unfortunately none of them ever do.

I DID NAZI THAT COMING

One night on the road last year I had a driver who hailed from Bosnia. He left because his city of Sarajevo became a war-torn hellscape, and he said to me: "What I am seeing happening here now is exactly what I saw in Bosnia then. Next-door neighbors who despise each other." He was telling me that hate on this level can only be sustained for so long before becoming actual war.

During campaigns, there's a lot of talk about who can unite us. No president can unite us. We have to unite ourselves. There are only two ways this country can go: either we come together and forgive our differences, or we turn into Sarajevo. Into the Balkan Wars of the nineties.

For decades Sarajevo was a diverse city where Serbs, Croats and Muslims lived together as friendly neighbors. In 1984, they hosted the Winter Olympics. Eight years later, people were getting shot by snipers when they went out for milk.

Nobody thought a war like that was possible in Europe that "late" in history—that Europe had passed the point of being vulnerable to such a thing. They hadn't, and never will, and neither will we.

Or think about Northern Ireland, which went through a period where political hatred, born of religion, turned into something called "the Troubles," which meant the hatred got so bad, it could not be contained by the usual means of disagreement. So people lived with bombings and sniping and urban warfare—what Tucker Carlson calls "sightseeing."

In America, our warring factions aren't Catholics and Protestants— but that same level of hatred, of "otherization," is happening between Democrats and Republicans. We've grown less religious, but that's because politics has become our religion. We used to pray for the nation. Now each side prays the other side doesn't destroy the nation. On one side, the Church of Woke wants to cleanse us of our past, and on the other the Cult of Trump wants to resurrect it.

Trump is often depicted as some kind of religious warrior, and out of office, he sometimes talks like an end-times religious nut. He speaks of an "epic battle" against "sinister forces" and says, "I am your warrior. I am your justice. And for those who have been wronged and betrayed: I am your retribution." Thanks, Batman. To get any closer to "smite the infidels" you'd have to be standing in a cave with a Kalashnikov and a turban.

"We will expel the warmongers," he says. "We will drive out the globalists, we will cast out the communists. We will liberate America from these villains and scoundrels once and for all." Big talk from a guy who can't even shut up his girlfriends.

But that's where we are: your fellow citizens who support the other party aren't just wrong, they're heretics who have to be destroyed. Political identities have become stronger than religious ones, stronger even than racial ones. Ninety-four percent of adults are now cool with interracial marriage—it's interparty marriage that's a deal-breaker for so many Republicans and Democrats, who don't want their kids marrying someone who belongs to the "other."

In 1960, only 5 percent of Americans had a negative reaction to the idea of marrying someone from a different political party; now it's 38 percent. For liberals, bringing home a Republican is the new *Guess Who's Coming to Dinner*. Only it's more like, *Guess Who's Coming to Dinner and Spending the Whole Meal Bitching About Mexicans*. In some families, even siblings have stopped speaking to one another, which makes it hard to get laid in the South.

Don't tell me it can't happen here. Yes—it *can* happen here. At Madison Square Garden in 1939, in liberal New York City, after Hitler had already done some awful things, twenty-two thousand Americans came out to cheer him on. I'm not saying Trump is Hitler. Hitler volunteered for the army. But he is a wannabe dictator. And he does have a knack for getting what he wants.

If Trump has taught us anything, it's that "It can't happen here" is a terribly outdated phrase. It not only *can* happen here, it *is* happening here.

Trump rallies are filled with words like "enemies of the people" and "human scum." They talk of people to be locked up. Liberals are described as weak, lame, coddling, oversensitive and limp dicked. Which are strong words from a bunch of mouth breathers, shitkickers, knuckle draggers, Bible thumpers, sister fuckers and rubes.

Yes, I've been guilty of saying things like that, but I'm going to try to stop. Because I've learned that the anti-intellectualism on the right doesn't come primarily from stupidity; it comes from hate. Telling people you think they're irredeemable and deplorable is what makes them say, "You know what? I'd rather side with Russia than you."

If we want to halt this descent into civil war, we have to stop hating each other. It's become so normalized now, we don't even notice how often someone online is wishing someone dead. Anyone we disagree with—about anything—is evil incarnate, and every argument goes from zero to homicide. It doesn't even have to be about something consequential: You insulted *Gossip Girl*? Prepare to die!

There's a moment in my stand-up act where I ask the audience—rhetorically—what should happen to all of the people who enabled Trump when he was in office. And about half the time someone shouts out "Kill them." Or "Hang them." Besides the fact that wishing people dead is a terrible place for your mind to be, if you're wishing them dead, you can be sure they're wishing *you* dead. You want a real war, liberals? You think you're gonna win the "I want you dead" war? You're not. They have way more guns and they know how to use them. And with all due respect, no one can do hate like a right-wing conservative.

When people despise each other, it doesn't matter what the "issues" are. When someone hates you, they don't hear the specifics of what you're saying, let alone want to work with you on an "issue." Today's Republicans don't have issues—oh, they have issues, just not like the ones they used to have. Balanced budget? They care about that as much as they care about the new season of *RuPaul's Drag Race*. "Owning the libs" is the only issue.

Obamacare wasn't a horrible or radical policy—it was even desperately needed by many of the people who fought it. But it came from the people they hated, so they hate *it*. Democrats keep thinking they can win over voters who hate them with better policies. They're dreaming. They're always asking, "Why do Republicans vote against their economic interests?" Because they hate you.

Comedians know this syndrome very well. You can have an act that kills—in a good way—but if you insult the audience, if you make them hate you: dead silence. They will not give you that laughter. And if they don't laugh, it's not comedy. It's alternative comedy.

BUBBLE JEOPARDY

Mark Finchem was the Republican nominee for secretary of state in Arizona in 2022, and Mark not only believes Trump won the 2020 election, he literally can't conceive that Biden could have. Why? He says: "I can't find anyone who will admit that they voted for Joe Biden."

Yeah, forget the meticulous audits, the hand recounts, the independent verifications run by Republican officials—this guy has never *personally* met a Biden voter. So they don't exist. You know, I've never been to a BTS concert, but I believe K-pop exists.

More than anything, this is what's wrong with our country. Our real division isn't between red and blue—it's between the people on both sides who aren't willing to mingle with Americans outside their political tribe and so have no idea what they're really like, and the people on both sides who *are* willing to do that.

Of course, Mark Finchem never met a Biden voter and probably thinks Democrats eat babies, because everybody *he knows* voted for Trump. Because he never leaves his hermetically sealed right-wing panic room, and I could say the same of many liberals who would never even talk to a Trump voter. I asked an old friend recently if he wanted to come by for a little party I was having, and when he found out one of the guests had voted for Trump, he told me he wasn't coming, saying, "I wouldn't breathe the same air." There's a word for people like this: "assholes."

When we confine ourselves to bubbles, alternate points of view become not just objectionable—they become unfathomable. This guy Finchem thinks Biden voters are literally a fiction, like wizards or the female orgasm. When he was pressed on this and asked, "Isn't it possible that lots of people you don't know personally did vote for Biden?" he replied, "In a fantasy world, anything's possible." Mark, have you ever been to a Whole Foods? Or talked to a woman under fifty?

In a nation based on pluralism, it's very dangerous that Americans are so in our silos, and it's largely because we've stopped living among each other. The latest census data revealed that Americans have hit the lowest rate of moving since they started tracking it in 1947, and while some of the reason for that is economic, much of the reason Americans don't move anymore is they just wouldn't feel welcome in too many places in their own country.

Would anyone ride the New York City subway wearing a MAGA hat? Would anyone go to a NASCAR race in a Biden T-shirt while they chant "Fuck Joe Biden"? That's where we are now, where other parts of the country are seen as scary no-go zones. People were afraid during the last presidential election to display lawn signs for the candidate of their choice if they were in a neighborhood where that was a decidedly minority opinion—that's like gang neighborhoods where you dare not get caught wearing the wrong color. America is like a prison now, where the inmates think they need to join one of the gangs to survive, and we dare not walk on the wrong side of the yard.

In January 2021, the *New York Times* published the headline "They Can't Leave the Bay Area Fast Enough" and followed it up that July with the headline "Tech Workers Who Swore Off the Bay Area Are Coming Back." Yeah, they saw all the red hats and said, "Fuck this. I'll take the wildfires."

LAST-HITCH EFFORT

If you want to understand why America is so divided, don't talk about Republicans and Democrats or red states and blue states—read the story "The City Mouse and the Country Mouse." That's the children's tale about two mice who learn that you're either city or you're country, and the same could be said for America. When you fly over it, you don't see red states and blue states, you see vast stretches of land where there's nothing— and then every once in a while, a city.

Every state's election map looks the same: a sea of red with a few blue spots. You can joke about Alabama all you want—yes, it's Trump country—but not Birmingham, because that's a city. It votes Democratic.

Something happens to you when you live in a city. You get mugged. But also, you have a multicultural experience. Cities are places with diversity and theater and museums and other gay stuff. I have nothing against rural life, but I've seen farms on TV, and they look dusty.

Why was Trump always poop-tweeting at three a.m.? Because he's from the city that never sleeps. He's such a New York guy he had his last *wife* delivered. He's a douchebag, but he's not a hick.

Blake Shelton is a good ol' boy from Oklahoma who sings about trucks and beer and things that happen down by the river, and I'd bet my house he voted for Trump; Gwen Stefani is the pop-princess hollaback girl from California, and I'll bet she didn't. And yet they got married and seem happy.

They make it work because—I assume—they see each other as more than just who they voted for. Their biggest issue with the person sleeping next to them isn't party affiliation, it's untreated sleep apnea. And they say "Yes, we're different, but that's also more fun, and we're gonna make that work *for* us." She's Whole Foods, he's Piggly Wiggly. She grew up playing punk, he grew up hunting skunk. She stands in line to vote, he stands in line to dance. She thinks guns are scary and he thinks the best cheese comes in a can.

They see the world differently *and* they love each other—what a concept! I'd like to try it in America, because that's how I feel about my country: you complete me, Tennessee. Because "You complete me" doesn't mean "We're exactly alike." In fact, it means we *are* different.

I don't want to live in a country without the red states. I like traveling there—when people talk to you in Oklahoma, they're not scanning the room to see if there's a bigger celebrity. Because, frankly, when I'm there, there never is. Also, they laugh like nobody's watching. They don't have a nondairy, gluten-free, hypoallergenic stick up their ass. Even the pro-lifers will laugh at a good dead baby joke.

James Carville and Mary Matalin, the epitome of the married couple who are political opposites, got hitched on Thanksgiving Day, and it's lasted thirty years. Their secret? Obviously, the hate sex. But also, they don't talk politics at home. Mary once told an interviewer, "Talking about the impact of the minimum wage is just not something that is high on our list of fun things to do." Exactly. Especially when there's so many other things you *can* talk about.

Let's take a hint from them, and next Thanksgiving, just celebrate it.

Don't try to "win" it. My childhood Thanksgivings were always in Princeton, New Jersey, because my father's sister married a country club Republican. I was aware my parents didn't like Republican politics—but they liked Uncle Hal. There was zero talk at Thanksgiving dinner about how wrong they thought his politics were. The ride home? That was a slightly different story.

But in general, politics and religion were just not subjects the adults talked about when I was a kid—they were considered private. It was thought to be impolite and nosy to go there. Politics was like Vegas: what happened in the voting booth stayed in the voting booth. Yes, we used to have no idea how much we hated each other, and it worked so much better.

Everyone these days says that the way to bridge our frightful partisan divide is to talk to the other side, so we can hear each other's point of view. No—that's exactly what you shouldn't do. It never works; no one ever flips to your side. Talk to them, yes, but not about politics. You'd have better luck trying to talk Tom Cruise out of Scientology. Just don't go there.

We never used to fight over politics 24/7. If somebody said, "Hot enough for ya today?" the other guy didn't say, "Yes, yes it is, largely because of your party's environmental policies!" True though that may be. But saying it at every opportunity doesn't help; people don't change their politics. Over the years, hundreds of people have come up to me and said, "I saw *Religulous*, and now I'm an atheist." Nobody has ever come up to me and said, "After listening to your warnings on Trump, I'm off the MAGA train."

They'll flip on God but not Trump. That cult is serious.

So when people ask, "How do we bridge the partisan divide?" I'll tell you how: shut the fuck up.

Stop talking politics to each other all the time. Especially on Facebook, which used to be an innocuous place to humblebrag and show cat videos, and now it's a cauldron of political hatred. It used to be a platform to *gain* friends; now it's more about rooting them out. What's with this "If you don't agree with what I just posted, unfriend me"? Gladly. We need to get back to what Facebook used to be: a place to see who from high school is gay, fat, bald or dead.

This making everything political is not a practice that is going to end well for us—liberals who won't eat Chick-fil-A, and conservatives who won't drink Bud Light. There are even reports that some hookers won't pee on you until you assure them it's "not a Trump thing."

CHEER NO EVIL

I'll admit it: I have a soft spot for this crazy, mixed-up country of ours. The place where I first learned to ride a bike and first ran after the ice cream truck; where I first served as an altar boy in our church and later sued the church for what happened. It's where I first played *Monopoly* during summer vacations, never imagining that going bankrupt in Atlantic City was a stepping stone to the White House.

You can unfriend someone whose politics you don't like, but you can't unfriend 47 percent of America. We have to see each other not as mortal enemies but merely as roommates from hell.

We've all been there with that scenario, right? The roommate who, if they were in the living room, you stayed in the kitchen, and if they were in the kitchen, you stayed in the living room, and if they were in the bathroom, you'd pee in a jar. You didn't give him his phone messages, and he dragged his balls across your pillow when you were out. You could go weeks without acknowledging the other person—it was like living with a ghost who never washes the dishes. Eventually you ended up ignoring each other's existence, living in the same place but not really seeing each other. Which is sad, but on the bright side, it does prepare you for marriage.

I've been in the bad-roommate situation where we literally got white tape and made a line through the middle of the apartment, something that's been tried for comic effect on more than a few sitcoms over the years. And it's tempting to want to divide America down the middle like that. But a country is not an apartment. Roommates can move out; patriots can't.

Think about how you can see politics so differently from people who share your very blood. We have to accept something about people: half of them have their taste in their ass.

Remember that the next time you think you can "own" somebody politically. It's never enough to just make a point anymore—it seems everyone has to "destroy" the person they're debating; you have to *own* people. Except the person who gets "owned" doesn't change their mind, they just make a mental note never to interact with you again.

Even if the Democrats win everything in 2024, the Republicans will still be here. They're not going to self-deport. They're in Congress, your office, sometimes your home. Home is where you learn that the three magic words in any relationship aren't "I love you"—they're "Let it go." You can't "own" your spouse. You sometimes just have to make peace with the fact that you're married to someone who believes in ghosts or won't throw out their baseball cards or thinks essential oils are essential. Or, yes, likes Donald Trump.

We have to drop this fantasy that we can *crush* the other side or *shred* or *pulverize* them. Those aren't real things. They're the middle three settings on the blender that no one has ever used. America is a big country filled with millions of people who don't think the way you do and never will, and you can't own, vanquish or disappear them. We're stuck with them and they're stuck with us. They're here, they're annoying, get used to it.

Because the pendulum always swings back. Even when we had a Civil War and physically owned the South—literally burned their cities to the ground and occupied their territory—Reconstruction only lasted for twelve years before the mint julep crowd took over again, and Jim Crow, the KKK and sharecropping became "Slavery 2.0." We tried to own the Germans after World War I, and that just got us World War II. It's a lesson that America forgot when the Soviet Union fell, and we continued to treat Russia as an enemy to be contained and not a new friend to be welcomed in.

In Japan after World War II, we staged wrestling matches between Japanese and American wrestlers and we made sure to sometimes make the American the bad guy—which was a huge morale boost to the Japanese people, and in fact made the matches so popular they almost single-handedly jump-started Japan's television industry, which led to Japan becoming the economic powerhouse it is today. Even though we dropped nuclear bombs on them, somehow much was forgiven simply because we let *their* wrestler kick *our* wrestler in the nuts. We need a little of that in America today, and if that means having to swallow the impulse to say "I told you so" and take a couple of fake kicks to the groin, well, then I regret that I have but two nuts to give for my country.

Finally, there's this: any talk about splitting our nation in two is dangerous, because it reinforces the belief that you can't even talk to "those people"—you just have to somehow nullify their very existence, by creating a country only of *your type of people*. It's always such a tempting thought, isn't it? If we could just keep the assholes out of where we, the good people, are, this would be a great place. But where do you draw the line as to how much someone can disagree with you before they're an asshole too?

The two congressladies from Karen County, Marjorie Taylor Greene and Lauren Boebert, seemed pretty joined at the hip for a while. They both love God, guns and gas stoves, but they reportedly had a bathroom fight in early 2023. When I read that, I wanted to ask Marjorie, who wants us to split in two: Does this mean Lauren doesn't get to live with you now in the new Free Republic of Jesus-ippi? And what about your own state of Georgia, which has a Republican governor and two Democratic senators—what are you going to do with the two and a half million Georgia residents who voted for the Democrats—put them on a plane to Martha's Vineyard?

What about the 43 percent of Republicans who are for gay marriage? Does that make them RINOs—"Republicans in name only"? And do RINOs get to live with you in Dumbassistan, or do they have to deport to Wokelahoma? What about the 11 percent of conservatives who

want strong borders but think the wall is stupid? What about the 12 percent of Bernie voters who listed their second choice as Trump? Sounds
like this new red-state country is going to have to *itself* split into two—or
maybe more, since there are many Republicans who want to legalize pot.
What I call "the good ones."

And same thing on the blue side: I assume abortion will be not just
legal in Newsomland but encouraged—but what about the 25 percent
of Democrats who oppose abortion? What I call the bad ones. Or the 28
percent who have a gun? Seems like we're going to need a lot more new
countries than just the two.

Or we could just stick with the one. The one where everybody gets to
disagree on everything except for one thing: you have to want to stay in
the marriage. You can't call yourself a "patriot" of the United States and
not be for the whole "united" part.

ACKNOWLEDGMENTS

Any book that is a compendium of material written for a TV show is a book by many writers. My name is on it, just like it's on the show itself, but this book is by Bill Maher and Chris Kelly and Billy Martin and Brian Jacobsmeyer and Jay Jaroch and Matt Gunn and Danny Vermont and Bob Oschack and Nick Vatterot and Amy Holmes and Samantha Matti. Producers Scott Carter, Sheila Griffiths and Dean Johnsen also are incredibly astute observers of our saucy democracy, and they say good things that find their way into the show and the book.

I will take credit for busting my nuts putting this thing together. I resisted doing this for so long because I remember what a lot of work it was just to put together New Rules compilations. But it turned out to be a labor of love. But it was a labor. Just reading through twenty years of editorials . . . Oy! I couldn't have gotten through this process without the longtime script supervisor extraordinaire Joaquin Torres.

I also relied on some of the stalwarts who do such a bang-up job at *Real Time*—namely, Joe Petro, David Stenson and Will Beeker, to look up shit, vet shit and generally keep it clean and honest. I trust them more than any news source, because they go through everything to find an answer, like AI, except they never occasionally go nuts. They also came up with a bunch of the pun-titles for the various essays.

You see, I have never been a pun guy—it's the one part of the show I leave completely to the writers. Other than that, what we have going has been one of the greatest joys of my life. I'll never know what it's like to play in a band, but it must be a transcendent feeling when you're in a band, and you're all good, and you're all playing off one another and making something greater than the parts with your cooperation and inspiration back and forth . . .

Paul McCartney said he'd rather have a band than a Rolls-Royce, and I feel the same way about a writing room. Also, Rolls-Royces are ugly.

Additional help from Chelsea Braun and Kennedy Howell let this process go much faster than it otherwise would. Also many thanks to Aja Pollock for knowing all the rules about grammar, spelling and research that authors have forgotten.

The publisher of this masterpiece is Jonathan Karp, who wrote me an email years ago, and I could tell he was a genuine fan. I'm so grateful he kept after me with just the right amount of space, and that this got done. I thank him and everybody who worked on this: designer Ruth Lee-Mui, art director Jackie Seow, managing editor Amanda Mulholland, production editor Jonathan Evans, publicist Larry Hughes, marketing director Stephen Bedford, audio producer Christina Zarafonitis, and audio publisher Chris Lynch.

INDEX

ABC, 48
abolition society, first, 232–233
abortion rights, 110, 138, 319, 355
Acevedo, Art, 151
ACLU, 119, 319, 320
Acreage Holdings, 172
addiction to products, 48–51
Adelson, Sheldon, 90
adult coloring books, 24
adult entertainment industry, 215
"adulting," 65
A&E, 121
Aeronauts, The, 228–229
Afghanistan, 276–278
African-Americans, *see* Black Americans
ageism, 76–78
agnosticism, 177–182
agriculture, water use for, 163–164
AIDS, 243, 299
Airbnb, 197, 325
air travel, 206, 238–239
Alabama, 90
alcohol consumption, 168–170
Algeria, 38, 39
Ali, Laila, 266
Alito, Samuel, 90, 187
Alley, Kirstie, 264–265
"All Lives Matter," 269
All Rise, 117
Amazon, 201–203, 218, 241
America
  ageism in, 77–78
  bad-faith arguments in, 145
  business model in, 204–209
  change in, 275
  compared to other countries, 276–278

  conservatives' sentimentality about, 90–92
  craving for authenticity in, 136
  decline in moving within, 348
  democracy in, 94
  division in, 342–355
  as dumb, 18–21, 76, 77 (*see also* knowledge)
  as a dysfunctional family, 93–94
  economy of (*see* economy)
  future historians' view of, xvii–xviii
  gun violence in, 220–225
  at its apex, xviii
  new normal in, 214
  origin of moral rot in, 49
  reflexive partisanship in, 5–8
  as republic, 95
  scams, graft, and greed in (*see* scamerica)
  Snitch Nation mindset in, 137–139
  spatial geographic inequality in, 202–203
  Trump's criticisms of, 92–93
  wages in, 220
  what people love or hate about, 273–278
  see also specific topics
American Families Plan, 28
American Rescue Plan, 165
Anderson, Erica, 320
Animal House, 30
animals, factory-farmed, 243–245
Aniston, Jennifer, 326
antibiotic-resistant diseases, 244
anti-intellectual trend, 22
anti-science, xvii–xviii
antisemitism, 131, 290

anxiety, 50, 170
Apple, 48, 56, 208
Arafat, Yasser, 39
Arizona, 166
Arkansas, 90
Aronofsky, Darren, 314
Arquette, Rosanna, 270
Ashcroft, John, 9
Asian-Americans, 108, 140, 259
Askew, Timothy, 260
Associated Press, 127
atheism, 177–182, 188, 194
Atlantic, xv–xvi, 302
Atlas Shrugged (Rand), 12
Australian immigrants, 278–280
authenticity, 135–137
authoritarian rule, sliding into, 96
avatars, 136–137, 309
awareness, raising, 19–21

Babbitt, Ashli, 8, 209, 210
baby boomers, 62, 213
Bachelor, The, 142
Bachmann, Michele, 177
bad-faith arguments, 145
Balenciaga, 66
Banks, Howard, 152
Bannon, Steve, 35, 274, 286, 305
Barr, William (Bill), 80, 189
Barrett, Amy Coney, 187–190
Baumbach, Noah, 314
Bayless, Skip, 16
Beamon, Bob, 87
Beatles, 234
Beck, Glenn, 86, 180
Begley, Ed, Jr., 238–239
Benedict, Pope, 190
Bengals, 15–17
Bennett, Bill, 188
Berlusconi, Silvio, 338
Bernstein, Leonard, 130
Beyoncé, 285
Bezos, Jeff, 201, 252
Bharara, Preet, 333
Bible, 64, 185–186, 227, 262–263
Biden, Joe, xix, 284
    age of, 77–78
    American Families Plan, 28
    Covid "relief" package, 113
    and election stealing, 95
    on January 6 insurrection, 6
    and marijuana legalization, 290
    Santos's district won by, 4

student debt cancellation, 108–109
    Texas voters for, 344
Bieber, Justin, 7
big business, 200–202
Bills, 15–17
birth rates, 249, 250
Bitcoin, 215–217, 239
Black Americans
    hopeful about America's future, 231
    incarceration of, 256, 271
    and political correctness, 140
    and racism in the South, 90
    and segregation in higher education,
        260–261
    voter protections for, 89
    and whites' appropriation of anger over
        racism, 267–269
Black Like Me, 131
Black national anthem, 259, 260
Blitzer, Wolf, 18
Boebert, Lauren, 1–2, 274, 354
Boehner, John, 8, 91, 172
Bon Jovi, Jon, 285
border wall, 280–281
Bork, Robert, 188
Bowie, David, 14
Bowman, Jamal, 275
Boy Scouts of America, 119–120
Brady, Tom, 87
brain hacking, 48
brand changes, 119–121
Brandeis, 122
Brando, Marlon, 288–289
Branson, Richard, 252
Breitbart, Andrew, 286
Brooks, Garth, 285
Brosnahan, Rachel, 131
Brown, Chris, 14
Brown v. Board of Education, 260
Buchanan, Pat, 188
Buddhism, 191
Budweiser, 20, 251
Buffett, Warren, 216, 242
bullying, 224, 230
bureaucracy, 156–159, 200
Burkina Faso, 277
Burns, Ken, 168
Burton, Tim, 314
Burundi, 277
Bush, Barbara, 340
Bush, Cori, 275
Bush, George H.W., 85
Bush, George W., xix, 35, 81, 87–89, 93, 343

business model, American, 204–209
BuzzFeed, 46, 126
Byzantium, 38

Cafferty, Emmanuel, 139–140
Cain, Herman, 177
California, 104, 162–164, 210, 245
Cameo, 197, 198
Cameron, James, 314
Canada, 170, 212
cancel culture, 132–148
    and authenticity, 135–137
    and comedy/jokes, 140–142
    in Hollywood, 141–146
    impact of, 139–140
    purity purge in, 137–139
    and revolutions, 132–135
    standing against, 146–148
    and Ukraine invasion, 7
capitalism
    and anti-capitalism, 201
    consumer product prices, 159
    in the field of money, 216
    as slavery by another name, 275 (see also
        free market)
    vulture, 207, 211–213
Capitol insurrection, see January 6
    insurrection
Carano, Gina, 142
carbon footprint, 217, 247
carbon-neutral lifestyle, 65–67
CARES Act, 165
Carlin, George, 117, 141
Carlson, Tucker, 121, 281
Carnival, 126
cars, 102–104, 239
Carson, Ben, 177
Carville, James, 113, 350
Catholic Church, 29
Catholics, 187–190
CBS News, 48
celebrities
    conservative, 285–286
    in government and politics, 282–284
    nepo babies, 265–266
    online, 75
Cena, John, 256–257
censorship, 52–54, 223
change, 38–40
    in America, 275
    in the Left, 132–135
    in political discourse, 58–60
    progress vs., 128

in socially acceptable standards,
    233–235
Chappelle, Dave, 117, 141, 147
Charlie Hebdo, 55
Cheney, Dick, 81, 82, 93
Cheney, Liz, 3, 80, 132, 146
child marriage, 26
Chili's, 195
China
    approach to problems in, 162
    Cultural Revolution in, 134
    detention camps of, 277
    GMO labeling in, 245
    high-speed rail in, 162
    Hong Kong returned to, 256
    human rights issues in, 255–258
    kowtowing to, 256–258
    obesity rate in, 304
    origin of Covid virus in, 258–259
    paid time off in, 199
    pretend parliament of, 96
    social credit system in, 219
    South–North Water Transfer Project
        in, 162
Chomsky, Noam, 19
Christianity, 38, 176–177, 182–186,
    262–263
Christie, Chris, 81
Christmas, 192–193
Chuck E. Cheese, 169
Churchill, Winston, 95
Citizens United, 90
Civil Rights Movement, 36
civil war and division, 342–355
    and commitment to unity, 352–355
    and divisionist history, 342–344
    hatred leading to, 344–347
    and partisan divide, 349–352
    and political bubbles, 347–349
Clay, Andrew Dice, 82
Cleisthenes, 36
climate change
    approach to fixing, 238–240
    and carbon-neutral lifestyle vs.
        consumerism, 65–67
    global warming, 217, 246, 296–297
    lies about, 236–237
    news sources on, 47
    and overpopulation/overuse of
        resources, 247
    and time wasted in approving green
        energy, 157–158
Clinton, Bill, 9, 44, 87, 189, 290, 335–337

Clinton, Chelsea, 305
Clinton, Hillary, xix
    campaign spending of, 43
    on fossil fuels, 100
    misinformation about, 302
    rural research/outreach by, 113
    on wins in 2016 election, 202–203
    work done by, 106
Clooney, George, 286
clothing industry, 242–243
Clyburn, James, 111
CNN, 8, 48
coal, 239–240
Coca-Cola, 164
Coen, Joel, 314
cognitive dissonance, 217
Cojones Awards, 146–148
Colbert, Stephen, 176
colleges and universities, 28–30
    admissions testing for, 267
    comedians who don't play at, 141
    "elite," indoctrination in, 33–35
    fraternities, 30–31
    free, 212
    legacy admissions to, 267
    paying for tuition, 198
    peril for professors in, 138
    segregated dorms and programs in, 34,
        260–261
    suggested terms to ban in, 121–122
    virtue signaling in, 287
    see also higher education; individual
        institutions
colonization, 36, 37, 39
Comcast, 48, 205
comedy clubs, 138–139
comic books, 64–65
commencement addresses, 31–33, 68–69
"commitment-phobic," 117
communism, 76, 133
Concussion, 13
Congress, 86–89, 342
Congresspersons, 1–5
    fights among, 11–12
    "religiously unaffiliated," 177
conservatism, xviii
conservatives
    2016 election of, 115
    on border wall, 354–355
    on capitalism, 212
    as celebrities, 285–286
    on democracy, 96
    governing by, 210

misinformation embraced by, 54
    on mob rule, 94
    and obesity crisis, 305
    real problem with, 89–92
    sentimentality about America among,
        90–92
    and social safety net, 210
    see also Republicans; the Right
Consolidated Appropriations Act, 165
conspiracy theories, 86
Constitution, 88–89, 189, 274
consulting, 160
consumerism, 65–67
consumer prices, 159–160
consumer products
    addiction to, 48–51
    costs of, 159–160
    fees for, 204–209
    online shopping for, 243
    packaging of, 241
    ratings of, 217–219
content creators, 74
Cooper, Bradley, 130
Cornell University, 147
corporate America, 207–209, 222–223,
        229
corruption, 90
Cotton, Tom, 35
Coulter, Ann, 83
Covid pandemic, 20
    as anti-regulation trigger, 103
    delivery services during, 196–197
    drinking during, 169
    and germophobia, 297–298
    government spending during, 214
    Great Barrington Declaration, 53
    misinformation on, 53, 54
    naming of virus, 258–259
    and obesity, 303–304
    online ordering during, 201–202
    parents' teaching responsibilities during,
        26
    "relief" package during, 113
    response to, 299–301
    sources of information on, 301–303
    stolen relief money from, 165–167
Covid virus, 257–259
creation science, 179–180
credit cards, 204
crime, 149–151
Crow, Sheryl, 285
Crowe, Harlan, 79
Crowley, Monica, 7

Cruise, Tom, 30, 257, 293, 326
Cruz, Ted, 11, 35, 183, 237
cryptocurrency, 66, 215–217
cultural appropriation, 9, 127–131, 267–269
Cummings, Elijah, 340
CumRocket, 215
Cusack, John, 326
Czechoslovakia, 38

Daily Beast, 46
Damon, Matt, 143–145, 322
Daniels, Stormy, 335–337
Darth Vader, 264
dating, 310–311
    see also love and sex
Davies, Edward, 181
Davis, Adelle, 295
Davitt, Christine, 137
Day-Lewis, Daniel, 130
Day the Earth Stood Still, The, 254
de Armas, Ana, 129
de Blasio, Bill, 154
deep state, 156–159
defense budget, 293
DeGeneres, Ellen, 116, 229, 268
democracy(-ies), 95–96
    as capitalism–socialism hybrids, 211
    direct, republics vs., 95
    in Hong Kong, 256
    Lee on, 94
    political parties' difference on, 94
    Republicans' threat to, xiv
Democrats, 97–114
    on author's alarmism, xviii
    "Believe Women" slogan of, 322
    and blame for Ukraine invasion, 6
    change in, 132–135
    and "crazy stuff," xiv, xix
    on crime, 150, 151
    on danger of Covid, 302
    and democracy, 94
    demographic issues for, 107–110
    divisions among, 355
    fundamental problem for, 99–102
    Gingrich on, 9
    insane excesses of, 110–114
    marijuana issue for, 172–173
    misinformation embraced by, 54
    paranoia about racism among, 107–108
    as party that protects feelings, 115–116
    political ads of, 99
    presidential candidates of, xix
    and presidential sex scandals, 335, 337
    and prudery, 9–10
    regulation issue for, 102–104
    and Republican message, 97–99
    Santos's appeal to, 4–5
    and socialism, 211
    and social safety net, 104–107
    view of Republicans by, 81
    voters' perceptions of, 110–114
Denmark, 212
Denny's, 218
Department of Homeland Security, 195
Depp, Johnny, 130
Derulo, Jason, 66
desalinization, 161
DeSantis, Ron, 35, 303
Diapers.com, 201
Diaz, Cameron, 264
digisexuals, 314–315
Dingell, John, 340
disabled people, xvi
diseases, naming, 258, 259
Disney, 48, 122, 223, 229
Disneyland, 169
diversity, equity and inclusion
    and cultural appropriation, 127–131
    including atheists in, 177
    liberals' lack of tolerance for, 116
    and Oscar quotas, 263–265
    racial, 84
    and segregation in higher education, 260–261
division, see civil war and division
Dogecoin, 215
Dolce, Domenico, 116
Dollar Store, 195
dollar stores, 195
Donohue, Bill, 55
drinking, 168–170
Driver, Minnie, 322
Druge, Matt, 84
drugs, 168–175
    alcohol, 168–170
    marijuana, 109–110, 170, 172–175, 230
    pills, 170–172
    prescription, 301
Duane Reade, 200–201
Duke, David, 84
Duke University, 198
dumbness, 18–21, 76, 77
Dunaway, Faye, 11
Dunning-Kruger effect, 22–23
Durham, John, 86

Eagles, 254
Earth, 236–254
  approach to fixing environment of, 238–240
  food supply on, 243–246
  health on, 296
  and lies about climate change, 236–237 (*see also* climate change)
  and Mars exploration, 250–254
  and online shopping, 243
  overpopulation of, 246–250
  post-apocalyptic, 254
  and scientific consensus, 237
Eastwood, Clint, 264
eBay, 197
economic exploitation, 209–210
economy
  2009 world economic crash, 216
  based on ratings, 217–219
  and big business as government, 200–202
  gig, 197–199
  middle class in, 207
  performance of, 207–208
  service, 205
  "sharing," 196, 199
  and spatial geographic inequality, 202
  see also employment; income; money
education
  commencement addresses, 31–33
  on gender, 228
  higher education system, 28–30 (*see also* colleges and universities; higher education)
  in history, 33, 35–40
  as indoctrination, 33–35
  lack of standards in, 23–24
  National Merit Scholarship awards, 267
  parents' interference with teachers, 27, 69
  student debt forgiveness, 108–109
  teachers' pay, 25–27
Edwards, John, 98
Egypt, 39
8chan, 221–222
elections
  2012, 90
  2016, 85, 202–203
  2020, 80–81, 95, 121, 347–348
  certifying the vote for, 121
  redistricting for, 87–89
  Russian interference in, 83, 84
  special interests' spending on, 90
  time allotted to, 18–19

  and voter fraud, 85, 95
  and voter suppression, 87–90, 101
Electoral College, 88
"elite" colleges, 33–35
Emerson, Ralph Waldo, 37
empathy, in liberalism, 131
employment
  change in wages, 195–196
  and Covid relief programs, 165–167
  higher education for, 28–30
  paid time off, 199–200
  of people of color, 230
  and robots, 198–199
enemies, 292–294
energy policy, 157–158
England, 199
entitlement, sense of, 141
environmental impact statements, 157–158
environmentalists, 238, 239
Enzi, Mike, 88
equality
  of outcomes vs. opportunity, 71, 73
  separate but equal doctrine, 260
  see also inequality
equity
  Trophy Syndrome as, 71–72
  see also diversity, equity and inclusion
Erewhon, 310
ESPN, 138
Ethereum, 215
ethnic cleansing, 38–39, 256
ethnicity, cultural appropriation and, 127–131
Etsy, 196
Europe, 55, 84, 199–200, 211–213, 319
Evancho, Jackie, 285
Evangelical Christians, 182–186
Every Body, xv
Everybody Lies, 136
evidence-based ideology, 180–181
evolution, 232–235
extinction crisis, 248

Facebook, 41–44, 48–50, 137, 308–309, 351–352
factory farming, 243–245
fake news, 44–46, 52–54
Falwell, Jerry, 179
Falwell, Jerry, Jr., 8
families, policies revolving around, 326–328
Families First Coronavirus Response Act, 165
farms, 163, 166, 211, 243–247

fast fashion, 242–243
FBI, 86, 87, 274
Feeding Our Future, 166
fees, 204–209
Fiddler on the Roof, 39
Finchem, Mark, 347–348
Finland, 212–213
First Amendment, 34
    see also free speech
fish, 244, 246
Fisher, Carrie, 115
Fixx, Jim, 295
Fleischer, Ari, 276
Flinders University, 122
Florida, 211
Floyd, George, 36, 151, 154, 155, 231, 268
flyover states, 203
food insecurity, 247
food supply, 243–246
football, 13–16, 20
foreign powers, party affiliation with,
    82–85
Foster, Jodie, 254
Foundation for Individual Rights and
    Expression, 34
Fourth Amendment rights, 36, 56–57
Fox, Megan, 321
Fox News, 45, 47, 100, 101, 125
fragility, 115–131
    and branding changes, 119–121
    and cultural appropriation, 127–131
    and Halloween costumes, 124–127
    and meaning of words, 117–119
    suggested terms to ban, 121–124
    and taking offense at everything, 115–116
    and trigger warnings, 122–123
France, 84, 162, 199
Franco, James, 129
Frank, Barney, 106
Franken, Al, 98, 322–324
fraternities, 30–31
freedom
    in art, 265
    in Hong Kong, 256
    loss of, 96
    peace of mind as, 212
    and ratings, 219
free market
    and big business, 200–202
    criticism of, 275
    libertarian obsession with, 12
    limits on, 212
    see also capitalism

free-range parenting, 70–71
free speech, 52–60
    and ACLU brand, 119
    on college campuses, 34
    for comedians, 140–142
    and illegal speech, 54
    jokes as, 330
    and misinformation/lies, 52–54
    in political discourse, 58–60
    and privacy of conversations, 56–57
    and reactions to jokes, 61–64
    and religious views, 55–56
Friends, 230, 257
friendships, need for, 222

Gabbana, Stefano, 116
Gadot, Gal, 130, 292
Gadsby, Hannah, 117
Gaetz, Matt, 8, 56
Galileo, 237
Gallego, Ruben, 111
Gap, 230
Garland, Texas, 276–277
Garner, Jennifer, 291
Gates, Bill, 217, 302
gay marriage, 229, 354
gay pride, 320
    see also LGBTQ rights
Gaza, 36
gender, teaching about, 228
gender apartheid, 258
General Motors, 195–196
generations, 61–78
    and ageism, 76–78
    and carbon-neutral lifestyle vs.
        consumerism, 65–67
    change in acceptable standards for,
        233–235
    and childishness, 64–65
    and kids' self-esteem vs. merit, 71–76
    parents of Gen Z, 68–71
    reactions to jokes by, 61–64
Gen Z, xvii
    on chance to be influencers, 74
    on chance to be online celebrities, 75
    characteristics of, 62–63, 68, 69
    clothes buying by, 243
    as crypto buyers, 66
    as environmentalists, 217
    life philosophy of, 126
    parents of, 68–71
    on property ownership and
        management, 76

Gen Z (*cont.*)
  sense of entitlement in, 141
  and socialism, 213–214
Gere, Richard, 11
Germany, 38, 84
germophobia, 297–298
Gibbons, Euell, 295
gift cards, 204
gig economy, 197–199
Gillibrand, Kirsten, 322, 323
Gingrich, Newt, 9, 188
Giuliani, Rudy, 93, 334
Giver, The, 254
global warming, 217, 246, 296–297
  see also climate change
Globe Theatre, London, 123
GMO labeling, 245–246
God, on our money, 194–195
Godfather, The, 288
Godzilla vs. Kong, 287
Google, 48, 53, 136, 256, 325
Gore, Al, xix, 87
Gorsuch, Neil, 187
Gosar, Paul, 274
Gottfried, Gilbert, 140
government
  big business as, 200–202
  bureaucracy of, 156–159
  celebrities in, 282–284
  farm subsidies from, 163
  graft and greed in, 162–163
  and paid vacation days, 199
  qualifications for, 282–284
  and socialism, 210–215
  "soft costs" in, 160
graft, in government, 162–163
Graham, Lindsey, 81, 294, 339
Grant, Ulysses S., 262
Great Barrington Declaration, 53
Great Depression, 214
Great Wall, The, 144
Greece, 77, 199
greed, 162–163, 199
Greene, Marjorie Taylor, 81
  and attitude toward enemies, 294
  beliefs of, 183
  and Boebert, 354
  on the FBI, 274
  on national divorce, 343
  and polyamorous tantric-sex, 8
  qualifications of, 2
Greenwald, Glenn, 55
Greitens, Eric, 97–98

Griffin, Kathy, 146
Griswold, Roger, 342
grocery stores, 169
groupthink, 15–16, 31
Gu, Eileen, 255, 257
Gucci, 195
guns, 173, 222
gun violence, 220–225
Guthrie Theater, Minneapolis, 122–123
Guyot, Paul, 285–286
Gyllenhaal, Jake, 130
gym memberships, 204

Hackford, Taylor, 314
Hagen, Sofie, 292
Haggard, Merle, 171
Haley, Nikki, 6, 212–213
Halloween costumes, 124–127
Hamas, 33, 34, 40
Hamlin, Damar, 15–17
Handmaid's Tale, The, 125–126
Hanks, Tom, 130, 285
Hannah-Jones, Nikole, 6
Hannity, Sean, 176, 188, 324
happiness, 212, 213
Hardy, Tom, 11
Harris, Kamala, 232
Harris, Tristan, 48
Harrison, Chris, 142–143
Hart, Kevin, 230
Harvard, 33–35
"hate speech," 117
hatred, 344–347
Hawley, Josh, 35
hazing deaths, 30–31
health, 295–307
  collective decisions on, 295–297
  and Covid pandemic response, 299–301
  and the immune system, 297–298
  mental, 223–224
  obesity, 303–307
  and quality of food supply, 244
  of single people, 327
  of a society, 86
  sources of information on, 300–303
health care, 200, 210–213
Heard, Amber, 130
"heartlanders," 171
heroes, 119, 310
higher education, 28–30
  fraternities in, 30–31
  as indoctrination at "elite" schools, 33–35
  see also colleges and universities

high-speed rail, 162
Hill, Katie, 9–10
Hilton, Paris, 75
Hispanics, 140
history
    abuse of, 226–229
    change throughout, 38–40
    divisionist, 342–344
    knowledge of, 33, 35–40
History Channel, 121
Hitler, Adolf, 346
HIV, 299
Hollywood
    "appropriation" in, 128–131
    and cancel culture, 141–146
    gun violence romanticized in, 223
    nepo babies in, 265–266
    and Oscar diversity quotas,
        263–265
    see also movies; showbiz
Hollywood Reporter, 291
Holocaust denial, 55
Home Depot, 310–311
Homeland Security, 299
homelessness, xv, 158–160, 288
HometownBuffet, 222
homophobia, 229, 278
Honduras, 277
Hong Kong, 256
Honolulu, 103
Hot Cars Act, 102
hotel bills, 205–206
House of Representatives, 2
Huckabee, Mike, 237
Huffington Post, 46
Hughes, Howard, 298
human evolution, 232–235
human rights issues, 255–258
Huntington, New York, 303
Hurt, William, 326
hypocrisy, in football, 17

I, Joan, 228
Iceland, 212
identity, 123, 178
identity politics, 99
I Feel Pretty, 290–291
IKEA, 244
immigration, 273–281
    of Australians, 278–280
    and border wall, 280–281
    and love for America, 273–278
incels, 310

income
    and education level, 28
    guaranteed, 109
    for one-third of Americans, 220
    teachers' pay, 25–27
income inequality, 195–197
Independent, 291, 292
India, 77
indoctrination, education as, 33–35
inequality
    income, 195–197
    spatial geographic, 202–203
infectious diseases, 243, 244
    see also specific diseases
influencers, 65, 74, 75
information bubbles, xiv–xv, 4
infrastructure bill, 109
innovation, 201–202
Instagram, 221
integrity, 98
intellectual property rights, 214–215
intelligence agencies, 92
International Women's Day, 277
Internet
    fake news on, 44–46
    and gun violence, 221–222
    "I'm embarrassed to be white" subgenre
        of, 270
    online shopping, 243
    "personalized content" on,
        46–48
    quality of information on, 43, 45
    virtue signaling on, 287
    see also social media; specific sites
interracial marriage, 230, 346
invasion of privacy, 56–57
Iran, 93
Iraq, 39
Ireland, 38
Irreversible Damage (Shrier), 320
Islamophobia, 55, 81
Israel, 6–7, 33–40, 161, 183
It's Complicated, 290

James, Bronny, 266
James, LeBron, 256, 266
January 6 insurrection
    Babbitt's death in, 209
    Biden on, 6
    and Evangelical Christianity, 182–183
    and loyalty to country, 94
    Mace on, 3
    Republicans' approval of, 274

January 6 insurrection (*cont.*)
  and Republicans' objection to certifying
    election, 121
  Santos on, 5
Japan, 77, 249, 354
Jaworski, Leon, 335
Jefferson, Thomas, 34, 262, 333
Jeffries, Hakeem, 145
jellyfish, 47
Jenner, Caitlyn, 282–284
Jenner, Kylie, 65–67
Jesus, slavery and, 262–263
Jetpuri, Mohammed, 277
Jews, 38–39, 131
Joan of Arc, 228
job(s)
  availability of, 74
  desired by Gen Z, 74–76
  governing as, 282–284
  parents' interference in hiring decisions,
    70
  ratings-dependent, 218
jobs programs, 211
John, Elton, 116
Johnson, Lyndon, 93
Johnson, Mike, 2
jokes
  and cancel culture, 140–142
  changed standards for, 233
  reactions to, 61–64
  Trump's reaction to, 329–330
Jones, Alex, 85–86, 294
Josephine, Charlie, 228
journalism, 42–46, 61–64
JPMorgan Chase, 200
justice system, 88, 256, 271

Kaczynski, David, 139
Kaepernick, Colin, 146
Kahn, Genghis, 37
Kansas, 175
Kappa Delta Rho, Penn State, 30
Kardashians, 74–75, 239
karma, 191–192
Kavanaugh, Brett, 187, 189
Keaton, Michael, 116
Kelly, General, 92
Kennedy, Anthony, 90
Kennedy, John F., 290, 339
Kennedy, Pagan, 295–296
Kerry, John, xix, 106, 239
Kid Rock, 146
Kilborn, Jason, 134

Kim Il Sung, 182
Kim Jong Il, 182
King, Martin Luther, Jr., 9, 36, 257, 260
knowledge, 18–40
  Americans' comfortable dumbness, 18–19
  and change, 38–40
  Dunning-Kruger effect, 22–23
  and fraternities, 30–31
  higher education system, 28–35
  of history, 33, 35–40
  indoctrination at "elite" schools, 33–35
  lack of educational standards, 23–24
  lies told to graduates, 31–33
  of old people, 77
  and political campaign ads, 21–22
  and raising awareness, 19–21
  social media as news source, 42–44
  and summer breaks, 24–25
  and teachers' pay, 25–27
  see also education
Knox, Belle, 198
Köbke, Michèle, 314
Kosovo, 39
Kushner, Jared, 35, 210
Kyle, Ted, 305, 307

Lamb, Conor, 111
land acknowledgments, 275
Landis, John, 11
language
  in political discourse, 58–60
  suggested terms to ban, 121–124
  use and redefinition of words, 117–119
Larry the Cable Guy, 141
Latino Americans, 111
Laurents, Arthur, 130
Lawrence, Jennifer, 45
Lee, Mike, 94, 250
Lee, Stan, 64–65
Left, the
  change in, xiv, xvi–xvii, 132–135
  crazies in, 133
  future historians' view of, xvii–xviii
  and Halloween, 125–126
  insane excesses of, 114
  things gotten wrong by, 95–96
  what is currently wrong with, xv
  see also Democrats; liberalism; liberals
legacy college admissions, 267
Leguizamo, John, 129
Lennon, John, 135
Leno, Jay, 22
Lewinsky, Monica, 335–337

Lewis, David, 87
Lewis, John, 106, 340
LGBTQ population growth, 318–320
LGBTQ rights
   and actors' roles, 129, 130
   and brand changes, 120
   and cancel culture, 143–145
   fake outrage about, 116
   gay marriage, 229
   and Ukraine war, 7
Libby, Scooter, 81
liberalism
   in colleges, 34
   Democrats' embarrassment about, 99
   empathy in, 131
   excesses of the Left vs., 114
   ideal of, xviii
   in Western civilization, 35–36
   wokeism vs., xiv, xvi
liberals
   on abortion, 110
   on Covid, 303
   desire to be sad among, 288
   and enemies, 294
   on extended education, 28
   as Fun Police, 126
   goal of, 105
   governing by, 210
   and gun violence, 223, 225
   in Hollywood, 263
   and obesity crisis, 305
   parts of country abandoned by, 202, 203
   social justice action by, 290
   on war against religion, 176–177
   what America means to, 275
   and white self-loathing, 269–270
   see also Democrats; the Left
libertarianism, 12–13
Liberty University, 179–180
Libya, 39
Lieu, Ted, 258
"Lift Every Voice and Sing," 259, 260
Limbaugh, Rush, 86, 174
Lincoln, Abraham, 133, 143, 262, 333–334
Lindell, Mike, 185
liquor, 168–170
Littlefeather, Sacheen, 288, 289
Lively, Blake, 261
loans, 204–205, 209
Locke, John, 36
Loesch, Dana, 285–286
London, 84
loneliness crisis, 221–222, 240

Lopez, Mario, 111–112
Los Angeles, 149, 160, 250
Los Angeles Times, xv, 74, 291, 320
Loughlin, Lori, 29
Loughlin, Olivia Jade, 29
Louis CK, 141
Love, Courtney, 116
Love Actually, 325
love and sex, 308–328
   characteristics of men, 316–317
   degrees of interactions, 321–324
   digisexuals or robosexuals, 314–315
   and driving, 318
   growth of LGBT population, 318–320
   initiating romance, 324–326
   office romances, 312–314
   policies revolving around families,
      326–328
   sexual harassment, 321–324
   and social media, 308–312
Lowell High School, 267
Lyft, 197
lying
   about climate change, 236–237
   about health, 301, 303
   and censorship, 52–54
   in Congress, 3–5
   manufacture of "facts," 85–86
   by politicians, 44
   by presidents, 87
   by Trump, 44, 87, 92
Lyon, Matthew, 342

Macdonald, Norm, 140
Mace, Nancy, 3
MacLaine, Shirley, 11
mad cow disease, 243
malls, 240–241
Malthus, Thomas, 249
Mandalorian, The, 142
Mandel, Howie, 297
Mann, Thomas, 86–87
Maoism, 182
Mao Zedong, 134
marginalized people, Western ideals and, 36
marijuana, 109–110, 171–175, 230, 290
marriage
   of children, 26
   gay, 229, 354
   interracial, 230, 346
   office romances leading to, 325
   and single people, 326–328
Mars exploration, 250–254

Marshall, Winston, 135
Martin, Steve, 115
mass shooters, 221–224
Matalin, Mary, 350
Mattix, Lori, 14–15
McCain, John, xix, 92, 283, 340
McCammond, Alexi, 137
McCarthy, Kevin, 79, 145
McCay, Clive, 295
McConaughey, Matthew, 282–284
McConnell, Mitch, 80, 89
McDonald's, 313
McVeigh, Timothy, 222
meat industry, 243–246
media, 41–51
    coverage of Trump in, 47–48
    information bubbles of, xiv–xv
    journalism, 45–46
    misinformation/lies in, 52–54
    music streaming, 73–74
    as news source, 42–48
    pride storylines in, 229
    and religion, 177
    revisiting ideas of the past in, 233–234
    smartphones, 49–51
    social media, 41–45, 48–49 (see also
        social media)
    violence in, 223–225
medical procedures, costs of, 159
Medicare, 210–212
Megiddo, Israel, 183
Mellencamp, John, 285
men
    and driving, 318
    involuntary celibacy of, 309–310
    and masculinity, 316–317
    testosterone loss in, 316
    women's relationships with, 316–317 (see
        also love and sex)
mental health, mass shootings and,
    223–224
mergers, 82–83
meritocracy, 71–76, 143, 266–267
Meta, 325
metaverse, 308–310
Me Too movement, 144, 322, 323
Mexico, 40, 170
Microsoft, 230
microtargeting, 47
middle class, 207, 209
Milich, Elisabeth, 26
military, 91–92, 274, 293
Mill, John Stuart, 34, 37

millennials
    alcohol use by, 68–169
    on chance to be influencers, 74
    characteristics of, 62–63
    clothes buying by, 243
    on communism, 76
    as crypto buyers, 66
    as environmentalists, 217
    future change in ideas of, 235
    jokes about, xvii
    life philosophy of, 126
    loneliness of, 221
    parents of, 70
    as religiously unaffiliated, 179
    and socialism, 213–214
    war within, 63
Miller, William, 186
Mirren, Helen, 131
misinformation, 52–54
Mississippi, 90, 203
mob rule, 94
Mohammad, Nazar, 276
money, 194–219
    American business model, 204–209
    big business, 200–202
    cryptocurrency, 215–217
    economic exploitation, 209–210
    fees, 204–209
    gig economy, 197–198
    God on, 194–195
    income inequality, 195–197
    as our god, 195
    paid time off, 199–200
    and ratings, 217–219
    "sharing economy," 196, 199
    and socialism, 210–215
    and spatial geographic inequality,
        202–203
monopolies, 200–202
Montignac, Michel, 295
Moore, Julianne, 254
Moore, Roy, 97
Moore, Michael, 176
Morey, Daryl, 256
Mormons, 101
Morocco, 39
Morrow, Vic, 11
movies
    about driving, 318
    Australian actors in, 279–280
    of human-machine interaction, 315
    love in, 325–326
    Oscar-nominated, 286–288

post-apocalyptic Earth in, 254
  see also Hollywood; showbiz
movie theaters, 169
MrBeast, xv–xvi, 66
MSNBC, 47
MTV, 121
Mueller, Robert, 333–335
Mueller report, 333–335
multiracial neighborhoods, 230
Mumford & Sons, 135
Murphy, Eddie, 11, 291
Murray, Bill, 11
music, 73–74, 146, 214
Musk, Elon, 248, 252
Muskogee drug treatment centers, 171
Muslims
    attitude toward America among, 277
    and "draw the prophet" contest, 276–277
    and gender apartheid, 258
    Islamophobia, 55, 81
    Ramadan, 178

Nakamoto, Satoshi, 216
Napoleon, 228
NASCAR, 229
national anthems, 259, 260
National Merit Scholarship awards, 267
national parks, 199
Native Americans, 140, 288–290
Navratilova, Martina, 116
Nazism, 182
NBC, 48, 111
Neeson, Liam, 144
Neiman Marcus, 195
Nelson, Craig T., 210
Nelson, Willie, 172
nepo babies, 265–266
Nestlé, 164
Netflix, 147, 325
Netherlands, 212
news feeds, 46–48
news sources
    bullshit nonissues as journalism, 45–46
    for campaign news, 101
    fake news, 44–46, 52–54
    news feeds, 46–48
    social media, 42–44
Newsweek, 237
New York Post, 269, 292
New York Times
    on the Bay Area, 349
    Littlefeather's obituary in, 289
    op-ed on baby boomers in, 62

on Paycheck Protection Program,
    166–167
on poor diet, 306
on the telegraph, 53
use of term "white supremacist" by, 118
virtue signaling at, 287
Nichols, Rachel, 138
Nichols, Tyre, 155
Nigeria, 38
Nike, 215
Nirvana, 118
Nixon, Richard, 9, 93
Norquist, Grover, 8–9
Northern Ireland, 345
North Korea, 96, 182, 277
Norway, 212, 213
Nugent, Ted, 82
nursing homes, 78

Obama, Barack, xvi–xvii, xix
    accomplishments of, 87
    accused of being foreign agent, 84
    Bush's wish for success of, 81
    celebrities at inauguration of, 285
    change of opinion in, 232
    "crazy stuff" doctrine of, xix
    and dating Michelle, 313
    on Democrats, 93
    and gay marriage, 290
    Giuliani's criticism of, 93
    qualifications of, 283
    as "secular humanist," 177–178
    on shovel-ready projects, 157
    on special interests' election spending, 90
    on Sterling episode, 56
    on unity of the USA, 259–260
    work done by, 106
Obama, Michelle, 304–305, 313
obesity, 303–307
Ocasio-Cortez, Alexandria (AOC), 111, 113,
    114, 275, 294
offense
    at Halloween costumes, 124–127
    taken at everything, 115–116
    taken at showbiz, 290–292
office romances, 312–314, 325
Ohio, 171
Olsen, Mary Kate and Ashley, 196
Olympics, 255
One Billion Americans (Yglesias), 248
online shopping, 243
OnlyFans, 197–198
oppression, 277, 278

O'Reilly, Bill, 35, 92, 188
Ornstein, Norm, 86–87
Oscars, 263–265, 286–288
O'Toole, Peter, 130
Outback Steakhouse, 195
overdose deaths, 171
overfishing, 246
overpopulation, 246–250
overreaction, in football, 17

packaging waste, 241
Padilla, Alex, 88
paid time off, 199–200
Palestine, 37, 39, 40
Palin, Sarah, xvii, 18, 26, 81, 177, 305
Palm Beach, 166
pandemic, *see* Covid pandemic
Paramount Global, 48
parents, 68–71
    during Covid pandemic, 26
    of Gen Z, 68–71
    and self-esteem of kids, 71–73
    teachers interfered with by, 27, 69
Parker, Kathleen, 56–57
partisanship
    partisan divide, 349–352
    partisan hate, xii–xiii
    reflexive, 5–8
Patel, Nimesh, 141
patriotism, 91–92, 301, 355
Paycheck Protection Program, 165–167
payday loans, 204–205
pedestrian deaths, 49
pedophilia, 56
Pelosi, Nancy, xvii, 106, 145
Pence, Mike, 80
Peng Shuai, 256
Penn, Sean, 129
Penney's, 195
Penn State, 30
Pennsylvania, 171
pensions, 212
People of Praise, 189
permits, 156–159
Perry, Rick, 177
PETA (People for the Ethical Treatment of
    Animals), 7–8
Philip Morris, 49
Philippines, 277
pills, 170–172
Pinker, Steven, 229
plastic recycling, 240
Playboy, 120

Poland, 38
Polanski, Roman, 11
police, 76, 111, 149–155, 274
political bubbles, 347–349
political campaign ads, 21–22, 99
political correctness
    Americans' view of, 140
    on college campuses, 30, 34, 125
    Lisa Simpson on, 233
    in naming Covid virus, 258
    see also cancel culture; language; woke
        ideology
political discourse, change in, 58–60
Politically Incorrect, xi
political parties, 1–14
    and characteristics of Congresspersons,
        1–5
    difference between, 86–89, 94
    fights among, 11–12
    foreign powers affiliated with, 82–85
    libertarian, 12–13
    and prudery, 8–10
    red and blue states, 343, 344
    and reflexive partisanship, 5–8
    see also individual parties
politics
    as binary, 111
    celebrities in, 282–284
    fact-free lifestyle in, 44
    identity, 99
    as local, not locally sourced, 113
    in medical decisions, 303
    as our religion, 345
    and partisan divide, 349–352
    social media personas in, 136
    views of democracy in, 94
Pollack, Martha, 147
Pompeo, Mike, 35
Pope, 44, 53, 190
population, 246–250, 327–328
pornography, 71, 197–198, 215
Portland Public Schools, 228
Portugal, 170–171
Povich, Maury, 327
power, 88, 230
prayers, 187
presentism, 226–229
presidential elections
    2016, 202–203
    2020, 80–81, 90, 95
    for Republicans, 83
    Russian interference in, 84
Priceline, 313

Pride Month, 229
Pritikin, Nathan, 295
privacy, 56–57, 137–139
private planes, 238–239
privilege, white, 230, 270, 271
processed foods, 49
progress, 128, 231
progressophobia, 229–231
Prohibition, 168
Project Better, 23
Project Greenlight, 143
protests, 55, 105
prudery, 8–10
Psychology Today, 50
Public Health England, 303
public safety, 149–151
purity purge, 137–139
Putin, Vladimir, 6, 7, 42–43, 83, 92, 284

QAnon, 7, 183, 184, 221
Quaid, Randy, 282–284
Quinn, Anthony, 338

race and racism, 230–231, 255–272
    accusations of racism, 257
    appropriation of anger over, 267–269
    and cancel culture, 143, 144
    in colleges, 34
    and cultural appropriation, 127
    entertainment diversity quotas,
        263–265
    guilt from slavery, 261–263
    human rights issues with, 255–258
    and naming of Covid virus, 258–259
    and nepo babies, 265–266
    and progressophobia, 229
    racism as America's number one bad, 272
    and Republican attitude toward Russia,
        83–84
    and SAT test, 118
    1619 Project on, 6
    social justice for Black Americans,
        259–261
    and societal progress, 231
    in the South vs. North, 90
    in sports, 266–267
    Supreme Court conservatives on, 89
    voter demographics, 107–108
    voter suppression, 89–90
    white power and privilege, 230
    white self-loathing, 269–272
    in woke ideology, 278
racial diversity, 84

racial injustice, appropriated anger over,
    267–269
raising awareness, 19–21
Ramadan, 178
Ramaswamy, Vivek, 35
Rand, Ayn, 12
ratings, 217–219
Ratzinger, Cardinal, 190
Raytheon, 229
Reagan, Nancy, 9, 290
Reagan, Ronald, 87, 93, 211–212
RealDoll X, 315
Real Time with Bill Maher, xi–xii
    Cojones Awards, 146–148
    editorials of, xii
    "Explaining Jokes to Idiots," 290, 329
    format of, xiii
    relationship with audience of, xix
recycling, 240, 241
redistricting, 87–89
redlining, 261
Redmayne, Eddie, 129
Red Sparrow, 45
Reeves, Keanu, 254
reflexive partisanship, 5–8
refugees, 38–40, 277–278
regulation, 102–104, 164
relationships
    between men and women (*see* love and
        sex)
    smartphones' influence on, 50–51
religion(s), 176–193
    atheism and agnosticism, 177–182
    Catholics on the Supreme Court, 187–190
    and Christmas, 192–193
    Evangelical Christianity, 182–186
    and free speech, 55–56
    and God on money, 194–195
    karma, 191–192
    labeling other ideologies as, 180–181
    liberals' war against, 176–177
    magical thinking in, 184
    in Palestine, 38
    politics as, 345
    Seventh-day Adventists, 186
    state, 182
    those "unaffiliated" with, 177–179
    "thoughts and prayers" phrase of, 187
"Reluctant Conservative, The," xviii
remote work, 197
Republicans, xiii, 79–96
    and 2020 election, 80
    anti-intellectual trend among, 22

Republicans (*cont.*)
  and blame for Ukraine invasion, 6
  brand change for, 121
  and cancel culture, 139, 146
  candidates of, 81–82
  central fraudulent ideas of, 86–89
  on climate change, 237
  and democracy in America, 94, 95
  demographic problem for, 83
  divisions among, 354–355
  and economic exploitation, 209–210
  free pass for, 92–96
  future acceptable candidates for, 82
  "good-as-it-gets," 81
  guns issue for, 173
  Latino voters as, 111
  manufacture of facts by, 85–86
  marijuana issue for, 172–173
  "mergers" for, 81–85
  message of, 97–99
  midlife crisis for, 106
  misinformation bubble of, 302
  Ornstein and Mann on, 86–87
  as party of patriotism, 301
  political ads of, 99
  political courage of, 100–101
  in presidential elections, 81
  on presidential sex scandals, 335–337
  and prudery, 8–9
  and racism, 107
  and real problem with conservatives,
    89–92
  redistricting by, 87–89
  and Russia, 82–85, 294
  Santos's appeal to, 4
  sentimentality about America among,
    90–92
  in showbiz, 285–286
  and socialism, 212
  spiritual advisers of, 8
  system rigged for, 88
  on Trump, 79–81
  Trump's influence on, xiii–xiv
  and voting, 87–88, 101
  on Waxman, 105
  what America means to, 273–274
republics, 95, 96
resources
  declining, 247–250
  exploring Mars for, 250–254
revolutions, 133–135
Reynolds, Ryan, 261, 262
Rich, John, 146

Richards, Keith, 295
Right, the
  on American Families Plan, 28
  argument of, xiv
  circular logic of, 95
  crazies in, 133
  future historians' view of, xvii–xviii
  hatred in, 346–347
  and health crisis, 305
  intellectual degeneration of, xviii
  military loved by, 91–92
  offense taken by, 9
  political ads of, 99
  see also conservatives; Republicans
Ringwald, Molly, 233–234
Rivers, Doc, 266
Roberts, John, 90, 187, 276
Robertson, Pat, 6–7, 35
robosexuals, 314–315
robots, 198–199
Rock, the, 282, 284
Rock, Chris, 141
Rockefeller, John D., 202
Roe v. Wade, 319
Rolling Stone, 73, 291
Romney, Mitt, xix, 4, 9, 80–81, 194
Roseanne, 141
Rousseau, Jean-Jacques, 36, 37
Rowling, J. K., 146
Roy, Chip, 2–3
royals, 123–124
Rubio, Marco, 211
Russia
  Carlson's value to, 121
  election interference by, 83, 84
  as enemy vs. as friend, 353
  Germans shoved out of, 38
  lack of racial diversity in, 84
  pretend parliament of, 96
  propaganda on social media from, 42–43
  Republican's attitude toward, 294
  as Republicans' "partner," 82–85
  and Trump, 86, 87
Ruth, Babe, 87
Ryan, Paul, 12, 79

Sabato, Antonio, Jr., 285
Salon, 46
Samoa, 101
Sanders, Bernie, 109, 212, 214
Sandy Hook shooting, 222
San Francisco, 150, 158, 267
Santorum, Rick, 9, 177, 188

Santos, George, 3–5, 44, 81
Sarajevo, Bosnia, 344–345
Sarandos, Ted, 147
SAT test, 118
Saudi Arabia, 39, 246, 277
Scalia, Antonin, 188–189
Scalise, Steve, 79
scamerica, 156–167
    and bureaucracy as true deep state,
        156–159
    costs of consumer products, 159–160
    stolen Covid relief money, 165–167
    water availability, 160–165
Schaaf, Libby, 268
Schumer, Amy, 290–292
Schumer, Chuck, 190
Schwab, Raymond, 174–175
scientific facts, 236
    about climate change, 236
    about Mars, 252, 253
    from medical establishment, 299–303
Scientology, 29, 30
Scott, Tim, xiv
Scott, Travis, 309
Sears, 195
Sears catalog, 240
segregation, in education, 260–261
Seinfeld, Jerry, 141
self-esteem, merit vs., 71–76
Semafor, 157
senators, number per state of, 88
Sengbe, Victor, 268
separate but equal doctrine, 260
service economy, 205
Seventh-day Adventists, 186
Sex and the City, 12
sexes
    maintaining binary in youth sports, xvi
    obvious physical differences between, xvii
    relationships between (see love and sex)
sexism, 229, 278
sexual harassment, 313, 321–324
shaming, 119, 305, 306
Shapiro, Ben, 343
sharing economy, 196
Sheen, Charlie, 82
Shein, 242–243
Shelton, Blake, 350
shopping malls, 240–241
showbiz, 282–294
    celebrities in government and politics,
        282–284
    conservative celebrities, 285–286

enemies portrayed in, 292–294
Native American issues in, 288–290
offense taken at, 290–292
virtue signaling in, 286–288
see also Hollywood; movies
Shrier, Abigail, 320
Shula, Don, 32
Shuttered Venue Operators Grant
    program, 166
Shyamalan, M. Night, 237
side hustles, 197
Siegel, Bugsy, 203
Silverman, Sarah, 141
Simpsons, The, 233
single people, 326–328
1619 Project, 6
"Sixteen Tons," 201
slaughterhouses, 244–245
slavery, 227, 232–233, 261–263
smartphones, 49–51, 56, 208, 224, 242
Smith, Kevin, 64
Snitch Nation mindset, 137–139
Snowden, Edward, 139
social engineering, 28
socialism, 210–215
social justice
    2020 protests, 259
    Floyd protests, 151, 268
    liberals' action on, 290
    and "merit first" concept, 143
    and royals, 124
    and use of word "violence," 118
    and Western Enlightenment, 37
social media
    avatars on, 136–137
    as crutch, 170
    and gun violence, 221–222
    influencers on, 74, 75
    lies in, 52–54
    as news source, 42–44
    purposeful addictive design of, 48–51
    quality of information on, 23, 24
    and relationships, 44–45, 308–312
    see also specific sites
social order, breakdown in, 149
social safety net, 104–107, 210, 212
Social Security, 211
Sondheim, Stephen, 130
Sonmez, Felicia, 62, 63
Sotomayor, Sonia, 187
South, the
    following Civil War, 353
    racism in, 90

South, the (*cont.*)
　　and Supreme Courts' Voting Rights Act
　　　ruling, 276
South Carolina, 90
Spacey, Kevin, 223
spatial geographic inequality, 202–203
special interests, election spending by, 90
species extinction, 248
Spicer, Sean, 305
Spielberg, Steven, 130, 314
sports
　　cultural appropriation in, 127–128
　　and human rights issues, 255–257
　　maintaining binary in, xvi
　　meritocracy in, 266–267
　　national anthems in, 259
　　in top-rated telecasts, 266
Sports Illustrated, 120
Springsteen, Bruce, 285
Sri Lanka, 199
Stalinism, 182
Standard Oil Company, 202
Stanford, xv
Staples, 19–20
Starbucks, 169
Starr, Ken, 335
Starr Report, 189
state religions, 182
states
　　rights of, 175
　　spatial geographic inequality in,
　　　202–203
Stefani, Gwen, 350
Sterling, Donald, 56
Stiller, Ben, 148
stock market, 207–208
Stone, Emma, 130
Stone, Roger, 324
Stone-Manning, Tracy, 247–248
Strangio, Chase, 320
Streep, Meryl, 254
Stripchat, 198
student debt, 108–109, 198
stupid logic, in football, 16–17
Supreme Court
　　appointment of justices to, 88–89
　　Brown v. Board of Education, 260
　　Catholics on the, 187–190
　　Harvard graduates on, 35
　　religions of justices on, 177
　　Roe v. Wade, 319
　　and voting rights, 89–90, 276
surfing, as cultural appropriation, 127

"survivor," 118
Swalwell, Eric, 145
Swan, Mitchell, 7
Sweden, 199, 212
Sweet, James, 226, 227
Swift, Jonathan, 52
Swinton, Tilda, 254
Switzerland, 199, 212
Syria, 39, 84

Taco Bell, 169
Taibbi, Matt, xiv–xv
Taiwan, 256–257
Takei, George, 104
Taliban, 276, 277
Target, 230
Tate, Andrew, 22
tax on whiteness, 272
teachers, 25–27
technological evolution, 233
technology, *see specific types of technology*
Teen Vogue, 137, 139
television, 266, 312
Tether, 215
Texas
　　abortion law in, 138
　　congressional districts in, 88, 89
　　Covid restrictions in, 302
　　on secession, 343
　　voting by minorities in, 90
Texas Tech, 28
TGI Fridays, 195
theaters, trigger warnings in, 122–123
Theron, Charlize, 11
Thomas, Clarence, 187
Thoreau, Henry David, 36, 37
"thoughts and prayers" phrase, 187
3 Doors Down, 285
Thunberg, Greta, 65, 238–239
ticks, 296–297
Timberlake, Justin, 127
time, 226–235
　　evolution of humans, 232–235
　　presentism, 226–229
　　progressophobia, 229–231
Time magazine, 289
TLC (The Learning Channel), 120
Top Gun movies, 257, 292–293
Trader Joe's, 147
trains, high-speed, 162
transgender people, 257, 319–321
　　see also LGBTQ rights
trauma, identity and, 123

tribalism, 5
trigger warnings, 122–123
Tritt, Travis, 146
Trophy Syndrome, 71–72
Tropic Thunder, 148
TrouserDeal.com, 196
Trump, Donald, 329–341
  on 2016 voter fraud, 85
  America run down by, 92–93
  anti-intellectual attitude of, 22
  appeal of, 82, 97, 99–100
  author sued by, 276, 329–330
  books written about, 337, 338
  and border wall, 280, 281
  California voters for, 344
  as cautionary tale, 283
  celebrity of, 283
  and change in political discourse, 58–60
  on Covid, 303
  on crime, 150
  and Daniels scandal, 335–337
  Democrats' on, 112
  as dictator wannabe, 346
  drug abuse in places won by, 171
  ego of, 331–332
  election lost by, xviii
  farm bailout by, 211
  FBI head fired by, 98
  fitness for presidency of, xix
  honor lesson of, 92
  inauguration guests of, 285
  indictments and trials of, 335–337
  investigation of "spying" on, 86
  on Jones, 85–86
  lies of, 44, 87
  Mace's condemnation of, 3
  Mars mission bill signed by, 252
  media platform of, 47–48
  on the military, 274
  and Mueller report, 333–335
  national debt under, 87
  and oligarchy, 343
  and patriotism, 91
  Pope on election of, 44
  popular vote lost by, 88–89
  potential eulogy for, 340–341
  primary reason for voting for, 112
  and Putin, 83, 92
  religious followers of, 182, 184–185
  as religious warrior, 345
  Republicans as party of, 121
  Republicans influenced by, xiii–xiv
  Republicans on, 79–81
  on the rigged system, 88
  and Russia, 86, 87
  Sanders voters for, 355
  sex life of, 335–340
  and social media as news source, 43
  speech of, 135–136
  supporters' perception of, 209, 351
  Ten Commandments of, 184
  and "thoughts and prayers" phrase, 187
  as worst president ever, 6
Trump, Donald, Jr., 324, 334
Trump, Melania, 338–339
Trumpism, 183
truth
  and manufacture of "facts," 85–86
  misinformation/lies vs., 52–54
  narrative conflicting with, 227
  in the news (*see* fake news)
Tunisia, 39
Turkey, 38
Turner, Kathleen, 326
Turner Classic Movies, 122
Tweeden, Leeann, 323, 324
Twitter, 43, 53

Uber, 197, 218
Ukraine war, 6–8, 121, 317
Unabomber, 139
unemployment, 28, 165–166
United Nations, 36–37, 40
unity
  commitment to, 352–355
  creating, 344
  symbols of, 259–260
Universal Basic Income, 109
Universal Declaration of Human Rights, 36
universal health care, 211–213
University of Michigan–Dearborn, 260
University of Missouri, 28
University of Ohio, 260
University of Wisconsin, 262
unreasonable search and seizure, 56
UN World Happiness rankings, 212
USA Today, 307
Usher, 285
U2, 285
Uyghurs, 256

vacation time, 199–200
Vanity Fair, 7
Venezuela, 277
"victim," 118
victimization, 36

Vietnam War, 93
Vindman, Alexander, 139
violence, 117–118, 145, 151–153, 220–225
Virginia, 90, 267
Virginia Tech, 222
virtual market, 216–217
virtual reality, 309, 310
virtue signaling, 286–288
Voltaire, 36
voter demographics, 107
voter fraud, 85, 95
voters
    being seen as a lawyer for, 107–110
    Democrats' issues supported by, 113
    Democrats' lack of appeal to, 110–114
    weed issue for, 173
voter suppression, 87, 89–90, 101
voting rights, 95, 101–102, 121, 274
Voting Rights Act (1965), 89–90, 276
vulture capitalism, 207

Walker, Herschel, 81, 98–99
Walker, Paul, 14
Walker, Scott, 177
Wallace, Mike, 49
Walmart, 2, 196
Walton, Alice, 196
Warner Bros. Discovery, 48
War on Drugs, 9, 174, 195
Warren, Elizabeth, 201
Washington, Denzel, 285
Washington, George, 262
Washington Post, xv–xvi, 56–57, 61–64
water availability, 160–165, 247, 249
Watergate, 335
Waxman, Henry, 104–106
weakness, in football, 17
weed, *see* marijuana
Weigel, David, 61–62
Weight Watchers (WW), 306
Welles, Orson, 53
West, Kanye, 284
West, water problems in, 160–161, 163–164
West Bank, 39, 40
Western civilization, ideals of, 35–37
Western Enlightenment, 37
West Virginia, 171
White Americans
    anger over racism appropriated by,
        267–269
    hopefulness about America's future in, 231
    self-loathing of, 269–272
white power and privilege, 230, 270, 271

"white supremacist," 118
Wigand, Jeffrey, 49
Williams, Jesse, 127
Winfrey, Oprah, 177
Winger, Debra, 11
Winslet, Kate, 254
Wisconsin, 171
woke ideology, 113–114
    abuse of history in, 226–229
    on America as rotten to the core, 278
    being offended as hallmark of, 115–116,
        290–292
    blaming election losses on, 113
    and Chinese Cultural Revolution, 134
    and cultural appropriation, 127
    dislike of, 140
    evolution of, xiii
    in Hollywood, 223
    and human evolution, 232–235
    and Jesus's position on slavery, 263
    "Jewface" in, 131
    and knowledge of history, 36
    liberalism vs., xiv, xvi
    and movie reviews, 290–294
    original definition of, 257
    and revolutions, 133–135
    seeing race first in, 257, 260
    on white power and privilege, 230
    "your truth" in, 54
    see also cancel culture
women
    and fraternities, 30
    International Women's Day, 277
    mass shootings blamed on, 222
    men's relationships with, 310–312 (*see
        also* love and sex)
Wonder, Stevie, 285
Woods, James, 285
word inflation, 117–119
working class, Republicans' con of, 209
world economic crash (2009), 216
World War II, 214
Wyoming, 158

Yale University, xv, 35, 124–125
Yglesias, Matthew, 248
YouTube, 53

Zelensky, Volodymyr, 317
Ziering, Ian, 198
Zombie Lie, 72, 129, 236, 237
Zucker, Jeff, 313–314
Zuckerberg, Mark, 308–309

ABOUT THE AUTHOR

Before hosting *Real Time* on HBO for the last twenty-one years, Bill Maher created and hosted *Politically Incorrect* on ABC. He lives in Los Angeles, California. He is the author of five previous books, including the novel *True Story*.